Charles Rogers

History of the Chapel Royal of Scotland

with the register of the Chapel Royal of Stirling, including details in relation to the rise and

progress of Scottish music

Charles Rogers

History of the Chapel Royal of Scotland
with the register of the Chapel Royal of Stirling, including details in relation to the rise and progress of Scottish music

ISBN/EAN: 9783743345843

Manufactured in Europe, USA, Canada, Australia, Japa

Cover: Foto ©ninafisch / pixelio.de

Manufactured and distributed by brebook publishing software (www.brebook.com)

Charles Rogers

History of the Chapel Royal of Scotland

HISTORY

OF THE

CHAPEL ROYAL OF SCOTLAND

WITH THE

REGISTER OF THE CHAPEL ROYAL OF STIRLING

INCLUDING DETAILS IN RELATION TO THE RISE AND PROGRESS OF SCOTTISH MUSIC

AND

Observations respecting the Order of the Thistle

BY THE

REV. CHARLES ROGERS, D.D., LL.D.

Fellow of the Society of Antiquaries of Scotland, and of the Royal Society of Northern
Antiquaries, Copenhagen,
Associate of the Imperial Archæological Society of Russia,
Member of the Historical Societies of Pennsylvania and Quebec,
Honorary Member of the Historical Societies of Michigan, Chicago, and New Jersey, and of the
Antiquarian Society of Montreal,
And Corresponding Member of the Royal Society of Bohemia,
Of the Historical Society of Berlin, of the American Ethnological Society,
And of the Historical Societies of New York, Maine, Virginia, Rhode Island, Maryland,
Minnesota, South Carolina, Missouri, Vermont, and New Brunswick,
Of the Numismatic and Antiquarian Society of Philadelphia,
Of the Historical and Genealogical Society of New England,
Of the Royal Society of Tasmania,
Of the Royal Heraldic and Genealogical Society of Italy,
And of the Natural History Society of Montreal

EDINBURGH
PRINTED FOR THE GRAMPIAN CLUB
1882

CONTENTS.

	PAGE
INTRODUCTION,	v
HISTORY OF THE CHAPEL ROYAL OF SCOTLAND,	xciii
REGISTRUM CAPELLÆ REGIÆ STRIVELINENSIS,	1

APPENDIX:

I. GRANT TO THE CHAPEL ROYAL BY THE REGENT, DUKE OF ALBANY,	95
II. PRESENTATION BY JAMES V. OF THE TREASURERSHIP OF THE CHAPEL ROYAL TO MR ANDREW DURIE,	97
III. APPOINTMENT OF JAMES CAMPBELL AS A MUSICIAN IN THE CHAPEL ROYAL,	98
IV. JOHN TAYLOR, THE WATER POET'S VISIT TO EDINBURGH,	99
V. LETTER OF LORD BINNING TO JAMES VI.,	99
VI. MR JAMES LAW'S MISSION TO LONDON,	100
VII. THE RIOT AT HOLYROODHOUSE ON THE 10TH DECEMBER 1688, AND SUBSEQUENT PROCEEDINGS IN RELATION TO CAPTAIN JOHN WALLACE,	102
INDEX,	115

INTRODUCTION.

From the surface of an inland sea, about four miles in breadth, which at a prehistoric period covered the strath resting between the Ochil Hills and the heights of Bannock and the Lennox, jutted three islets, of which the most considerable became, long after the waters had receded, the site of a rude fortalice, latterly of a royal palace. At the dawn of history the place was known as Strivelyn, a compound word signifying a rock surrounded by a marsh. Such was its true description; but the swamp has ceased, while in the plain, now rich and verdant, meander the rivers Forth, Teith, and Allan, the delight of the angler and the glory of the poet.

Topographically in the centre of Scotland, Stirling became a focus of the national life. In its castle the sovereign held court and council, in its streets were the dwellings of the nobles, and in its environs were practised the sports of chivalry. Within its Chapel Royal did kings delight to worship; it was their place of confession and the sanctuary of their household.

Associated with regal power, Stirling Rock stood

forth as a great altar in the field of freedom. A cradle of the arts, there was cherished in its halls that music which, wedded to the national song, has endeared Scotland to its sons, and through their minstrelsy has endeared it to the world.

Of the Chapel Royal of Stirling, any history would be imperfect which did not refer to the grace and beauty of its site. From Stirling Castle may be descried a prospect singularly picturesque. Bordering the ancient swamp, now a cultured garden, do sylvan-clad mansions rest on a prehistoric sea-beach, while the ennobling panorama is bounded by towering heights and majestic mountains. At every point far as the eye can reach are scenes famous in romance or historically celebrated. Where on the east the Forth enfolds Cambuskenneth Abbey, terminated that struggle between the Scots and Picts which enabled Kenneth, son of Alpin, to establish monarchical order on tribal misrule. Towards the south at Falkirk, in two military engagements, fought centuries apart, did the national cause suffer inglorious discomfiture. In the same direction at Kildean, an ill-advised monarch was worsted and slain. Close by on the south Scottish liberty triumphed at Bannockburn. On the north at Sheriffmuir the first insurrection on behalf of the exiled House of Stewart began and terminated.

When Stirling Castle became a royal residence has not been ascertained; it was a favoured resort of

Alexander I. This sovereign, surnamed the Fierce, from his vigorous character, was withal beneficent and pious. To the town of Stirling he, in 1120, granted a charter of incorporation, and founding a chapel in the castle, he, in honour of his departed mother, the sainted Queen Margaret, attached it to Dunfermline monastery.*

During the reign of David I. (1124-1153) a controversy arose between the administrators of the Chapel Royal and the ecclesiastical authorities at Eccles, a parish which comprehended Stirling, and that extensive territory embracing the modern parishes of Larbert and Dunipace.† The dispute related to the disposal of tithes and of the dues of sepulture; it was adjusted at the Castle of Edinburgh in presence of the king, his son the Prince Henry, and the principal nobility. In the following document the decision is embodied:

DE CONCORDIA ECCLESIARUM DE ECCLES ET STRIUELIN.

Hec est concordia que facta fuit apud Castellum Puellarum, coram rege Dauid et Henrico filio eius et baronibus eorum, inter R. episcopum Sancti Andree et G. abbatem de Dunfermelyn, de ecclesia parochiali de Eccles et Capella Castelli de Striuelin: Recordati fuerunt barones regis, et in hac recordacione omnes concordati sunt, quod ea die qua Rex Alexander fecit Capellam dedicare supradictam, donauit et concessit eidem Capelle decimas dominiorum suorum in soca de Striuelin; que eadem die fuerunt dominia sua, siue acreuerunt siue decreuerunt. Et

---

* Reg. de Dunfermlyn, 4, 8.
† Sketches of Early Scotch History, by Cosmo Innes, Edinb. 1861, 8vo, pp. 16, 17.

preterea considerauerunt quod ecclesia parochialis de Eccles habere debebat uniuersas decimas que proueniunt de hurdmannis et bondis et gresmannis cum ceteris consuetudinibus quas debent ecclesie; et qui mortui fuerint siue sint de mancipiis dominiorum siue de parochia supradicta corpora eorum iaceant in cimiterio parochiali prenominato cum rebus quas debent habere mortui secum ad ecclesiam nisi forte fuerit quod aliquis de burgensibus aliquo subito casu ibi moriatur. Et si dominia postea creuerunt uel in sartis uel in fractura ueteris terre antea non culte, decimas eorum habeat predicta Capella; si uero eodem modo creuerunt terre aliorum hominum parochialium, ecclesia parochialis decimas eorum habeat; et si homines plures quam solebant dudum modo manent in dominio supradicto, decimas eorum et omnium hominum quicumque illud excoluerint dominium habebit capella, et ecclesia parochialis habebit eorum corpora qui in dominio manent; et si terre que tunc non fuerunt de dominio creuerunt in mansuris hominum, parochialis ecclesia eorum decimas habebit; et hiis omnibus predictis hominibus ipsa eadem omnes rectitudines christianitatis propter sepulture dignitatem faciet. Hiis presentibus testibus, G. episcopo Dunkeldensis, A. abbate Sancte Crucis, W. abbate de Striuelin, H. priore de Coldingham, O. priore de Jeddeworth, O. priore Sancte Crucis; et de laicis, Duncano comite, Gospatric comite, H. constabulario, W. de Sumeruile, Dauid Olifard, W. filio Alani, H. Camerario, Henrico filio Swani; et aliis multis.*

The preceding instrument may be thus rendered:

"This is the agreement which was entered into at the Castle of the Maidens, before King David, and Henry his son, and their barons, between R[obert] bishop of St Andrews and G[alfrid] abbot of Dunfermlyn, regarding the parish church of Eccles and the chapel of the Castle of Stirling. The King's barons remembered, and in that remembrance all agreed, that on the day when King Alexander caused the aforesaid chapel to be dedicated, he gave and granted thereto the tithes of his domains in

* Reg. de Dunfermlyn, 8, 9.

the lordship of Stirling, as they were his at the time, whether they increased or decreased: And further, they considered that the parish church of Eccles ought to have the whole tithes accruing from the herdsmen, bondmen, and gresmen, with other dues which they owe to the church; and those of them who may die, whether servants of the demesne lands or of the parish, their bodies should lie in the burying-ground of the parish, with such things as the dead ought to have with them to the church, unless by chance any of the burgesses die there suddenly. And if the domains shall increase, either by the grubbing out of wood or the breaking up land not before tilled, the chapel shall possess the tithes; and if the lands of other men of the parish increase, the parish church should have their tithes; and if more men dwell in the demesne than in times past, the tithes of these and of all cultivators shall go to the chapel, while the parish church shall have their bodies; and if the lands which were not of the demesne increase in the number of dwellings, the parish church should have their tithes; and to all the church shall minister Christian rites, on account of the dignity of sepulture. These witnesses were present— G[regory], bishop of Dunkeld; A[lwin], abbot of Holyrood; W., abbot of Stirling; H[erbert], prior of Coldingham; O[sbert], prior of Jedburgh; O[sbert], prior of Holyrood; and these laymen—Duncan, earl [of Fife]; Gospatric, earl [of Dunbar]; H[ugh de Morville], Constable; W[illiam] de Somerville [of Carnwath]; David Olifard [justiciar of Lothian]; W[alter], son of Alan [the Steward]; H[erbert], Chamberlain; Henry, son of Swan, and many others."

The history of the chapel is continued in the following instrument of excambion, of the reign of William the Lyon [1165-1214]:*

"Willelmus Rex Scottorum omnibus probis hominibus tocius terre sue, clericis et laicis, salutem. Sciatis me concessisse et dedisse et hac carta me confirmasse Deo et ecclesie Sancte

* Reg. de Dunfermlyn, 38, 39.

Trinitatis de Dunfermelyn et monachis ibidem Deo seruientibus et Capelle Castelli mei de Striuelin in excambium terre sue quam primum clausi in parco meo quando parcum meum primum clausi, terram que est inter terram suam quam habent extra parcum et diuisas terre de Kirketun et ex alia parte terram que est inter Cambusbarun terram Petri de Striuelin et terram Rogeri filii Odonis, sicut magna strata uadit ad Cuiltedouenald, sicut Ricardus de Moreuilla, constabularius, et Robertus Auenel, justiciarius, et Radulphus vicecomes, et Petrus de Striuelin perambulauerunt: Tenendam in perpetuam elemosinam, ita libere et quiete, sicut alias elemosinas suas tenent: Testibus, Ricardo de Moruilla, constabulario, Roberto Auenel, justiciario, Alano filio dapiferi, Adamo filio Thome, Rogero de Valoniis, Radulpho vicecomite de Striuelin, Petro de Striuelin, Waltero de Berkelai, Ricardo clerico apud Striuelin."

Rendered into English, the preceding instrument reads thus:

"William, King of Scots, to all good men, clerical and lay, greeting: Wit ye me to have granted and given, and by this my present charter confirmed to God and the Church of the Holy Trinity at Dunfermline, and the monks there serving God, and to the chapel of my castle of Stirling, in exchange for their land, which I find included in my park when I first enclosed my park,* the land which is between their land which they have outside of the park, and the boundaries of the land of Kirketoun; and, on the other side, the land which is between Cambusbaron, the land of Peter of Stirling, and the land of Roger, son of Odo—as the high road leads to Cuiltedouenald, as Richard de Moreville, constable, and Robert Avenel, justiciary,

* The King's Park at Stirling, a portion of table-land lying between the south-western edge of the castle rock and the hamlet of Cambusbarron, is still attached to the Crown, under care of the Commissioners of Woods and Forests. When, in 1264, "a new park" at Stirling was to be laid out, allusion was made to "the old," being that doubtless which was constructed at the instance of King William the Lyon.—Exchequer Rolls, i. 24.

and Ralph the sheriff, and Peter of Stirling perambulated it: To hold in perpetual alms, as freely and peaceably as they hold their other alms. Witnesses—Richard de Morville, constable; Robert Avenel, justiciar; Alan, son of the Steward; Adam, son of Thomas; Roger de Valoniis; Ralf, sheriff of Stirling; Walter of Berkelay; Richard the clerk. At Stirling."*

Included in the schedule of documents found in the King's Treasury of Edinburgh, on St Michael's Day 1282, by Thomas de Carnoto, Ralph de Bosco, and William de Dumfries, is a bull of Pope Alexander IV. [1154-1261], granting indulgence to the King's Chapel.†

In the account of Sir Robert Erskine, Sheriff of Stirling, rendered at Dundee on the 2d April 1359, appears a sum of fifty shillings as having been paid to the chaplain officiating in the chapel of St Michael in the Castle of Stirling, his salary being five pounds a year, payable at the king's pleasure.‡

Robert, Earl of Fife, High Chamberlain, in his account presented at Stirling on the 18th March 1384, records a payment for two thousand large nails with pointed heads for the door of the chapel at Stirling Castle.§

During the regency of the Duke of Albany the chapel

* In the Register of Dunfermline the various confirmations include the Chapel Royal of Stirling, with "all things thereto belonging" (pp. 57, 63, 66, 81, 154, 157, 418).

† Acta Parl. Scot., i. 107, 108.

‡ Exchequer Rolls, i. 577. The Irish ecclesiastic, St Malachi or Michael, visited David I. "in quodam castello suo," and healed his son, the Prince Henry (Forbes's Kalendars of Scottish Saints, 398). In commemoration of this event the name of the Irish saint may have suggested a dedication of the Chapel Royal alike to himself and to the chief of the apostles.

§ Exchequer Rolls, iii. 676.

was partially rebuilt. For the work of renovation the chamberlain, John Stewart, Earl of Buchan, presented at Perth, on the 12th June 1412, an account showing an expenditure of £22, 3s. 8d.*

In 1425 David Broun, canon of the King's Chapel, is named as one of the auditors of exchequer.† In the account of Alexander Gulde and John Richardson, custumars of Stirling, rendered 31st May 1434, is included a payment of ten shillings for bread, wine, soap, and wax issued for the use of the chapel.‡

Under 1434 appears a payment of £7, 6s. 8d. as the salary of the chaplain officiating in the Chapel of Stirling Castle.§

In an account rendered to the exchequer on the 21st June 1435, there is a payment of five shillings for bread, wine, soap, and wax for the Chapel of Stirling Castle, also for two vials for the use of the altar.∥

Hitherto the King's Chapel, known also as St Michael's, was a very small structure, while, as we have seen, the humble chaplain, at first recompensed with five pounds a year, was afterwards rewarded with a salary one-half beyond that sum. From the reign of James III. the institution became differently constituted.

James III. succeeded to the throne in 1460 when a child of nine years. From his grandfather, James

---

* Exchequer Rolls, iv. 164.   † Ibid. iv. 379.
‡ Ibid., iv. 565.   § Ibid., iv. 592.   ∥ Ibid., iv. 605.

I., inheriting a love of music, he drew to his court at Stirling those who cherished the harmonic art. Of these the most notable was William Rogers, a doctor of music, who came to the Scottish court in the train of the English ambassador.* Rogers, it is believed, was educated in the same school which produced Hamboys, a noted performer, and the author of a musical treatise usually but incorrectly attributed to Thomas of Tewkesbury.†

With the royal household Rogers was connected prior to the 29th November 1469, when by a charter under the great seal he obtained the lands of Traquair, which, on the forfeiture of Lord Boyd, had reverted to the Crown. In the charter it is set forth that the lands were granted him for important service, while in the instrument of sasine he is described as *scutifero meo familiari*, that is, a squire of the royal household.‡ If we suppose, as is probable, that he was connected with the court at least one year before he received his lands, the king must have been in his seventeenth year when he elected him into favour. Doubtless the English musician would to the young and ardent sovereign expatiate on the interesting character of the richly endowed schools of music connected with the English cathedrals and principal

---

* Ferrarius Continuation of Boethius, 1574, pp. 391, 392.

† Hawkins' History of Music, 1776, ii. 345, 346; Bishop Tanner's Bibliotheca, Lond. 1748, p. 373.

‡ Traquair Papers, quoted by Dr William Chambers in his History of Peeblesshire, Edinb. 1864, p. 85.

churches. He would also set forth the munificence of Edward IV., in whose household were thirteen minstrels, who discoursed music to him at meals, and at such other seasons as they were specially commanded to render service.*

By such animating details would be excited the enthusiasm of a prince supremely moved by one passion, and who, inexperienced in government, might readily conceive that what had been effected in the sister country could without difficulty be accomplished in his own. James determined that St Michael's Chapel should be rebuilt and constituted both as a royal chapel and a musical college.

It was most probably when he was about to reconstruct the chapel that James summoned to his court those artificers, of whom his patronage became attended with tragic events. The artificers included Robert Cochrane, an architect; James Homyll, a robemaker; and Leonard, a worker in skins. John Ramsay, a youth of elegant accomplishments, also obtained special favour. For the progress of events we are indebted to Lindsay of Pitscottie. After setting forth the discomfiture of Henry VI. by Edward IV., his successful rival, Lindsay remarks, that James III., "being in good peace and rest the most part of that year, went to Stirling and remained there." The chronicler then details how James "founded a college, which he named the

* Hawkins' History of Music, ii. 290-292.

Chapel Royal." Now, Edward IV. took Henry VI. prisoner on the 14th April 1471, and if Lindsay's narrative is correct, the Chapel Royal was constructed somewhat posterior to that date. Lindsay's relation is confirmed by entries in the treasurer's accounts. These accounts are extant only from 1473, but in that year, under " Expensis for the Chappell," occur the following items :

"In the first, to Schire Johnne of Rende* to pay for a pres kist [press chest] to the chapell to keep the graith [equipments], ... xvj^s vj^d

Item, for the makin of thre albis, three amytis,† and a towale for the hie alter, ... vj^s

Item, for mess bred for the hale yere, . . xv^s

Item, for a pund of sens [incense], . . . iiij^s

Item, for jli of Birgis threde [Bruges thread] to mend the vestamentis, ... ij^s vj^d

Item, for the mending of a caip, ... iij^s

Item, for the cariagis of the chapell grath on Sanct Margretes day fra the Abbay [Cambuskenneth] to the castell and to the Abbay, ... xviij^d

Item, given to the King and the Qwene to offir in the castell on Sanct Margretis day a Franche croune and half a ross noble, extendand to . . . xxvij^s vj^d."

These items in connection with the Chapel Royal are included in the treasurer's statement of 1474 :

"Item, gevin to Schire Johnne Story, collector for the chapell, for the hail offerandis for this yere, . . . xx^{li}

---

* Sir John of Rende or Rhynd was of a Perthshire family. Will of Rynde is, in 1473 and subsequently, named in the Treasurer's Accounts as supplying textile fabrics for the king's use.

† The amyt or amice was an oblong portion of linen, richly embroidered, worn on the neck at mass.

Item, to the King and Qwene to offir on Sanct Petris day, ilkane
j croune, ... xxiiij^s
Item, to the King and Qwene to offir vpone Sonday, the xiij day
of Julij, ilkane j croune, ... xxiiij^s
Item, fra Sandris of Turing ix° Nouembris and deliuerit to
Master Johne Patonsone, vj elne of brade clath for ij
tovellis to the Kingis alter, price elne iij^s, . summa, xviij^s
Sum totale of thir expensis of the chapel, . xxx^{li} vij^s vi^d."

The preceding entries refer to the Chapel Royal solely in its ecclesiastical relations. Of the king's intentions respecting it as a musical seminary we shall learn in the sequel.

Prior to the reign of James I., our knowledge of Scottish music is extremely circumscribed. The bagpipe belongs to the prehistoric period, as well as some other Scottish instruments in their simpler forms. Among the sculptured decorations of Melrose Abbey, founded in 1136, a piper is represented. To the pipers of David II., in 1362, was made a payment of forty shillings.* Especially cherishing the harmonic art, James I. excelled in music, both instrumental and vocal. In his poem, "Peblis to the Play," he celebrates the bagpipe in these strains:

"The bag pipe blew and they out-threw
  Out of the townis untauld,
 Lord! sic ane schout was thame amang
  Quhen they were owre the wald.
   .   .   .   .   .   .

"With that Will Swain came sweitand out,
  Ane mickle miller man;
 Gif I sall dance, have done, lat se
  Blaw up the bag-pipe than."

* Exchequer Rolls, ii. 115.

James I., according to Buchanan,* played on all musical instruments, and could in singing compete with the best vocalists of his age. Writing in 1646, Tassoni remarks that James composed music, but this assertion is not supported by any earlier authority.

Sir Richard Holland, in "The Howlat,"† a poem composed in 1453, enumerates twenty-three instruments as existing in his time. We quote the passage:

> " All thus our lady thai lovit with lyking and lyst
> Menstralis and musicianis, mo than I mene may,
> The Psaltery, the Sytholis, the soft Sytharist,
> The Crovde, and the Monycordis, the Gittyrnis gay;
> The Rote and the Recordour, the Ribupe, the Rist,
> The Trumpe and the Talburn, the Tympane but tray;
> The Lilt Pype and the Lute, the Fydill in fist,
> The Dulset, the Dulsacordis, the Schalme of Assay;
> The amyable Organis vsit full oft;
> Claryonis lowde knellis,
> Portatiuis and Bellis,
> Cymbaclanis in the cellis
>   That soundis so soft."

The Psaltery was a one-sided instrument of triangular form, mounted with three rows of strings; the Sitholis, so called from *cistella*, a small bone, was a sort of whistle; the Sitharist or Cither, an instrument of which the strings were twanged with a quill; the Croude, a species of violin; the Monycord, a one-

* Rerum Scot. Hist., lib. x., sec. 57.
† The Buke of the Howlat. 1823, edited by David Laing, Edinb. Stanza 59.

stringed instrument; the Gittern or Gythorn, a species of guitar; the Rote, a hurdy-gurdy; the Ribupe or Rebeck, an instrument of three strings; the Rist, probably an instrument emitting music by percussion; the Trumpe, the *Jeu-trompe* or Jew's harp; the Recorder, a large flageolet; the Talburn or Tabor, a small drum; the Tympane, a large drum; the Liltpipe, a shepherd's pipe or stock and horn; the Lute, an instrument with originally eight strings; and the Fydell, a pear-shaped instrument, with four strings, resembling the modern violin. The Dulset and the Dulsacord were varieties of the Dulcimer or rudimentary Pianoforte. The Schalme was a species of hautbois. The Organ was then an instrument of ten or fourteen pipes. The Clarion was a trumpet; and the Portative, a portable organ, afterwards known as the regals. The "Bellis Cymbaclanis" were a sort of tambourine, producing music by percussion.

The luter or lute-player of James III. wore a livery of green. In August 1473, "Heroun, clerk of the chapell," received at "the Kingis commande" eleven shillings "to his passage to the scolis," while in the following September a payment of five pounds was made to "Johnne Broune, lutare, at his passage our sey to lere his craft." Broune* was doubtless sent to Bruges, for in the subsequent December appears a payment for "a barell of salmond that was send to a lutare to Bruges, at the Kingis command." In 1474

* Treasurer's Accounts, i. 43-67.

the king's "litill lutare, the page," was also sent to Bruges.

These entries might imply that Rogers, who received the honour of knighthood, and held rank as a courtier and landowner, was not expected to instruct in the elements of music. He remained in constant attendance on the royal person. The result was such as, among an untutored people and in a turbulent age, might have been anticipated. The nobles and barons conspired against the stranger knight, and determined his overthrow. In 1478 he was forced to surrender the lands of Traquair at a nominal price. For seventy marks[*]—of which forty were to be paid "at Martinmas next ensuing," and the remaining thirty eight days before Christmas—he surrendered his lands to James Stewart, Earl of Buchan, the king's uncle, executing in his favour, on the 19th September 1479, an instrument of sasine. Nor did this surrender satisfy either cupidity or revenge. In league against the musician, Buchan was joined by the king's two brothers, the Duke of Albany and the Earl of Mar. The latter was by the king thrown into prison, and there died; the former escaped to France, but afterwards joined Edward IV., when, in June 1482, he entered Scotland with an army. To resist the invasion, James, on the 22d July, assembled an army at Lauder; but mutiny

[*] Chambers's Peeblesshire, pp. 85, 86. The lands of Traquair now produce a rental of about £6000.

supervened; for he was accompanied by Rogers, also by his favourites, Ramsay and Cochrane, of whom the last, having lately been created Earl of Mar, was on this account peculiarly obnoxious. Heedless of the enemy's approach, the Earl of Angus led a party, which seized the royal favourites, and hastening them to Lauder Bridge, there hanged Rogers and Cochrane from the parapet. On account of his youth and the king's entreaties, Ramsay's life was spared.*

By nearly all the historians it has been alleged or assumed that in the Lauder massacre were included the whole of the king's artistic associates. It is certain that James Homyll, the robemaker, survived, since he is mentioned both in relation to a royal pension and otherwise, some years subsequently. The warrant for his pension may not inappropriately be introduced.

"James, be the grace of God King of Scottis, to our Chawmerlane of Striuelyneschire that now is and that sall happin to be for the tyme, greting: Wit ye that we, being at oure perfect aige, and eftir oure last General Revocatioun, for the singular [favour] that we have to oure familiare sartein and workman for our persoun, James Homyll, we have gevin and assignit and be thir present lettres, gevis and assignis to him ane yerly pensioun of twenty pundis of usuale money of our realme, for all the dayis of his life, for his lele, treu, and thankfull seruice done and to be done til ws; to be pait to the said James furth of the maills and proffittis pertening til ws within Striuelyneschir be oure Chawmerlane therof that now is and sall happin to be for the tyme, at tua usuale termes in the yer, Witsunday and Mer-

* Drummond of Hawthornden's History of Scotland, Glasg. 1749, 12mo, p. 131.

times in winter, be evin porciones, but ony reuocatioun, impediment, or again calling of ws or oure successouris quhatsumeuer, induring the lyftyme of the said James: Quharfor we charge straitly, and commandis you oure said Chawmerlane that now is and sall happin to be for the tyme, that ye yerly content and pay to the said James, at the termes forsaid, the said sume of tuenty pundis, as his fee for all the dayis of his life yerly, of our said proffitis and fermes of Striuelyneschir, nochtwithstanding our said late general revocatioun, vnder all the hiest pain and charge that eftir may folow: The quhilk soume of tuenty pundis we sall mak be allowit to you yerly in your comptis be the auditouris of our chekker, ye schawand thir oure letres anys before the saidis auditouris and registrat in   Rollis, and bringing the said James acquittance and ressait of the said soume yerly, to scheu for your warant: And thir our letres, being registrat, deliueris thame agane to the said James, to remane with him for all the dais of his lyfe, as said is: Gevin vnder oure priue sele, at Edinburgh, the tuenty day of Janvar, the yer of our Lorde a thousand four hundreth sevinty and sevin yeris, and of our reynne the auchtene yere." *

Being involved in a charge of treason along with the Earl of Buchan, Homyll had his goods confiscated prior to the 10th July 1488. †

Having slaughtered two of his associates, the dissatisfied nobles conducted the king to Edinburgh, and there warded him in the castle. Marching to the capital, the English army would have aided in placing the Duke of Albany on the throne; but the royal brothers becoming reconciled, the king's authority was restored.

Among those whom James received into his royal

---

* Rotuli Scaccarii Scotie, No. 280.
† Acta Parl. Scot., ii. 201; Treasurer's Accounts, i. lxiii.

favour were William and Robert Schevez. These persons appear in 1473 as officers of the wardrobe,* but Robert is not mentioned subsequently, and may have died young. "Master William Sevas" is, in the Treasurer's Accounts, frequently named. According to Buchanan, he had studied medicine at Louvaine under a distinguished preceptor, but had recommended himself to the Scottish sovereign rather as an astrologer.† One of his early offices was that of physician to the court; he was thereafter constituted an auditor of exchequer and archdeacon of St Andrews. ‡

On the ground that he was ignorant of theology, William Schevez was by Archbishop Graham of St Andrews refused institution, a proceeding which involved the primate in grievous persecution. Schevez was elevated as coadjutor-bishop, and having at length accomplished Graham's deprivation, was about the year 1478 consecrated as his successor.

On the assassination of Rogers and Cochrane, Archbishop Schevez became the king's principal adviser. Resolved on the endowment of the Chapel

---

* Treasurer's Accounts, i. 13, 18, 20.

† Rerum Scot. Hist., lib. xii., c. 37. In the library of the University of Edinburgh, a MS., bound in a thick folio volume, bears, after the colophon, the signature *Scheuez*, to which is added in the same handwriting, *Lib. Villielmi Sanctiândree Archiepi*. The MS., a treatise on medicine, is dated 1393, and is entitled, *Geraldus de Solo super nono Almansoris*. It was purchased at the sale of Dr John Jamieson by Principal Lee, at whose death it was acquired by its present custodiers.

‡ Treasurer's Accounts, i. 21, 23, 75.

Royal as a musical school, James embraced what seemed a favourable opportunity for effecting his purpose. In the conduct of some of its members the priory of Coldingham had become a reproach; it was also the victim of cupidity, for two powerful barons—Patrick and James Home—had usurped the revenues, and refused to restore them, in defiance of ecclesiastical censures. Utterly defenceless, the monks sought and obtained refuge in the priory of Lindisfarne.* Under the circumstances, James was persuaded by Schevez that annexation to the Chapel Royal of the revenues of Coldingham Priory would at once punish profligate churchmen, and restore to a proper use that which had been unjustly appropriated. The step was in 1485 approved by Parliament, and thereafter Schevez proceeded to obtain the Papal sanction. Innocent III. having acceded to the royal wish, Parliament in 1487 decreed that any attempt to oppose or disturb the act of annexation should be construed as treason.† This enactment was not unnecessary, for Patrick and James Home had already determined to resist any attempt to dispossess them of the priory revenues. They were warmly supported by the Hepburns, their opulent neighbours. Obtaining a further ally in the Earl of Angus, that powerful nobleman obtained to their

---

* Raine's Priory of Coldingham, Surtees Society, ix., x., xi.; Hunter's History of the Priory, 1857, 68-71.
† Acta Parl. Scot., ii. 171.

cause the adhesion of the Earl of Argyll, and the Lords Gray, Lyle, and Drummond; also of many of the lesser barons. In the words of the Act by which they afterwards sought excuse, they renewed the old charge that the king "counsellet and assistet to him in the inbringing of Englishmen to the perpetual subjection of the realm." Personally they sought the support of Henry VII.* The insurrection in favour of the Homes became general, while at Leith and the castle of Dunbar the insurgents obtained both ammunition and money. In the formidable combination contemplating the overthrow of his benefactor, Schevez abandoned the royal cause, and, joining the disaffected, bestowed upon them his episcopal benediction. Under the persuasion of Schaw of Sauchie, governor of Stirling Castle, the Duke of Rothesay forsook his royal father, and consented to become the nominal leader of his opponents. Among his northern subjects James mustered a considerable army, and at their head met the rebels at Blackness. An amicable arrangement ensued, and the king, under the belief that his opponents were satisfied, disbanded his army. But the insurgents were still in the field, and when James with his armed attendants proceeded from Edinburgh to Stirling in June 1488, he found the castle closed against him. A body of rebels whom he found in the place he drove across Stirling Bridge, and, pursuing them to the

* Rymer, Fœdera, xii. 340.

house of Keir, three miles to the northward, set fire to that mansion. On the 11th June his followers encountered the main body of the insurgents at Sauchie, near Bannockburn. There he experienced defeat, and, in endeavouring to escape, fell from his horse. Severely stunned, he was borne into a peasant's hut, where, recognised by one of the enemy, he was cruelly slain.*

Prior to his father's death, the Duke of Rothesay had assumed the government; when he became actual sovereign, he bestowed on his father's adversaries high offices of state. Yet, if we believe Lindsay of Pitscottie, he was not satisfied that making war upon his father was an act wholly to be justified. Proceeds the chronicler:

"The king remained a while in the castle of Stirling, and daily passed to the Chapel Royal, and heard matins and evening-song; in the which every day the chaplains prayed for the king's grace, deploring and lamenting the death of his father; which moved the king, in Stirling, to repentance, that he happened to be counselled to come against his father in battle, where-through he was murdered and slain. To that effect he was moved to pass to the dean of the said Chapel Royal, and to have his counsel how he might be satisfied, in his own conscience, of the art and part of the cruel act which was done to his father. The dean, being a godly man, gave the king a good comfort; and, seeing him in repentance, was very glad thereof. But yet this godly man durst not utter his mind unto the king, so far as his conscience served him; because the king was young and youthful, and had no constancy to keep counsel or secret thought, albeit it was for his own profit. And also this godly

* Treasurer's Accounts, i., Preface, lxvii., lxviii.

man dreaded the lords, and them that were conspirators of the king's dead, his father, thinking that these murderers would be discontent, and utterly displeased at him, if he had given the king his counsel, so far as his conscience dyted him. Therefore he continued the same till he saw the king farder in age, and other counsellors about him. In the meantime he gave him fair words, and put him in good hope of forgiveness thereof, by God's mercy in Jesus Christ." *

That James IV. provided for the due continuance of divine service in the Chapel Royal is evidenced in the Treasurer's Accounts by the following entries:

"1488. To the clerkis of the chapell for thair service at Ywle, at the kingis commande, . . . xxx^{ti} li.
1489. To the clerkis of the kingis chapell, at the kingis commande, ... xx^{ti} li.
To the clerkis of the chapell for Ywle, . . xxx^{ti} li.
To the clerkis of the chapell that wer in Lythgow quhen the Imbassatouris was thare, at the kingis commande, ... xxx^{ti} li.
1490. On Sonday the ij° Janvar, to the clerkis of the chapell for thair service at Ywle, . . . xv li."

When the king moved from one residence to another, there were borne along with him by his attendants a cupboard of plate, a wardrobe of vestments, and a box containing the chapel gear. In reference to the last, the Treasurer's Accounts of 1484-89 contain the following entries:

"For the carying of the chapell grayth fra Edinburgh to Lythgow before Ywle, and agane to Edinburgh efter Ywle, xx^s.
To Schir Johne of Rind, for iiij hors to Striuelin with the

---

* Lindsay of Pitscottie's History of Scotland, Edinb. 1728, fol., p. 93.

INTRODUCTION.   xxvii

chapel gere and himself, and fra Striuelin to Edinburgh
agane, ...   xxxij s.
For wesching of the chapel gere, and for a kist to turs it
in, ...   iiij s.
To iiij hors to turs the sammyne graith [convey the same equip-
ments] to Edinburgh, ...   xx^s.
To Schir Johne Rynde for the carying of the chapell graytht to
Lythgow, ...   xviij^s vi^d."

Under the year 1494, the Treasurer's Accounts exhibit the following charges in connection with the chapel furniture :

"Expens made apoune the kingis chapell—
Item, in the first, gevin to the Lard [Laird] of Lundy,* to mak
tua towallis to the altar of Striuiling, and to mak ane new
alb to the sammyne, xvj ellis of braid clath, price of the
ell iij^s., summa, ...   xlviij^s.
Item, for the mending of the sepulture [niche in chancel], the
chapell dure [door], and Judas crois,†   .   .   iij^s.
Item, for a lok, stapill, and nalis,   .   .   .   ij^s.
Item, bocht j^c estland burdis [Dantzic wainscot] for the silour-
ing [ceiling] of the chapell in Striueling, price   .   x^{li}.
Item, gevin to the browdstar [embroiderer] to mend the vest-
imentis of the Kingis chapell, be command of the King,
xviij pirnis of gold, bocht fra James of Turing, price   ix^{li}.
Item, to the sammyne, xj vnce of silk, price of the vnce iiij s.,
summa, ...   xliiij s.
Item, to the sammyne, xvij ellis of bukerame, price of the ell
iij s., summa, ...   lj s.
Item, to the sammyne, iiij vnce of rubannis, price of the vnce
vj s., summa, ...   xxiiij s.

* Sir John Lundy of that ilk was governor of Stirling Castle.
† The Paschal Candlestick, usually of brass, had seven branches, from the seventh or middle one of which a tall piece of wood, painted like a candle, and called the Judas of the Paschal, rose nearly to the roof, on the top of which was placed at Eastertide the Paschal candle of wax.

Item, to the sammyne, a half pund of raw silk, price xxvj s. viij d.
Item, to the browstar himself, for three termes fee, at the Kingis command, xx^{li}, summa, . . xl li. xviij s. viij d."

In the love and practice of music James IV. did not yield to his royal sire. On succeeding to the throne, he continued to support such musical performers as had already been employed at court. Jacob, an accomplished luter—probably one of Sir William Rogers' pupils *—is, in the Treasurer's Accounts, named as receiving his reward in 1489 and subsequent years. Owing to his improvidence Jacob in 1500 pledged his lute, when he received, by the king's order, a portion of money to "louse" or redeem it. While ordinary lute-players received a quarterly allowance of fourteen shillings, Jacob had a salary of double that amount. In 1496 "Lundoris the lutare" and "John Wardlaw the lutare" are named in connection with the household. During the previous reign harpers are unnamed; but in May 1490, an ersche (Irish) harper had, at the king's command, a recompense of eighteen shillings. In 1496 and 1497 James Mylsone the harper, Pate the harper, and Fowlis the harper, and the "harper with a [one] hand," received rewards. In 1502 five harpers are named.

Performers on the clarsha, a kind of harp used

---

* Writing in 1529, Ferrarius, the continuator of Boethius, remarks that he had met with several persons who boasted that Sir William Rogers had instructed them (Boethius' History, 1574, pp. 391, 392).

chiefly in the Highlands, and strung with brass wire instead of catgut, were also entertained at court. In the Treasurer's Accounts, Martyn, otherwise Martyn M'Bretne, clareschaw, is named in 1490 and 1492. In 1505 there are payments to Alexander, harper, Pate, harper-clarsha, and his son the Ersch clarsha, "ilk man ix^s." In the same year, Makbuty the clarsha received from the king five French crowns to defray his travelling expenses to the Isles.

Among the household minstrels were Nicholas Gray, and one Jame, who played on the dron—that is, the bagpipe. English pipers came to the castle gate at Edinburgh in 1489, and there played before the king; these, in August 1491, were rewarded at Linlithgow with seven unicorns.*

A performer on the viol, a three or four stringed instrument, was designated a fithelar or fiddler. These fithelars were employed at court in 1489. In 1497 are named "the brokin-bakkit fithelar in Sanct Androus," and "ane fidelar that playit to the king at Durrisdeer; also "ane fidelar in Dunbar," and "Widderspune, the foulare, that tald tales and brocht foulis to the king."

The monycord was constantly borne with the king in his state progresses. In April 1497, John Hert received nine shillings for "bering a pare of moni-

---

* A gold coin struck in the reign of James III., and exhibiting a unicorn supporting a shield with the royal arms. Its value was eighteen shillings Scottish money.

cordis of the kingis fra Abirdene to Strivelin," and in the same year nine shillings were paid for "tursing of the kingis organis betuix Strivelin and Edinburgh." John Goldsmyth, in Inverness, was, in 1502, indemnified in seven shillings and eightpence—his advances "for ane cais to turs the organis in, vij^s and viii^d," while "to ij childer that bure the organis and their bellysis ouir the Month and again" were paid xxviii^s.

Payments to vocal performers were not uncommon. In 1489 "Cunnynghame the singar" received a demy—that is, a French gold coin of fourteen shillings value; and in the same year Wilzeam, sangster of Linlithgow, had ten pounds for "a sange bwke he brocht to the king be a precep." In April 1490, Henry the minstrel, known as the metrical chronicler of Sir William Wallace, is, under the designation of "Blind Harry," recompensed with "eighteen shillings." "Tua women that sang to the king," in June 1496, had a fee of thirteen shillings; and minstrels "that playit Mons [the famous cannon Mons Meg] doun the gate," received (April 1497) eighteen shillings. In the same month "tua fithelaris that sang Graysteil to the king" had a gratuity of nine shillings.

Not forgetful of his father's desire for the establishment of a musical college, James IV. at length took steps towards this object. Having in 1501 opened negotiations with the court of Rome, pro-

ceedings ensued, which are detailed in the *Register*.
In instrument No. I. it is set forth how that

"James Abercromby, abbot of Scone,* and David Arnot,
archdean of Lothian,† judges and executors for the church of
St Andrews in the matters underwritten, along with a colleague
specially deputed by the Apostolic See, had received a letter of
Pope Alexander the Sixth,‡ by the king's hands. From that
letter it appeared that the Pope had got a petition from the
king, representing that, in the Chapel Royal of the blessed
Mary and St Michael, within the palace of the castle of Stirling,
in the diocese of St Andrews, one dean, and several others,
chantors, chaplains, and clerks, daily celebrated mass, and discharged other important functions; that the king had caused
the chapel to be renovated, and adorned it with books, cups,
and other ornaments. The king, it had also been set forth, had
assigned some of his own immovable property, with a view to
the chapel being erected and endowed as a collegiate church,
with a common chest, seal, chapter, and other insignia. Thereupon the king had desired that the provost of the church of St
Mary of the Rock,§ at St Andrews, and in his royal patronage,
should be erected into the deanery of the said church, and that
the provost of the church of St Mary should be dean of the
collegiate church, preside over the other persons therein, and
have the cure of the souls of the king and his household;

* This ecclesiastic was probably a scion of Abercromby of that ilk.
There was an abbot James of Scone in January 1493; also in 1516 (Gordon's Monasticon, Glasg. 1868, i. 35).

† Son of John Arnot of that ilk, by his wife Katherine, daughter of
Melville of Carnbee. Subsequently provost of Bothwell, he was chosen
abbot of Cambuskenneth in 1503, an office he retained till 1509, when he
was preferred to the bishopric of Galloway. He died in 1526 (Keith's
Scottish Bishops, Edinb. 1824, 277, 278).

‡ The infamous Roderic Borgia, who, under the title of Alexander VI.,
was Pope from 1492 till 1503.

§ Kirkheugh Church, at St Andrews, has long disappeared; but the
foundations, on a promontory near the present harbour, have been excavated. The church was designated "capella domini regni Scotorum."

and who, while residing in the church of St Mary, should be provost, and while in the church to be erected should be dean, so that there should not be two dignities, but one only, having the pre-eminence in both churches. There should also be a subdean to act in the dean's absence; a sacristan to have charge of the jewels and other ornaments; also sixteen canons, and as many prebends skilled in song, with six boy clerics, competently trained in song, or fit to be instructed therein. These should, it was desired, perform divine worship both day and night, and should not be bound to observe any other mode of worship, unless the king so determined. And whereas two canons only had been wont to reside in the Augustinian priory of Rostnot [Roseneath], albeit its revenues were worth one hundred and twenty pounds sterling yearly, and were sufficient for the support of six, and even more, canons of the order; and that, in the church of Dunbar, the canons generally served by substitutes, it was by the king desired that a suitable portion should be reserved from the revenues of the priory for six canons, of whom the existing prior should be one, and that the residue be applied to the deanery and other offices of the collegiate church; and that the canonries and prebends of Dunbar, and other benefices with and without cure in the city or diocese of St Andrews, or wherever they are in the patronage of the king or of other laics, yielding revenues to the value of £2000 Scots, being £500 sterling or thereby in the year, should be united to the collegiate church, a suitable portion being reserved for the perpetual vicars. Of the residue of the revenues of these benefices, it was desired that a proportion should be distributed among the dean, subdean, and other officers of the collegiate church. By these means, it was set forth that divine worship would be increased in the chapel. The king further offered to assign, as endowment to the collegiate church, other patrimonial goods of the yearly value of £500 Scots. In consideration of the royal request, and on the full understanding that the promised endowments would be forthcoming, the Pope, commending the king's pious and laudable purpose, commanded the erection of the Chapel Royal into a collegiate church, reserving to the king the right of presentation of suitable persons to the offices of subdean, sacristan, canons, and prebends, and also the right of instituting and degrading the said six boys. The Pope further exempted the collegiate church and its officers from visitation, correction, jurisdiction, lordship, and power of the Archbishop of St Andrews, and of others his ordinaries whomsoever, and his officers and vicars; subjecting the church, its subdean, and other officers to the jurisdiction of the dean, and the dean to the immediate protection of the Apostolic See; and granting all privileges enjoyed by other collegiate churches in Scotland. The Pope likewise empowered the dean to absolve the king and queen, and their children, in cases reserved to the Apostolic See, except for crimes against ecclesiastical liberty, heresy, and rebellion or conspiracy, against the person or state of the Roman Pontiff or Apostolic See, or other crimes of a like nature."

This Papal rescript was dated at St Peter's, Rome, on the 2d May 1501, in the ninth year of Alexander's pontificate:—On the receipt of these letters the judges made examination, and found that the king, besides the endowments specified in his memorial, had assigned to the collegiate church possessions of the value of £500 Scots yearly, viz., £93, 6s. 8d. from the lands of Castellaw, in the county of Edinburgh; £94, 13s. 4d. from Strathbraan, Glenshee, and Auchtnabaid, in the county of Perth; and £312 from Kyntore and Lochaber, in the counties of Elgin and Forres: Whereupon, at the king's request, James, Abbot of Scone, and David, Archdeacon of Lothian, erected the chapel into a collegiate church, with common coffer, seal, chapter, and other collegial insignia, and the said provostry of St Mary of the Rock of St

Andrews into a deanery, and applied and assigned the residue of the revenue of the priory of Rostnot (Roseneath) to the dean and others, after deducting 400 marks Scots for the six canons of St Augustine, who should do the service of the priory. They further united the canonries and prebends of Spot, Belton, and Dunse, the archpresbytery and rectorship of Dunbar, Ayr and its chapel, Dalmellington, Crieff, Kyncardine with its annexed chapels, Petty Bracklyn, Duchell, and the parish churches of Kyrkandrews, Balmaclellan, Kells, Forest, Glenholm, Buitt, Ellem, and Cranschaws, all of which are in the patronage of the king, and their revenues do not amount to the sum of £2000 Scots yearly, distributing the possessions thus :—500 marks to the dean, 240 marks to the subdean, to one canon £100, to seven canons 100 marks each, to the other eight canons £20 each, with suitable daily *distributions*, to the six boys 90 marks, and reserving from the fruits of the curates of the united benefices a suitable portion for the perpetual vicars, from Kyrkandrews 24 marks, with residence to each parish church. Besides, they assigned a portion from the provents of the canonries and prebends of Pyncarton, first as the presbyters or their *remoreable* clerks who have served in these four canonries or prebends have been accustomed to receive; also to each of these four, one mark Scots for the presbyters or clerks who may serve in the churches or benefices without cure;

imparting to the king the power of publishing statutes for the direction of the church, and to the dean the right of presenting persons to the subdeanery; granting to the dean, or in his absence to the subdean, the oblations and casual revenues. The instrument was subscribed by notaries public, and sealed with the seals of the judges and with the great seal. The presentation of the Papal Mandate was made by the king to the judges at the Palace of Falkland on the 1st September, and the other acts of erection and publication at the castle of Stirling on the 6th September 1501, in presence of Andrew,* Abbot of Lindores, and other witnesses.

In the Register next in chronological order is a mandate by Pope Alexander VI., dated 19th March 1501-2, addressed to the Abbot of Holyrood and the Archdeacon of Lothian, whereby, in accordance with the bull of Paul II., he empowers these delegates to take account of the possessions and goods assigned by the king to his Chapel Royal, as set forth in the royal petitions. Among these are named the rents of Kyntore and Lochaber to the annual value of £70 sterling; also other churches in the king's patronage which should yield a revenue of £80 sterling. Should they find the proposed exchange and union to be to the evident advantage of the collegiate church, they

---

* Andrew Caveris, Abbot of Lindores, was appointed Master of Work, at Stirling, 26th January 1496-7, receiving on his entry a payment of £106, 13s. 4d. (Lindores Abbey, by Alexander Laing, LL.D., Edinb. 1876, 4to, 528).

were to give licence to the dean and chapter to receive other immovable goods, if the king should desire to assign such, in place of the foresaid possessions and goods, or to unite other churches to the value of £80 yearly, with the king's assent; providing also that through this union the several churches should not be deprived of their obsequies, or the cure of souls be neglected.

No. II. of the Register is a rescript of Pope Alexander, dated 16th April 1502, in which the erection of the Chapel Royal as a collegiate church is confirmed, it being provided that the cantor should have precedence of the sacristan, and enjoy a stipend of £100 Scots. By a further rescript of the same date (No. 10), it is set forth that the revenues of the church of Ayr, in the diocese of Glasgow, were of the value of £80 yearly; of Kincardyne, in the diocese of Aberdeen, £100; of Crieff, in the diocese of Dunkeld, £50; and of Petty Bracklyn and Duchell, in the diocese of Moray, £40 each; and that these were reserved for the new canonries and prebends, £50 for Glasgow, £50 for Aberdeen, and 30 marks Scots for each of those of Dunkeld and Moray, the residue to be applied to the collegiate church.

No. III. is a letter of conservation, dated St Peter's, 16th April 1502; it is addressed to the abbots of Holyrood, Cambuskenneth, and Paisley, on behalf of the dean and others serving the Chapel Royal. In the letter it is set forth that whereas the dean and subdean had shown that archbishops and other ecclesiastics, also members of the laity, might detain their goods and other possessions, or abet those who detained them, or might inflict injuries on them, and that it would be difficult to have recourse to the Apostolic See in every quarrel; therefore the Pope commanded the abbots, or two or one of them, personally or by others—even should they be without the district in which the abbots are deputed conservators and judges—not to permit the petitioners in any of their rights to be molested, but with the Papal authority to exercise ecclesiastical censure, and invoke the secular arm if need be, so that they may not be summoned to trial out of the place of their church under pretext of any other *conservatoriæ*, but may be held to answer in presence of the said abbots or their deputies. Moreover, if the places for citation of molesters be not safe, the judges are to affix citations where it is likely they may come to the notice of those cited, notwithstanding the constitution of Pope Benedict VI. and other Popes as to judges, delegates, and conservators, not to be summoned to judgment, or in other edicts which might interfere with the jurisdiction of the abbots in this matter, and notwithstanding any privileges granted to churches, monasteries, and orders, even the Cluniac and Cistercian. Further, the Pope decreed that none of the conservators might be hindered by any canonical impediment in the prosecution of any thing, even should another have commanded it.

A Papal mandate, dated 16th April 1502, and addressed to the abbots of Cambuskenneth and Paisley and to the archdeacon of St Andrews, sets forth that to the Chapel Royal had been appropriated the residue fruits of the churches of Ayr, Kincardine, and Crieff; also of Petty Bracklyn and Duchal. In this mandate the delegates are enjoined to publish the Papal letters when and as frequently as might be needful. They are instructed to aid the dean and other members of the collegiate church in enjoying quiet possession of their goods, and in the execution of their duties are to inflict such ecclesiastical censures as should be needful. In the event of the bishops of Glasgow, Aberdeen, Dunkeld, or Moray interfering with the chapel or its officers, they are to invoke the secular arm.

On the 13th March 1503, the endowments were confirmed by Parliament in an act of the following terms :

"The quhilk day our sourane lord with autorite of Parliament ratifiis and apprevis the fundatione to infeftmentis maid to the college of Striuiling callit his Chapell Riale baith of Kirkis Prebendis Chanonrijs and landis and the vnionis of the samyne efter the forme of the fundacione writtis and euidentis maid theruppon notwithstanding ony anexationis or vnione maid of the saidis landis prebendis or kirkis of befor."*

The first dean of the collegiate church was James Allardyce, Provost of Kirkheugh, formerly a member

* Acta Parl. Scot., ii. 240.

of the royal household. Allardyce died soon after entering upon office, when, on the king's request, the connection between the church at St Andrews and the Chapel Royal was dissolved. One of the king's early associates was Sir David Beaton of Balfour, who had become Treasurer of the kingdom. His younger brother James was a churchman, and under royal favour his promotion became easy. He was precentor of Caithness[*] in the cathedral church of Dornoch in October 1497, and from this office he advanced step by step till he became Archbishop of St Andrews. His nephew, David Beaton, was the celebrated cardinal. In the Register of the Chapel Royal, one of James Beaton's preferments, hitherto unknown to historians, has been recorded. On the 4th January 1503, he is described as Rector of Kirkinner, in Wigtownshire, in which capacity he assented to his benefice being transferred from the Priory of Whithorn to the Chapel Royal. The instrument of transfer, No. IV. of the Register, proceeds thus :—" George, Bishop of Whithorn, consequent on a petition by the prior and chapter of the church at Whithorn, representing that the parish church of Kyrkynnere, belonging to them would, if united to the collegiate church of Stirling, be of no little advantage to its dean and chapter, especially as the king granted to the prior and chapter of Whithorn the church of Kyrkandris, and on the supplication in the said petition to the

[*] Bannatyne Club Miscellany, ii. 162.

bishop to give his consent to the king's donation, and to annex the church of Kyrkynner to the said collegiate church, the bishop cited Mr James Betoune, rector of Kyrkynnere, and all others interested, to appear at Whithorn to show cause, if any, why the union should not take place; whereupon the bishop, sitting as judge, the prior and chapter, and Mr David Abyrcrumby, subdean of Dunkeld, as procurator for Mr James Betoune, rector of Kyrkynnere, appeared, and asked the bishop's consent to the annexation; and the bishop having inspected the king's charter, granted the foresaid church of Kyrkynnere to the collegiate church of Stirling, conferring on the prior and chapter of Whithorn the right to take possession of the church of Kyrkandris; providing also that the said churches be not defrauded of the due obsequies, and the cure of souls in them be noways neglected; and for the removal of all doubt the royal charter is incorporated in full." This instrument is dated at Edinburgh, 8th December 1503, and is subscribed and sealed by the bishop and by the chapter 4th January 1503-4, and attested by notaries public.

No. VI. of the Register is a notarial instrument, attesting that on the 9th December 1503, Mr James Betoune, rector of Kyrkynnere, asserted that the patronage of that church belonged to the prior and convent of Whithorn, and constituted Masters David Abircrommye, subdean of Dunkeld, Fergus Makdowel, official of Whithorn, James Akynheide, and

John Abircrommye, his procurators, to see and hear the annexation of the said church by George, Bishop of Whithorn, and in his name to give consent thereto. This instrument was, at Mr James Betoune's request, taken in the church of St Giles, Edinburgh.

No. VII. is a notarial instrument by Mr David Abircrummy, subdean of Dunkeld, as procurator for Mr James Betoune, into the hand of Thomas Kyrkaldy, notary public, of the resignation of the church of Kyrkynnere; taken in the lodging of Alexander Livingstoune, in the burgh of Stirling, on the 12th January 1503.

The next instrument, No. VIII., is a mandate by Pope Julius II., whereby, in terms of the king's petition, desiring the appointment of a treasurer as the fourth dignitary of the church, next to the cantor, with ten canons and a like number of prebendaries, together with similar portions to the other sixteen prebendaries, the Pope commands the abbots of Dunfermline, Scone, and Cambuskenneth to institute these offices accordingly, and which were to be in the patronage of the king. The mandate is dated at St Peter's, Rome, the 4th June 1504.

No. IX. is a confirmation by Pope Julius II., whereby, on the petition of the king and the dean and chapter of the church of the Blessed Mary and St Michael, at Stirling, narrating the grant by the king of the church of Kyrkandris to the prior and chapter of Whithorn, and the annexation of the church of

Kyrkynnere to the church at Stirling, and the possession thereof by the said church on the demission of James Betoune, the rector, and that the said petitioners stated that the revenues of the church of Kyrkynner did not exceed £80 sterling; he approves and confirms the annexation of the church of Kyrkynner: It is dated at Rome, 4th June 1504.

To make room for Beaton's promotion as Prior of Whithorn, and to prepare for his further advancement, James IV. petitioned the Pope to revoke the act whereby the collegiate church was united with the Provostry of Kirkheugh. Accordingly Pope Julius II., by rescript dated 3d July 1504 (No. XV.), restricted the Provost of Kirkheugh to his former function, and conferred the office of dean on the bishop of Whithorn. By the same instrument, subsequently confirmed (No. XVII.), the Pope united to the deanery the bishopric of Whithorn, which was afterwards styled the bishopric of Galloway. George Vans, Prior of Whithorn, was appointed to the conjoined office, while Beaton attained the place of prior. The union of the Chapel Royal with the see of Galloway would have subjected the royal family to episcopal jurisdiction, but this contingency was averted by a Papal rescript, No. XIV. of the series. In that rescript, dated 3d July 1504, Julius exempts the members of the king's household from the jurisdiction of bishops, archbishops, and other ordinaries. He further provides that the abbots of Dunfermline and

Cambuskenneth and the Provost of the church of Fesulan,* should uphold the cause of the exempted.

No. V. is a Papal rescript of the 4th June 1504, in which the canonries and prebends of Dunbar, Balmaclellan, the Forest, Buyth, and Ellam (Ellem), also the prebend of Crieff, are annexed to the collegiate church.

In 1508 Beaton was appointed bishop of Whithorn and dean of the Chapel Royal. A mandate of Pope Julius (No. XVI.), dated 8th September 1508, and addressed to the Archbishop of Siponto,† and the abbots of Cambuskenneth and Lindores, incorporates a bull providing that the bishop-elect should exercise ordinary rights over the churches united to the Chapel Royal, such as the rectors of these churches might have exercised had those churches not been united with that institution. The rectors were charged

---

* At Faslane, anciently Fassalane, at the head of the Gareloch, stood a small chapel, dedicated to St Michael, of which the ruin remains; in the same vicinity were other three chapels. But the designation of " Provost of the church of Fesulan " was more likely to be applied to the chief of a monastery of canons regular, which, dedicated to the Virgin, is believed to have constituted the religious establishment at Roseneath.

† Siponto is an archdiocese with one suffragan in the Neapolitan territory of Italy; the modern name is Manfredonia. In 1506-11, the Archbishop of Siponto was Antonio Maria dal Monte, an eminent jurist; he was translated to the see at Padua, and was afterwards a cardinal; his nephew was Pope Julius III. He died in 1533 (*Ughelli Italia Sacra*, tom i., 1106, vii., 859). How an Italian ecclesiastic should be introduced into a bull relating to church arrangements in Scotland is not very obvious. As Pope Julius II. despatched from Rome a special legate with a sword of state to James IV. in 1507, the conjecture may be permitted that that legate was the Archbishop of Siponto, who may have remained in Scotland up to the date of Pope Julius's mandate of September 1508.

not to suffer the elect of Whithorn and of the Chapel Royal to be molested against the tenor of these letters.

James Beaton held his conjunct office for one year only; he was thereafter advanced to the archbishopric of Glasgow. His successor was David Arnot, one of the commissioners in erecting the Collegiate Church, who in No. XVIII. of the Register is, in reference to a document subscribed by him dated on the 5th March 1511, described as "David, bishop of Whithorn and of the Chapel Royal of Stirling." As "bishop of *Candida Casa* and of the Chapel Royal of Stirling," he appears as a witness on the 10th October 1515, and again on the 7th February 1523.*

No. XIII. of the Register is an inventory of vestments, jewels, and books which belonged to the institution. Translated it reads thus:

These are the ornaments, jewels, and volumes kept in the collegiate church of the Blessed Mary and Saint Michael of Stirling, on 4th November 1505, under care of a prudent man, Mr David Trail, sacristan.

OF A BLACK COLOUR.

First, a chasuble,† a stole,‡ a maniple§ with fringe, an

---

* Registrum Domus de Soltre, etc.; Charters of Trinity College and other Collegiate Churches in Midlothian. Bannatyne Club, 1861, pp. 289, 331.

† The chasuble was a mantle of colour and quality suited to the rank of the wearer, usually bordered with gold.

‡ The stole, an embroidered scarf, was worn on the shoulders.

§ A narrow scarf, fringed at each end, the maniple was held in the hand, or worn on the arm of the officiating priest.

alb,* and an amice† of satin of black colour, having a fold of black buckrum; and this chasuble has embroidery of black velvet: Item, three copes, ‡ also of black velvet new and valuable, bearing the arms of our lord the King; one of which is sewed with threads of gold after the manner of glistering stars: Also a chasuble and two tunics of black velvet, sewed with golden threads; two stoles, three maniples with fringes for three albs and three amices of the same colour and texture: Also a pendiculum § of black velvet, sewed with golden threads in the manner of glistering stars, intended for the high altar, and which has a fold of blue buckram:|| Also one narrow and long cloth of black velvet, upon which are sewed with threads of gold these words—"His mercy is over all His works;" it has a fold of blue buckram: Also one cope of black damask, having the embroidery of velvet somewhat red: Likewise a chasuble of black damask, having embroidery of reddish velvet: Also a pendiculum of black damask for the high altar: Also a small and short old cope of silk, of black and red colour mixed, but rather more black than red: Also a chasuble, three stoles, three maniples with the fringe for three albs and three amices of black camelot,¶ with fold of buckram of the same colour. This chasuble was a fringe of black damask with certain red lines.

Of Blue Colour.

First, two copes of blue or sky coloured damask, with golden threads sewed like the rays of the sun; these are large and precious, having their hoods and the embroidery of precious cloth

---

* Made of fine linen, the alb was fitted closely to the body and worn with tight sleeves.

† A linen garment in the form of an oblong square, the amice was originally worn as a hood; it was latterly suspended from the shoulders.

‡ A sleeveless garment which surrounded the body, the cope was furnished with a hood and by a clasp fastened across the breast.

§ A small hanging.

|| True cotton stuff, considered precious.

¶ Camlet, a fabric originally composed of camel's hair, was afterwards made of silk.

of gold, and they have a linen cloth for preserving them: Also a chasuble, two tunics,* one stole, three maniples, with the fringe for three albs and one amice of damask, of the same colour, quality, and texture with the two copes immediately before named. These two tunics have the embroidery of precious cloth of gold. With these tunics are kept one stole and the fringe for one amice of gold, very precious.

Also one pendicule for the high altar, of blue damask sewed with golden threads like the rays of the sun, bearing a very beautiful salutation of Our Lady: Also one other pendicule for the high altar, of damask of the same colour and goodness with the pendicule immediately preceding, bearing a most excellent image of God the Father, and of Our Lady, and the images of certain angels. This pendicule has in it many pearls for its adornment; and these two pendicules have a linen cloth for their preservation: Also two smaller pendicules, of sky or blue coloured velvet, joined together with golden threads, one of them bearing an image of the Holy Trinity wrought in gold: Also one chasuble, two tunics, two stoles, three maniples, and with fringe, and three albs and three amices of velvet of blue colour, and having embroidery of cloth of gold: Also two pendicules for the high altar of blue taffety, one of which bears in the middle of it an image of the crucifix sewed with golden threads, and these two pendicules have a fold of white fustian.

OF RED COLOUR.

Two copes of precious cloth of gold, having hoods and embroidery also of cloth of gold, of red colour. These have a linen cloth for their preservation, and are the best copes in the church, and of great price: Also two copes of cloth of gold and red velvet, having a linen cloth for keeping them: Also two copes of cloth of gold and velvet mixed, with embroidery of cloth of gold, and fringes of silk threads round about them, with linen cloth for keeping them: Also two copes, one chasuble, two tunics, one stole, one maniple with fringe for one alb and one amice of red satin, wrought with threads of gold like the

* Linen dresses, with tight sleeves, worn by the subdeacons.

branches of trees. These two copes have linen cloth for their preservation : Also one precious cloth of gold of red colour ordained for the honour of the Eucharist when it is carried without the church, having a linen cloth for its preservation : Also four wooden staves of red colour for bearing aloft the said cloth upon the Eucharist: Also one small valuable frontlet of cloth of gold, and with golden threads hanging down, bearing the arms of the king and divers other arms, and certain images of saints, and which has upon it many pearls for its decoration : Also one cope of red velvet, with embroidery of black velvet: Also one cope of red satin cramasy, with embroidery of green damask: Also one chasuble of red satin cramasy, with fringe of green satin : Also a silken casket of square form, red without and white within, for keeping the communion cloths. Therein is included one cassock for the chalice, under a square figure of gold, sewed together, and richly wrought with many pearls : Also one new chasuble, one stole, one maniple with fringe for one alb and one amice of precious red cloth of gold, richly sewed and wrought, having a fold of blue satin. This chasuble has embroidery of cloth of gold sewed with golden threads, and is of great price: Also an old embroidery of cloth of gold suitable for a cope: Also another old embroidery of cloth of gold, for a cope ; and these two embroidered cloths are of red colour : Also one old frontlet of silk of divers colours, bearing various arms wrought thereupon, and of moderate value.

Of Whitish or Dun Colour.

One chasuble, two tunics, two stoles, three maniples with fringe for three albs and three amices of damask of dun colour, having embroidery of cloth of gold : Also two old silk cloths, wrought with golden threads of dun colour : Also one small old silk cloth wrought with golden threads of dun colour : Also one old velvet cloth of dun colour, intended, as appears, for the pulpit.

Of Green Colour.

One old chasuble, one stole, one maniple bearing the arms of the king and queen, which came from Dacia, of green damask, and with fringe for one alb and one amice of the same colour and texture: Also one cloth of verdour of divers colours, but chiefly green: Also two cloths of burd Alexander,* having a fold of linen cloth for covering both: Also one chasuble, with the arms of the king, two tunics, two stoles, three maniples with fringe for three albs and three amices of green damask: Also one chasuble bearing the king's arms, one stole, one maniple with fringe for one of green damask; this chasuble has embroidery of black velvet.

Of White Colour.

Two copes of white cloth of gold, having linen cloth for their preservation. One cope of white damask, sewed with golden threads like the shining sun, and the embroidery of cloth of gold.

Two chasubles, two stoles, two maniples with fringe for two albs and two amices of white damask, these chasubles having embroidery of black velvet. One chasuble, two tunics, two stoles three maniples with fringe for three albs and three amices of white damask, having embroidery of cloth of gold, and fold of red buckram; they are new and precious; and the said tunics have silken cords hanging behind, and bearing the arms of the king before, and of the king and queen, daughter of the King of England, commingled behind.

Of Purple Colour.

Two chasubles of purple velvet, with embroidery of cloth of gold, two stoles, two maniples, and with fringe for two albs and two amices of the same colour and texture.

Also two brass candlesticks, somewhat large; eight pewter phials; one small bell hanging before the church door; three large bells which came from the city of London, having been bought there by the king, founder of the church. One beautiful complete horecudium,† made by Sir James Pettygrew. Two

---

* Striped silk cloth brought from Alexandria.

† Or *horetudium*, supposed to be a striking clock or timepiece.

flaccots * of pewter, a pewter cross, gilt, bearing the image of the crucifix. Three small bells; a wooden cross of red colour, having a long staff. A long stick for carrying the image of the crucifix without the church. Two large desks of wood, standing in the choir. Three pairs of organs,† of which one is of wood and the other two of pewter or lead. Three servicalia,‡ to be placed under the missals on the altar. A table with three leaves, whereon are depicted an image of Our Lady carrying her Son in her arms, with two angels carrying musical instruments. A table on which is written "Pridie, etc." A large chest closed with two locks, for keeping the ornaments of the church. The Judas bells and the traitor,§ for the work of darkness on the week of our Lord's passion. A leather box, suitable for keeping the evidences of the church. Moreover, they have in painting many arms of the king and queen for celebrating ceremonies; one having three leaves on which are painted, under glass, an image of the crucifix, and four saints also under glass on the sides. A tabula, || bearing the form of the countenance of our Saviour, is called the vernakill: Also a tabula, on which is painted an image of Our Lady: Also a casket of pewter for the chrism.

Concerning the Jewels.

A large casket of silver for carrying the Eucharist; and a jewel of great weight and sumptuously wrought, and bearing on

---

* A flask or flagon, a narrow-necked vessel used for holding sacramental wine.

† A large organ was erected in Canterbury Cathedral so early as the twelfth century, and such were common in the abbey churches of England a century prior to the Reformation. The three pairs of organs of the Chapel Royal were evidently a species of regals intended to be carried about by the choristers.

‡ Cushions.

§ The Judas bells and an image of the traitor are not included in any other ecclesiastical inventory which has come under our notice.

|| The tabula was an instrument made of bone which the precentor held in his hand during service; it was occasionally ornamented with gold or silver.

the top of it an image of the crucifix; two silver vials gilt about the top; three silver candlesticks of notable weight; a censor with nave and spoon, of silver, for incense. The teistyr,* of silver gilt, bearing the image of the crucifix, and of Our Lady, and John the Evangelist; it has also many gems of various colours set in it, and is a notable jewel. One jewel of silver gilt has a belfry on the top of it, in which is placed a particle or portion of the wood of the holy cross; and this jewel is adorned with many pearls, and there are inclosed therein, as is verily believed, many relics of the saints. One small jewel of silver gilt, having the image of the crucifix on the top, stretched somewhat upward. A ring of pure gold having the likeness of the head of John the Baptist. Also four chalices and four pots of silver gilt, and of considerable weight. One small casket of silver gilt, of a round form, for keeping the Eucharist. One large and precious jewel of pure gold, bearing the image of Our Lady carrying her Son dead upon her knees, and divers other images. This jewel has on its top an image of the crucifix, and is wrought with great skill; it also bears many gems and divers pearls, and for preservation is enclosed in a leathern case. Three small candlesticks of silver gilt, bearing the arms of the King of England, were brought to Scotland with our queen, who is daughter of the King of England.

Of the Volumes.†

Two missals on paper, printed in letters. Two missals on parchment, printed. One old missal on parchment, written with the pen. Book of the Gospels written on parchment. Book of the Epistles written on parchment. Two old psalters written on parchment. Four large music books written on parchment,

---

* A small ornament with a canopy.

† This inventory is dated 4th November 1505, being eighteen months before Walter Chepman, in 1507, under the special sanction of the Privy Council, introduced into Scotland the art of printing. Prior to the operation of Chepman's press Scottish monastic libraries consisted of breviaries, missals and matin books, psalters, and copies of the Gospels and Epistles.

having divers capital letters gilt.* Two large breviaries printed on parchment. One large breviary printed on paper, many of the leaves torn. Two volumes in parchment, with notes of counterpoint. Two legends written on parchment, one of which concerns temporal things, the other relating to the saints. Ten processionals, † written on parchment, and annotated. Three Gradalia, ‡ written on parchment, and the large gradale, written on parchment, given to the king by the deceased abbot of St Colme. A large breviary, printed on paper. A small breviary, printed on paper. A volume called "Ordinary in usum Sarum," written on parchment. A small missal printed on paper. The vail of the temple divided into two parts, for *Quadragesima*. Also seven small linen cloths, adorned with crosses, and ordained to cover the images of the saints in the time of *Quadragesima*, etc.

From Gavin Douglas's "Palice of Honour," composed prior to 1509, it would appear that the instruments of music then in use did not materially differ from those enumerated in the " Howlat."

> "In modulatioun hard I play and sing
> Faburdoun, priksang, discant, countering,
> Cant organe, figuratioun, and gemmell;
> On croud, lute, harp, with mony gudlie spring;
> Schalmes, clariounes, portatiues, hard I ring,
> Monycord, organe, tympane, and cymbell,
> Sytholl, psalterie, and voices sweet as bell. §

* These letters were, no doubt, illuminated by Sir Thomas Galbraith, a priest descended from a powerful family in the Lennox, who, under James IV., was connected artistically with the Chapel Royal. In the Treasurer's Accounts " Schir Thomas Galbrecht " is named, in 1491, along with " Jok Goldsmyth and Craford " as receiving each three unicorns, " for the singyn of a ballad to the king in the mornyng." Sir George Galbraith, probably a brother of Sir Thomas, was Royal Master of Works at Dumbarton.

† Books containing parts of the service relating to processions.

‡ The Graduals were books containing portions of the service of the Mass.

§ The Poetical Works of Gavin Douglas, edited by John Small, Edinb. 1874, 8vo, i. 20.

During the reign of James III. those musical performers who received royal gratuities were chiefly Flemings. But James IV. encouraged and recompensed minstrels from Italy, tabroners from France, and harpers, pipers, and trumpeters from England. On the 1st January 1507, there appears in the Treasurer's Accounts a payment of ten pounds eleven shillings as made to sixty-three persons, who included " menstralis, trumpetis, tambroneris, fithelaris, lutaris, harperis, clarscharis, and piparis." Italian minstrels were regarded with especial favour. In September 1503, four Italian minstrels received six shillings to "fie [hire] thaime hors to Linlithgow, and to red [clear] them of the toun."

In August 1515, Bestians (Sebastian) Drummonth had a donative of ten pounds to aid his expenses in visiting his friends in Italy.

Vocalists were also employed and recompensed. In August 1504, "tua Inglise wemen that sang in the king's pailzeoune [pavilion]" received twenty-three shillings. "The crukit [lame] vicar of Dumfriess, who sang to the king at Lochmaben," had, in September 1506, a gratuity of fourteen shillings. The two following entries belong to the year 1508:

'Feb. 16. Item, to Wantonnes that the king fechit and gert her sing in the quenis chamer, . . . xiij s.
Mar. 6. Item, to Wantones and her tua marrowes that sang with her, ... xiij s."

On the 12th September 1512, Nicholas Abernethy,

the king's "sangster," received from the Treasurer a payment of twenty pounds.*

In acquiring a knowledge of their art, young musicians were aided at the public expense. In the Treasurer's Accounts, under the 27th March 1512, is the following entry:

> "Item, to foure scolaris, menstrallis, be the kingis command, to by thame instrumentis in Flandris vij^{li} gret, answerand in Scottis money to xxi li. and help thair expensis and fraucht Lvjs. And therefter, becaus thai plenyeit thai gat our litill expens and fraucht deliverit uther Lvj,   xxxvj li. xij s."

To "the chanoun of Halyrudhous" (canon of Holyrood) were paid in 1506 seven pounds for repairing "the organis in Strivelin." In 1511 "Gilleam," described as "organist makar of the kingis," was given

> "For expensis maid be him on the said organis in gait skynnis and parchment for the bellis [bellows], in nailles and sprentis of irne, in glew, papir, candill, coill, &c.,   viij^{li}. iijs."

In supporting and encouraging musical studies, James V., who commenced his reign in 1513, was equally ardent as his royal predecessors. He performed on the lute. For lutes purchased for his use, William Galbraith received forty and fifty shillings, and for a lute procured for him in 1540, John Barbour was paid a like sum.

In his *Complaynt of the Papyngo*, composed about

---

* Treasurer's Accounts.

the year 1512, Sir David Lyndsay thus refers to Stirling and its Chapel Royal:

> Adieu, fair Snawdoun! with thy touris hie,
>   The Chapell Royall, park, and tabyll rounde!
> May, June, and July walde I dwell in thee,
>   War·I ane man to heir the birdis sounde,
>   Quhilk doith agane thy royall roche redounde.*

Among the preferments of the celebrated John Mair or Major were the offices of canon and treasurer of the Chapel Royal. In the records of the University of Glasgow† he in 1518 is described thus: *Egregius vir magister Johannes Major doctor Parisiensis ac principalis regens collegii et pedagogii dicte universitatis canonicusque capelle regis ac vicarus de Dunlop.* In the same register he is in 1522 designated *Theologie professor, thesaurarius capelle regie Strivilingensis*, etc.

Quoting *Richardinus* (*Exegesis in can. S. Augustini*, fol. 87), Father Hay describes Alexander Paterson, sacristan of the Chapel Royal, as joint-author with the abbot of Inchcolm of a work "For Singing the Mass." The words quoted by him are, *Et illius etiam venerabilis viri Alexandri Patersonen Sacrarii Regalis Collegii Stirlingen, Quae non minus devotionem accendunt quam bonam delectationem.*‡

---

* Poetical Works of Sir David Lyndsay. Dr Laing's edit. Edinb. 1871, 12mo. i., 86.

† Ann. Univ. Glasg.—Records, No. i.

‡ Ane Account of the most renowned Churches, Bishopricks, Monastries, and other Devote Places, from the first introducing of Christianity into Scotland, etc. Written by Mr Richard Augustine Hay, Cannon Regular of St Genof's of Paris, Prior of St Pierremont, etc., 1700, tome i., p. 234.

In his "History of the Reformation," Knox refers to oppressive measures adopted against one of the musicians of the Chapel Royal, who had been suspected of heresy. We quote the Reformer's words: "Richart Carmichaell, yet leving in Fyfe, who being young, and ane singar in the Chapell Royal of Striveling, happened in his sleepe to say, 'The devill tak away the preastis, for thei ar a gready pack.' Hie, thairfor, accused be Sir George Clapperton, Deane of the said Chapell, was compelled tharefore to burne his bill." The date of Carmichael's prosecution is not given, but according to the chronological arrangement of Knox's work, it must have occurred between the years 1530 and 1536.* There was passed under the Privy Seal, 25th March 1539, " ane letter maid to Richard Carmichaell, remittand to him his eschete gudis pertenying to our Soverane throw being of the said Richard abjurit of heresy."

In annotating Knox's History, Dr David Laing has shown that Clapperton was subdean only. He first appears in the Treasurer's Accounts as "Maister Elimosinar to the Kingis grace;" he was afterwards Provost of Trinity College, near Edinburgh.† By an instrument, dated at Edinburgh, 22d March 1546-47, he was as subdean of the Chapel Royal of Stirling named as one of the judges delegated by letters of Antony, grand penitentiary of the Pope, in a process

* Knox's History of the Reformation. Dr Laing's edit. Edinb. 1846, i. 45.
† Reg. Mag. Sig., vol. xiv.

ratifying the gift of lands to the abbey of Kilwinning.* Subsequent to the Reformation he continued, though John Duncanson acted as minister, to be styled subdean of the Chapel Royal, and received two-thirds of the benefice. As vicar he was, on the 14th September 1562, granted a life-rent of the teinds of Kirkinner.† He died in April 1574, and in his testament, written at Stirling in his "awn dwelling-house" on the 5th of that month, he names Mr Robert Pont, Provost of Trinity College, to act as oversman and one of his assignees—a circumstance which, as Dr Laing remarks, would induce the belief that he had embraced the Reformed doctrines.‡

No. XVIII. of the Register continues the clerical history of the institution. In an instrument dated 1st December 1537, Henry (Wemyss), "bishop of Whithorn and of the Chapel Royal," along with the members of the Chapter, ordain

"Sir John Lambert, prebendary of the Chapel and scribe of the Register, to inscribe in the books a notarial instrument, under the hand of J. Prymrois, taken in the Chapel Royal, near the town of Edinburgh, 5th March 1511, certifying that Sir John Broune, perpetual vicar pensioner of the parish church of Creyf, had compeared in the presence of Mr David Abbercrunimy, principal official of Whithorn and of the Chapel Royal of Stirling, subdean of the said Chapel Royal, on the one part, and Sirs Wm. Sterheid and John Goldsmyth, canons of the Chapel Royal and

---

* Eighth Report of Historical MS. Commissioners' Report. Part i., p. 309.
† Analecta Scotica, i. 2.
‡ Register of Confirmed Testaments, 21st Sept. 1574.

prebendaries of the same church, on the other part; that in support of his claim for the augmentation of his yearly pension as being too meagre for his support, Sir John Broune produced two writings, one subscribed by James IV., dated at Edinburgh, 25th September, the other subscribed by David, bishop of Whithorn and of the Chapel Royal of Stirling, and dated at Edinburgh, 5th March 1511, whereupon the said vicar demanded augmentation of his pension; and that on consideration the judge ordained that the said vicar should have yearly from the fruits of Creyf 24 marks Scots, and two acres of arable land adjoining the said church from the town of For (?), a garden, houses, pasture, and fuel, paying yearly to the bishop the procurations due and wont, synodal fees, and the ordinary expenses to the dean," etc.

Bishop Henry Wemyss is in certain chartularies designated "fratre regis" and "fratre naturali regis." He was an illegitimate son of James IV. by a daughter of the House of Wemyss.* He appears in March 1540 as still holding office as bishop of *Candida Casa* and of the Chapel Royal.† In his conjunct offices he was succeeded by Andrew Durie, abbot of Melrose, who died in 1558.‡

On the 8th January 1548-49 William Hamilton, archdeacon of the Chapel Royal, and official general of Glasgow, granted a decree for transuming the deed of foundation of the collegiate church of Glasgow.§

John Carswell, a pious and learned churchman, latterly Bishop of the Isles, was sometime prebend of

* Russel's Keith's Scottish Bishops. Edinb. 1824, p. 278.
† Liber Col. Nost. Dom. de Glasg., p. 222.
‡ Russel's Keith's Scottish Bishops, p. 278.
§ Liber Col. Nost. Dom. de Glasg., p. 3.

the Chapel Royal. In the disbursements by Collectors of Thirds of Benefices, the sum of £26, 13s. 4d. appears to have been paid him as prebend.* Originally a brother of the abbey of Icolmkill, Carswell was in 1558 appointed to the parishes of Southwick and Kingarth by Clapperton, subdean of the Chapel Royal. At the Reformation he embraced the Protestant doctrines, and was appointed Superintendent of Argyle; he was in 1566 promoted as Bishop of the Isles. Bishop Carswell died in 1572 at an advanced age.†

James Paterson, sacristan of the Chapel Royal, and rector and vicar of Kirkinner and Kirkcowan, was probably a relative of Alexander Paterson, the former sacristan. In the charter-chest of the Earl of Selkirk at St Mary's Isle‡ is preserved a charter by James Paterson, in which as sacristan of the Chapel Royal and rector of half the rectory and vicarage of Kirkinner and Kirkcowan, he grants to Roger Gordon, son of the late William Gordon of Cracklaw, half of the two mark-lands of the kirklands of Kirkcowan and Kirkinner of old extent, with the manse, buildings, and garden, situated near the parish church of Kirkinner, upon the glebe thereof,—it being provided that the same shall be " prompta et parata ad recipiendum me et meos servitores quoties et quando mihi visum fuerit

---
* Russel's Keith's Scottish Bishops, p. 307.
† Fasti. Eccl. Scot. iii., 11, 445, 447.
‡ Fourth Report of Historical MS. Com. Part. i., p. 517.

ibidem, vel in *lye clachane*, sumptibus et expensis meis permanere, ac etiam cum officio ballivatus predictarum terrarum cum curiis exitibus," etc. This charter is dated at Kirkinner on the 3d November 1547; it is countersigned by " Alexander [Gordon], Bishop of Whithorn," who in 1558 attained the episcopate,. and had probably thereafter attached his name to the charter to complete its validity.

Queen Mary commenced her personal reign in Scotland in August 1561, and on the 11th January following James Paterson, sacristan of the Chapel Royal, handed to Servais de Conde, one of the Queen's valets, an inventory of vestments and ornaments belonging to the institution. This inventory, of which the original is preserved at Craufurdland Castle, is in these terms :

"The Inventor of the Quenis Grace Chapell Royale geir and ornamentis now heir in the Paleiss of Halyruidhous deliverit be Schir James Paterson, sacristane, at the Quenis command to Serues de Conde,* Frencheman and varloit of Oure Souverein Ladeis chalmer, be Maister Archibald Craufurd, her [Gracis] Maister Almoner, to be keipit in the Wardrop of Edinburgh.
" Imprimis, twa blew damaiss capis stripit with gold.
" Item, tua reid welwouss [capis] champit with gold.
" Item, ane fyne caipe of claith of gold on blew weluouss feild.
" Item, thrie black weluouss caipis for the mort, ane of them st[ern]it with gold,
" Item, tua tunikillis with ane chesabill of blak weluouss for

* On the 20th January 1564-5 "Servais de Condez, Verlat of her hienes chalmer," was appointed to the keeping of the Palace of Holyroodhouse. George Chalmers' MSS. ; Laing's MSS., University of Edinburgh.

the mort stand, with thric albis, amittis, stolis and fannonis, and purse.
" Item, tua auld alter towallis.
" Item, ane frontole and ane pendikill of blak weluouss st[ern]it with gold.
" Item, four tunikillis, twa chesabillis of fyne clayth of gold, with thrie albis, stolis, fannonis, amittis, and purse.
" Item, ane Mess Buik of parchment, with ane nottit Antiphonale of parchment.
" Item, ane coffer, with lok and key, within the quhilk thair is part of this forsaid garniture.
" Item, ane pendakill of silk, ane frontoll of gold and purpour velvat.
   " All this geyr receivit be me, Seruais, varlot of chalmer to our Soucrane, at hyr command, the eleuint daye of Janver, anno 1561, befor me David Lamerol.
     "S. DE CONDEZ, vallet de chambre de la Royne.
"A Lillebour, 11me Janvier 1561."

The Inventory was rendered into English and French. The English translation proceeds:

" Memorandum of the ornamentis of the Kirk quhilk I ressauit fra the Kepair of the Chapel of Striueling 1562.
" First, twa auld caippis of blew dames droppit with floure delice of gold, with the foirbrestis maid in histories.
" Alsua, ane cover of the alter, with the vnderpand, all of fresit claith of gold with blew, and diuidit equalis in bredis of claith of gold figurit with reid, freinyeit with silk of the same cullour.
" Mair, twa auld caippis of reid veluot, figurit with flouris of gold, furnisit the foirbreistis with counterfait gold.
" Mair, twa tvnicles, ane chasuble, and a caip, all of claith of gold, figurit with blew veluot, the foirbreistis of broderie work of gold and silk.
" Mair, twa tvnicles, thre caippis, ane chasuble, with the cover of ane alter and the vnderpand all of blak veluot droppit with starnis of gold. The foirbreistis of thame of reid veluot enrichit with the armes of Scotland and histories.

"Mair, ane chasuable and twa tvnacles of claith of gold, pyrnit with blak, furnisit with the foirbreistis of fyne gold.
"Mair, foure stoillis and sex fannonis, with fyve beltis maid of quhite threid.
"Mair, six abbis and foure amytis with twa auld alter claithis.
* " Worne."

The original of the French translation which follows is preserved at Preshome among the Papers saved from the wreck of the Scots College at Paris.

"Memoyre des Ornement D'Eglise que je resceu du Secretain de la Chapelle de Strellin, 1562.
"Premierement, deux vielle chappe de damas bleu, semee de fleur de lis d'or avec les orfres fect d'istoyre.
"Plus, ung parrement d'autel avec le soubassement, le tout de toylle d'or frisee de bleu, et meparty de toylle d'or figurree de rouge, frange de soye, de mesmes coulleur.
"Plus, deux vielle chappe de velours rouge figurree de fleurs d'or, garny d'orfre d'or de masse, a savoir faux or.
"Plus, deux tuniques et une chasuble et une chappe, le tout de toylle d'or figurree de velours bleu, garny d'orfres fect d'or nues.
"Plus, deux tuniques, troy chappe, et une chasubles, avec ung parrement d'ostel et le soubassement, le tout de velours noyr, semez d'estoilles d'or. Et les orfres des dicts ornement sont de velours rouges enriche des armes d'Ecosse et histoyrre.
"Plus, une chasuble, et deux tuniques de toylle d'or, broche de noyr, garnye d'orfres d'or fin.
"Plus, quatre estolles, et six fanons, avec sincq sainturre fect de filz blanc.
"Plus, six aubes, et quatre amycts avec deux vielle nappe d'autel.
"Usee."*

* A Collection of Inventories and other Records of the Royal Wardrobe, etc., 1488-1506 (edited by George Thomson). Printed at Edinburgh 1815. Inuentaires de la Reyne Descosse Douairiere de France, Catalogues of the Jewels, etc., of Mary, Queen of Scots, edited by Joseph Robertson. Edinb. 1863, pp. xxvii., cxli,, cxlii., 59 ; Illustrations of the Reigns of Queen Mary and King James VI., pp. 11, 12.

From the care bestowed on the catalogue of its trappings and ornaments at the commencement of her personal reign, it may be inferred that Queen Mary was led to actively interest herself in the collegiate church, while the removal of the articles to Holyrood-house would induce the belief that even at this period the substitution of that palace as the chapel's headquarters was in contemplation. Probably the intention may have been induced by an event which took place at Stirling not long subsequent to the queen's return from France. It is reported by Randolph that when on the 14th September 1561 "her grace's devout chaplains would, by the good device of Arthur Erskine, have sung a high mass, the Earl of Argyle and the Lord James so disturbed the quire, that some, both priests and clerks, left their places with broken heads and bloody ears." He adds, "It was a sport alone for some who were there to behold it; others were there that shed a tear or two, and then made no more of the matter."*

The transference to Holyroodhouse of the endowments of the Chapel Royal with its musical school would have involved changes difficult and inopportune. It was therefore not proceeded with. At Holyrood the queen employed musicians, who were recompensed in common with the other members of her household. Her performers on the viol were John Feldie, Moreis Dow, William Hay, John Dow, and

* Chalmers' Life of Queen Mary, i. 54.

John Ray. On the 8th January 1561-2 the Treasurer paid to "John Feldie and his bairns, violaris," for their services at last Yule £20. Each violar had a salary of £10 a year, exclusive of perquisites. In 1562 the queen's musicians received white taffety to be coats and hose, or trousers, with red and white taffety for their bonnets.

In 1561 and 1562 the queen employed three performers on the lute. John Adesone, valet of the chamber and lute player, received in 1562 a payment of £24. John Hume, chief of the luters, will be mentioned subsequently. James Heron and James Ramsay played on the shalme, or pipe and whistle. In 1563-4 Ramsay had a salary of £59, 4s.†

Singers or "sangsters" were also employed in the royal household. In August 1565 the Treasurer paid for clothes and Paris hats to five "sangsters," probably supplied to them on the occasion of the queen's marriage with Darnley. As a vocalist David Rizzio obtained his first connection with the court. A native of Piedmont, Rizzio came to Scotland in December 1561 in the suite of Monsieur Moret, the ambassador of Savoy. At this time there were three valets of the queen's chamber, who each sung a part, but a fourth for bass was wanting. As a bass singer Rizzio was

---

* Treasurer's Accounts. Chalmers' Life of Queen Mary, i. 72, 73.

† Register of Signatures, Book i.; Chalmers' Life of Queen Mary, 72-73; Letters of Mary, Queen of Scots, collected by Prince Lebano, edited by Agnes Strickland, ii. 288.

appointed a valet of the chamber. It is recorded that on the 8th January 1561-2 the Treasurer paid "by a precept to David Ricio, virlat in the Queen's Grace chalmer," £50. In the entry of a further payment made to him on the 14th of the following April, he is described as "David Ricio, Italian, chalmer's cheild."* In an account of payments made in 1564 by George Wishart of Drymme, deputy of Sir John Wishart of Pitarrow, the Comptroller, Rizzio appears to have then received a salary of eighty pounds, which was paid quarterly.†

Having served as valet-musician for three years, Rizzio was, in December 1564, appointed successor to M. Roulat, the queen's French secretary, who was removed for misconduct.‡

A considerable verse writer, and skilful in music, both vocal and instrumental, David Rizzio obtained the queen's favour, and it is believed he warmly supported Darnley's suit. On the 28th February 1565-6, there was paid to him, by the queen's precept, the sum of £2000, "in part of ten thousand marks for the duty of the Cunzie house, owing to Her Majestie for two years."§ His assassination at

* Treasurer's Accounts. The expression chamber-chield was the usual Scottish designation of a valet of the chamber.
† MSS. of George Chalmers in Laing's MSS. Collection, University of Edinburgh.
‡ Randolph to Cecil, 13th December 1564; Keith, 268.
§ Thorpe's Calendar of State Papers, Lond., 1858, 8vo.; Randolph's Letters to Cecil in 1565, Public Record Office and Cottonian Library; Goodal, i. 205; Chalmers' MSS. in Dr Laing's Collection, University of Edinburgh.

Holyroodhouse in the queen's presence, on the 9th March 1566, was one of the most tragic events in her troubled reign. Six weeks after his death, his brother Joseph came to Scotland with M. Castelnau de Malvisie, when he was appointed French secretary in his stead.* He also acted as a musician. But his character was defective, for, in January 1566-7, he fled to England with a friend's money, when the queen, though unsuccessfully, requested Drury to send him back. †

At the period of Rizzio's slaughter, Mary was advanced in pregnancy about six months; her child was born in the Castle of Edinburgh on the 19th June 1566. Prince of Scotland, and heir-apparent of two kingdoms, the royal infant was an object of solicitude to the Reformers. Soon after her recovery the queen was waited upon by Mr John Spottiswoode, superintendent of Lothian, who offered the congratulations of the Church, and at the same time expressed a hope that the future sovereign might be baptized by a Presbyterian minister. Mary accepted the congratulations, but waived the proposal as to the baptism; she had already determined that her son should be baptized in her own faith.‡

Probably the queen hesitated as to whether the baptism should be solemnised at Edinburgh or Stir-

---

* Randolph to Cecil, 25th April 1566; Keith, Appendix, 129.
† George Chalmers' MSS., Laing's MSS., University of Edinburgh.
‡ Spottiswoode's History of the Church of Scotland, Edinb., 1851, ii. 40.

ling. On her arrival from France, in August 1561, when she ventured to restore the mass at Holyrood, a riot had supervened; and, as we have seen, a similar attempt at Stirling in September had been attended with a demonstration scarcely less violent. But at Stirling was situated the Chapel Royal, and if there former sovereigns were not baptized the place was nevertheless associated with stirring events in the monarchical history. To Stirling Castle Mary removed her son, on the 22d August, and preparations for the baptism were commenced forthwith. To defray costs, the Privy Council, on the 6th October, levied a taxation of £12,000. That taxation was made, the Privy Council record bears, in consideration that "sum of the grettest princes in Christendome hes ernestlie requirit of our soveranis that be thair ambassatouris thai may be witnessis and gosseppis at the baptisme of thair Majesteis derrist sone the native prince of this realme, quhais requisitioun being bayth ressonabil and honorabill, thair Majesteis hes glaidlie condiscendit thairunto, and dalie lukis for the arryving of the saidis ambassatouris."*

The birth of an heir to the Scottish throne was promptly reported to Queen Elizabeth, through Sir James Melvill, who also conveyed to her majesty the request of his royal mistress that she would act as godmother. Accepting the proffered honour, the English queen delegated as her representative at

* Privy Council Records, ii. 485.

the baptism the Countess of Argyle, who, while Mary's natural sister and personal friend, was also a member of the Reformed Church. But the English queen, besides appointing a delegate or "gossip" to represent her at the baptism, despatched to Scotland as special envoy the Earl of Bedford, who, a noted Protestant and the protector of the exiled lords, was sure to be made welcome by the Scottish nobility. Bedford travelled to Scotland with forty attendants; he was met at Coldingham by Melvill on behalf of the queen, while the Protestant gentry of Haddingtonshire also offered their respects, and joined his procession. At Edinburgh Bedford and his attendants were accommodated for a night in the Duke of Chatelherault's quarters at Kirk o' Field; next day they resumed their journey to Stirling. On Saturday the 14th December, Bedford was at Stirling Palace admitted to an audience by Mary, who had, in order to his reception there, hastened from Holyroodhouse. Before her majesty, Bedford placed a gold font, which, in his written instructions, he was commissioned to "say pleasantly was made as soon as we heard of the prince's birth, and then 'twas big enough for him; but now he being grown is too big for it; therefore it may be better used for the *next* child, provided it be christened before it outgrows the font." The font weighed 333 ounces, rendering the value £1048, 13s.*

* Keith's History of Scottish Affairs, 1845, 8vo, ii. 479.

The Privy Council precept became payable on the 30th November, and preparations being completed, the baptism was fixed to take place on Tuesday the 17th December. At five o'clock on the afternoon of that day the nobility, gentry, and burgesses assembled in the Castle. The barons drew up in double columns between the Palace and the Chapel Royal, as a guard of honour; each in his hand carried a waxen taper, or bore a symbol of office. At the sound of clarions and other instruments, a body of handsome youths passed to the Chapel between the columns bearing torches. The Countess of Argyle,* having in her arms the royal infant, followed next; she was supported on the right by the Count de Brienne, ambassador of France, and on the left by Monsieur le Croc, substitute deputy of the Duke of Savoy. Following the Countess came the Earl of Athole, bearing a large waxen candle, the Earl of Eglinton, holding "the salt-fat," Lord Sempill, supporting the holy rood, and Lord Ross, bearing a ewer and basin. When the procession reached the Chapel, those who professed the Protestant doctrines remained outside, including the English ambassador, and the Earls of Murray, Bothwell, and Huntly.

Within the Chapel already were assembled with

* By the General Assembly, which met at Edinburgh on the 25th December 1567, the Countess of Argyle was ordered to make public repentance in the Chapel Royal of Stirling, upon ane Sunday in time of preaching, "for assisting at the prince's baptism, performed in a papistical manner."—*Booke of the Universal Kirk.*

the queen, Archbishop Hamilton of St Andrews, and the Bishops of Dunkeld, Dunblane, and Ross, accompanied by the prior of Whithorn, and several deans and archdeacons. As representative of Queen Elizabeth, the Countess of Argyle presented the child at the altar, the baptismal rite being celebrated by the archbishop. The application of saliva, or "the spittle," was omitted, in deference to Mary's express wish. When the solemnities were concluded, the heralds declared aloud the prince's name and titles, as "Charles James, James Charles, Prince and Steward of Scotland, Duke of Rothesay, Earl of Carrick, Lord of the Isles, and Baron of Renfrew." This proclamation, followed by the din of clarions, was thrice repeated. Thereafter the choristers sung appropriate airs, accompanied by the organs. At the door of the Chapel, the English ambassador assured the queen that, though two earls only had entered the building, twelve were in waiting upon her.

The solemnity of the baptism was followed by a great banquet, served in the palace. Writes a contemporary chronicler:

"Thaj all past to the greit hall to the supper, quhair at ane tabill sat the quenis majestie at mydburd, the French ambassatour at the rycht hand, the Inglis ambassatour at hir left hand, and Monsieur de Lacrok, ambassatour for Savoy, at the burd-end. And thair servit the quenis majestie, the erle of Huntlie, carvoure, the erle of Murray, coppar [cupper], and the erle of Bothwill, sewar [server]. The French ambassatour was servit be the erle of Mar, carvoure, the erle of Cassilis, coppar, and the erle of Atholc, sewar. The Inglis ambassatour, be the erle of Eglingtoun, coppar, the erle of Rothes, carvoure, and the erle of Crawfurd, sewar. The duke of Savoyis ambassatour, be the maister Maxwell, carvour, and the lord Boyd, coppar, and the lord Levingstoun, sewar. The ordour of the cuming of the meit was this, efter the herauldis, maisseris, trumpetouris, and swescheouris [musicians], being thre maister houshaldis in rank, viz., Fyndlater in the mydis, Seinzour Francisco de Busso at the rycht hand, and Gilbert Balfour at the left, thair come in George lord Seytoun, him allane; and efter him come Archibald erle of Ergile, allane; and ilk ane of thame bure ane fair quhite staff in thair handis; and the lordis, barronis, and nobilles bure fair greit torches, quhilk wer in greit haboundance, and weill ordourit; and efter dansing and playing in haboundance, the saidis lordis that nycht depairtit to thair lugeingis."*

For several days following the baptism sports were conducted in the palace, and in "the valley," a hollow of Stirling Rock; while festivities and musical fetes occupied the evenings. On Thursday, the 19th December, a display of fireworks varied the entertainment. "Thair wes," writes the author of the *Diurnal*, "masry [masquerading] and playing in all sortis, befoir supper; than ane fort halding in Striueling besyid the Kirk-yaird, quhairin wes artailzerie, schote fyre ballis, fyre speris, and all vtheris thingis plesand for the sicht of man; this done, our souerane ladie past to the castell, and thair maid James, prince of Scotland, the duke of Rothissay, erle of Kyle, Carrick, and Cunnynghame, and barroun of the barronie of Renfrew, and maid certane knychtis."† At the supper

* Diurnal of Occurrents, 1513-1575, 103, 104. Edinb. 1835, 4to.
† Diurnal of Occurrents, 105.

which followed, an occurrence took place which might have terminated seriously. Jealousy had already been awakened between the French and English, for the former were displeased that the queen had extended a marked attention to her English visitors, while they conceived themselves proportionally neglected. This feeling was shared by the queen's French servant, De Bastian, master of the ceremonies, who resolved at the banquet to offer an affront to the English visitors. In the manner of the period, the table containing the viands was ushered into the hall by men draped as satyrs, accompanied by musicians, playing on various instruments. The satyrs were removed to make way for the advancing table, but in performing this office they seized their tails and wagged them among the guests. The long-tailed English, was an epithet of contempt applied by the Scots to their southern neighbours, and of which the English were abundantly aware. There was consequently among this portion of the guests a strong feeling of displeasure, and a number of them resolving not to share the feast, turned their backs upon the table. So indignant was Christopher Hatton,* an English gentleman, that he informed Sir James Melville that but for the queen's presence he would have slain De Bastian on the spot. The queen, who was in conversation with the Earl of Bedford, turned round on

* Subsequently Sir Christopher Hatton, latterly Privy Councillor and Lord Chancellor. Queen Mary presented him with a valuable chain having her portrait attached.

remarking the tumult, and having learned its cause procceded, with the earl's help, to restore harmony and order.*

Of the taxation levied by the Privy Council a portion was appropriated in gifts to the ambassadors and prominent members of their suites. To the Earl of Bedford, the queen presented a chain of diamonds. John Hume, who conducted the musical arrangements, received for himself and staff the sum of £177, 10s. 8d. Hume was clothed in a livery of fine velvet, and wore "a hat and velvet bonnet, rapier and belt."†

Lord Darnley was not present at his son's baptism. From the queen he had become estranged at the time of Rizzio's murder, but there had been a partial reconciliation after her confinement. Mary had lived with him at Stirling from the 30th August till the 11th September, also for several days at Craigmillar Castle towards the end of November. But he thereafter came to Stirling alone, and it does not appear that subsequently any communication passed between him and the queen. He occupied private apartments in the burgh, and there remained sullen and solitary amidst the joyous demonstrations of December. On the morning of the baptism, if we are to believe the French ambassador, he was intoxicated, and would have exposed the court to disgrace but for

---

* Sir James Melville's Memoirs, p. 152. Edinb. 1735.
† Chalmers' Life of Queen Mary, i. 72, 73.

the envoy's interference. On the 24th December he proceeded to Glasgow. The end was near; he was assassinated at Kirk o' Field, near Edinburgh, on the 10th of February. Whether this terrible solution of a state difficulty was directly countenanced by the queen is a moot point of history. Yet her early union with Bothwell, who was unquestionably privy to her husband's murder, was clearly a blunder which could be repaired only by abdication. On the 24th July 1567, she resigned the crown in favour of her infant son, who was, as James VI., generally recognised. During the twenty years of her unhappy life which remained, Mary experienced some solace in cultivating those musical arts which she had cherished as a queen. Unwilling to arouse the jealousy of her royal sister and rival, Melville answered Queen Elizabeth's question as to her skill with the remark that she played "reasonably well as a queen;" in truth she excelled in music, especially as a performer on the lute and virginals.* At least one of the court musicians adhered to her during her imprisonment and exile; "John, the musician who played the base violin," is named, in 1574, as one who bore messages to her in England from her adherents in Scotland.†

Under charge of the Countess of Mar, the young prince remained at Stirling. When he became king, he had assigned him as part of his household four

---

* Chalmers' Life of Queen Mary, i. 73.
† Thorpe's Calendar of State Papers relating to Scotland. Lond., 1858, 8vo, ii. 916.

violaris, viz.—"Mekill Thomas Hudsoun,* Robert Hudsoun, James Hudsoun, and William Hudsoun." These, with their attendant, "Thomas Fowlarton," were accommodated in the castle.† Among the more dignified members of the household was Alexander Gordon, Dean of the Chapel Royal, second son of John, Master of Huntly, by Jane, natural daughter of James IV. Gordon in his youth was companion of James V. He was designed for the bishopric of Caithness in 1514, but the see did not become vacant. Elected in 1547 to the diocese of Glasgow, the Pope gave the preferment to James Beaton, but to relieve Gordon's disappointment constituted him Archbishop of Athens, with the promise that he would receive the next Scottish bishopric. He became Bishop of the Isles in 1558, and sat in the Parliament of 1560 which ratified the Confession of Faith. Joining the Reformers he was appointed Bishop of Galloway and Dean of the Chapel Royal; he was afterwards nominated an Extraordinary Lord of Session. Through his influence at court, he was mainly instrumental in procuring for the Reformed clergy a provision from the thirds of benefices. But he imperfectly discharged his own clerical duties, owing to his being deeply engrossed with secular affairs. Charged with negligence he exposed himself to the censure of the

* This person, who seems to have been of gigantic stature was, in 1586, appointed Master of the Chapel Royal. (See *postea*.)
† Chalmers' Life of Queen Mary, i. 177.

General Assembly, but having promptly acknowledged his error and readily submitted to discipline, he was allowed to retain his ecclesiastical offices. He died in November 1575.*

As regarded the spiritual instruction of the young king, the services of Dean and Bishop Gordon were not available. An instructor was recommended by Buchanan, in the person of John Duncanson, minister of Stirling, and formerly Principal of St Leonard's College. A convert from the old faith, Duncanson was one of the few ecclesiastics who cordially accepted the Reformed doctrines. He was appointed vicar of the Chapel Royal on the 17th March 1568,† having already by the General Assembly been nominated "minister of the King's House," as under the new system the office of chaplain at court was designated.

The organs and ornaments of the Chapel Royal were preserved when those in cathedrals and other churches were wrecked and ruined. But what the multitude had spared, the Earl of Mar, as Captain of the Castle, caused to be swept away. His act was indemnified by a Parliament convened by the Regent Lennox, which assembled at Stirling on the 28th August 1571. That Parliament passed a resolution, which, from its curious interest, we present in full:

* Fasti Eccl. Scot., i. 775 ; Brunton & Haig's College of Justice, 128 ; Keith's Bishops, 279, 307.
† Fasti Eccl. Scot., i. 156.

"My lord regent's grace thre estatis and haill body of this present parliamet calling to mynd how at the coronatioun of the kinge ma^{tie} o^r souane lord accomplishit and solempnizat vpouñ the xxix day of Julij, the zeir of God J^m v^c and threscoir sevin zeiris, the nobilitie prelattis commissioners of burrowis and vtheris his hienes faythfull and trew subjectis purpoislie convenit for that effect, nawis neglecting the caus of God. Bot with the first louking thereto specialie to the estait of the Chapell Riall within the castell of Striueling quhair his hienes persouñ wes than and presentlie is resident and nurischit Thoucht it tendit to goddis honor that the said Chapell suld be purgit of all monumentis of ydolatrie or vthiris thingis quhatsumeuir dedicat to superstitioun. That the puir word of God my^t be trewlie prechit and his sacramentis richtlie and sinceirlie ministrat therein. Thairfoir thai gaif special and expres cōmand and charge to Johnne Erle of Mar, Lord Erskin, Capitane of the said Castell of Striuiling that he suld caus the said Chapell w^{t}out delay be purgit and reformit in maner and to the effect abouewritten quhilk cōmandiment he dewlie put in executioun declaring himself ane noble man and a fauorar of godlines. And the same being cōsiderit be my lord regent's grace, the thre estatis and haill body of this present parliament foirsaid, thai haif allowit and approvit and be this present act allowis, approvis, and findis guid the said reformatioun and purgatiouñ of the said Chapell Royall, done and accomplishit be the said Erle of Mar and vtheris at his . . . the sercheing and seiking of all monumental veshells, vestiments . . . apparelling quhatsumeuir quhilk war within the said Chapell . . . war dedicat or appertenit thereto. And the dispositiouñ and away p . . . decernand and declarand that the said erle and vther personis makaris . . . reformatioun and purgatioun of the said Chapell Riall for that d . . . incur ony skaith or danger in thair personis, landis, or guidis . . . callit or accusit for the samin crīnalie nor ciuilie be . . . way in tyme cuming. Notwithstanding ony lawis or cost . . . euir maid or to be maid quhilk may appeir to extend in the . . . Dischargeing be this present act all iugeis and ministeris of . . . within this realme present and tocum of all calling, accusing, or in ony . . . proceding aganis the said erle or vtheris pesonis makars of the f . . . reformatiouñ and purgatioun at his cōmand their airis and their executoris for that . . . deid or ony thing depending thairvpouñ and of thair offices in that part for euir."*

Another enactment, passed at the Parliament held at Stirling in August, was attended with a serious result. The Duke of Chatelherault, his sons, and Kirkaldy of Grange, were, as supporters of the dethroned queen, subjected to forfeiture. Learning what had occurred, Kirkaldy resolved to surprise the Parliament and arrest its leaders. Seizing the horses which appeared in the public market at Edinburgh, he, on the evening of the 2d September, left that city at the head of 200 mounted troops, and 300 infantry. Reaching Stirling before daybreak, he seized several of the nobility. Among these was the Regent Lennox, who surrendered to Spence of Wormiston. There had been no intention to injure the Regent, but a shot fired by one Captain Calder, a fierce adventurer, wounded him mortally. In a dying state he was carried to the castle, where he evinced deep concern as to the safety of his grandson, the young king. He only survived till the following day. His remains were honourably interred in the Chapel Royal, and near the spot a monumental tablet was afterwards placed by his widow, in testimony of her affection. †

* Acta Parl. Scot., iii. 62.
† Spottiswoode's History, ii. 163-166; Chambers's Life of James I., 40-46.

In relation to an appointment to a canonry in the Chapel Royal, the Privy Council, which assembled at the Palace of Holyrood on the 6th July 1573, were considerably exercised.* By a letter of gift under the Privy Seal, issued on the 26th August 1571, by the late Regent, William Drummond, son of Sir Robert Drummond of Carnock, was appointed to the canonry called " the parsonage and vicarage of Alloway." But Mr David Lindsay, " Commissioner of the Kirk" for the western district, refused admission on the ground that the presentee had not personally produced his letter of gift. In defence it was pleaded that this instrument was presented by his elder brother Patrick, the presentee being at the University of St Andrews prosecuting his studies, and, besides that the inclemency of the season prevented his making long travel. The case was complicated, inasmuch as Mr David Lindsay had appointed to the canonry "ane James Dalrumpill," and had refused the late Regent's letter when it was by the presentee actually produced to him. As Lindsay made no answer to the complaint, a decree was in his absence pronounced in Drummond's favour. It proved inoperative, and Dalrymple was within a month afterwards presented to the parsonage and vicarage by the Crown. Dalrymple died in 1580.†

The Chapel Royal at Stirling seems to have been

* Privy Council Register, i. 254-256.
† Fasti Eccl. Scot., ii. 84.

very partially used subsequent to the purgation; it was probably closed after the court removed from Stirling Castle to Holyroodhouse. It was not to be wholly abandoned. In January 1593-4 the king communicated to the Privy Council that he expected the queen shortly to bring him an heir. This announcement caused a parliament to be summoned; it met on the 28th January, when anticipatory of the interesting event, and consequent baptism, a general taxation was sanctioned. Of the sum of £100,000 voted on the occasion, it was ordered that one-half was to be contributed by "the spiritual estate," £33,333, 16s. 8d. by "the freeholders," and the balance, £16,666, 13s. 4d., by the burgesses of the royal burghs.*

Prince Henry was born on the 19th February, and henceforth baptismal concerns occupied the king's chief attention. With a view to the baptism being celebrated in the same ancient palace where he had himself been received into the Church, James caused the fragile and ruinous structure of the Chapel Royal to be removed, while he personally superintended the erection of a new and more commodious edifice on the same site. Of the entire proceedings thereanent, as well as in regard to the event of Prince Henry's baptism, a narrative minute and circumstantial was published at the time, evidently under the king's own direction. This publication, which embraces fifteen

* Acta Parl. Scot., iv. 50-52.

pages small quarto, is printed in black letter. A copy, almost unique, is preserved in the Grenville Library. The title is " A true Reportarie of the most triumphant and royal Accomplishment of the Baptisme of Frederick-Henry, Prince of Scotland, solemnized the 30 Day of August 1594 : Edinb., R. Waldegrave." The tract, considerably altered, was reprinted at London in 1603, with the title "A true Accompt of the Baptism of Henry Frederick, Prince of Scotland, and now Prince of Wales." It was again reprinted at Edinburgh in 1787, and it has been reproduced in the third volume of Nichol's " Progresses of Queen Elizabeth," 1805; in the second volume of the Somers Collection ; also in *Scotia Rediviva*, a collection of Scottish Historical Tracts, published in 1826. The "Reportarie" commences thus :

"The noble and most potent prince of Scotland was born in the castle of Striviling the 19 day of February 1594, upon which occasion the king's majestie sent for the nobles of his land, and to all the capitall burrows thereof, to haue their aduise how he should proceed for the due solemnization of his royal baptisme, and what princes he should send too; when they were all compeared with great diligence and good will, he proponed unto them, that it was necessary to direct out ambassadours to France, England, Denmark, the Low Countries, the Duke of Brunswicke, his brother-in-law, and to the Duke of Magdelburg, the queenis majestie's grandfather, and to such other princes as should be thought expedient. Likewise he thought the castle of Striviling the most convenient place for the residence of this most noble and mightie prince, in respect that he was borne there; as also, it was necessary, that sufficient preparation might be made for the ambassadours that should be invited to come, for honour of the crown and countrey. And besides all this, because the Chapell Royal was ruinous and too little, concluded that the old chappell should be utterly rased, and a new erected in the same place, that should be more large, long, and glorious, to entertain the great number of straungers expected. These propositions at length considered they all, with a free voluntarie deliberation, graunted unto his majestie the summe of an hundred thousand pounds money of Scotland."

That the new Chapel Royal might be properly reared and decorated, the king, proceeds the "Reportarie," gathered together "the greatest number of skilled workmen," and himself superintended their operations. The foreign ambassadors, each as he arrived, was received by the king, and entertained by him "at his own charges."

Chiefly intent on celebrating the splendour of the baptismal arrangements, the author of the "Reportarie" omits special reference to the architecture of the new chapel, or its structural decorations. But we are informed by the historian, Robert Johnstone, who lived contemporaneously, that the ceiling was garnished with gold, and that the walls were magnificently adorned with pictures, sculptures, and other ornaments.*

The 30th day of August was fixed for the baptism, and ceremonial arrangements entrusted to Sir Patrick

* Rerum Britannicarum Historia auctore Roberto Johnstono (1572-1628) MS. Advocates Library, fol. 153.

Leslie, commendator or "Lord of Lindores,"* and to Mr William Fowler,† Master of Works, at Stirling or Edinburgh. These, according to the author of the "Reportarie," faithfully discharged their duties, and "by their travell, diligence, and invention, brought it to that perfection which the shortness of the time and other considerations could permit."

During the two days which preceded the baptism, chivalric sports were conducted in "the valley." In course of these sports appeared in female attire as Amazons, Sir Patrick Leslie, master of the ceremonies, already noticed; also Sir Walter Scott of Buccleuch, and Mr John Bothwell,‡ described as "Abbot of Holyrood." On the morning of the 30th Mr Patrick Galloway, "minister of the King's House,"

* Sir Patrick Leslie was second son of the fifth Earl of Rothes. Enjoying the favour of James VI., he was appointed commendator of Lindores, and on the 25th December 1600 was created Lord Lindores.

† Mr William Fowler appears to have been the son of a merchant in Edinburgh, who traded with Paris, probably for silks and articles of *vertu*. Lord Herreis died suddenly in the lodgings of William Fowler at Edinburgh, on the 20th January 1582-3. After serving as Master of Works, Fowler was appointed by James VI. Secretary to his Queen; he also received the honour of knighthood. He composed verses; and a sonnet from his pen addressed to the Countess of Erroll is contained in the Hawthornden MSS., in keeping of the Scottish Society of Antiquaries. Sir William Fowler's sister, Susanna, was wife of Sir John Drummond of Hawthornden, and mother of William Drummond the poet (Privy Council Register, ii. 329, 433; iii. 549; Calderwood, viii. 232; Lord Strathallan's Genealogie of the House of Drummond, *passim*).

‡ Though described in the "Reportarie" as Abbot of Holyrood, Mr John Bothwell was not an ecclesiastic. Son of Adam Bothwell, Bishop of Orkney, he had from James VI., with whom he was a favourite, three several charters, 1591-1592, of the lands and jurisdiction of the Abbacy of Holyrood. On the 20th December 1607, he was raised to the peerage as Lord Holyroodhouse, the abbey lands being in his favour erected into a temporal lordship.

preached in the new Chapel Royal for the first time. "He," writes the author of the "Reportarie," "learnedlie and godlie entreated upon the text of the 21 of Genesis." The young prince was thereafter baptized by Mr David Cunningham, Bishop of Aberdeen. The bishop afterwards "ascended the pulpit, when, after he had delivered in verse a certaine praise and commendation of the prince, then he converted the rest of his Latine oration, in prose, to the ambassadours, every one in particular, beginning at the ambassadour of England, and so continuing with the rest; wherein he made mention of the chronology of each of these princes, and recited the proximitie and nearnesse of blood that they had with Scotland, concluding his oration with exhortation and thanksgiving to God for that good occasion and prosperous assembly." "Thereafter," proceeds the "Reportarie," "the provost and prebends of the Chappell Royall did sing the 21 psalme of Dauid, according to the art of musique, to the great delectation of the noble auditorie."

The religious service concluded, sixteen barons and gentlemen were dubbed knights; when, as the author of the "Reportarie" quaintly relates, "great quantity of divers especes of gold and money were cast over amongst the people."

A banquet followed, which, in its preparation, had no doubt taxed the ingenuity of the age. Proceeds the chronicler: "The kinge, queene, and ambassadours were placed all at one table, being formed of three parts, after a geometricall figure in such sort, that euery one might haue a full sight of the other." As the banquet proceeded a great chariot, bearing fruits and delicacies, was drawn into the apartment. It had been contemplated that a lion, as impersonating the monarchy, might drag in the chariot, but in consideration for the nerves of the more sensitive, a moor, richly attired, "bore forward the chariot, being attached to it by great chaines of gold." Next entered, or rather sailed into the banquet-hall a ship floating in an artificial sea, at the approach of which volleys from thirty-six brass guns surprised and startled the assembly. The ship, which was in the keel 18 feet long, and to its topmost flag 40 feet in height, bore a cargo of fishes. These are enumerated as "Hearings, whitings, flooks, oysters, buckies, lampets, partans, lapstars, crabs, spout-fish, and clammes."

"Whilst the ship was unloading," adds the author of the "Reportarie", "Arion, sitting upon the galey nose, which resembled the forme of a dolphine fish, played upon his harpe; then begane his musick in greene holyne howboyes, in fine parts. After that followed viols, with voices in plaine counterpoint," discoursing Latin hexameters, composed for the occasion. "A stil noise of recoders and fluts," and "for the fourth, a general consort of the best instruments," concluded the first portion of the entertainment.

A concert followed. "There was sung, with most delicate dulce voices, and sweet harmonies, in seven partes, the 128th Psalm, with fourteen voices." Rejoicings were prolonged till past midnight.

Since the preceding pages were printed,* a detached document, discovered in the General Register House, would serve to show that about ten years prior to the construction of the new fabric in 1594, a proposal for such a renovation had, through the Lord High Treasurer, been submitted to the Privy Council. The proposal was made by Sir Robert Drummond, the King's Master of Works, and it is embodied in the form of a report on the condition of the Royal Palace. The report, embraced in two folio sheets, is inscribed on the back, " Ane fforme and Invitowre of the expenssis appeiranlie to be maid in the Kingis hienes Paleyssis as is withein writtin. Apud Halyrudhous septimo Maij anno [millesimo] v° Octuagesimo tertio. Productum per Robertum Drummond de Carnok militem coram dominis scaccarij."

That portion of the report relating to the Castle and Chapel Royal of Stirling we present entire:

"THE APPEIRAND EXPENSSIS TO BE MAID UPON THE CASTELL OF STIRLING.

"Item, the Castell of Stirling is rwingows † in sic sort that the greit hall thairof is in poynt of tynsall ‡ be the altering of

---

* Other important documents in relation to the early history of the Chapel Royal of Stirling, lately discovered in the General Register House, will be added in the Appendix.

† Ruinous.   ‡ Loss.

f

the same quhilkis conswmeis the wallis in resaueing watter and als the thak* of the same is reywin and resaweis watter in sic sort that it sall rott the rwif of the said hall.

"Item, the foirentres the towris thairof ar naikit and without skalze.†

"Item, to mend the greit windois in the cowrthall in the new vork twa dissone ‡ vane scott,§ Thre dissone daillis withe ffoure corballis of aik; Price off the tymmer and the workmenschip to ane hunderethe merkis.

"Item, the Westqwarter thairof to be all tane downe to the grownd, thane to big and beild the same vp agane in the maist plesand maner that can be dewyssit: Quhilk qwarter off the said paleys is the best and maist plesand sitwatioune off ony of his hienes palayes be ressone it will hawe the maist plesand sycht of all the foure airthis: In speciall Perk || and gairdin ¶ deir thairin vp the Rawerais** of Forth, Teyth, Allone, and Gwddy to Lochlomwnd, ane sycht rownd abowt in all pairtis, and downe the Rewear of Forthe quhair thair standis many greit stane howssis: Provyding thair be ane fair gallery beildit on the ane syd of the said work, withe ane tarras †† on the vther syde of the said work: And this ffoirsaid gallerie and tarras to be beildit and bigit vpone the heich pairtis off the ffoirsaid work.

"Item, the ffoirsaid westqwarter the rwif thairof is all brokin and falling downe, necessar it is the tymmer and skailze thairon to be takin downe presently and laid vp in howssis ffor suppleing the Kingis grace workis.

"Item, the Chapell Royall, the thak thairof resaweis weit and rane in sic sort that the Kingis hienes may nocht weill remane within the same in tyme off weitt or rane.

"Item, to witt the said Chappell Royall in Stirling, the rwif thairof hes bene wrang wrocht mekill vnder sqware that

---

* Thatch. † Slates. ‡ Dozen. § Wainscot.
|| The Royal Park of Stirling.
¶ The Royal Gardens, occupying the southern slope of the castle hill, and extending to the plain beneath.
** Rivers. †† Terrace.

the thak of the same is off skailze, and is ane werray licht thak.

"Notwithstanding thair is many kyppillis* thairof brokin, swa it is necessar to pwt ane new rwif vpone the said Cheppell, and the said rwif to be mekill abone the sqware : Thane the gayvellis † of the said Cheppell, the stane work and paittis mane be reassit to ane greit heicht, agreabill to the new rwif thairof ffor remembrance off this wark : In cais the westqwarter off the ffoirsaid palays wer beildit and bigit as is ffoirsaid, thane it wer necessar ffor the owtsett off the said palcys and making of the cowrt and clois large and mair to ane better ffassioun, to tak away the Cheppell and to big the same neirby the northe bak wall in ane vther sort off biging to the pwrpois that oure Qweyne, withe hir tryne off ladyis, may pas fwrthe off this new dewyssit work into the said Cheppell loft,‡ and the Kingis grace saitt to be bigit directlie annent the pwppeit thairof: This being done the clos and cowrt will stand neirby vpone sqware in all pairtis, qwhilkis workis wilbe large expens.

"It is nocht wnknawin to zour lordschipis that the new work off the Castell of Stirling is the maist substantious work and maist plesand withein the same zitt the sitwatioun thairof is nocht gwid nor plesand, in respect thair can na plesand sycht be had swa giff this vther new work wer beildit the Kingis hienes wald mak his recedence in the westqwarter.

"Item, ffor beilding or biging of ane kennell hows withein the said Castell in the nedder bailze : Suma in expenssis all maner of wayis, extendane to fyve hunder merkis or thairby : And gif awld tymmer and skailze be taikin of the westqwarter to fwrneis the foirsaid hows, the expenssis thairof to be of ane les price."

The description of the older Chapel as being partially constructed of turf and insufficiently thatched would point to the poverty of palatial architecture,

* Cupples.   † Gables.   ‡ Gallery.

as contrasted with that of the cathedrals; while it is not uninteresting to find the court architect providing for the comfort of the queen and her ladies, the king being only in his seventeenth year and unmarried.

The architect, or master of works, Sir Robert Drummond, claims special notice. Descended from the ancient House of Drummond, he was the fifth of his family who owned the lands of Carnock, Stirlingshire. Born about 1518, he seems to have succeeded as the King's Master of Works, his kinsman John Drummond,* who held a similar office under James IV. and V., and was doubtless architect of the new Palace at Stirling, reared by the latter sovereign. Sir Robert was twice married, his first wife, Margaret Kirkaldy, being sister of the famous Sir William Kirkaldy of Grange. His second wife, Marjorie Fleming, was sister of Robert, Lord Elphinstone. His second son, born of the second marriage, was Sir John Drummond of Hawthornden, whose son William was the celebrated poet. Sir Robert died in 1592, and his epitaph has been written in verse by the poet, Alexander Montgomery.†

The Chapel Royal of Stirling, reared in 1594, after serving the special purpose for which it was prepared, was afterwards exposed to neglect, its internal decora-

---

* Lord Strathallan's Genealogie of the House of Drummond, pp. 62, 264, 265.

† Malcolm's Genealogical Memoirs of the House of Drummond, Edinb. 1808, p. 32; Lord Strathallan's Genealogie of the House of Drummond, pp. 71, 74, 250, 267; Alexander Montgomery's Poems, Edinb. 1820, p. 244.

tions being defaced and scattered. After being used as an ordinary barrack it was modernised and renovated, one portion being adapted as a garrison schoolroom, and another fitted up as a repertory of arms. The architecture is Saxon; two columns, surmounted by an entablature, adorn the entrance.

Subsequent to the endowments of the Chapel Royal being transferred to Holyroodhouse, the office of "minister of the constabulary of Stirling" was created. When the Act of Union between the kingdoms, of 1707, provided that a garrison should be established at Stirling Castle, the two offices of minister of the constabulary and chaplain of the garrison seem to have been combined. Thomas Davidson, lecturer in the Tron Church, Edinburgh, was, in June 1709, commissioned by Queen Anne as chaplain to the garrison. He was ordained to the charge, and admitted a member of the local Presbytery.* In 1759 the chaplaincy of Stirling Castle was conferred on Dr William Robertson, the historian, who at the same time held office as minister of Lady Yester's Church, Edinburgh. Dr Robertson was succeeded by Dr Robert Moodie, minister of Clackmannan, after whose death in 1832 the office, which had for upwards of a century been virtually a sinecure, was again associated with active service. The editor of this work was, in succession to the Rev. Robert Watson, appointed chaplain of Stirling Castle by a royal

* Fasti Eccl. Scot., ii. 685.

commission, dated 25th January 1855, and was ordained to the cure. He retired in August 1863, and to the office no commissioned chaplain has since been appointed.

To the Chapel Royal of Stirling as a collegiate church does the accompanying Register belong. Styled *Registrum Capellæ Regiæ Strivelinensis*, it is contained in a folio volume of fifty-one leaves, each leaf being authenticated by Sir James Primrose, who in 1602 was appointed clerk to the Privy Council. Written in a large distinct hand, all the folios are entire save one, the 49th, which is lost. There are eighteen separate documents of dates between 1501 and 1537, including charters of erection and endowment, and a list of vestments, jewels, and other ornaments ; also a list of books which in 1505 was possessed by the institution. The documents are generally in Latin. Marginal comments on the different instruments have, with one or two exceptions, been added at a later period. The Register is preserved in the Advocates' Library, and is now printed for the first time. The brief analysis of it, published in 1828 by Sir John Graham Dalyell, conveys a very imperfect idea of its contents.

In producing a volume chiefly founded on materials obtained from unprinted sources, we have necessarily incurred obligations of kind service. To Mr John Small, of the University of Edinburgh, we are indebted for important suggestions and useful cooperation. Mr Thomas Dickson, of the General Register House, has courteously extended facilities of search, and by rendering available several unprinted documents, has added to the value of our historical details. In the transcription, the Rev. Walter Macleod has exhibited his wonted skill and unwearied diligence.

3 BRANDON STREET, EDINBURGH,
December 1881.

HISTORY

OF THE

CHAPEL ROYAL OF SCOTLAND.

FATHER HAY, in remarking that at the Reformation the revenues of the Chapel Royal were valued at £5000 sterling, adds, "Comparring this with the course of money att the time of James the fourth, the rent of this Royall Chapell can be no less than five thousand merks Scots money, that is 330 pound sterling, payable out of the lands, and the soume of five thousand pound sterling payable out of the benefices, being recover'd, and reduced to ane ordinary rentall, which soume [they] would easily afford. . . . These of greatest worth were out of the Chapell's possession in James the sixt's daye, in the Priory of Rosneth, belonging to the Canon Regulars." *

For a time John Duncanson, "minister of the King's House," retained the incumbency of Stirling along with the vicarage of the Chapel Royal. He

* Hay's Scotia Sacra MS., Advocates Library. The date of the MS. is uncertain. Hay was born in 1601, and attained an advanced age.

resigned his parochial cure subsequent to the 16th
January 1571, and it is probable that not long afterwards he accompanied his royal charge to the Palace
of Holyrood. Here was constituted as a new Chapel
Royal an inconsiderable structure, which stood on the
south side of the Palace, and which had been used
for worship by the Court, both before the Reformation and subsequently. Of this erection we obtain
some account by referring to Sir Robert Drummond's
MS. report on the Royal Palaces. This report,
which is dated 7th May 1583, contains the following
entries :

"THE PAYLEIS OFF HALYRWDOWS.

" Item, To repair the Cheppell of the said paleys to the Kingis
Majesties honowre, ane honorabill saitt to be maid to his
hienes, togidder withe ane chanchelar* wall of tymmer
withe ane trym powpeit and formes and saittis encirclat
rownd abowt as effeiris and without the chanchelar wall
certane formis to be maid.
" Item, Foure dissone of vanescott to the Kingis Majesteis saitt
and powpeit ; price thairof, ane hunder merkis.
" Item, Ten corballis to fwrneis the said workis ; price thairof,
twenty pundis.
" Item, Half ane hunder dellis to the foirsaid work, . xx^{lib}.
" Item, Twentie fyre† treis to the sollis and binding of the saidis
formis, price, . . .
" Item, For boltis bandis of irone and iron naillis with ane
lotte gleu and . . . thairto ; price thairof, $xiij^{lib}$ vj^s $viij^d$.
" Item, Ffor workmenschip to the said Cheppell, twa hunder
merkis.
" Item, To gett tymmer to big the heidis of the twa Rowndis

* The *cancellus*—a perforated screen, in this instance made of timber.
† Fir.

abone the principall zett at the entres thairof; price of the said tymmer ane hunder pundis; and the expenssis to big the twa Rowndis ffoirsaidis, twa hunder merkis.

"Item, to repair and mend the est gallerie with tymmer and sklaitt, as effeiris; price thairof, . . .

"And giff swa be to reis the principall hows that garrownis may be laid upone the principall hows thairof."

Within the Chapel of Holyroodhouse mass had been performed immediately subsequent to Queen Mary's return in August 1561; and it was this fabric which became the CHAPEL ROYAL OF SCOTLAND in substitution for the deserted structure at Stirling. The building was removed in 1671, when the Palace was made to assume its present quadrangular form.

The remainder of Mr John Duncanson's history may now be related. As the king's chaplain or minister he received some share of ecclesiastical honours. A reply, prepared by Duncanson to Tyrie the Jesuit's refutation of Knox's answer to a former work, was revised and issued by the General Assembly of March 1573, and of the succeeding Assembly he was chosen Moderator. In 1574, he was appointed sub-dean. By the Church in 1576, and again in 1578, he was authorised, with others, to prepare the Second Book of Discipline. He died on the 4th October 1601, having attained nearly his hundredth year. It appeared after his decease that while his office of subdean yielded a revenue of £200 sterling, he had not for a course of years received payment, and for a grant of the arrears a petition was, by his son, presented to the king.*

During his latter years Duncanson had, as his colleague in the office of king's minister, the celebrated John Craig. Deprived of his father, who fell on the field of Flodden, when he was under his twelfth year, Craig became tutor to Lord Dacres. He afterwards joined the Dominican monastery at St Andrews. Some time imprisoned under the charge of heresy, he afterwards travelled in France, and proceeded to Rome. Under the patronage of Cardinal Pole, he was admitted into a convent at Bologna. By reading the Institutions of Calvin he was led to embrace the Reformed doctrines, and being again charged with heresy he was condemned to suffer at the stake. On the death of Pope Paul IV. in 1559 he obtained his liberty. After some stirring adventures and perils he became a minister at Vienna, there obtaining the countenance of Maximilian II. Returning to Scotland he, in 1561, was chosen minister of the Canongate, from which office he was, in 1563, translated to St Giles Church. From the pulpit he denounced the marriage of Queen Mary with Bothwell. In 1571 he was translated to Montrose, and in 1573 to New Aberdeen. He returned to Edinburgh in 1580 as king's minister, for which " the Assembly blessed the Lord and praised the king." Craig drew

* Fasti Eccl. Scot., i. 150 ; ii. 671 ; Miscellany of the Wodrow Society, i. 455, 456.

up the Confession of Faith, which, subscribed by the king in March 1580, was also adopted by the nation. Of three General Assemblies he was elected Moderator. He died on the 12th September 1600, in his eighty-ninth year.*

Another colleague of Duncanson in the pastorate of the Chapel Royal was Patrick Galloway. From the parochial cure of Fowlis-Easter he was translated to the Old Church, Perth. While holding the latter office he incurred the king's displeasure by supporting the Earl of Gowrie, and for a time had to retire to England. Permitted to return, he regained the king's favour, and with the approval of the Church accepted in 1589 the office of royal chaplain. He preached in the Chapel Royal, Stirling, at the baptism of Prince Henry, and ministered in the Chapel Royal of Holyrood till 1607, when he was translated to St Giles Church, Edinburgh. He died prior to the 10th February 1625-6. His eldest son, James, was raised to the peerage as Lord Dunkeld.†

In 1596 John Edmestoun, minister of Dunning, was appointed minister of the King's House, but still retained his parochial charge. He was succeeded in 1602 by Andrew Lamb. A native of Fifeshire, Lamb was ordained minister of Burntisland in 1593. Translated to Arbroath in 1596, he remained there till 1600, when he was elected to the second charge of

---

* Fasti Eccl. Scot., i. 5, 82, 150 ; iii. 462, 843.
† Ibid., i. 8, 151 ; ii. 610.

South Leith. His preferment as minister of the King's House, or chaplain of the royal household (with the teinds of Kirkinner and Kirkcowan) was sanctioned by the General Assembly. On the 24th March 1603, he was appointed commendator of the Abbey of Cupar. He preached at Holyroodhouse on the morning of the 5th April 1603, immediately before the king's departure from Scotland to occupy the English throne. Consecrated, in 1609, Bishop of Brechin, he was transferred to the see of Galloway in 1619, when he also became Dean of the Chapel Royal. Afflicted with blindness he latterly resided at Edinburgh where he died in 1634.*

Mr James Nicolson, minister of Meigle, was, in 1602, nominated as minister of the King's House ; he was appointed to the see of Brechin in 1607. He died before consecration. †

An Act of Parliament was passed in 1579, enjoining the magistrates of burghs, and provosts of colleges to provide " sang scuilis " in their several localities. In order to the greater efficiency of the Chapel Royal as a musical seminary, the king's chief " violar," Thomas Hudsoun, was, by a royal letter, dated 5th June 1586, appointed " Master " of the institution ; he was also appointed chief of the king's " vther chantorie collegis." His appointment was confirmed by Parliament in 1592. And thereon follows the provi-

* Fasti Eccl. Scot., i. 103, 151, 393, 777 ; ii. 528, 777, 785, 889.
† Ibid., i. 151 ; ii. 837.

sion : "And becaus thair is ane greit pairt of the fruittis and rentis of the kirkis and benefices pertening to the said Chappell Royall disponit and assignit to the ministeris serving the cure of the saidis kirkis : Thairfoir His Majestie, with auise foresaid, ordanis and commandis his hienes collectour generall and thesaurair of the new augmentationis to answer and mak payment zeirlie to the said Thomas of samekle as he sall want of the zeirlie fruittis and rentis of the saidis kirkis and teyndis thairof, be the benefices or stipendis assignit or disponit to the ministeris furth of the same. And for the remanent prebendaries and rentis of the said Chappell Royall, foundit vpoun temporall landis and disponit to quhatsumevir vtheris nor to the said Thomas, and vse of the saidis musicianis at ony tyme sen the dait of his said gift : Findis and declaris that he hes guid richt and actioun to persew for reductioun and annulling thereof, to the effect that the same may be josit and vsit according to the effect and meaning of the said gift and prouision in all pointis. And becaus it is speciallie prouydit be the said letter that the said Thomas sal haue payit to him zeirlie in his fie, be the Collectour Generall off the superplus, of the thriddis of benefices within this realme, the sowme of tua hundreth pundis monie, ay and quhill samekle of the rentis of the same Chappell Royall be recoverit be him as will extend to the same sowme." The Act concludes by declaring that the king should not fill up the vacant prebendaries so as to deprive Hudsoun of his office.*

The interests of the musicians serving in the Chapel Royal were further secured by the following Act, passed in 1594:

" Our Souerane Lord and Estaitis of this present Parliament, considdering that his Maiesties maist noble progenitoris of guid memorie conforme to the example of vther ciuile and Christiane princes foundit the Chappell Royall of Striuiling, and disponit certane landis, rentis, and benefices thairto for interteynement of ane certane nowmer of Musicianis, to mak residence and seruice in his hienes house and Chappell at all tymes requisit, neuirtheless be the inoportune sute of sindrie personis in his Maisties minoritie, the rentis of the said benefice ar sua alterit and disponit that the saidis musicianis are not hable to mak residence nor thair is na thing left to thame to leif vpoun, bot that the said erectioun and fundation appearis alluterlie to decay: THAIRFOIR his hienis and estaitis foirsaidis, retretis, rescindis, cassis, and annullis all takis, pensionis, or vther dispositionis quatsumever maid be his hienes of the few males and dewties of few landis and of the dewties of the takis of teyndis of the said benefice or ony part of the same to quatsumeuir persone or personis at ony tyme heirtofoir—And decernis the saidis takis, pensionis, and vther dispositionis foirsaidis of the few males of the saidis landis and of the dewties of the takis of the teyndis thairof to be null: Saulffand allanerlie and exceptand the assignationis maid to the ministeris resident and servand the cures of the kirkis of the said benefice."†

A solitary reference sums up the musical history of the Chapel Royal from the period of Hudson's appointment as chief musician up to the close of the sixteenth century. That reference, contained in "the

* Acta Parl. Scot.; iii. 563, 564.   † Ibid., iv. 75.

Inventory" of Sir Walter Scott of Branxholm, dated at Hawick, 11th April 1574, is in these terms :

"Item, to Schir James Castellaw,* preceptor to the sex barnes foundin within our Soverane Lòrdis Chapell Royall of Striueling, as for the said barnis pairt of Sanct Marie Kirk of Lowis, for certane zeiris preceding the xx day of Februar, anno Lxxxiij four scoir threttene pundis vjs viijd." †

The preceding extract shows that the office of preceptor or "master of the six bairns" was, in 1574, held by James Castellaw, whom we shall find discharging the duties many years afterwards.

On the 14th May 1601, Mr William Chalmer (probably of the family of Drumlochy) was admitted "lwter" of the Chapel Royal.‡ In 1605 he obtained a royal signature for a grant of a yearly pension for life of the third of the prebendary of Kippen, extending to £8, 17s. 9⅓d. ; the third of the nunnery of Manuel, extending to £42, 12s. 10½d. ; and out of the thirds of Arbroath, 15 bolls, 2 firlots, 2 pecks of meal; that is to say, out of Kirktoun 8 bolls, out of Colistoun 6 bolls meal, and out of Brakis the rest—extending in all to £50 ; and 16 bolls meal or thereby, in consideration of "the gude, trew, and

---

* The name Castellaw is clearly of territorial origin. It was the designation of lands, situated at the base of Turnhouse Hill, parish of Glencross, Edinburghshire, the teinds of which belonged to the Chapel Royal. There were four prebendaries of Castellaw among the offices of the Chapel Royal.
† Edinb. Com. Reg., iii., 18th November 1574.
‡ Privy Seal Register, lxxiii. 292.

thankfull service done to his majesty in the office of lectorie in his Majesty's house." In the instrument of gift which is dated at Hampton Court, on the 27th September, and at Edinburgh, 31st December 1605, the grantee is described as "Mr William Chalmer," his Majesty's "servitour." *

In the Register of Presentations appears, under the 8th July 1605, a royal precept for a grant under the Privy Seal to Symeoun Ramsay, son of the late —— Ramsay, indweller in Dalkeith, of the prebendary of the Chapel Royal of Stirling, founded on the parsonage and vicarage of the Kirk of Kells, in the shire of Wigtown, during his lifetime, "for his better sustentatioun and intertenement at the scuillis, and to encourage him to continow in the studie of letters and exerceis musick." The office, it is further set forth, was vacant by the decease of Andrew Gray.†

For many years, notwithstanding feeble attempts after a better state of things, the revenues of the institution were almost wholly secularised. John Gib, who was appointed groom of the Privy Chamber when the king was under the age of nine years, acquired an easy ascendancy over his royal master. This is abundantly evidenced by his having bestowed upon him a succession of immunities and offices. That he might enjoy the revenues, Gib was

---

* Register of Presentations to Benefices, iii., fol. 116.
† *Ibid.*, iii., fol. 108.

constituted "Prebendary of the Chapell Royall of Striuiling, callit the personage of Dalmellingtoun in the dyocis of Glasgw." This office he received by a letter under the Privy Seal, dated 9th February 1585-6. In the instrument of gift it is set forth that it was granted on the death of "Schir Andro Buchquhan, last prebender and possessour thereof."* The gift was followed by a letter under the Privy Seal, dated 14th September 1588, in which Gib was authorised to receive the third part of the parsonage teinds of Dalmellington, belonging to the Chapel Royal. Nor by these grants was the king's liberality towards his early "chamber-chield" in any way exhausted. On the 18th February 1604-5, James constituted his attendant receiver and administrator of the chapel rents. The following is embraced in a royal letter of this date:

"That our souerane lord considdering quhow heirtofore his maiestis royal predicessoures of most blissit and happie memorie, Kingis of his hienes realme of Scotland, alsweill for advancing of the liberall science of musick, as to induce those quha haid attenit to any perfectioun in that airt, to addict thameselffis to the service of thair maiestie's chappell, did speciallie erect and found within thair castell of Striueling ane chappell royal, to remain at their awin gift and presentatioun in all tyme heirefter, and that for training up and educatioun of such personis in the said service, as micht thairefter be most able to serve in the said chappell: and upoun the same respect, and for maintenance and sustenance of thais quha war of the said chappell royall, they did doite and provyde sufficient rentis and revenewis. The quhilk

* Privy Seal Register, liii., fol. 103.

first fundatioun being so advysedlie set doun, hes nevertheles beine within thir few yearis transgressit be the inopportune inquyring of unqualifeit persones to be presentit to the places of the said chappell being unfit for the same, and altogidder voyde and ignorant of ony knawledge in the said science of musick, quhairthrow baith his maiesties chappell hes beine unprovydit of thais quha could serve thairin and the rentis and emolimentis gevin to the said chapell royall hes beine intromettit with be sic quha can nawayes serue thairfore. And now, it being his maiesties most gratious will, mynd, and intentioun to have the said chapell royall in all thingis restorit to the former integritie according to the first fundatioun and institutioun of the same, and that the rentis thairof be employit to na uther use quhatsumever: Thairfore, with advyse of the lordis of his maiesties privie counsell of Scotland, makand, constituand, and ordinand his maiesties trustie servitour, Jhonn Gib, ane of the gromes of his hienes bed chalmer, during all the dayes of his lyftyme, factour, receaver, and intromettour with the haill teindis, fruitis, rentis, proffittis, and emolimentis quhatsumever belangand and perteining, or quhilkis at ony tyme heirtofore hes beine dotit and provydit to the said chapell royall, alsweill that quhilk be the vacand places in the said chapell may be presentlie mellit [meddled] with, as all utheris presentlie possessit be sic as ar provydit quhen ever the same sall onnawayes vaik be thair deceis, to be imployit upoun sufficient persones qualefeit in musick and able to attend and serve his hienes within the said chapell; and vtherwayes, according as it sall pleas his maiestie to direct; with power," etc.*

Disgusted with an act of sovereignty which suppressed a national institution, and deprived its proper officers of the means of living, the Scottish Parliament of 1606 ventured on a protest. They passed an Act which, as illustrative of the intelligence and patriotism of the period, we present unabridged.

* Privy Seal Register, lxxiv., fol. 287.

"Oure Soueraue Lord being of intentioun not onlie to mantene the honour, prerogatiue, and Majestie of his crowne of this his native kingdome of Scotland, bot also to repair and redress sic thingis as are done to the harme and preiudice of the samyn : to the effect that quhan it sall pleis God to gif his maiestie and his royall successouris occasioun to resorte to his said kingdome the dignitie and ancient markis of soueranitie thairof may be so inviolablie observit as may best stand with his majesties honour, the reputation of the cuntrey, and deserve guid reporte and estimatioun amongis strangeris : And understanding that his maist nobile progenitor of happie memorie King James the fourt, following the commendable example of vtheris civill and vertuous princis, foundit ane Chapell Royall constitute of ane sufficient number of persones for serveing his majestie and his successouris in Musique: and mortefeit, doted, and disponit to the said Chapell Royall and memberis thairof diuers kirkis and rentis for thair leving and intertenement, quairof the funda- tion is now sa far neglectit as thair is nather ony sufficient num- ber of qualefeit persones appointit for service thairin, nather is the kirkis, rentis, and revenus thairof keipit in thair awin integritie according to the fundationis, mortificationis, dispositionis, richtis, and securities maid to the said Chapell Royall and memberis of the samyn thairanent : Bot be the contrair the saidis landis, kirkis, teyndis, patronages, proffeittis, and rentis ar analeit, dismemberit, diminischit, and sa mony wayes enormelie hurte, that his majestie and his successouris sall nocht at their cumming to this cuntrey almaist find ony recorde or apperance of the said fundatioun or ony monument of that Royall institutioun; the inlak quairof will breid dirogatioun to the honour of the realme, quhilk onlie among all the Christiane kingdomes will be the meane vant that civill and commendable provisioun of ordinar Musick for recrea- tioun and honour of thair princis : For remede quairof and to the effect that be his Majesties exampill the subiectis of the said kingdome may be the forder encouraged to interteny thair fundatiounis of Musick scholis, quhairby zouth may be in- structit in that liberall science quhilk quicknes the ingyne, gives plesant and harmeless recreatioun to all Estaitis and estaittis of

persones, and is ane haly exercise agreable to the religioun, and
commandit of God for geving of thankis and praise to his holie
Majestie:—Our Souerane Lord with advyse and consent of his
haill estaittis of this present Parliament ratifeis and appreves
the said fundatioun and institutioun of the foirsaid Chappell
Royall, insafar as concernis the seruice of his Maiestie and his
successouris in Musick and all vtheris thingis nocht repugnand to
the trew religioun presently professit and be the law establissit
within this realme: And all landis, kirkis, teyndis, rentis, and
commodities quhatsumeuir mortefeit gevin and disponit to the
samyn or to ony of the memberis thairof: And becaus it is
knawin that nather the said seruice can be done vnles the persones appointit for the samyn have thair competent intertenement and auld levying, nather can their levingis be obtenit
gif the patronage of thair benefice be taken from his Majestie
and the rentis thairof from the said chappell and memberis of
the samin,—THAIRFOIR his Majestie and Estaittis foirsaidis
retrcittis, rescindis, cassis, and annullis all alienationis and dispositionis of landis, kirkis, and patronages of the kirkis and
beneficces belonging or quhilkis heirtofoir ony wayes belongit to
the said Chappell Royall, and patrimonie thairof, and memberis
of the samyn, and all dispositionis, takkis, rentallis, pensionis,
and utheris richtis, titillis, and securiteis quhatsumeuir of the
landis, kirkis, teyndis, fruittis, rentis, dueteis, and commoditeis
thairof annaleit, disponit, gewin, or sett to quhatsumeuir persone
in hurte and prejudice of his hienes patronage of the said
Chappell Royall or in diminutioun of the best and greatest
rentall thairof: And decernis the indoubtit and full richt of
the saidis haill patronages of all and sindrie kirkis quhilkis in
ony tyme bigane wer dottit or annexit to the said chappell—
sall now and in all tyme cumming belang and pertene to our
said souverane lord and his successouris: And that the Maisteris
and Memberis of the said Chappell Royall alreadie establisit
or heirefter to be provydit or establissit be our Souerane Lord
and his succesouris to haue indoubtit richt to the haill landis,
kirkis, teyndis, rentis, proffittis, dueties, or commoditeis quhilk
in ony tyme bigane belangit or appertenit to the said Chappell

Royall and memberis thairof: And lykwayes decernis and
ordanis that the nullitie of the saidis alienationis, dispositionis,
and securiteis of the saidis patronage or thair landis, kirkis,
richtis, and rentis maid to thair preiudice to ony vther persone
in maner foirsaid be ressavit be way of exceptioun or reply
without ony necessitie of actioun, persute, or reductioun of the
samin : And that the samin sall nocht, nor may nocht, in ony tyme
cumming be lauchfullie possessit bot be the ordinar memberis
alanarlie of the said Chappell Royall being astrictit to serue
his Maiestie and his successouris in Musick and vtheris Godlie
and lauchfull exerceis agreabill to the fundatioun and nocht
repugnant to the trew religioun presentlie professit within
this realme nochtwithstanding ony richt, titill, or dispositioun
thairof gevin or ratifeit in parliament or vtherwayes in contrair
the premissis in ony time bigane quhilkis his Majestie
and Estaittis forsaiddis declaris to haue bene fra the beginning and to be in all tyme cumming null and of nane
availl, with all that hes followit or may follow thairvpon as
gif the samin had nevir bene grantit nor maid: Exceptand
alwayes and Reserveand the aduocation, donatioun, and richt
of patronage of the Kirkis of the said Chappell Royall quhilkis
were disponit of befoir to George, Erle of Dunbar, or ar
disponit to him in this present Parliament, sua that the saidis
kirkis, fruitis, rentis, profeittis, dueteis, and emolumentis of
the samen, the aduacation, donatioun, and richt of patronage
thairof sall nawayes be comprehendit in this present act,
bot sall remane with the said George, Erle of Dunbar, his airis
and successouris as their heretable patronages: As gif this
present act had nevir bene maid and nochtwithstanding the
samin, and all vtheris actis and statutis maid of befoir and in
this present Parliament ffrome the quhilkis the saidis patronages
is and sall be exceptit. And also exceptand and reserveand
furth of this present Act and haill contentis thairof the Takkis
of the Teyndis of the Kirk of the Sanctmarie Lowis and pen-
dicles thairof set to Walter Lord Scott of Balcleugh and all the
takkis sett to him of all vtheris Teyndis of whatsumeuir kirkis
perteining to the said Chappell Royall." *

* Acta Parl. Scot., iv. 298.

The Act of 1606 was passed in the king's name, and formally received the royal sanction. But James was still strongly disposed to provide for his favourite attendant, irrespective of every other consideration. Accordingly, in utter disregard of the Scottish Estates—in disregard, too, of those serving the Chapel Royal, he asserted his determination to convert the revenues of the institution into a source of permanent emolument to the companion of his childhood. From Whitehall, on the 15th April 1610, he issued a mandate in these terms :

"Ane letter maid, with advyse of his hienes richt trustie, and familiar counsallour, Mr Johne Prestoun of Pennycuik, his maiesties generall collectour, makand mentioun that his maiestie calling to mynd the lang, guid, trew, and thankfull service done to his hienes continuallie sen his infancie be his maiesties trustie and secreit servitour Johne Gib, grume in his hienes bedchalmer, and his maiestie being always of guid mynd and intentioun to remvnerat his said faithfull seruice with rememberance of his hienes guidwill, as occasioun sall offer: And remembering that albeit his maiestie hes maid and constitute the said Johne maister of his hienes Chapell Royall of Striviling, yit the said Johne rypis na proffeit nor commoditie thairby: Bot the patrimonies, fruitis, and rentis of the kirkis annexit to the said Chapell Royall ar bestowit and imployit to wrang useis: Thairfore, and unto the tyme his maiestie tak full deliberatioun and resolutioun tuitching the sattelling of ane constant platt how the fruitis and rentis of the said Chapell Royall sal be imployit according to the first foundatioun, his maiestie, of certane knawledge and proper motive, with advyse foirsaid, hes gevin, grantit, and disponit, and be thir presentis geveis, grantis, and dispones to the said John Gib all and sindrie the teynd scheavis and utheris teyndis, fruitis, rentis, emolumentis, maillis, fermes, canis, customeis, caswalities, proffeitis, and dewties of all and sindrie the Kirkis of Air, Alloway, Damellytoun, Dalrumpill, Balmaclellane, Kiellis, Creiff, Glenholme, Suddick, Kirkcoune, Kirkkenner: And als of all and sindrie the Kirkis of Kingarth, in Buit St Marie Kirk of Lewis, and lykways of all and sindrie the fyve prebendaries of Strabrane, and of the four prebendaries of Castellaw, and siclyke of all and sindrie the landis of Strawbrane, Castellaw, and fourtene aikeris of the landis of Raplache, quhilk war and ar ane pairt of the patrimonie and propertie of the said Chapell Royall. And that in yeirlie pensioun to the said Johne Gib during all the dayis of his lyftyme, togidder also with the haill byrun, teyndis, fruitis, rentis, emolimentis, maillis, fermes, cainis, customes, caswalities, proffeitis, and dewties quhatsumever of the haill foirsaidis kirkis, landis, and prebendaries restand awand unpayit in the parochinaris and fewaris handis and utheris addebetit in payment thairof. . . ." *

Effectually to carry out the Royal intention a further mandate was issued from Oatlands on the 3d July 1612, in which Gib was constituted King's Factor and Commissioner for settling all tacks and assedations connected with the Chapel Royal. Of that instrument an excerpt follows:

" Ane letter maid, makand mentioun that his maiestie remembring that heretofore his hines by his gift under his hines privie seill of the dait, the fyftene day of Apryle the zeir of God j^m vi^c and ten, gave, granted, and disponed to his hines trustie and secreit serwand Johne Gib, groome of his maiesties bed chalmir, all and sindrie the teynd scheavis and other teyndis, fructis, rentis, emolimentis, maillis, fermes, caynes, customes, caswalities, proffeitis, and dewties of all and sindrie the Kirkis of Kingarth in Bute, Air, Alloway, Damellintoun, Bamaclellane, Darympill, Quelton, Kelles, Kerkennare, Kirkowane, Suddick, Glenhome, St Marie Lowes . . . Creif . . . the [five] prebendaries of Strabrane, the four prebendaries of Castellaw

* Privy Seal Register, lxxix., fol. 110.

And siclyk of all and sindrie the landis of Strabrane, Castellaw, and fourtene aikeris of landis of Raploch, quhilkis war and ar ane pairt of the patrimonie and propertie of his maiesties Chaipel Royall of Striviling, and that in zeirlie pensioun to the said Johne Gib duiring all the dayis of his lyftyme, togidder also with the haill byrun teyndis, fruitis, rentis, emolimentis, maillis, fermes, caynes, customes, caswalitiss, proffeitis, and dewties quhatsumever of the haill foirsaidis Kirkis, landis, and prebendries, resten awand unpayit in the parochinaris and fewaris handis, and utheris addebtit in payment thairof of all and quhatsumever zereis bygane preceiding the dait of the said gift as in the same gift maid to the said Johne thairupone at mair lenth is conteyned. Quhilk gift his maiestie hes of certane knawledge and propper motive ratifeit and approvin, and by the tennour heirof for his hignes [sic] and his successouris ratifeis and approveis in the haill heidis, claussis, and articles, provisionnis, conditionis, and circumstanceis quhatsumever specifeit and conteyned thairin: And willis, grantis, declairis, and ordanes that the generalitie heirof sal be als goode, valide, effectuall, and sufficient in the selff in all respectis as giff the foirsaid gift war at lenth word be word insert herein dispensing thairanent by thir presentis.

"And fardir, our said souerane lord, in coroboratioun of the foirsaid gift and for the said Johne his better securitie . . . His Maiestie with advyse of his trustie and familiar counsallour, Sir Johne Arnot of Birswick, Knycht, his hines generall collector deput, hes maid, constitute, and ordeyned, and be the tennour heirof makis, constituteis, and ordainis, the said Johne Gib duiring all the dayis of his lyftyme his hignes factour and commissionar to the effect vnderspecifeit, geveing, granting, and commiting his maiesties full power and commissioun to the said Johne to sett takkis and assedationes prouyding that the same be with advyse of the Erle Dumfermling, chancellar, Sir Thomas Hammiltoun of Byres, Knycht, clerk of the register, and Mr Willame Oliphant of Newtoun, his maiesties aduocat, and not to indure abone nyntene zeiris, to quhatsever persone or persones he pleissis without diminutioun of the auld rentall of all and sindrie the tynd scheaves and other teyndis, fruitis, rentis, emolimentis, and dewties quhatsoever of all and sindrie the aforesaidis Kirkis and prebendaries abone-named, quhilkis takis and assedationes, ane or mae, to be sett be the said Johne Gib, his maiestie, with aduyse foir-said, hes declaired, decernid, and ordanid, and be thir presentis for his hines and his successouris, declairis, decernes, and ordanis sall be als guid, valide, effectuall, and sufficient in the selff in all respectis to the ressaucaris, thair airis, assignayis, and successouris, as gif the saidis takis and assedationis war past be his maiestie himselff, or his hines successouris, and be the personnes and prebendaris of the foirsaidis Kirkis gif thai war on lyff, with consent of the haill patrones and chapter of the said Chaipel royall and under thair seillis with all uther solemnities requisit, and lvkways with speciall and full power to the said Johne to mak and sett the gersoumes and compo-sitiones of the saidis takis, and to intromet with, uptak, and resaue the samyn gersummes and compositiounes of the saidis takis, togidder with the haill zeirlie dewties of the saidis teyndis contenit in the saiddis takkis, and to use and dispone upone the samyn to his awin proper use, at his pleasour, and speciallie as-signis the said yeirlie dewtie of the foirsaidis Kirkis and pre-bendries, teyndis, fruitis, and rentis thairof to the said Johne, in payment to him of his foirsaid zeirlie pensioun during all the dayis of his lyftyme. . . ."*

The preceding instrument was issued, doubtless at Gib's request, to meet a possible contingency. Gavin Hamilton, bishop of Galloway,† died in the

* Privy Seal Register, lxxxii., fol. 45.

† Second son of the proprietor of Orbistoun, in the county of Lanark, Gavin Hamilton studied at the University of St Andrews, where he gradu-ated in 1584. He is described as having " usurped " the vicarage of Lanark, but in 1590 he was lawfully admitted to the second charge of Hamilton. Translated to Bothwell in 1593, he was, with other brethren, appointed by the General Assembly to attend to the plantation of churches. In 1604 he returned to Hamilton as minister of the first charge ; he was, on the 3d March 1605, promoted to the bishopric of Galloway, and was consecrated

preceding February, and a movement for a reunion of the office of Dean of the Chapel Royal with that bishopric had supervened. Such a reunion implied that at least a portion of the Chapel revenues would fall to be restored. Notwithstanding Gib's prevision and the legal instrument for upholding his claim, the movement for reviving the Deanery made progress. On the 10th April 1612, about three months before Gib had secured office as administrator of the Chapel's rents and teinds, the Archbishop of Glasgow received a letter from the king, in which his majesty commanded him to appoint Mr William Birnie to the office of minister of Ayr, inasmuch that he had "of long tyme resolved to restore the ancient dignity of our Chapell Royall—and considering that Air is a church thereupon depending." The king added, "Mr Birnie had been chosen to serve there, the rather becaus we have a mynd to prefer him also to be Deane of our said Chapell."*

Notwithstanding Gib's strategic movement in July, those who guided the royal counsels in April successfully resumed them in September, when Birnie was constituted " Dean," and " Master of the Chapel Royal," which in the instrument of gift was declared

---

21st October 1610. With that bishopric he held the Commendatorship of Whithorn, and also the Abbacies of Dundrennan and Glenluce, yet his emoluments were insufficient for his support. In circumstances of indigence he died in February 1612, about the age of fifty-one.

* Original Letters relating to the Ecclesiastical Affairs of Scotland, Edinb. 1841, 4to, i. 282.

to be "heirefter callit his Majesties Chappell Royal of Scotland." That instrument proceeds :

"Oure Soverane Lord ordanis ane letter to be maid under his hienes previe seall in dew forme berand that his maiestie calling to mynd quhow that his hienes Chappell Royall of Scotland being foundit and erectit of auld be his majesties maist noble progenitores for the honor of the realme, ornament, and decoratioun of the kirk thairof, consisting of ane deane or maister and ane certane number of prebendares quhais cure [is] to reid and sing divine service in the said Chappell for the use of his maiesties court and household within this kingdome, and considring that the said Chappell and service appointit to be usit therin hes now of lang tyme bene intermittit in default of ane deane and maister to quhome it cheiflie belongis to provyd prebendares and men skeilfull in musick for service of the said Chappell according to the first fundatioun thairof, his maiestie being now of full purpois to haif the samyn restorit and redintegrate to the first integritee and everie thing that is requyrit for the ornament thairof sufficientlie provydit, hes nominat and presentit his weill belovit Maister Williame Birnee, minister, to the place, office, and dignitie of Deane of the said Chappell Royall, Diletur gevand and grantand to the said Maister Williame during all quia.* the dayis of his lyftyme all and sindrie the landis, kirkes, teyndis, frutes, rentis, emolumentis, custumes, and dewteis quhatsumever pertenyng to the samyn, with all dignities, honores, priviledgis, immunities, and liberties injoyit at any tyme befoir by any deane of the said Chappell quhilk ar not repugnant to the religioun presentlie professit, and agreable to the lawes of kirk and realme, with speciall power to the said Mr Williame to chuise, nominat, and elect ane sufficient number of prebendares, skeilfull in mwsick being apt and qualifeit for uther divine service, to serve in the particular charges and services of the said Chappell Royall, and to gift and confer vnto thame the

* Probably the sentence commencing *diletur quia* is left incomplete, owing to some uncertainty on the part of the responsible official as to John Gib's privileges and rights.

benefices, prebendarees, and vther thair levingis belongand to thame and thair places according to the first institutioun, and finallie to do all and everie thing that servis for the restablischment of the said Chappell and service thairin, till the samyn be broucht to the first perfectioun that is requyrit: And becaus the place of residence of his Majesties Counsall and Sessioun, and cheif remanaing of his hienes court quhan he sall happin to be in this kingdome is and will be at the toun of Edinburgh; and that it is expedient the said Chappell be erectit in the maist conspicuus place, and quhair maist resort is of court and counsall, his maiestie thairfoir ordanit the place of speciall residence thairof to be at Halyrudhous in the palice of the samyn, and ordanis the said Mr Williame Birnee, deane electit of the same, to tak sufficient ordour for satling the said Chapell haill memberis and office berares thairin, at the said Palice of Halyrudhous in sic forme and maner as belongis, dispensand, lyk as his maiestie be thir presentis dispensis with the claus and conditioun contenit in the first institutioun thairof gif any sic be, quhairby it is appointit that the said Chappell be resident at Striveling and callit the Chappell Royall thairof, and willis the said Chappell to be heirefter callit his Majesties Chappell Royall of Scotland: And be reddy alwayes to attend his maiesties service in quhatsumever pairt of that kingdome quhair his Majestie sall happin to be personallie present, and keip his majesties residence for the tyme: And ordanis the said lettre to be extendit in the best forme with all clauses neidfull, and with command in the samyn to the Lordis of Counsall, Sessioun, and Eschecker, to grant and direct letres of horning vpone ane simple charge at ten dayes, sequestratioun, arreistment, poinding and vtheris, at the instance of the said Mr Williame for causing him be ansuerit, obeyit, and payit of all and sindrie the landes, kirkes, teyndes, fruites, rentis, and dewties of the said deanery and benefice thairof in all tyme cuming during his lyftyme, as accordis. Gevin at Tibollis the tuentie day of September, the zeir of God j^{m}vj^c and tweff zeiris.*

Diletur.

Son of Birnie of that ilk, Mr William Birnie was

* Register of Presentations, iv., fol. 80.

born at Edinburgh in 1563. After graduating at the University of St Andrews in 1588, he abandoned literature for merchandise, but sustaining heavy losses, he returned to his studies, and entered the Church. By James VI. he was presented to the vicarage of Lanark in 1597, and in 1603 was by the king constituted master and *economus* of the hospital of St Leonards. He countenanced the brethren confined at Blackness in 1606, but continued to enjoy the royal confidence. His appointment to the parish of Ayr in conjunction with the deanery of the Chapel Royal has been referred to. When it was resolved to unite the deanery with the bishopric of Galloway, Birnie consented to surrender his office. As a compensatory arrangement he was, on the 16th June 1614, presented to the parsonage and vicarage of Alloway. By this gift his revenues were believed to be augmented one thousand pounds Scots. Yet the increase seems to have been nominal, for the teinds of Alloway were not available. Consequently Birnie was celebrated in these lines—

"He waited on his charge with care and pains,
At Air, on little hopes and smaller gains."

An earnest and devoted pastor, he displayed feats of agility and strength, which made him famous. He died on the 19th January 1619 at the age of fifty-six.*

* Fasti Eccl. Scot., ii. 86, 306.

In the see of Galloway, the new bishop was William Cowper, minister of Perth, who received his commission on the 31st July 1612, his appointment being afterwards sanctioned by Parliament. Like his predecessor, he held the office of Commendator of Glenluce, and also possessed the revenues of the Priory of Whithorn. On Birnie's resignation he was, on the 2d June 1615, appointed Dean of the Chapel Royal. The following is the instrument of gift:

"Our Souerane Lord ordanes ane Lettre to be maid vnder the great seill in dew and ampill forme, to and in favouris of the reverend father in God, William, bishop of Galloway, makand mention that forsamikle as be ane Act of lait parliament, halden at Edinburgh in the moneth of October, the yeir of God Jaj vj⁰ and twelff yeiris his Majestie and Estaittis of the said Parliament ffor great and waichtie causis exprest in the said Act dissolvit, annullit, retreittit, and rescindit ye Act of annexatioun quhairby all the kirk lands within the kingdom of Scotland were annexit to the Croun, in sa far as the samen Act micht or may be extendit to the Abacie of Tungland and Glenluce and priorie of Quhitherne haill landis, lordschippis, barrones, and vtheris pertening and belanging yairto, to the effect that the saiddis abbacies and priorie with all that hes pertenit and belangit to the samen, alsweill temporalitie as spiritualitie thairof, micht be unitit and incorporat to and with the said bishoprik of Galloway to remayne thairwith inseparable for ever lyk as his Majestie and estaitis foirsaidis be vertew of the said Act of Parliament, unite, annexat, and incorporat to and with the said bishoprik, the foirsaids abacies and pryorie, and with all lands, lordschippis, barrones, burrows, superiorities, kirkis teyndis great and small, functiones, offices, iurisdictiones, and vtheris alsweill of ye temporalitie as spiritualitie yairoff, to remayne abyd and continow with the said bishoprik of Galloway and with the said William, now bishop of Galloway, and his successouris efter him inseparablie in all tyme cuming: And ordanit that ane Lettre of donatioun sould be past and exped in favouris of the said reverend father vnder the greit seill thairvpone in dew and ample forme as at mair lenth is contenit in the Act of Parliament conforme to the quhilk and efter sufficient tryell and consideratioun takin be his Maiestie that the Chappell Royall of Striviling of auld in the dayes of umquhile king James the fourt, his hienes grandshir of maist excellent memorie, wes vnitet to the said bishoprik of Galloway, togidder with all landis, kirkis, rentis, offices, iurisdictiones, dignities, and immunities pertening to the said Chappell Royall, and that the bishoppis of Galloway fra tyme to tyme efter the erectioune of the said chappell wer deanes thairoff and chaiplanes to his maiestie predecessouris: Thairfore our said Souerane Lord, with advys and consent of the lordis of his hienes secret counsall of his said kingdome of Scotland, hes ratifiet, approvin, and perpetuallie confermit all and quhatsumever giftis . . . and declaires and ordaines that the said reverend father and his successouris bishoppis of Galloway ar and salbe in all tyme cuming chaplainis to his Maiestie and his successouris as deanes of the said Chapell Royall of Stirling, and remanent vther benefices abone namit, anexat, and incorporat to and with the said bishoprik, in maner above specefeit als lairgelie and amplie in all respectis as onie bishope of Galloway, deane of the Chappell Royall, pryour and abbot of the saidis pryorie, and abbacies bruikit and joysit at ony tyme heirtofoir: And ordanes that the present chaptour of the said bishoprik of Galloway with the said bishoppes seill and chaiptouris seill now vseit salbe sufficient in tyme cuming for the samen bishoprik, Chapell Royall, and vtheris benefices abonewrettin, vñitit, and anexat thairto for all fewis, infeftmentis, takes, and vtheris to be grantit to the said reverend father in tyme cuming: And that the said Lettre be furder extendit with all claussis necessar and preceptis to be direct ordourlie heirvpone in forme as effeires. At Theoballis the second day of Junii, the zeir of God Jm vj^c and fyftene zeiris."*

* Register of Presentations, iv., fol. 118.

h

Having become dean, Bishop Cowper made a vigorous effort to recover the misappropriated revenues. To his royal patron he, in January 1616, communicated thus :

" I have intended action against all such as praesentlie possesses the rents of the Chappell, and shall doe what in me lyes to recover them; not for ony benefit to me, being hartlie content to quyt all the rent theirof that your Hienes Chappell may be provydit of musitians, and the churches belonging therevnto of pastors. . . . And so soone as livings may be provyded for the musitians, it shalbe my great contentment to be their praesident, in sending up to God, everie day, prayers and praises for your Maiestie and your Royall children. I remember in the last conference concerning it, your Hienes called it, *Insigne Imperii*, and what your Maiestie estemes ony honorable ensyne of your royall estait, we were most vnthankful servants if we sould not follow it, and willinglie come vnder it, sen your Hienes hes geuen so monifold prooffes of rare pietie and wisdome, never streatching out your royal scepter to the uttermost, bot tempering things lawfull with the law of expedience. In end, all my sute is, your Maiestie wold be pleased to giue commandement to the Lordis of your Hienes Session, that they do iustice in such actions as shall come before their Lordships perteining to the Chappell. Sundrie noble men haue I to do with, bot the caus is your Maiestie's, and not myne." *

Whatever commands, if any, James conveyed to the Lords of Session, do not appear. But John Gib was arranged with; he accepted for his claim against the Chapel revenues 3000 marks, which sum was paid him by the bishop.

* Original Letters relating to Ecclesiastical Affairs in Scotland. Bannatyne Club, Edinb. 1851, 4to, ii. 466.

Yielding from his youth a reluctant support to the Presbyterian clergy, James VI. fully determined, after ascending the English throne, to induce his northern subjects to embrace the Anglican ritual. With this object in view he began in 1616, or earlier, to propose a visit to his native kingdom. Preparations for his reception were commenced accordingly. On the 18th July 1616, the treasurer was ordained by the Privy Council to advance 20,000 marks for the works at Stirling, Edinburgh, and Holyrood, in view of the king's visit.*

There was temporary inaction, but as James had at length fixed the period of his advent, operations were commenced in earnest. On the 4th February 1617 the Privy Council passed the following Act :

" Forsamekle as the necessitie of reparatioun and accomplisheing of his Majesteis workis at his majesteis pallace of Halyruidhous is so vrgent in respect of the neir approtcheing of the tyme appointit for his majesteis comeing heir that choise mon be maid of craftismen frome all the pairtis of the cuntrey to furder the saidis worke : And thairfoir the Lordis of Secreit Counsall ordanis Lettres to be direct chargeing the prouest and baillies of the burrowis of Dundie, St Andros, Dysert, Crail, Pittinweme, and Johne Scrymgeour of Dudop, constable of Dundie, to compeir and to bring, present, and exhibite with thame the personis particularlie vnderwrittin nychtbouris and inhabitantis of the saidis townis, with thair workloomes, befoir the Lordis of secreit counsall, vpoun the ellevint day of February instant : That is to say, the saidis prouest and baillies of Dundee to bring and exhibite Andro Wilsoun, maistir maisoun, Thomas Norie, James

* Privy Council Register.

Hunnyman, Johne Norie, Dauid Norie, Johne Donaldsoun, George Hunnyman, Thomas Buquhannane, and Adam Lowry, maisonis, and Johne Smyth, painter. The saidis prouest and baillies of Dysert to bring and exhibite Thomas Hird, and . . . Hird, maissonis, the saidis prouest and baillies of St Androis to bring and exhibite Roger Greene, quheilwrycht, Andro Wilsoun, Thomas Wilsoun, Thomas Robertsoun, Dauid Robertsoun, Hew Phrew, James Phrew, Alexander Miller, Thomas Pady, Johne Wilsoune, maissonis, and Dauid Greg, painter: and the prouest and baillies of Pittinweyme to bring and exhibite with thame, Johne Cowye, Williame Cowye, and Thomas Masoun, maissonis; and the said Johne Skrymegeour of Dudop, to bring and exhibite with him the said Johne Smith, painter, yf he be in his company to the effect the saidis craftismen may be imployed in his Majesteis workis foirsaidis at Halyruidhous, quhair thay salbe weele vsed with reddie and thankfull payment for thair labour, vnder the pane of rebellioun and putting of the prouest and baillies of the burrowis foirsaidis and the said Johne Skrymgeour of Dudop to the horne with certificatioun to thame, and thay failzet Lettres salbe direct heiropoun to putt thame thairto."*

The magistrates of Glasgow and Linlithgow were, on the 10th of February, charged in like manner to supply their quota of workmen. The Privy Council minute proceeds:

" Forsamekle as the necessitie of perfyteing and accomplisheing of his majesteis werkis at the Castell of Edinburgh and palice of Halyruidhous is verie vrgent in respect of the neir approcheing tyme of his majesteis heir comeing as the grittest expeditioun and diligence that can be vsit is litle eneugh, and the saidis werkis being so necessare for the honour and credite of the cuntrey mon be preferrit to all vther werkis of private personis, and proficienttis mon be had frome all the pairtis of the

* Privy Seal Register, Acta 1615-17, fol. 75.

cuntrey to forder and advance the saidis werkis: Thairfore the Lordis of secreit counsall ordanis lettres to be direct chairgeing the prouest and baillies of Glasgw and Lynlithgw to send to his majestcis palice of Halyruidhouse, the personis particularlie vnderwrittin, with thair workloomes: That is to say, the said prouest and baillies of Glasgow to send in James Rankene, Dauid Sclaiter, John Rankene, Johne Boyde, Johne Stewart, James Richie, and James, Johne, Dauid, maissiones; and the said prouest and baillies of Lynlithgw, to send in Nicoll and John Gibsonis, maissonis, and at thair comeing to Halyruidhouse, that thay put thame selffis to the maister of his majesteis werkis or his deputis who attendis the werke at Halyruidhous, whare thay salbe put to worke, salbe weele and kyndlie vsit, and sall ressaue honest and thankfull payment for thair labouris, within foure dayes efter the saidis prouest and baillies beis chairgeit thairto vnder the pane of rebellioun," etc.*

Further edicts were issued on the 20th February, in which certain skilled workmen at Culross were charged to enter service; another on the 27th February, when James Aytoun and other expert artificers at Edinburgh were enjoined at once to repair to "Halyruidhous with their workeloomes under pane of rebellioun."†

The king contemplated operations at Holyrood Palace which his counsellors in Scotland would not have ventured upon. It was his supreme desire that the Chapel Royal of Scotland, now situated at Holyroodhouse, should be specially adapted and fitted up for episcopal worship. Towards this end he despatched artists from London, who were charged to wholly renew the Chapel in its interior arrange-

* Privy Seal Register, Acta 1615-17, fol. 76.   † Ibid., fol. 78-80.

ments. The existing furniture was to be taken out, and all traces of Presbyterian worship obliterated. Not only so, but an altar was to be constructed, which, richly decorated, was to support elegantly sculptured candlesticks and other ornaments. The stalls of the prebendaries and choristers were to be adorned with carved and gilded figures of the apostles and evangelists. The English workmen completed their operations in March, as would appear from the following entries in the Treasurer's Accounts :

"THE EXPENSIS DEBURSIT IN HIS MAJESTIES EFFAIRIS AND DIRECTIONES OF HIS HIENES COUNSALL IN THE MONETH OF MARCHE 1617.

" Item, to Nicolas Stone, carvar, citiner of Londoun, for making of Stall seattis wrocht and enriched in all soirtis with bases, fries, cornes, armes, figuris, with fair daskis, befoir the saidis stallis and seattis within his hienes Chapell Royall of the palace of Halyrudhous, the sown of iiij^c ^{lib} sterling as the contract, and his acquittance produceit vpoun compt beiris, extending in Scottis money to the sowme of .   v^m iiij^c ^{lib}.
" Item, to Mathow Guidrig, painter, for painting and guilting his majesteis Chapell Royall in the palace of Halyrudehous the sowme of four hundreth merkis sterling money extending in Scottis money to the sowme of iij^m ij^c ^{lib} as the contract and his acquittance produceit vpon compt beiris,
.   .   .   .   iij^m ij^c ^{lib}.
" Item, to the said Nicoll Stone and Mathow Guidrig, for thair awin consideratioun and thair menis drink silver L ^{lib} sterling money, extending in Scottis money to vj^c ^{lib} as the precept and thair acquittance, produceit vpon compt beiris,
.   .   .   .   vj^c ^{lib}."

The king's procedure in connection with a structure in which his royal mother, amidst the execrations of the populace, had been present at mass fifty-six years before, was singularly indiscreet. Wild rumours spread everywhere, especially among the citizens of Edinburgh, that "the mass would surely follow the setting up of images." Bishop Cowper apprehended popular violence and a desecration of the sacred structure. So along with the archbishop of St Andrews and the bishops of Aberdeen and Brechin, and several of the ministers of Edinburgh, he entreated the king "to stay the affixing of the portraits." James expressed indignation. In a letter dated "Whitehall, 13th March," he chided the bishops and ridiculed their apprehensions. "Yee could," he wrote, "endure the dieuels to be figured for ornament of your churches, but can not allow that the patriarches and apostles should have like place." Then he informed the expostulating ecclesiastics that he was independent of their mediation with the people, since he remarked, "They have experience of Oure favour, and Wee of their love, so as nather the one nor the other is to be doubted of." Reminding the bishops of the tumult at Edinburgh, on the 17th December 1596,* he sums up, "The pastor, not the

* This tumult, long remembered as the *Seventeenth of December*, took place at Edinburgh in this fashion :—Against what he termed "unlawful convocations of the clergy," James had issued an edict; one Black, a Presbyterian minister, was prosecuted for slandering him and his queen; and certain nobles, members of the Romish faith, who had been exiled, were allowed to return. So on Friday, the 17th December, some malicious person shouted out that certain Presbyterian ministers, who had convened

people, is the cause of their misleading; so Wee doubte not to giue them contentment, and that at Oure being there, they will in such poyntis rather trust Vs, and conforme themselues to Oure so well warranted desires, nor the passion of any preacher there of whatsoeuer degrie." While ventilating his indignation, James consented to "stay the erecting of the portraits," "not," as he said, "for ease of their hearts, or confirming them in their error, but because the work could not be done so quickly in that kind as was first appointed." Referring to the royal epistle in a letter to his friend, Patrick Simson, minister of Stirling, dated the 26th of May, Bishop Cowper writes, " Concerning images, we have gotten them discharged, upon a letter we wrote, subscribed by the bishops, Mr Patrik Galloway and Mr Johne Hall; but yit, with a sharpe rebuke and checke of ignorance, both from his Majestie and Canterburie,* calling our skarring at them *scandalum acceptum set non datum*. We beare the reproofe the more patientlie, becaus we have obteaned that which we craved."†

in St Giles Church, were about to slay the king, who was then in the adjoining structure of the Tolbooth, whereupon a multitude assembled and made a prodigious clamour. The demonstration was as pitiable as it was uncalled for, and it would have been speedily forgotten but for James's own imprudence in seeking revenge for unintended injury.

* George Abbot, Archbishop of Canterbury, a mild prelate, was used as an instrument by James VI. in persuading the Scottish clergy to conform to Episcopacy. But the real author of the letter was no doubt William Laud, then the king's chaplain.

† Calderwood's History, vii. 245 ; Spottiswoode's History, iii. 239 ; Original Letters, etc., ii. 499.

The Scottish authorities were willing that the Chapel Royal should not lack in decorations of an inoffensive character. Under April 1617, the Treasurer's Accounts present the following entry:

" Item, to James Rae, merchand burges of Edinburgh, for certane crammassie velvit, Spanies teffitie, and clinking pasmentis, coft fra him, to be ane cloth to hing befoir his majestie in the kirk, as the compt with his acquittance produceit heirvpoun beiris, . . iij^c lx^{lib} iij^s vj^d."

The musical arrangements were also fully attended to. The following outlays by the Treasurer are entered—the first in May, the second in July:

" Item, to Mr Dalam, organ maker, in consideratioun of his paines and travillis, tuentie angellis, as the precept and his acquittance produceit vpon compt beiris, Inde, . .
. . . . . . j^c xxxiij^{lib} vj^s viij^d.
Item, to Alexander Chisholme and Adam Wallat, musitianes, for furnissing to everie ane of thame a suit of apperrell, as the precept with his acquittance produceit vpon compt beiris, ... vj$^{c\ lib}$."

On the 16th May 1617, James arrived at Edinburgh, and on the day following, being Saturday, choral service in the Chapel Royal was celebrated in his presence. There, too, was the Holy Communion dispensed on Whit-Sunday, the 8th June, when a few noblemen and several bishops partook kneeling. Bishop Cowper refused to kneel, but at next Easter he fully complied with the English ritual.* The

* Calderwood's History, vii. 246, 297.

struggle between Church and King, begun in the Chapel Royal of Scotland in May 1617, did not terminate till the Stewart dynasty was dethroned and exiled.

James proceeded to Stirling, and on the 19th July, within the structure of the Chapel Royal there, he received a deputation from the University of Edinburgh, the several regents conducting in his presence a philosophical debate. In compliment to the disputants, the king decreed that the University of the capital should be styled "The College of King James." *

Before the king left Scotland, he, on the advice of Laud, gave orders that musical service in the Chapel Royal should be conducted daily. The command was not acted upon. A solitary musical demonstration took place on the 19th August, when Bishop Cowper baptized a son of John Murray, groom of the bedchamber, afterwards Earl of Annandale. On that occasion, writes Calderwood, "there was playing of organes, and singing of nuns and boyes, both before and efter sermone. The bishope came doun, efter sermone, to a table standing in the floore, covered with fyne linnen or cambridge [cambric], where there was also a basen of silver and a lawer, with some cuppes."† In a letter to his Majesty, dated 15th September, Bishop Cowper detailed these occurrences. The letter proceeds :

* Life of King James the First, by Robert Chambers, Edinb. 1830, ii. 244, 245.
† Calderwood's History, vii. 277.

"Most Gratious and Sacred Soueraine,

"Please your Hienes, I have as yet done no service in the Chappell, except the baptising of John Murray his sonne, where the organes and musitians, four on everie part, men and boyes, agreit in pleasant harmonie, to the contentment of all, becaus they vnderstood what wes soung. The organes hes bene too commonlie visited, the organist shew me that the spakes that raises the bellowes had bene somewhat vnskilfullie vsed be ignorant people. I shew it to my Lord Chancellar,* who hes commanded to keip them more carefullie, yet the myce and dust of the house will do them evill if convenient coverings be not provyded for them in tyme. For this your Maiestie wilbe pleased giue direction to the Thesaurar; as also for intertenment of the Organist, who can both mak and mend and play vpon them in ordour, for the rent present the Chappell hes will scarse sustene the Prebendaries that ar, except the Lordis help to restore the living that hes bene taken from it, as I hope they will. As for me I see no appearance of a loodging allowed for me; four chalmers are offered me, wherein a man may not possiblie turne a halbert; they can not conteine the half of my familie, and some of them wanting chimneyes, can not be for studentes. How the rest of the houses ar disponed, your Majestie will learne of others better nor of me. Neither key of Chappell nor organe loft is committed to me. I wryt no thing be way of complaint, but that your Maiestie, vnderstanding how matters ar, may giue direction as best pleases your Hienes. Sen everie Minister of the countrey hes a manse at his Kirk, I think your Maiesties will shalbe, that your Hienes Deane haue ane also, either within or without, convenient for his estait. Otherway hard to me to wait vpon dailie service there. Bot referring all to your Maiesties good pleasure, I humblie tak my leaue, and rests your Maiesties humble seruant and dailie oratour,   WILLIAM, BISHOP OF GALLOWAY.†

"Cannogait, Septembre 15, 1617.
"To his Maiestie."

* Alexander Seton, Earl of Dunfermline.
† Original Letters, ii. pp. 509, 510.

His complaints being unredressed, Bishop Cowper supplicated the king anew. "As to the house," he writes, in April 1818, "your maiestie is informed, the Commissioners of your Highnes affaires hes appointed for me, I took my Lord Secretaire to sie it; the best of them [the rooms] is not the lenth of a speare, and four of them scarse able to conteine one bed. I hope my Lord Secretarie will shew your Maiestie the truth. I have committed no fault that I suld be shutt vp in a prison, their being larger rowmes anew possest by others. Bot that your Maiestie be not fashed with such triffles, if it may be your Highnes pleasure to command the Treasurer to discharge me on termes taxation. I am bound to pay for Galloway, and that for this half yeare onlie. I shall so long as I liue furnish a house to my self; and yet more nor this is given everie yeare in pension to some preachors. In good faith, Sir, I spended that summe in attending your Maiestie at your incomming; my self and ane other lived at the King's table; bot my retinue vpon my charges, man and horse, six dailie in number."

Writing in May or June, after mentioning the sum he had paid to Gib,* the bishop adds—"It is hard for me to giue of my oune poore portion for restitu-

* Gib was not satisfied with the sum of 3000 marks paid him for the surrender of his grants, for as titular of Dalmellington he continued to draw the parsonage tithes of that church. Increasing in wealth as he grew in royal favour, he was at length, in 1624, dubbed a knight; he passes from the scene as Sir John Gib of Knock (Life and Times of Robert Gibb, by Sir George Duncan Gibb, Bart. Lond. 1874, 8vo, ii. 50-65).

tion of the Chappel, and to serue in it without house, maile [rent], or stipend ; for in truth I am forced to give all to the præbendaries." *

As the king remained silent, the disappointed bishop entreated on his behalf the good offices of his friend John Murray. Writing to this influential personage on the 10th August 1618, he proceeds : " It is verie hard that I suld giue my owne geir to redeme a rent to the Musitians ; for in gud faith I may not spend abone an hundreth merkis of our money of all the rent of the Chappel in the yeare. And then to pay for my house mail three hundreth merkis yearlie, and more." †

Bishop Cowper's request was at length acceded to, for on the 9th January 1619, the Privy Council gave orders that he should be paid the sum of £1928, 17s. 8d., being arrears on account of house rent. The bishop died on the 15th February thereafter, in his fifty-third year.

In a brief autobiography Bishop Cowper relates that in his eighth year he was taken by his father from Edinburgh to the school of Dunbar, where he remained four years. Sent at the age of thirteen to the University of St Andrews, he there prosecuted his studies for three years. Rejecting proposals to enter into business, he proceeded to Hoddesdon, near London, where he assisted a fellow countryman named Guthrie in con-

* Original Letters, ii. 562, 563 ; *Ibid.*, ii. 558, 559.
† Original Letters, ii. 572.

ducting a school. Afterwards he studied theology at London. In his nineteenth year returning to Edinburgh, he became a licentiate of the Church. He was appointed minister of Bothkennar, Stirlingshire, but there, owing to "the weaknesse of the soil in winter and the unwholesome waters," his health was seriously impaired. Translated to Perth in 1595, he there remained nineteen years, when he was offered the bishopric of Galloway. In his biographical sketch he complains that he suffered through misrepresentation, yet it is undeniable that he was one of the forty-two ministers who, in 1606, subscribed a protest to Parliament against the introduction of Episcopacy, and that his subsequent acceptance of a bishopric afforded ground for animadversion. Not only so, but if we are to credit the author of a contemporary narrative respecting the Chapel Royal, he was chargeable with providing for his relatives out of church funds under his control, without any due regard to the discharge of duties for which these funds were made applicable.*
He was nevertheless imbued with pious sentiment, was an erudite theologian and a faithful pastor. His theological works, consisting of sermons and expositions, collected in 1623 in a folio volume, are composed in an easy style, and abound in striking illustrations. Among his works is a defence of Episcopal government against the unjust imputations of Mr David Hume of Godscroft.

* See *postea*.

Among the original documents embraced in that volume of Sir James Balfour's Collection, entitled, "Church Affaires from the zeire of God 1610 to the zeire 1625,"* is a folio manuscript, entitled, "Informatione anent the first and present esteat of the K. M. Chapell Royall." This document, which seems to have been prepared as a report on the condition of the Chapel, immediately subsequent to Bishop Cowper's death, proceeds thus :

"King James the fourt of gude memorie, in the zeir [1501] foundit the Chapell Royall of Sterling, appointing for the fundation xvi. chanonis, nyne prebendaries and sax boyis, with yearly rent as followes: The fundation is confirmed be Popis Alexander and Julius.

" The saxtein chanonis, besyd the deane (who had a rent of five hundreth mark assigned to him furth of these foundit and mortified revenues) ar these—

1. The subdeane. His rent wes the half of Kirk Inner and Kirkowen in Galloway, which payit to him, besyd the service of the cure at the kirkis, fourteen scoir markis yeirly, now payis only xl. mark. Andrew Cowper, brother to the late B of Galloway, is titular.

" 2. The sacristan, who had the iust vther half of the saidis kirkis, payit of old as the vther dilapidat, payis now as the vther xl. mark zeirly. The said Andro Couper is titular of this also.

" 3. The chanter; 4. the Thesaurer; 5. the Maister of the bairnis. Eche one of these had a rent 100 lib. zeirly furth of S. Marie of the Lowis. One William Scot that dwelleth in the border is chanter, who can not serve nor will not reside. Mr Thomas Gray is Thesaurar—in lyk maner non resident—never comis to the Chapel. James Castellaw is Maister of the bairnis; he attendis dayly, bot the rent is diminisched to 100 mark, being first 100 lib. The revenues of this kirk, ar set in long taks to the Erle of Bakleugh, worth 2000 lib. zeirly.

* Advocates Library. MSS. 33, 3, 12.

"6. The chanceler, his rent wes the Kirk of Sowthweik, whilk now the organist hes. It payes 100 marks be zeir. It had also ane kirk in Bute, whilk now payis 50 mark be zeir, and the trumpeter Fergison hes it. Thir ar called the sax dignities.

"7. The person of Kellis hes now 100 lib. zeirly. A child, Thomas Cowper, nevoy to the late Bischop, is titular—can not serve.

"8. The person of Balmaklellan hes only 50 marks; Patrick Dumbar, titular, attends and is skilfull.

"9. The person of Glenwhom hes 50 mark, and hes sold it to my L. Wigton. Vaikand.

"10. The person callit Air *primo* hes 100 lib. zeirly. The foirsaid Andro Cowper titular of this also.

"11. The person of Alloway hes 80 mark zeirly. Another child, James Cowper, nevoy to the late Bischop, is titular, and can not serve.

"12. The person of Dalmellinton hes 80 mark. Johne Gib his ma^{ties} servant is titular. No attendance.

"13. The person of Dalrumpill hes 50 mark. Andro Sinklar, titular, attendis and is skilfull.

"14. Culton now devyded betuix tuo personis, the said James Castellaw and Barnard Lyndesay,* his majesties servant; eche of them has xl. lib. zeirly. Barnard Lyndesay can not attend.

---

* Bernard Lindsay was one of the *chamber chields* of James VI. who attained to special favour. Son of Thomas Lindsay, Searcher-general of Leith and Snowdoun Herald, he received from the king in acknowledgment of service a ruinous structure at Leith, called "The King's Work," which he substantially renovated. It was granted to Lindsay as a free barony, on the condition that one of the cellars was to be kept in repair for holding wines and other provisions for the king's use. When James returned from Denmark with his queen, on the 1st May 1590, they proceeded to the King's Work at Leith, where they remained an entire week. Lindsay, it is recorded, constructed a large tennis-court, where the king and notable foreigners engaged in recreation. The site of the King's Work is now occupied by the Custom House, and a principal street in Leith is named Bernard Street. Lindsay is, in Walton's Life of Sir Henry Walton, mentioned as having introduced Sir Henry to James VI. under his assumed name of Octavio Baldi, ambassador of the Duke of Florence. Accompanying the king to England, he acquired the lands of Lochhill in Edinburghshire, and others (Lord Lindsay's Lives of the Lindsays, i. 319, 385, 441; Acta. Parl. Scot. iv. 315; Walton's Lives).

"15 and 16. Creif, having tuo personis foundit, the said Mr Thomas Gray one, and a child callit Henry Mow the vther. Eche of them hes 80 marks zeirly. This kirk is set in taks. It is worth 22 chalderis zeirly by the Vicarage.

"Thir ar the xvi. chanonis.

"The nyn prebendars ar, fyve in Strabran, whairof the said Patrik Dumbar hath one, and Sthephan Tillidaf the vther four; ilk prebendarie is xx lib. zeirly. The vther four ar in Castellaw, whairof the said James Castellaw hath one, William Duncanson that dwelleth into Pole [Poland], another, and James Keith, who attendis and is skilfull, the vther two. Thir prebendis ar worth eche of them 35 mark zeirly.

"The sax boyis had 90 markis among them, whairof their is none this day; and of all the xvi chanonis and nyn prebendis, only sevin attendis, and hes no meanes, so that only they sing the common tune of a Psalme, and, being so few, ar skarse knowen.

"Item, thair is aikeris besyde Sterling, called the Raploch,* foundit and perteining to it, bot hes never payit this long tyme.

"Item, 312 lib. zeirly furth of Kintyr and Loquhaber, payit ever till of late zeiris.

"Thir abonewritten kirkis and rentis are reknit in the fundation to have payit to the chapell then in the 1501 zeir 2000 lib. zeirly, whilk is more then ten thousand lib. now, and this day payis only tuell hundreth lib., and most of it to non residentis.

"REMEDIES.

"First. To restore the 312 lib., whilk wes duly payit furth of Loquhaber and Kintyre furth of the king's duties all the dayis

---

* Raploch, a place where archery was practised, as the name implies, is situated at the western base of Stirling Rock; it is occupied by a modern hamlet. On the 22d August 1607, Archibald Cunnynghame of Ladyland was served heir of Robert Cunnynghame, his father, in fourteen acres of land at Raploch, commonly called *Preistis Akris*, lying near the castle of Stirling (*Inq. Speciales* Stirling, No. 60).

of King James the fourt and fyft, and of late ceased, these boundis ceasing to be ciuill, whilk now, blessed be God, is vtherwayes, and suld be restored.

"Secondly. To assay be course of law to repair the dilapidat estait of this benefice, diminution of rentall being so evident, and be the lawis of Scotland a clear irritation of ane tak; besyd that, these takis wanting the patron his consent (who is his majestie), can not subsist, and to this effect to writ to my lord advocat and Secretar to have a cair herein as of his Majesties proper service.

"Thirdly. Seing thair hes been mortified to the chapell besyd the abone written rentis, evin in the fundation, the pryorie of Restenot,* the prebendaries of Spot, Belton, Duns, Pinkarton, lyand within the college kirk of Dumbar, Kinkairn in Mar, Pettie Brachly and Duthell in Murray, Ellam and Cranschawis in Lamermuir, all this as conteined in the fundation,—Item, be act of parliament the pryorie of Coldingame is annexat to the chapell, of all whilkis the chapell hes nothing† to try (seeing the titulars of the chapell hes never renuncit these kirkis and benefices) how they are lost, and [that] either by law or composition some zeirly dutie may be had furth of them.

"Lastly. If no better meanes can be had, a new fundation must supplie it, or els all will cease. And a howse to the Dean to dwell in wald be giuen, or to pay the meill [rent] of it, as wes befoir."

By an Act of Parliament, passed in 1606, which recalled alienations of land that had formerly belonged to the institution, an exception was made in favour of Walter, Lord Scott of Buccleuch, in respect of the church of St Mary Lowes, in Ettrick Forest.

* Roseneath is here meant.
† The annexation of Coldingham Priory with the Chapel Royal, though legally proceeded with, was not practically carried out.

Consequent on that exception, there proceeded under the Privy Seal, in 1612, a royal letter, ratifying to Walter, Lord Scott of Buccleuch,* a lease of the teinds provided for his predecessor. That document is of the following import:

"Ane lettre maid, ratefeand, and approwand, and for his maiestie and his successores, perpetuallie confirmand the tak and assedatioun maid, set, and grantit be William Scott, Chanter of his hienes Chapell Royalle of Striuiling, Mr Thomas Gray, thesaurer thairof, and James Castellaw, Maister of the sax bairnis of ye samyne Chapell, with consent of the prebendaris and chapter of the said Chapell royall, and of Mr James Gray, maister thairof, and commissionar for his maiestie in that pairt; to vmquhile Sir Walter Scot of Branxholme, knyght, thairefter styllit Walter, Lord Scott of Bukglugh, and to his airis maill beirand the armes and surname of Scott, and thair assignayis quhatsumever, ane or ma off all and sundrie the teynd schevis, and utheris teyndis, fruittis, rentis, proffeittis, proventis, emolumentis, and dewties quhatsumever, baithe greit and small, baithe personage and viccarage, of the paroche kirk and parochin of Sanct Marie kirk of Lowis, lyand in Ettrick forrest, and within the Shirrefdome of [Selkirk], and of all landis, rowmes, and possessionis within the samyne, for all the dayes, yeiris, termes, and space of the lyftime of the said vmquhile Sir Walter, and efter his deceis, for all the dayes, yeiris, space, and termes of nyntene zeiris, and efter the ische of the saidis nynetene zeiris, for all the dayis, zeiris, space, and termes of the second nynetene zeiris; and efter the ische of the saidis second nynetene zeiris, ffor all the dayes, space, zeiris, and termes of the thrid uther nynetene zeiris successive nixt efter the entrie of the said vmquhile our traist cousing and counsallour Walter, Lord Scott of Bukglugh, and

---

* Sir Walter Scott of Buccleuch, a man of great courage and devoted patriotism, was a meritorious favourite of James VI. He was, on the 16th May 1606, raised to the peerage by the title of Lord Scott of Buccleuch.

his forsaidis thairto, quhilk was and begane at the dait vnderwritten of the said tak and assedatioun, for payment of certane zeirlie dewtie thairin contenit as the samyne, of the dait, at Edinburgh, the fourtene day of September, the zeir of God jm vj^c and thrie zeires, at mair lenth proportis in all and sundrie pointis, passis, heidis, articlis, claussis, and conditionis and circumstancis quhatsumever thairin contenit, efter the forme and tennor thairof, with all that hes followit or may follow thairvpone: Attoure our said Soverane Lord willis and grantis, and for his maiestie and his successors decernis and ordaines, that this his hienes present ratificatioun is, and sals be, as valide, effectuall, and sufficient in all respectis to his hienes traist cousing Walter, now Lord Scott of Bukglugh, sone and air to the said vmquhile Walter, Lord Scott of Bukglugh, his airis maill and assignayis, for bruiking and joysing of the teyndis, als weill personage and viccarage abonewritt, during the haill lyftymes, zeirs, and space abone specifeit, contenit in the said Tak and assedatioun, to rin as gif the samyne Tak had bene sett with consent of oure said soverane lord, and hed bene subscryuit be his Maiestie, and seillit with his hienes previe seill, at the dait abone written of the said tak and assedatioun, &c., At Edinburgh, the last day of December, the zeir of God Jm vi^o and Tuelff zeiris: Compositio fourtie merkis." *Per signaturam.* *

The instrument by which Bishop Cowper, as Dean of the Chapel Royal, ratified the preceding mandate, contains additional information as to the officers of the institution and on other points, and is therefore here presented without abridgment:

" Be it kend till all men be thir present Lettres, we, William, be ye mercie of God Bishop of Galloway and of the Chappell Royall of Striveling, with advyse and consent of our chaptor, channonis, and prebendaris of the said Chappell Royall, for greit

---
* Privy Seal Register, lxxxii., fol. 83.

and weightie causes and considerations moveing us theirto, To
have ratifeit, approvin, and perpetuallie confeirmet, and be the
tennor heirof ratifies, approvis, and perpetuallie confeirmes
thai Lettres of tak and assedatioun, maid and grantet be
William Scott, chantour of the said Chappel Royall of Strivil-
ling, Mr Thomas Gray, Thesaurer yairof, and James Castellaw,
maister of the sax bairnis of the samyn Chappell, all three
dewlie provyded respectiue to the personage and viccarage of
the parochyn and paroche kirk of Sanct Marie kirk of ye Lowis,
lyand in Attrick Forreste, within the Shreiffdome of [Selkirk]
and haveand guid richt respective to ye teyndis, fruites, rentis,
dewties, profeitis, proventis, comodities, and emolumentis pertening to the saidis personage and vicarage, to umquhil Walter
Lord Scot of Balcleuche, stylet for the tyme Sir Walter Scot of
Branxholme, Knycht, and his airis maill beirand the airmes
and surname of Scott, and yair assigneyis quhatsumever, ane or
mair, of all and sindrie the teynd schaves, and uther teyndis,
fruitis, rentes, profeites, proventis, emolumentis, and dewties
quhatsumever, baith greit and small, alsweill personage as vicarage, of the said paroche kirk and parochin of Sanct Marie Kirk
of Lowis, lyand as said is, and of all landis, rowmes, and pos-
sessiounis within the samyn, for all the dayis, yeiris, and termes
of the lyftyme of the said umquhill Walter Lord Balcleuche, and
efter his deceis for all the dayis, yeiris, space, and termes of nynteine
yeiris, and efter the ische of the saidis nynteine yeiris, for all the
dayis, space, and termes of the second uther nynteine yeires, for
all the dayis, space, and termes of the thrid and uther nynteine
yeiris successive next efter the entrie of the said umquhill Walter
Lord Balcleuche, and his foresaidis yairto, quhilk were and
began at the dait underwrittin of the foresaide tak, and yairefter
to indure during the lyftyme of the said umquhill Walter Lord
Balcleuche, and after his deceis, during the saidis thryse thrie
and tryple nynteine yeiris successive, ay and quhill the saidis
lyftyme and lyfrent of the said umquhill Walter Lord Balcleuche,
and yairefter the saidis thrie and tripell nynteine zeiris successive be fullillie compleit and outrune but interval or inter-
ruptioun, for payment zeirlie of the particular dewties respective

underwritten, viz., to the said William Scot, chantour foresaid, and his successouris chantouris of the said Chappel Royall, that happenis to be dewlie provydid, and to have guid richt respective as said is of the sowme of ane hundreth pundis guid and usuall money of this realme of Scotland, and to the saide Mr Thomas Gray, Thesaurer foirsaid, and his successouris Thesaureris of the said Chappell Royall that happenis to be dewlie provydet, and to have guid richt respective as said is of the sowme ane uther hundreth pundis money foirsaid, and to the said James Castellaw, maister of the saidis sax bairnes, and his successouris maisteris of the saidis sax bairnes that happenis to be dewlie provydit, and to have guid richt respective as said is of the sowme of ane hundreth merkis money abone written, at four termis in the zeir, Beltane, Lambis, alhalowmeis, and Candilmes, be equall poirtionis alanerlie, and als the said umquhile Walter Lord Balcleuche and his foirsaidis, relevand thame and thair saidis successouris, at the handis of the viccar pensionair of the said kirk for the tyme, of all maillis and dewties quhilk he may clame furth of the samyn zeirlie duiring the spaces foirsaidis, in oniewayis siclyk, and in the samyn maner als the said umquhill Walter Lord Balcleuche, and his predecessouris, takismen, and possessouris of the fruits of the said paroche kirk did of befoir, quhilk tak is of the dait, at Edinburgh, the fourteine day of September, the zeir of God Jaj vj^c and thrie yeiris, and sicklyk ratifies, approvis, and perpetuallie confeirmes that letter of confirmation under the privie Seill, granted be our Soverane Lord the Kingis Majestie, of the foresaid uther letter of tak, quhilk confirmatioun and ratificatioun foirsaid is of the dait the last day of December, the zeir of God Jaj vj^c and twelf zeiris: In all and sundrie heidis, poyntis, claussis, articleis, and conditiounis specifeit and conteinit in the foirsaidis lettreis of tak and ratificatioun thairof abovewritten: Attour we will and grant, and for us and our successouris declair and ordainis, that thir our Lettres of ratificatioun and confirmatioun abovewritten ar and salbe as guid, valeid, and effectual to ane nobill and potent Lord Walter, now Lord Scot of Balcleuche, sone and air of the said umquhill Walter Lord Scot of Balcleuch, his father, and to his aires

maill, assigneyis, and successouris, as gif the foirsaidis lettres of tak and confirmatioun tharof above specifiet were hereintill at lenth et de verbo in verbum ingrost and set down: As also that ye foirsaidis lettres of tak and confirmatioun of the samyn hes bene, ar, and salbe guid, valide, effectuall, and sufficient richtis and securities to the said nobill Lord and his foirsaidis for bruiking, joysing, collecting, using, and disponing upoun the above written teyndis, baith personage and viccarage, of the foirsaid parochin of Sanct Marie Kirk of Lowis during the haill zeiris, space, and tyme mentionat in the saidis lettres of tak, provyding nevertheles that we, the said William Bishop of Galloway, be na maner of way obleist in warrandice tharof, but fra our owin propper fact and deed allenarlie, and for the mair securitie we ar content and consentis that yir presentis be ingrost and registrat in the bukis of cunsall ad futuram rei memoriam, and to that effect constitutis
our prouris, &c. In witness quhairof to thir presentis (quhilk ar writtin be James Hardie, servitor to Ion Gilmour, Wryter), subscrybet be us the said William Bishop of Galloway, and als be our said Chaptour, Channonis, and prebenderies of the said Chappell Royall, our awin propper seill, togidder with the said Chaptour seill, ar appendit, at Edinburgh and
the secund day of Apryll and   dayis of
the zeir of God Jaj vj^c and seventeen zeiris, before thir witnesses, Andro Scot, chirurgeone burges of Edinburgh; the saidis Jon Gilmour, and James Hardie, and Mr James Scot, our servitor, and witnesses to other subscriptionis. (Signed) Guilielmus, Candidæ casæ and capellæ regiæ Sterlingen, eps; Williame Scott, Chantor; J. Duncanson, prebendar of Castellaw;   Couper, prebendar of Kirkynner; Johne Chrainthall, prebendar of Kellis; W. Murray, person of Crieff; Mr Thomas Gray, Thesaurer of his majesties chappell; James Castellaw, Maister of the bairnis; John Ross, prebendar of Strabran consentis; Patrik Dunbar, ane of the prebendaries of the Chappell Royall, callit ane of ye prebendaris of Strathbran; Andro Scot, Witness; J. Gilmour, Witness; Mr James Scott, Witness; J. Hardie, Wit-

ness; Gilbert Watt, Witness to the subscriptioun of William Scott, chantour." *

To the conjunct offices of Bishop of Galloway and Dean of the Chapel Royal, Andrew Lamb, Bishop of Brechin, and formerly "Minister of the King's House," was appointed in 1619 in succession to Bishop Cowper. Lamb's earlier history has been related. Owing to feeble health, or in terms of the royal wish, he, after holding the deanery two years, demitted it, when an important change was effected. The office of dean, so long associated with the see of Galloway, was separated from it, and united with the bishopric of Dunblane. The precept for a charter of the office and its emoluments in favour of Adam Bellenden, Bishop of Dunblane, dated at Theobalds, 16th July 1621, narrates that partly owing to the absence of the deans of the Chapel Royal of Stirling, and partly because of the great distance of the bishopric of Galloway from the Chapel, divine service had of late years been rarely performed therein, and that the Bishop of Galloway could not conveniently attend thereto, and had therefore, with consent of the chapter of his diocese, demitted his office of dean

* No. 48 in Process, Deans of the Chapel Royal v. Johnstone and Others, 1863-69.

into the king's hands. Therefore, with advice of the lords of the Privy Council, the king detached the deanery from the bishopric of Galloway and from the Crown, and erected the same into a separate benefice, to be designated the Deanery of the Chapel Royal: And whereas John Murray of Lochmaben had resigned the lands and barony of Dundrennan and other lands which belonged to the abbacy, together with an annual rent of ten chalders of victual out of the lands of Markill* and Traprane, in the constabulary of Haddington, which was disponed by the deceased Francis, Lord of Bothwell, and Lady Margaret Douglas, his spouse, to the late Mr Thomas Craig, advocate, and Helen Heriot, his spouse: Therefore his majesty gives, mortifies, and unites the said lands and annual rent to the deanery of the Chapel Royal; and constitutes Adam, Bishop of Dunblane, dean thereof, to hold of the Crown, for rendering prayers and supplications to God Almighty for the happiness and good estate of the king and his successors, and performing divine service at all times requisite in the Chapel Royal; also the sum of 300 merks Scots, and to provide the elements necessary for the communion in the said church. The bishop of Dunblane and his successors were bound to pay to the ministers serv-

* The rents accruing from these lands will be subsequently referred to. In 1606 a considerable part of the land which originally belonged to the monastery of Markhill or Markle, in the parish of Prestonkirk and county of Haddington, was resumed by the Crown, and by Act of Parliament annexed to the Chapel Royal.

ing in the church of Dundrennan a yearly stipend of two chalders of oatmeal.*

The annexation of the Chapel Royal to the bishopric of Dunblane having been sanctioned by the Parliament, which assembled on the 4th August 1621,† the Privy Council proceeded to recover from the widow of Bishop Cowper the charters and other writs of the institution. Bearing the documents entrusted to her late husband, Mrs Cowper appeared before the Privy Council on the 8th March 1621-2. The relative proceedings are thus set forth in the Register :‡

> " Apud Edinburgh, Octauo Martii 1621. Sederunt—Chancellair, Thesaurair, Wyntoun, Melros, Lauderdaill, L. Erskine, Carnegie, Mr of Elphinstoun, Previe Seale, Thesaurair-depute, Justice-Clerk, Aduocat, Kilsythe, Bruntyland, Marchinstoun, Innerteill, Ridhous, Curriehill, Fostersait, Sir Andro Ker, Sir Peter Young, Conseruatour.
>
> " The quhilk day, in presence of the Lordis of Secret Counsaill, compeirit personallie Grissell Andersoun, relict of vmquhile William, Bishop of Galloway, and for obedience of the chairge execute aganis her at the instance of Adam, Bishop of Dunblane, Deane of his Maiesties Chappell, sho produceit and exhibite befoir the saidis Lordis the bullis register and euidentis of his Maiesties chappell, quhilkis wer in hir lait husbandis custodie and keiping, and quhilkis wer delyueret to him vpoun inventair, and his acquittance be command and directioun of the saidis Lordis, quhilkis bullis register and euidentis being consignit in the handis of the clerk of his Maiesties counsaill,

* Privy Seal Register, xxix., fol. 182.
† Acta Parl. Scot., iv. 649.
‡ Privy Council Register, Jan. 1621 to Mar. 1625, vol. 12

the saidis Lord ordainis and commandis him to delyuer the same vpoun inuentair and acquittance to the said Adam, Bishop of Dunblane, Dean of his Maiesties chappell, to be keipt be him as Deane of the chappell in tyme comeing, and to be maid furthcomeand be him to his successouris, anent the delyuerie quhairof thir presentis with the said bishop his acquittance salbe vnto the said clerk of the counsaill ane warrand."

In the following minute of the Privy Council the delivery of the documents to Bishop Bellenden is circumstantially recorded:

"Apud Edinburgh, decimo tertio Martii 1621. Sederunt —Chancellair Preuie Seale Melros, Thesaurair-depute Lauderdaill, Justice-Clerk, Marchinstoun, L. Erskine, Aduacat, Sir Andro Ker, Carnegie, Kilsaithe, Sir Peter Young, Mr of Elphinstoun, Inuerteill.

"The quhilk day, in presence of the Lordis of Secrett Counsaill, compeirit Mr Robert Nairne, aduocat, as procuratour for Adam, Bishop of Dunblane, Deane of his Maiesties chappell, and gaif in the acquittance vnderwritten subscryued with the said bishop his hand, desiring the same to be insert and registratt in the bookis of Secreit counsell ad futuram rei memoriam, quhilk desire the saidis Lordis finding resounable thay haif ordanit and ordanis the said acquittanis to be insert and registrat in the saidis bookis off the quhilk the tennour followis: I, Adam, Bishop of Dunblane, Deane of his Maiesties chappell, be the tennour heirof grantis me to haif ressauit fra James Primrois, clerk of his Maiesties counsell, the Register bullis lettres and writtis vnderwrittin, quhilkis wer produceit and exhibite befoir the Lordis of Secreit Counsaill vpoun the aucht day of Marche instant, be Grisell Andersoun, relict of umquhile William, Bishop of Galloway, laite deane of the said chappell, for obedience of the chairge execute against hir to that effect, and be the saidis Lordis decreit and sentence wer ordanit to be delyuerit vpoun inuentiar to me as the said decreit bearis.

"Ane commissioun maid and gevin be Pope Alexander [the sixth to the ab]bottis of Haliruidhous and Scoone and Archideane of Lo[thian for the erecti]oun of the Chappell Royall of Struiling in ane colledge [be means of] the mortificatioun and vnioun of certane dewteis to the   oute of Restennett the kirk of Dunbar and otheris. The said [commissioun] beareing daite at Roome the saxt of the nones of May [J v^c and ane] and in the nynt yeir of his Popedoome.

" Ane confirmatioun maid be the said Pope Alexander of the erectioun of the said colledge kirk, with the mortificatiounis and vniouns thairin contenit daitit at Roome the xxvj of the kalendis of May Jm vc and tua in the tent yeir of his Popedoome.

" Ane erectioun of a conseruatorie for the said colledge kirk, maid and gevin be the said Pope Alexander quhairby the Abbottis of Haliruidhouse Cambuskynneth and Paislay or ony of thame wer appointit to be conseruatouris of the said colledge, daitit at Roome the said saxteene of May Jm v^c and tua in the tent year of his Popedoome.

" Ane vnioun or applicatioun of the fruitis of channonreis and prebendaryis of the kirkis of Air, Creiff, Kincairdin, Pettie Bracklie, and Duchall, to the Chappell Royall of Striuiling, maid be the said Pope Alexander the saxt at Roome the saxteene of the kalendis of May Jm v^c and tua in the tent yeir of his Popedoome.

" Ane commissioun maid and gevin be the said Pope Alexander the saxt to the Abbottis of Cambuskynneth, Paislay, and Archideane of St Androis, ffor assisting of the Deane and Chaptour of the Chappell Royall of Striuiling in the peceable possessioun of the foirsaidis vnited kirkis, daitit at Roome the saxteen of the kalends of May Im v^c and tua in the said tent yeir of his Popedoome.

" Ane Ratificatioun maid be Pope Julius the secund of the vnioun of certain Channonreis and Prebendaryis of Dunbar, Balmaclellane, Bute Forrest, and Ellem, to the Chappell Royall of Striuiling, with ane vnioun to the same chappell of the fruitis of the Channonrie and Prebendarie of Creiff, daitit at Roome pridie nonas Junij Jm vc and foure in the first yeir of his Popedoome.

" Ane Confirmatioun maid be the said Pope Julius the secund

of the vnioun of Kirkinner to the said chappell, and contening ane new vnioun thairof, daitit at Roome pridie nonas Junii Jm v⁰ and foure in the first yeir of his Popedoome.

"Ane Commissioun maid and gevin be the said Pope Julius the secund to the Abbotis of Scoone, Dunfermlyne, and Cambuskynneth, for erectioun and establisheing of ane thesaurarie and ten Channonreis to the Chappell of Striuiling, datit at Roome pridie nonas Junij Jm vc and foure in the first yeir of his Popedoome.

"Ane Bull of the said Pope Julius the secund, ordaining and appointing the Bischop of Galloway to be Deane of the Chaippell Royall of Striuiling, daitit at Roome the fyft of the nones of Julij Jm v⁰ and foure in the first yeir of his Popedoome.

"Ane vnioun maid be the said Pope Julius the secund of the Priorie of Restenneth and Inchemahomo, and of the Prouestrie of Lincluden to the Chappell Royall of Striuiling, daitit at Roome the thrid of the nones of Junij Jm v⁰ and aucht in the fyft yeir of his Popedoome.

"Ane Bull and Lettre quhairby Pope Julius the secund deceirnit and ordanit the Bischop of Galloway as Deane of the Chappell Royall of Striuiling to haif the hail iurisdictioun, richtis, and preuiledges ouer the kirkis vnite to the said chappell, whilk the ordinarie had befoir the vnion, daitit at Roome the saxt of the Ides of September Jm v⁰ and aught in the fyft yeir of his Popedoome.

"Ane Register booke of parchement, with trie brodis couerit with broun ledder, contening fiftie-three leavis of parchment, quhairof fiftie-one leavis are markit be the said James Prymrois, and the first and last leavis of the said Register are vnmarkit, haveing no thing writtin thairupoun, and of the leavis that ar merkit the threttie nyne leaffe and the fourtie leaffe hath no thing writtin vpoun thame: In the quhilk Register the particular Bullis Lettres and Writtis being quotit and intitulat as thay ar heir sett doun ar insert and registratt.

"Processus super erectione ecclesiæ collegiatæ de Striuiling, begynning at the first leaffe of the said register and ending at the aucht leafe thairof.

"Confirmatio erectionis ecclesiæ Collegiatæ de Striuiling cum erectione cantoriæ, begynnand at the nynt leaffe and ending at the threttene leaffe of the said Register.

"Conseruatoria ecclesiæ Collegiatæ de Striuiling begynnand at the fourteene leaffe and ending at the saxtene leaffe of the said Register.

"Vnio ecclesiæ de Kirkinner begynnand at the saxteen [leaffe and] ending at the nyneteen leaffe of the said Register.

"Secunda applicatio sive vnio fructuum de Creif et g darum de Dunbar et ecclesiarum de Ellem Bute et Balma[clellan begyn]nand at the nyneteene leaffe and ending at the xxiii leaffe.

"Constitutio procuratorum ad prestandum consensum rector[is] de Kirkinner et ad resignandum post vnionem factam begynnand at the xxiii leaffe and ending at the 24 leaffe of the said Register.

"Instrumentum publicum super resignatione de Kirkinner vnder the signum and subscriptioun of Thomas Kirkaldy, preist and notair, begynnand at the 24 leaffe and ending at the 25 leaffe of the said Register.

"Commissio ad erigendum thesaurariam et decem canonicatus et prebendas, begynnand at the 25 leaffe and ending at the 27 leaffe of the said Register.

"Confirmatio vnionis ecclesiæ de Kirkinner, begynnand at the 27 leaffe and ending at the 28 leaffe of the said Register.

"Applicatio prima fructuum de Air, Kincairdin, Creif, et Pettie Brachlie, begynnand at the 28 leaffe and ending at the 31 leaffe of the said Register.

"Bulla si inquidentem, begynnand at the 32 leaffe and ending at the 33 leaffe of the said Register.

"Conseruatio penes applicationem fructuum de Air, Kincardine, Creif, et Pettie Brachlie, begynnand on the 34 leaffe and ending at the same leaffe of the said Register.

"Ornamenta Jocalia et volumina que habentur in ecclesia Collegiata beatæ Mariæ et Sancti Michaelis de Striuiling et ponuntur sub firma custodia discreti viri Magistri Dauidis Trail sacristæ dicte ecclesiæ quarto die mensis Novembris de anno domini millesimo quingentesimo quinto, begynnand at the 35 leaffe and ending at the 38 leaffe of the said Register, Preuilegium familiarium Regis et Reginæ, grantit be Pope Julius the Secund the fyft of the nones of Julij jm v° and foure, begynnand at the 41 leaffe and ending at the 42 leaffe of the said Register.

" Mutatio decani ecclesiæ Collegiatæ de Striuiling, begynnand the 42 leaffe and ending at the 43 leaffe of the said Register.

" Confirmatio bullæ super funeralia Jura eclesiastica et Jurisdictione ecclesiarum vnitarum, begynnand at the 44 leaffe and ending at the 46 leaffe of the said Register.

" Bulla super funeralia Jura ecclesiastica et Jurisdictione ecclesiarum vnitarum maid be Pope Julius the Secund, at Rome, the saxt day of Ides of September jm v° and aucht, begynnand at the 47 leaffe and ending at the 49 leaffe of the said Register.

" Ane lettre quhairby Henrie Bischop of Galloway and Deane of the Chappell Royall of Striuiling, with consent of the channonis, ordanit the erectioun of the Kirk of Creiff to be insert in the Register of the said chaippell be Deane Johnne Lambert, keepair of the said Register. The said Lettre bearis dait the first of December jm v° xxxvj, and is writtin on the fiftie leaffe of the said Register.

" Ane Instrument maid and consaved in favouris of Deane Johnne Broun, Vicair Pensionair of Creiff, anent the augmentatioun of his pensioun whilk he had oute of the Kirk of Creiff. The said Instrument bearis dait the fyft of Marche jm v° and ellevin, and begynnis at the fiftie leaffe and endis at the fiftie ane leaffe of the said Register.

Off the quhilkis particulair bullis, lettres, writtis, and Register, I, the said Adam, Bishop of Dunblane, grantis the ressett, and exoneris and dischargeis the said James Prymrois, the said Grissell Andersoun, and the airis and executouris of the said laite Bishop of the same for euer: And oblissis me and my airis to keepe the same suirlie for the vse and behoove of me and my successouris, Deanis of the Chappell, and to mak the same furthecomeand to thame quhen it sall pleis God to appoint the tyme: And for the mair securitie I am content and consentis that this present Inventair contening my discharge, as said is, be insert and registratt in the Bookis of Preuie Counsaill ad futuram rei memoriam, and for registring heirof constitutis Mr Robert Nairne my procuratouris: In Witnes quhairof, I haif subscryruit thir presentis, with my hand, at Edinburgh, the xiij day of Marche, the yeir of God jm vj° and tuentie ane yeiris, befoir thir witnesses, James Bellenden, my eldest sone, Laurence Keir and Johnne Aitkine, seruitouris to the said James Prymrois: Sic subscribitur, Ad. B of Dunblane, James Bellenden, witnes; Laurence Keir, witnes; Johnne Aitkyn, witnes." *

With a zeal not less warm than that evinced by his predecessor, Bishop Bellenden sought to restore the Chapel Royal to its former opulence. In a letter to the king, dated from the Canongate, the 17th May 1623, and despatched to court by Mr James Law, treasurer of the institution, the Bishop writes :

"The estait of the Chapell Roiall being well foundit for the tyme be your Maiesties most worthie predecessors, hes resauit suche ruine sen the Reformation by most schamefull dilapidations as hes bene seen be those that at your Maiesties command hes visited the samin; for their wer foundit saxtein Prebendaries besyd the Deane, and nyne boyes, whilk had a reasonable provision assigned them above thre thowsand lib., Scottish money, be yeir, whilk now will not be twell hundreth libs., Scottish money yearly. Your Maiestie hes sufficiently provydlt the Deane his dutie, and for the prebendaries, what remedie can be had to recover ony pairt be law sall be assayed. The best meanes to supplie the rest is by mortifieing of some church rent whilk is at your Maiesties gift as yet vndisponit to the vse of the Chappell, for by this course your Maiesties patrimonie is not burdenit, and in the searche of these church levingis that remainis vnerectit, the beirar, Mr James Law, hes made grit searche, and taken panes to try owt the samin, with some vther

* Privy Council Register, Jan. 1621 to Mar. 1625, fol. 13.

overtures for the bettering of the Chapell, whilk I wald your Maiestie might be pleased to consider, etc." *

With his wonted impetuosity, James sanctioned Bishop Bellenden's proposal, by granting a signature authorising the members of the Chapel Royal to receive the fruits of other chaplainries, prebendaries, and altarages throughout the kingdom. As such a royal order was likely to excite much disaffection, Sir Alexander Napier, the Treasurer-Depute, in a letter dated 1st August 1623,† entreated the king to rescind it. It was rescinded accordingly.

Unaware of the counter movement, the bishop-dean and the prebendaries re-despatched to court their treasurer, James Law, ‡ with a memorial to the king renewing their request. This memorial, dated 5th August [1623], set forth that several of their number had only three pounds sterling by the year, others no recompense whatever, adding, "the haill rent dew to ws all not exceiding ane hundreth merkis sterling." The memorialists then thanked the king for his own "royall and religious dispositioun for re-paireing the breaches thereof, especiallie in such a tyme when the erecting of it finds so vniversall ane oppositioun and contradiction of all sorts of people, from the highest to the tumultuarie vulgar." They next refer to the king's inclination " to re-erect the

* Original Letters, p. 715. † *Ibid.*, p. 720.

‡ Mr James Law was, it is conjectured, the eldest of the three sons of James Law, Archbishop of Glasgow. See Appendix for a letter addressed by Law to the king.

same by his maiesties own hand, no less by doting thereto a competent mantenance than by building a princelie and glorious fabrick." A prayer follows for the better endowment of the institution, the memorialists desiring to have conferred upon it "beneficcs, chaplanries, and certane small few dewties of kirklands," which are described as being " of sa litle value and so troublesome to be collected, that few or nane of them are in vse to pay any dewtie in your Maiesties Exchecker, at the least have bene of the nature of cancealled dewties." The memorial is subscribed by these sixteen members of the institution :

Ro. Wynram.*	An. Cowper.	Ad. B. of Dunblane
Mr James Law.	S^r. James Keith.	and Deane of the
J. Laurie.	S. Tullideff.	Chapell Roiall.
Robert Ros.	J. Castellaw.	Walter Troupe.
A. Hay.	Mr Ja. Weland.	Patrik Dunbar.
Ro^t. Weir.	Humphray Watson.	Johne Watsone.

To the prayer of this memorial, James, with his usual lack of consideration, gave full effect, and in its terms promulgated a royal mandate. Much indignation followed, more especially among those of the higher clergy, whose revenues would have been considerably abridged. But James was, on the 27th March 1625, gathered to his fathers. His mandate was virtually recalled by Charles I. in the following

* Probably of the same family as the celebrated sub-prior of St Andrews. Robert Wynram was connected with the Wynrams of Libberton. He was Albany Herald. (See page clii.)

royal letter, dated 25th August 1626, and addressed
to the bishop-dean:

"Right, etc.—Understanding that it is a course much more
just and honorable that our Chappell royall within that our
kingdome, and the persounes serving therein, should be main-
teined by those meanes appoynted for that purpose at the first
fondation thereof, then otherwise by prosecuting of that course
intended by our late deare father, by making disposition of
some Chappallanaries, preybends, and alterages belonging to our
Crowne: Therfore it is our pleasure that (desisting from that
former course) yow make searche of the old fundations of that
Chappelle, and of the rents alloted there vnto, in whose handes
they are for the present, what right they haue to the same, and
of all other circumstances that may best giue light to the
knowledge thereof: And therefter that the samen may be in
readines to be showen wnto ws at our comming to that our
kingdome, to the effect wee may giue order for making competent provisions for the personnes serving in the said Chappell.
So expecting your diligence in the premissis, wee bid, etc.
Windsor, the 25 of August 1626." *

On the same day the king's advocate was commanded to arrest such proceedings as might be
competent on the order of the late king. To the
advocate the king's letter proceeded thus:

"Trustie and weil-beloved Counsellor, we, etc., being informed that yow caused charge diverse of the Bishops and
Minesters of that our kingdome for production of theire rights
and fundamentall titles to such Chapelaneris, preybendes, and
alterages, as they possesse, for furtherance of the course intended
by oure late deare father to helpe the Chappell Royall: And
seing wee haue resolued to provyd for the same out of the rents

* Sir William Alexander's Register of Royal Letters, MS. in General
Register House.

alloted therevnto as the most lawfull meanes, whereof wee haue written to the Deane thereof, Our pleasure is that yow desist from further perseuing the saidis Bishops or Ministers for the said cause vntill you be further warranted by ws for your so doeing, for it is not our mynd that anie of them be troubled in the possession which they enjoye till wee be pleased to giue further order concerning the same. Thus wee bid, etc. Windsore, the 25 of August 1626." *

On the 7th July 1624, Robert Wynram, Albany Herald, was, in reward of service, appointed "an ordinary musitianer of the Chapel Royal." From the instrument of gift, an excerpt follows :

"Our Souerane Lordis most gratious and sacred Majestie, being crediblie informit off the qualificatioun, literature, and guid conversatioun off his hienes lovat, Robert Winrahame, Albanie Herauld, for vsing and exercing off the airt and science of Musik within his Majesties Chappell Royall, quhairoff he hes given ane sufficient pruiff and tryell as ane ordinar musitianer within the said Chappell this lang tyme bygane, and thair withall calling to mynd the guid, trew, and thankfull service maid and done to his hienes be the said Robert Wynrahame, the tymes of his employment as herauld in his Maiesties service, and vtherwayis within the boundis of Orknay, Zetland, and vtheris partis of the Hielandis, and vtheris alsweill be sey as land, quhairin he was in grit perrell and dainger off his lyff: Thairfore his Majestie, to recompence the said Robert Winrame for his guid and thankfull service, quhill ane better casualtie and occasioun fall out, ordaines ane gift and presentatioun to be maid under the privie seall in dew forme, nominattand and presentand the said Robert Winrame to be ane ordinar Musitianer of the said Chappell Royall of Strivling, and givand and grantand and disponeand to him the office, place, charge, and

* Sir William Alexander's Register of Royal Letters, MS. in General Register House.

functioun thairoff, for all the dayes of his lyftyme, togidder with that pairt of all and sindrie the teind scheiffis, fruitis, rentis, emolumentis, and dewties quhatsumever of the Paroch Kirk of Sanct Marie Lowis, quhilk perteinit to that chantorie and prebendarie of the said Chappell Royall of Stirling, sometyme perteining to umquhill Sir George Gray, possessour thairoff for the tyme, and belanging to the said Chappell Royall as ane pairt of the patrimonie of the samyn, now vaikand, in his Maiesties handis, and at his hienes presentatioun and dispositioun, be deprivatioun of William Scott, sone to Walter Scott of Goldilandis,* last pretendit chantour, prebendar, and titular thairoff, etc." †

The efforts of Bishop Bellenden, persistently exercised, for his better endowment as dean, likewise for increased remuneration to the other members of the institution, led to some further action on the part of the Crown. The following royal letters, addressed to the Privy Council, "the Advocatts," and the Commissioners of Teinds and of Exchequer, also to the Lords of Session, are severally dated 16th May 1627. Each seems worthy of a place.

"TO THE COUNSELL.

"Right, etc.—Whereas it pleased our late deare father that all those, as well of the Privy Counsell as of the Sessioun, should euery Sonday and holyday repayre to our Chappell Royall, haveing for this effect commanded that the seates of the prebandaryes or singing men should be distinguished from others of the Nobility, Counsell, and Sessioun : Seing that course hath beene soe seriously recommended by our said father, and that it

* William Scott held office in the Chapel Royal as a sinecurist, under favour of the Lords of Buccleuch, as titulars of St Mary of the Lowes.
† Register of Presentations of Benefices, vi., fol. 7.

is fitting and decent for diverse respects, Our pleasure is, that at your being in our burgh of Edinburgh, or other parts adjoyneing, yow repayre euery Sonday and holyday to the said Chappell: And likewise that yow be carefull that all such goode orders as were appointed by our said late deare father concerning the said Chappell may be remidied and settled: And as in this, soe in all other thingis concerning the said Chappell, the deane and members thereof yow give your best advice and assistance, which wee will take as acceptable service done vnto vs. Soe we bid yow, etc. Whitehall, the 26 of May 1627.*

"TO THE ADVOCATTS.

"Whereas diverse benefices haue beene annexed to our Chappell Royall in that our Kingdome, the particulares of some whereof wee remitt to be delivered vnto yow by the reverend father in God and our right trusty and well-beloved counsellour the Bishope of Dumblane, deane of our sayd Chappell: And being willing that the said benefices should, according to the first intention, be fully setled vpoun the samen, Oure pleasure is that yow carefully informe your selves of the best course for the recouery thereof by law, or otherwise that yow vse your best meanes for transacting with the possessours, whereby, if the said dutyes can not at this tyme be recouered, at least some yearely rent thereof may be had for their better mantaynance, which will be a meanes that they be lesse burdenable to our Exchequer, concerning which purpose wee haue for your better assistance wryttin to our Colledge of Justice. Soe recommending this vnto yow as a purpose which wee specially respect, wee bid, etc. Whitehall, the 16 of May 1627.†

"TO THE COMMISSIONARES.

"Whereas it pleased our late deare father both effectually, at diverse tymes and vpoun goode consideratiounes to requyre that

* Sir William Alexander's Register of Royal Letters, MS. in General Register House.
† *Ibid.*

such benefices and other small church liveings which were annexed to our chappell royall in that our kingdome, by the first foundatioun thereof, might be fully setled thervpoun. And seing our fathers intention therin is just and many wayes requisite for our vse, the vse of oure successours and the credite of that our Kingdome: Therefore, in reguard that in your proceeding according to your commissioun the said things belonging vnto the sayd chappell are to be treated of among yow, oure pleasure is that a speciall care be taken by yow for the modifying to euery one of the chaplaines out of that church rent, appropriat vnto him some such competent and reasonable meanes, and after such maner as may most conveniently be done, such things being performed by them as is requyred by our commissioun. And whereas we are informed that the Abbacy of Dundranan was purchaste by our late deare father and mortified for the vse of our said Chappell, though wee doubt not but that at your takeing of the estate of that Abbacy amongst others into your consideratioun yow will consider the differences betweene it and other erectiounes, yet wee have thought goode hereby to acquainte yow with our pleasure herein, which is that yow take such a course therein as shall be most aggreeable to our said father's intention, and as may most conveniently be done, according to the course intended by vs at this time. And whereas it hath beene humbly moued vnto vs that the tithes of the half of the lands of Markhill, whereof the stock being Ten Chalders of victuall, is likewise mortified for the vse of the said Chappell, might be acquired and added therevnto for the vse forsayd, though wee like well of any thing that may tend to the advancement of soe goode a work, yet wee would not determine therein without your speciall advice who are cheefely entrusted with the affaires of this and the like nature: Therefore our pleasure is that yow consider of the samen and take such a course therein as may most conveniently and lawfully be done: All which specially recommending to your care wee bid yow farewell. Whitehall, 16 of May 1627.*

* Sir William Alexander's Register of Royal Letters, MS. in General Register House.

"To the Exchequer.

"Whereas it pleased our late deare father to wryte vnto yow that whensoeuer any takismen of our Chappell Royall should be putt to our horne, his escheit of soe much as was held of our said Chappell should be gevin to the deane and members thereof for their better mantaynance till they were otherwise provyded: These are therefore to will and requyre yow that whensoeuer the escheit of any such person doth fall in our hands that soe much thereof as is held of our said Chappell, be gevin to the deane and members thereof whom yow shall cause finde cautioun not to dilapidate or diminish the value of any benefice or other particular granted to our said Chappell, but to preserue the same in their integrity to their successours, according to the pleasure of our late deare father, heretofore signified to this purpose: And it is our further pleasure till the said Chappell rents be established that yow, our Tresurer and deputy, pay yearely out of the first and readiest of our rents of that our Kingdome, for the vse of the said Chappell, an annuity of three thousand merks Scottish, to be disposed and distributed by the deane of the said Chappell as he shall think expedient for doeing, etc. Whitehall, 16 May 1627.*

"To the Session.

"Whereas wee haue beene pleased according to the example of our late deare father for trying of such benefices as were mortified for the vse of our Chappell Royall in that our Kingdome, being willing that they should be recouered (if neede doth soe requyre), by law or otherwise, that the possessours should be delt with, that some yearely rent should be had for the better mantaynance of the deane and the members of the said Chappell, oure pleasure is that whensoeuer any such action concerning the samen shall be intended before yow with the most convenient diligence that can be vsed, proceede in justice therein according to the equity of the cause, and that for the well of the said Chappell yow show as much fauour as can be lawfully granted,

* Sir William Alexander's Register of Royal Letters, MS. in General Register House.

otherwise, at your being so desired by the said deane, or our advocatts, or either of them, that yow mediate, or cause mediate with the said possessours for allowing a yearely rent for the vse foresayd, which wilbe a meanes that they will be lesse burdenable to our exchequer: All which wee recommend vnto your care, and bid, etc. Whitehall, the 16 May 1627." *

A complaint by Bishop Bellenden against Sir David Lindsay of Balcarres, afterwards Lord Lindsay, as to the withholding of tithes led to the following royal letter being addressed to him as "the Laird of Balcarres:"

"Trustie, etc.—Being informed that the reverend father in God, and our right trustie and wellbeloved counseller the Bischop of Dumblaine, the Deane of our Chapple Royall, cannot haue that wse at your handis in the tithes of some landis belonging to him, as heretours haue in the samen parochen in which his landis doe lye, but is forced to pay a farr greater dwetie proportionabillie then they doe, a course in oure judgment contrair to that which should be keept with men of his profession: And sieing our intentione is that everie heretour may haue his owne tithes for ressonable satisfactione to be given to those who haue or pretend right thairto: And that the said bischop declairis himselff to what shalbe found ressonble vpon his part: Thairfore wee haue thought good heirby to desire you that the said bischop haue his owne tithes vpon such satisfactione as our commissioners for surrendars shall determine, or as you yourselff did giue for them, ffor wee doe not heirby intend any lose to you, but that this maeter betuix yow and him may be composed in a fair and amiable maner according to equitie and conscience, as you wold expect any lawfull fauour from ws in the like; or in any other kind. Sic, etc. Bagshot, 17 August 1627." †

* Sir William Alexander's Register of Royal Letters, MS. in Genera Register House.
† *Ibid.*

Already we have seen that Charles I. had commanded the members of Council and Session to attend Divine service in the Chapel Royal on Sundays and holidays, in seats appropriated to them. In 1629 the injunction was emphatically renewed, the king giving positive command that in July of that year the Holy Communion should, at the sound of trumpets,* be dispensed in the Chapel Royal, and that all members of the Privy Council, and of the College of Justice, and other servants of the Crown should, under the highest penalties, repair to the Chapel and there join in that sacred ordinance. The decree proving inoperative, Charles despatched to the Privy Council, on the 6th November 1629, the following mandate:

"Right, etc.—Whereas wee formerlie gaue ordour that by sound of Trumpett the communione should be administrated in our Chappell Royall, in July last, that all of our privie counsell, college of justice and members thareof, and others mentioned in our lettres writen to that effect, might be required to communicatt, and that such of them as wold not should alsoe be required to forbeare the executioune of thare seuerall charges in our seruice, vntill they brought a certificat of thare receaving the communione from the Deane of that Chappell. But now understanding that some papistes affected haue neglected this course,

* History, under like conditions, curiously repeats itself. It is impossible on reading the narrative of this despotic order to avoid recalling a similar order made by an eastern potentate long previously. "Nebuchadnezzar the king made an image of gold, . . . he set it up in the plain of Dura, in the province of Babylon. . . . Then an herald cried aloud, To you it is commanded, O people, nations, and languages, that at what time ye hear the sound of the cornet, flute, harp, sackbut, psaltery, dulcimer, and all kinds of music, ye fall down and worship the golden image that Nebuchadnezzar the king hath set up."—*Book of Daniel*, iii. 1, 4, 5.

Wee, out of our care and affectione to the mantenance of the professed religeone, are heirby pleased to will and require you that according to our former pleasour herein you remoue from our counsall table all such whoe are dissobedient in that kind. Whitehall, the 6 of November 1629." *

A portion of the monastic lands of Markle, Haddingtonshire, was recovered by the Crown, and in 1606 attached to the Chapel Royal, and with it were conjoined the lands of Traprane in the same vicinity. Patrick Hepburn of Smeaton, whose possessions surrounded these lands, had made a claim upon the tithes, and in consequence the following royal letter was addressed to the President of the Council :

" Right, etc.—Whareas wee are informed that our late royall father did purchase the landis of Markle and Trappone and did appropriat them to the vse of our Chappell Royall, the tithes of which landis bieing as yet in the possessione of the Laird of Smeetoun bieing willing for the better and more speedie helping of these persones whoe serue in the Chappell, that some present course be taken for thare mantenance and wese of the tennentis of these landis : Oure pleasoure is that by the advise of the Deane of the Chappell, and our aduocatt, you vse your best and most readie endeuouris for dealing with the said Laird for buying these tithes for him : But if you find just caus for reduceing thareof to the vse afoirsaid that you proceed tharein as you shall think most fitt, and vpon your certiefieing of ws what shalbe thought expedient to be done vpon your parte wee will accordinglie giue ordour for doing thareof: Willing that you in the meantyme, in our name, require our chancellare and keeper of our seall not to pas any new grant of thes landis or titillis in fauour of any persone till our forther plesure be knowen tharein,

* Sir William Alexander's Register of Royal Letters, MS. in General Register House.

willing you likewyis to signifie vnto the said Deane that when any competent benefitt shalbe thought fitt by the Commissioners for tithes to be appropriat to the patrimonie of his see, wee will accordinglie giue way therevnto. Sic. etc. Whitehall, the 6 of November 1629." *

Negotiations with the Laird of Smeaton by the Privy Council having proved tardy, Charles I. communicated with the Commissioners of Exchequer, in a letter dated 2d October 1630, of which the import follows :

"Right, etc.—Whareas wee are informed that ane annuelrent out of the Landis of Markhill and Trapren was bought and mortified by our late deir father for the vse of our Chappell Royall, which tharefter was ratiefied in parliament : And that now it is feared that if any dispositioune or deid should be made ws and our successouris of or concern[ing] these Landis or chappells right to that annualrent wilbe endangered, though wee sie noe just caus to suspect any thing yet to avoid any feare that may come in that kind : Oure pleasure is that you consider if thare be any such necessitie for taking a course to prevent what herm is feared, and if you find it necessarie that you make ane act of exchecquer tharevpon, or otherwayis that you doe thairin as you shall think most fitt for that purpose, which wee if need be shall further authorise as you to this effect shall best advise ws, soe we bid you, etc. Hamptoune Court, the second of October 1630." †

Between the authorities of the Crown in the interests of the Chapel Royal, and the Laird of Smeaton, matters were at length adjusted. As

* Sir William Alexander's Register of Royal Letters, MS. in General Register House.
† Ibid.

President of the Council, the Earl of Menteith consented to pay to the laird the sum of £500 sterling to compensate his right to the disputed teinds. The arrangement is described in the royal letter which follows, addressed to the Treasurer:

"Right, etc.—Whareas our right trustie, etc., the Erle of Monteith hath by expres command from ws, for the vse of our Chappell Royall, agreed with the Laird of Smeetoun for the tithes of the Landis of Markhill and Trapren for payment vnto him of fyue hunderith poundis sterling. Bieing willing (if convenientlie it can be done this yeir) that the tithes of theis landis for this crop may be hade for the vse of oure said chappell. Oure pleasure is that with all convenient diligence you pay vnto the said Laird of Smeetoune the said soume of 500^{lib} sterling, and that out of the first and reddiest of our rentis, casualities, and vther dueties whatsoeuer due vnto ws within the said Kingdome, and for your soe doing these presentis shalbe vnto you a sufficient warrant and discharge. Given at Hamptoune Court the 10 of October 1630." *

On the 17th March 1628 was appointed to the Chapel Royal, as a prebendary and musician, Edward Kellie, respecting whom we are informed in the instrument of gift that he had been "seruitour to George, Viscount of Diplene (afterwards Earl of Kinnoull), Heich Chancellar of Scotland, also one of the Chapel's ordinar musitianes." The instrument of gift is in these terms:

"Our Souerane Lord being crediblie informit of the qualificatioun, literature, and gude conversatioun of his lovitt Edward

* Sir William Alexander's Register of Royal Letters, MS. in General Register House.

Kellie, servitour to His Majesties right traist cousing and counsellour, George, Viscount of Diplene, Lord Hay of Kinfawnes,
Heich Chancellar of Scotland, for vsing and exerceing the airt
and science of musik within his majesties Chappell Royall of
Stirling, whereof he hes gevin ane sufficient pruiff and tryell as
ane of the ordinar musitianes of the samen this lang tyme
bygane: Ordaines thairfore ane gift and presentatioun to be
maid vnder the previe seall in dew forme, nominating and presenting the said Edward Kellie to be ane of the ordinar prebendaris and musitianes of the said Chappell Royall, gevand, grant-
and, and disponand to him the office, place, functioun, and charge
thairoff, during all the dayes of his lyftyme, togidder with that
pairt of all and sindrie the teind scheivis, fruittis, rentis, emolumentis and dewties quhatsumever of the paroche kirk and par-
ochine of Sanct Marie Lowis, quhilkis pertenit to the chantorie
and prebendarie of the said Chappell Royall of Stirling, sometime pertening to umquhile Sir George Gray, possessour thairof,
for the tyme, and belonging to the said Chappell Royall as ane
part of the patrimonie of the samyn now vakand in his Maiesties
handis, and at his hienes presentation and dispositioun be deprivatioun of William Scott, sone to Walter Scott of Goldilandis,
and of Robert Winrahame, Albanie Herauld, last pretendit prebendaris and titularis thairof, or of ane or vther of thame as
being vnable and vnqualified to vse and exerce the place of ane
musiciane in the said Chappell Royall, and refusing to compeir
before the Deane and chaptour of the said Chapell Royall to
give tryell of the samyn and throw not residence to serve
thairintill, etc." *

Proving most prominently zealous, Kellie was, on
the 26th November 1629, appointed Receiver of
the chapel rents and other revenues; also Director
of Music. On his officially reporting as to the in-
efficiency and non-residence of persons sharing the

* Register of Presentations to Benefices, vi., fol. 45.

revenues, the Privy Council were in a royal letter instructed to discharge all such as continued inefficient and refractory. That letter follows :

" Right, etc.—Being informed by Eduard Kellie, our seruand, of the insufficiencie, non-residence, and dissobedience of some heaving charge in our chappell royall to the ordouris prescryued by the dean thareof, and his assistance for setling of the same in a fitt and decent maner, assuming vnto themselves by former giftis of thare offices what freedome and imunitie they think fitt, whareby the seruice to be performed by them is neglected, Oure pleasure is, after due examinatioune and finding of what heirin is alledged to be due, that you discharge such insufficient and refractorie personis, iff they shall not be found (after such triall as you shall think requisit) able to discharge a duetie in thare seruices, and most willing heirefter both to better thare judgmentis in thare professiones, and to obtemper to all the good ordouris alreadie and heirefter to be prescryued by the Dean and his assistances, and for your so doing, etc. Soe wee bid, etc. Whithall, the 28 Junij 1630."*

A royal letter, bearing the same date as the preceding, and addressed "to the Exchequer," authorises the cancelling of a precept of six thousand marks, which Kellie had received from the king. This letter proceeds:

" Right, etc.—Whareas Eduard Kellie, our seruand, hath been a humble suittour vnto ws, that his accomptis touching the setling of the Chappell Royall by our directione and furnesing of thingis tharevnto belonging might be hard, and vpon satisfactione made vnto him of such moneyis as should be found justlie due vnto him a precept of sex thousand merkis procured by him

* Sir William Alexander's Register of Royal Letters, MS. in General Register House.

from ws might be takkin bak by you to be cancelled, wharein finding his demand reasonable and his former panis to meritt some meritt [reward], find encouragement from ws to continow in our seruice in that kind: Oure plesoure is that what moneyis shall appeare due vnto him vpon his accomptis that with all convenient diligence you caus pay the same vnto him, remitting the consideratione of his panis till wee shalbe pleased to sie the effect thareof ffor doing whareof, etc. Whitehall, the 28 Junij 1630."*

The king's determination to provide for the musicians of the Chapel Royal was further evinced by the following communication addressed to his majesty's advocate:

"Right, etc.—Whareas wee are resolued to be serued in our Chappell Royall in that our kingdome with such musicians borne within the same as are continualie or placed of new by the deane of that chappell and by Eduard Kellie, our seruand, to the effect they may be the mare able to discharge our seruice tharein: Oure pleasure is, and we doe heirby will and require you, that with all convenient and possible diligence you caus pay out of the reddiest of our rentis or casualities whatsoeuer in that our kingdome, vnto the said Eduard into the behalff of the said musicians all such arrears of thare feeis as shalbe found justlie due vnto them or any of them, conforme to any gift or giftis granted by ws tharevpon least our said seruice at our cumming thither be ather neglected or they not fitt to be in such a place and charge, and for your soe doing, etc. Whitehall, the 8 of February 1630."†

A further royal letter to "the King's Advocate" relative to the due maintenance of the musicians, was

---

* Sir William Alexander's Register of Royal Letters, MS. in General Register House.
† Ibid.

issued from Greenwich on the 9th June 1631. It proceeds thus :

"Trustie, etc.—Whereas by our gift wee did appoynt a certaine soume to be payed foorth of our Exchequer there to the musicians of our Chappell royall for theire maintenance yearlie till such time as the rents of the old fundation of the said Chappell should be established, and seing as wee are informed the soume appoynted by our said gift is not sufficient to mantaine such a nomber in any competencie as our servants: Therefore, and for there better maintenance and disburdening of our Exchequer of the said yearlie soume, Wee are verie willing that our said Chappell royall and our musicians thereof be established in the old rents and casualities alloted thereto att, or since the fundation thereof according to its own rights, lawes, and practique of our said kingdome: Our pleasure is that in all actions intended or to be intended att the instance of the deane of our said Chappell, or of our seruant, Edward Kellie, touching that purpose, yow compeare for our interest and giue them your best assistance against [any] person whatsoever in so farr as yow can laufully doe: Which oure will take as acceptable seruice done vnto vs. Greenwitch, the 9 of June 1631."*

To prove his zeal in the restoration of the Chapel Royal, Kellie set forth that at his own cost he maintained an organist and other performers. These commenced duty on the 24th October 1630, and on the 9th June the king addressed to the Exchequer the following notification :

"Right, etc.—Whereas wee appoynted our seruant, Edward Kellie, for the ordering of our Chappell royall, and being cre-

* Sir William Alexander's Register of Royal Letters, MS. in General Register House.

diblie informed that he hath well furnished it with an expert organist, singing men and boyes, and other things thereto belonging, whereof wee doe hereby approue as good seruice: And being lykwise [informed] that the said organist and six boyes haue been since the 24 of October last, and are as yett at the only charge of our said seruant, Wee being vnwilling that he should any wise suffer for his seruice done vnto vs: Our pleasure is, and wee doe hereby will and requyre yow, that with all convenient diligence yow receaue his accompts of his disbursments for the maintenance of the said organist and boyes since the said 24 of October last, and accordinglie that yow make payement vnto him, his heires or assignes thereof, and of the arrears of his former accompts allowed by yow preceeding the said day, and that some course be taken whereby he may be disburdened of the lyke charge in all tyme comeing. Greenwitch, the 9 of June 1631."*

These various proceedings, adopted at the instance of the Chapel's Receiver and Director of Music, induced his Majesty's advisers to obtain from Kellie a special report respecting the institution. Entitled, " Information touching the Chappell-Royal of Scotland," and dated " Whitehall, 24th January 1631," the report proceeds thus :

"To the King's most excellent Majestie, the Information and Petition of your Majestie's humble servant, Edward Kellie, touching your Majestie's Chappell-Royal of Scotland.

"When first your Majestie intended to goe into your kingdome of Scotland, I was employed by your Majestie, and such of your Councill of the kingdom as were then at courte, to provide psalmes, services, and anthymnes for your Majestie's said chap-

* Sir William Alexander's Register of Royal Letters, MS. in General Register House.

pell-royal there, as in your chappell here. Thereupon I caused make twelve great books, gilded, and twelve small ones, with an organe-book, wherein I caused write the said psalmes, services, and anthymnes, and attended the writing thereof fyve monethes here in London. At that tyme, alsoe, I provided the same musick that was at your Majestie's coronation here, with one Bible for your Majestie, and two great Bibles for the Deane and for the Readers of the said chappell. Thereafter I procured your Majestie's warrante for deposeing all insufficient persons that had places in your said chappell-royall, and for placing others more qualified, upon examination, in their roomes. Herevpon I carryed home an organist, and two men for playing on cornets and sakbuts,* and two boyes for singing divisions in the *versus*, all which are most exquisite in their severall faculties. I caused the said organist examine all the aforesaid musick-bookes and organ-bookes; and finding them right, convened all the musicians of your Majestie's said chappell, some whereof (being efter triall found insufficient for such service) I deposed, and choosed some others in their roomes, whereby I made vpp the number of sixteen men, beside the organist and six boyes, who all of them sung there psalmes, services, and anthymnes sufficiently at first sight to the organe, *versus*, and chorus; soe being confident of their abilitie to discharge the service, I desired the lordes of your Majesties honourable councell, and others of authoritie, skilfull in that faultie, to heare them; which lordes, after their hearing, in token of their approbation, gave me a testificate under their hands, witnessing that I had fully performed my former vndertakings, and showing that the like service was never done there before by any soe well, or in soe good order. This testificate I have here to show your Majestie. Then, for my assurance in tyme coeming, I took bond of the said musicians, that they should be ready at all tymes to vndertake and discharge the seruice. This bond I have here alsoe to showe. Herefter your Majestie was gratiously pleased, by your letters under your highnes privie seall,

---

* A bass wind instrument of the trumpet kind, similar to the trombone.

with the consent of the Deane of your said chappell-royall, to constitute mee collector and distributer of the rents pertayning to your said chappell, and to see such good orders established in the same, as the service therein might be well and faithfully done, and that none but persons sufficiently qualified should have any place there, and that they should be all keept at daily practise; and for that effect your Majestie appointed mee ane chamber within your pallace of Halyrudehouse, wherein I have provided and sett vpp ane organe, two flutes, two pandores with violls, and other instruments, with all sorts of English, French, Dutch, Spaynish, Latin, Italian, and old Scotch musick, vocall and instrumentall. In the said chamber the said organist and the boyes do remain, and the remanent musicians and vnder officers doe meet therein tuice a week to practise and to receive directions for the next service. For observance of these meetings, and many other good orders, I have likewise taken bond of the said musicians, which bond I have also here to showe. In tyme of service within the chappell, the organist and all the singing men are in black gownes, the boyes are in sadd coloured coats, and the vsher and the sexten and vestrie-keeper are in browne gownes. The singing men doe sit in seats, lately made, before the noblemen, and the boyes before them, with their bookis lay'd, as in your Majestie's chappell here. One of the great Bibles is placed in the midle of the chappell for the reader, the other before the Deane. There is sung before the sermon ane full anthymne, and after sermon ane anthymne alone in versus with the organe. And thus every one attendeth the charge in his place in a very grave and decent forme.

"At this tyme, for your Majestie's now intended journey into your said native kingdome, and for your highnes coronation therein, I have not as yet had any commandment. Nevertheless I am always in readinesse, in manner aforesaide, with the said musick of your Majestie's coronation, and all other musicke necessary, with cornets, sakbuts, and other instruments, with men to play thereon, ready vpon advertisement.

"If, therefore, it shall please your most sacred Majestie to ratifie these my former powers and warrantes, for ingathering of the rents and ordering your said chappell as I have begunne, your Majestie's exchequer by that meanes will be disburdened: And I, your Majestie's servant, shall vndertake either to give your Majestie good assurance, by a new testificate from your councell, of my present abilitie for performance of the service with greater credite to your Majestie's native kingdome than it can be done by strangearis, and with no greater charge vnto your Majestie then is allready due; or else I shall give tymouse advertisement vnto your highnes that your musicians here may be conveyed thither for the service, which vndoubtedly will be a great and needless charge, if your Majestie's servants at home can doe the same, all things being provided and ready for the purpose.

"These premisses I most humbly refer vnto your Majestie's speedy resolution and answer herein. And because this information hath no man else to [be] answerable for what is in it but my selfe, whoe have formerly given proofe of my care and affection to your highnes service; Therefore that your Majestie may be assured that I attempt nothing but what is faire, and what I am confident to performe, as I shall be answerable for, according to my vndertaking, I have subscrived these presents with my hand, at Whitehall, 24th Januarii 1631, after the English account.   E. KELLIE."*

The king's long promised visit to Edinburgh was at length fulfilled. Charles arrived at Holyrood Palace on the 15th June 1633, and by the civic authorities was received at a splendid demonstration. Next day being Sunday, he attended morning service in the Chapel Royal, when the dean, Bishop Bellenden, preached.†

For the coronation extensive preparations had

* Dauney's Ancient Scottish Melodies, Edinb. 1837, 4to, pp. 365-367.
† Spalding's Memorials, 1850, i. 35.

been made by Sir James Balfour, Lyon-King-at-Arms, and Tuesday, the 18th instant, was fixed for the ceremonial. On Monday evening Charles proceeded to the castle, where he remained for the night. Next morning at eight o'clock he, in the great hall of the castle, seated on a chair of state, received a congratulatory address from the nobility and barons, presented by the Lord Chancellor. A procession was formed, in which, preceded by trumpeters, the nobility, clergy, and officers of state took their places, each according to his degree. Next came the king, attired gorgeously in crimson velvet, his train borne by four noblemen. Dismounting at Holyroodhouse, he walked to the Abbey Church, having borne over him a canopy of crimson velvet fringed with gold. The Archbishop of Glasgow rode in the procession, but the Archbishop of St Andrews waited at the western door of the church to receive his Majesty.

The king, as he entered the building, knelt upon the floor. When he rose up, Bishop Bellenden, as dean, conducted him to a seat, and then presented to him Mr James Hannay, minister of the Abbey Church. Preceded by the choristers, discoursing appropriate music, his Majesty now moved forward to the dais, while the crown, sceptre, sword, and spurs, also the anointing oil, were placed near the communion table. Having sat down, he, after an interval, occupied a chair near the pulpit. Dr David Lindsay,

Bishop of Brechin, preached from that passage in the first Book of Kings,* relating to the anointing of Solomon as King of Israel. At the close of the discourse the king reascended the dais, where the Primate presented him to the people. Just as the words "God save the king" had been ejaculated by all present, the choir sung an anthem. Then the king deposited an oblation in a cup of gold, when the archbishop, who received it, administered the coronation oath. Again the choristers discoursed sacred music, and the litany was, by the Bishops of Moray and Ross, read and sung. The archbishop having invoked the Divine blessing, the Duke of Lennox, as great chamberlain, disrobed the king of his upper garment. Under a canopy near the pulpit he now seated himself, when the archbishop approached with the consecrated vial of oil. By the archbishop's hands the king was anointed on the head, breast, elbows, and palms of the hands; also above and between the shoulders. Near the communion table he was next, by the great chamberlain, clad in the state robes of James IV.; he was thereafter girt with the sword of state, and, having received other symbols of sovereign authority, was by the Archbishop of St Andrews solemnly crowned. The clergy and barons having severally expressed their allegiance, were permitted to kiss the king's left cheek. Charles now partook of the Holy Communion, and thereafter left

* 1 Kings, i. 39.

the church, wearing his crown and carrying the sceptre.*

To this description, derived from the narrative of Sir James Balfour, may be added some particulars of the coronation detailed by John Spalding, the industrious annalist. According to this accurate observer, the Archbishop of St Andrews, and the Bishops of Moray, Dunkeld, Ross, Dunblane, and Brechin wore white rochets. There were also, remarks the annalist, among other offensive emblems, a crucifix wrought in tapestry on the communion table, towards which the surplice-clad bishops made obeisance. The other Scottish prelates, adds Spalding, wore black gowns. †

In their accounts of the coronation, both Balfour and Spalding omit reference to a great functionary present on the occasion, who was then exercising a most disastrous influence upon his sovereign. This was William Laud, Bishop of London, and Dean of the Chapel Royal of England. He accompanied James VI. to Scotland in 1617 as his chaplain, and had since attained to great authority. He will shortly reappear.

Charles opened parliament on Wednesday the 19th June. On the occasion was passed an Act "for the rehabilitatione of Francis Stewart," de-

* See "The Memorable and soleme Coronatione of King Charles, crowned King of Scotland at Holyrudhouse, the 18th Junii 1633," Balfour's Historical Works, iv. 354, 389.

† Spalding's Memorials, i. 36, 37.

scribed as "eldest lawfull sone of vmq¹ Francis, sometyme Erle Bothuell." Consequent thereon, Bishop Bellenden protested that "the expeding of the act sould not be prejudiciall to the said Bishop of Dumblane and his successors, deanes of the chappell royall, anent the lands of Markill and Traprain, lyand withine the constabularie of Hadingtone, dotted and mortified be his Majestie's father of eternal memorie, to the vse of his Majestie's chappell royall in Striveling, and annexit to the bishoprick of Dumblane." On behalf of the restored earl, the king assented to the protest. In the same parliament the late king's gift of the Abbey of Dundrennan to the deanery of the Chapel Royal was ratified and confirmed.*

On Monday the 24th June, being St John's Day, the king proceeded in state to the Abbey Church, and there, after a solemn offertory, touched about one hundred persons for the king's evil. Round the neck of each he suspended by a white silk riband a piece of gold. †

Spalding, who mentions the place of coronation as "the Abay Kirk," relates that "vpon Tuysday the 25th of Junij, the king hard deuotion in his owne cheppell royall." He adds: "Doctor William Forbes, minister at Abirdein, teichit in his blak goun, without surpluce or rotchet. His text wes at

* Acta Parl. Scot., v. 56, 72.
† Balfour's Annals, vol. ii., p. 261.

the 27th verss of the 14th chepdour of Sanct Johnes Gospell. The Englishe seruice wes said befoir and efter sermon, as thair vse wes, the cheplanis and novices haueing thair white surpluces on. The Bischop of Dumblane, as cheplane of the cheppell royall, had his rotchet and whyte sleivis on, bot none of our Scottis bischopis except he had the lyk, bot onlie blak gounes."* A moderate Episcopalian, Spalding regarded the white sleeve as a badge of Popery. He reports that Charles worshipped in "the cheppell royal" on Sunday the 30th June. It was for the last time.

With most of his suite, Charles left Scotland for London on the 15th of July. Laud still lingered in the north; he visited Archbishop Spottiswoode at St Andrews, and Bishop Bellenden at Dunblane, discoursing to both of approaching changes, and endeavouring to ascertain how far these prelates might be of service.

Laud had just returned to London when, on the 4th August, he was invested with that high dignity to which he had long aspired, and the duties of which he had some time virtually performed. He was elevated to the archdiocese of Canterbury, and so became primate. But high-handed action in the Church of England was then somewhat impracticable. Scotland, less potent in respect of wealth, and

* Spalding's Memorials, i. 39, 40.

its people in respect of loyalty more pliant,[*] must in the first instance be won. But neither Archbishop Spottiswoode nor Bishop Bellenden were sufficiently advanced for work to be done at Edinburgh. Compliant as to costume, they were Protestant at heart. Laud, with the craft of the conspirator, ever sought to relieve of duty those who refused to yield to his authority. Edinburgh was in the archdiocese of St Andrews; it was now separated from it, and a new diocese constituted, of which it was made the centre. As first bishop, Laud named Dr William Forbes, who, though preaching to the king in his black gown, was found ready to acquiesce both in the Liturgy and Canons. To Bishop Bellenden was, on the 8th October, addressed a royal letter, embodying certain "articles," concocted by the English primate. These documents proceed :

"Reverend Father in God and Trusty and Wel-beloued Counsellour,—Wee greet yow well. Wee have thought goode, for the better ordering of Divine Service to be performed in oure Chappell Royall there, to sett doune some Articles vnder oure owne hand to be observed therein, which We send yow here enclosed. And it is oure speciall pleasure that yow carefully see everie thing performed, according as Wee have directed by these oure enclosed Articles: And likeuise that you certifie to the Lords of oure Privie Counsall if any of these appointed by oure former

[*] A speech of James, Earl of Arran, afterwards Duke of Hamilton, spoken in 1689, seems to interpret that sentiment of loyalty, which led so many Scotsmen to strongly adhere to the House of Stewart. Referring to the dethroned and exiled James VII., Lord Arran remarked, "I must distinguish between his Popery and his person; I dislike the one, but have sworn and do owe allegiance to the other."

letters to them to communicate in oure Chappell Royall, shall not accordingly performe the same, to the effect such order may be taken by our Counsell therein, as by our sayds former letters to them Wee did appointe. Wherein, expecting your diligence and care, Wee bid you farewell. From our Court at Whitehall, the eight^{day} of October 1633.

" To the Reverend Father in God, and oure
Right Trusty and Welbeloued Counsel-
loure the Bishope of Dunblane, Dean of
our Chappell Royall within oure Kingdome of Scotland.

"THE ARTICLES FOR HIS MAJESTIE'S CHAPEL ROYAL.
October the 8th, 1633.

"CHARLES REX,
" Our express Will and pleasure is that the Dean of our Chappel, that now is, and his successors, shall be Assistant to the Right Reverend Father in God, the Archbishop of St Andrews, at the Coronation, so often as it shall happen.

" That the Book of the Form of our Coronation lately used, be put in a little box, and laid into a standard, and committed to the care of the Dean of the Chappel successively.

" That there be Prayers tuice a-day, with the Quire, as well in our absence as otherwise, according to the English Liturgie, till some course be taken for making one, that may fit the custom and constitution of that church.

" That the Dean of the Chappel look carefully that all that receive the Blessed Sacrament there, receive it kneeling; and that there be a Communion held in that our Chappel, the first Sunday of every month.

" That the Dean of our Chappel that now is, and so successively, come duly thither to prayers upon Sundays, and such Holy-days as that Church observes, in his Whites and preach so, whenever he preacheth there; And that he be not absent from thence, but upon necessary occasion of his Diocese, or otherwise, according to the course of his preferment.

CHAPEL ROYAL OF SCOTLAND. clxxvii

"That these Orders shall be our Warrant to the Dean of our Chappel, that the Lords of our Privy Council, the Lords of the Sessions, the Advocates, Clerks, Writers to the Signet, and Members of our College of Justice, be commanded to receive the Holy Communion, once every year at the least, in that our Chappel Royal, and kneeling, for example's sake to the kingdom. And We likewise command the Dean aforesaid to make Report yearly to us, how Wee are obeyed therein, and by whom; as also, if any man shall refuse, in what manner he doth so, and why?

"That the Copes* which are consecrated to our use, be delivered to the Dean to be kept upon inventory by him, and in a Standard † provided for that purpose; and to be used at the celebration of the Sacrament in our Chapel Royall." ‡

In the "articles" there is skilful handling. The *Form of the Coronation*, which was to be honourably preserved, was a religious ritual approved by Laud. Then the Dean is honoured in being constituted Assistant of the Primate in conducting future coronations. Thus distinguished he is privileged to conduct daily service in the Chapel Royal, according to the Book of Common Prayer, till a special Service Book is got ready. The English Prayer Book would pioneer other forms which Laud had in preparation. But Bishop Bellenden as Dean was called on to adopt a course from which the most emboldened would have shrunk. He was to enjoin the Lords of the Privy Council, the Lords of

---

* Communion Cups; chalices.
† An upright cupboard similar to a modern wardrobe.
‡ Wodrow MSS. Folio, vol. lxvi., No. 12.

Session, the Advocates, the Writers to the Signet, and their Clerks, to partake in the Chapel Royal of the Holy Communion (on their knees) at least once a year. And in default he was to report them to the sovereign. Of the Bishop-Dean there was demanded a further and special test. The cups used by the king at his coronation—one into which he had dropped an *oblation* or piece of gold, the other that from which he had tasted wine in the Communion service—the Dean was charged to revere as specially "consecrated;" and as such was to preserve in "a standard" constructed for that purpose. These king-touched vessels were only to be used by those communicating in the Chapel Royal.

Notwithstanding the enticing words wherewith "the articles" commenced, they closed with requirements against which every Protestant minister would certainly revolt. Cups consecrated to Christ in the blessed Sacrament could derive no further or special sanctity from the royal touch. Nor would any ecclesiastic, worthy of his office, compel men to partake of a sacred ordinance utterly regardless of their personal inclination. While usually requiring a strict and uncompromising obedience, Laud meanwhile exhibited towards Bellenden a conciliatory policy. By the Parliament of 1633 had been continued an impost granted some years before as a temporary aid to the king's brother-in-law, the Prince Palatine. Obnoxious generally, this impost was a special source of complaint on the part of Bishop Bellenden. For his relief Laud procured him the following royal letter, which was issued just a week after the despatch of " the articles." It proceeds thus :

"Trustie, etc.—Being willing that the reverend father in God, the bischop of Dunblane, deane of our Chapell, and his successours deanes thairof, be freed from hence furth of all taxations and impossitions whatsoever in so far as may concerne ther owin personall esteats and goodis, and as for the rents payable to them belonging to the said chappell, we ar lykwayes willing that they have what favour may be convenentlie affurded vnto them without prejudice of the course establisched for the levyeing of our taxations. Our pleasur is that having to this purpois conferred with our right, etc., the Erles of Morton and Traquair, our Theasaurers principall and deputie, Our Clerk of Register, and the said bischop, you draw up such a warrand to be signed by us, and to pass our sealls as shal be sufficient for frieing of him and them of the premisses or what further they and you in your opinions think we may convenientlie doe, and that you send the same docat by you for our hand to be returned and exped accordinglie. Whythall, 15 Oct. 1633."*

Grateful for past favours, Bishop Bellenden accepted "the articles" without offering a protest. Against remonstrance there were several reasons. The injunction to daily service gave a further claim to personal recompense or to promotion, and also effectually served to plead the cause of the musicians. Besides, the Bishop had some legal business in the courts at Westminster, which a hint from the English

* Sir William Alexander's Register of Royal Letters, MS. in General Register House.

Primate to the presiding judge might help satisfactorily to adjust. At the commencement of the following letter Laud refers to the influencing of judges without scruple or hesitation:

"You are much beholding to my Lord Sterlinge; * and for my selfe, I did you the best service I could, and am glad your troublesome suites are at an end. I hope that which the Kinge hath now done will preserve you against your pressing necessityes, thurough which I pray God send you a good passage: But for Westminster foes, they did very much wrong you, whoever they [were] that made those relations to you of that great sume; for my former [letters told] the trueth to you.

"Concerning your preferme[nt, until any better] place falls, I can promise nothing; but I assure [you his Majestie] hath a very good opinion both of you and your service; and, therefore, I [can not] doubt but that he will take you and your estate into his consideration. All this time you have given his Majestie good content, and he expects that you continue in that course; and lett him still receive a note whoe they be that conforme, and whoe not, for I see his Majestie is resolved to go constantlie on, and therefore you must not fayle.

"I have considerd howe much reason you speake concerning the poor singing men, and have receivd their petition, which you sent enclosd. I must needs say their case deserves a great deale of commiseration; and the very first time that I gott accesse to his Majestie, after the receipt of your letters, I acquainted him with their necessities, and he, like a gracious and a good Prince, was very much moved with it, and commanded me to deliver theire Petition to my Lord Sterling, that some course might be taken for them; and this, God willing, I will doe soe soone as ever I can meete with that Lord, which I hope will be this day, and soe soone as I can drive it to any good

* Sir William Alexander, Earl of Stirling, the Scottish Secretary at Court.

issue, you shall heare from me. Soe, in hast, I leave you to the grace of God, and rest,
"Your Lordship's very lovinge Friend and Brother,
"W. CANT.*
"Lambeth, January 14, 1633-[4]."

With his legal affairs at Westminster satisfactorily adjusted, Bishop Bellenden ventured to serve as dean after his own fashion. By Mr John Row † we are informed, with reference to the king's command, as to the Lords of the Privy Council and others receiving the communion in the Chapel, kneeling, on the first Sunday of every month, that Bellenden required obedience in a manner of his own. In connection with the December celebration he, in the Scottish mode, preached on the preceding Saturday by way of preparation, while his teaching was such that the ordinance was postponed till Sunday the 15th of the month, and even then there were few participants.‡ The bishop having also omitted daily service, his procedure, as might indeed have been anticipated, moved Laud with indignation. And a fit opportunity for expressing it occurred not long afterwards, when, on the unexpected demise of the Bishop of Edinburgh, Bellenden made application for the office. The following letter from Laud to Bellenden is endorsed "Anent the Liturgie and his sermon," and it is

* Wodrow MSS., folio, vol. lxvi., No 13.
† Row's Historie of the Kirk. Wodrow Society, 1842, p. 370.
‡ Ibid.

evident that the discourse referred to was that preached early in December. Laud's letter proceeds :

"S. IN CHRISTO.

"My very good Lord,—I am right sorry for the death of the Bishop of Edinburrow, the loss being very great both to the King and the Church. I acquainted his Majesty how needful it was to fill that place with an able successor; and when mention was made of divers men to succeed, I did, as you desire, show his Majestie what your desires were, and what necessityes lay upon you. After much consideration of the busynes his Majestie resolued to give the Bishoprick of Edinburrowe to my Lord of Brehen; and for yourselfe he commanded me to write expresly to you that he did not take it well, that contrary to his express command you had omitted prayers in his Chappell Royall, according to the English Liturgye, with some other omissiouns there, which pleased him not; besides, his Majestie hath heard that there have lately been some differences in Edenburgh about the sufferings of Christ, etc., and that your Lordship was some cause of them; or, at least, such an occasion as might have bred much disturbance, if the late Bishop of Edenburrow, his care and temper, had not moderated them; and this his Majestie is not well pleased with neither. And this hath been the cause, as I conceive, why his Majestie hath past you over in this remove; and you shall doe very well to applye yourselfe better both to his Majesties service and the well ordering of that Church, lest you give just occasion to the Kinge to passe you by, when any other remove falls. I am very sorry that I must write thus unto you; but the only way of helpe lyes in yourselfe and your owne carriage: and, therefore, if you will not be carefull of that, I do not see what any friend can be able to doe for you. Therefore, not doubting but you will take these things into serious consideration for your owne good, I leave you to the grace of God, and rest,

"Your Lordship's very loving Friend and Brother,

"W. CANT.*

"Lambeth, May 6th, 1634."

* Wodrow MSS., folio, vol. lxvi., No. 15.

Bishop Forbes, tidings of whose demise had been conveyed to the court, held his high office only a few weeks. Consecrated in the Chapel Royal on the 28th January 1634, he died on the 12th April thereafter. Just before his death he had, in a charge to his clergy, exhibited his strong adhesion to the royal will, and his departure had therefore, as Laud expressed it, been held as a loss, "both to the King and the Church." By acting upon his own principles, rather than those of the Court, Bellenden now realised that he had missed preferment; he resolved henceforth to make a liberal sacrifice of his convictions. If we rightly interpret the primate's next letter, he must have despatched to the king more than one missive expressive of obedience. His pleas in extenuation of his nonconformity are by Laud in the following letter fully adverted to :

"S IN CHRISTO.

"My very good Lord,—My hast at this time forces me to write very briefly; and these are to lett you knowe that I write nothing in my former letters but as the Kinge was informed, and myself by him commanded. I have now read your Lordship's letters to his Majestie, which hath in some part satisfeit him, but not altogether. And for the first, his Majesty saith, that though the gentlemen of the Chapell Royall did absent themselves for feare of arrests, having not to pay; and that that might hinder the service in the Chappel in a solemne and formall way of singing by them; Yet his Majestie thinks you might have got a Chaplaine of your owne to have read the English Liturgye, that soe the work, for the maine part of it, might have gone on. And for the payment of those menn I think your Lordship knowes I have done all the good offices I cann, but have it not in my power to mend all the difficultyes of the time.

"Concerning the disturbance that was in Edinburrow, if any wrong was done your Lordship, that must lye upon them whoe misreported you to the King, who ere they were. And howsoeuer, the Kinge took it not ill, you advised the then Bishop of Edinburgh to appease the differences, for that was very worthily done and discreetly done by you. But as far as I remember, the charge layed upon you to the Kinge was, that in your own sermon, which you preach'd about that time, you did rather side with one partye than either represse or comepose the difference. Though I must needs confess to your Lordship, that by reason of the multitude of businesses which lie upon me, I cannot charge my memory with the particular.

"You have done very well to acquaint the Lords of Counsell and Session, etc., with his Majesties resolution concerning the Communion in the Chappell Royall. And I doubt not, if you continue to doe that which his Majestie lookes for in the course of the Church, and which is most just and fit to be done, but that you will easily recover his Majesty's favour, and find the good of it. So in hast I leave you to the grace of God, and rest,
"Your Lordship's very loving Friend and Brother,
"W. CANT.*
"Lambeth, July 1, 1634."

As Bellenden was now willing to impose the Holy Communion on all whom the king and Laud had enjoined to receive it, the latter was content to renew expressions of approval, also to indicate recompense. He wrote thus:

"S IN C.

"My very good Lord,—I have a second time moved his

* Wodrow MSS., folio, vol. lxvi., No. 16. The letter is endorsed "Anent Reading of the Liturgie and his Sermon at Edinburgh."

Majestie concerning them that obeyed or disobeyed his commands in receiving the Communion in the Chappell at Hallyrudhous, and you shall not fayle to receiue his Majesties answer by my Lord [of Rosse], so that I shall not need to be farther troublesome to you in that parti[cular].

"His Majesty is fully satissfyed that the English . . . in . . . the Chappell Royall before my Lord of R[osse] . . . and in all things else, one . . . satisfied me concerning . . . his Majestie such satisf . . . doubt not but your L . . . so much to your fi . . . Your . . . gentlemen of the Chap . . . to moue his Majestie conce . . . and he told me that a little before his . . . d since the . . . your Lordship half the money was payed unto them. And that the other half was payed before to one, I thinke, of theire company, whom themselves employed to receive it; who, it seems, was a bancroft [bankrupt], and either ran away with their money, or misspent it, or else serued his own turn with it. Now, what to say to this I cannot tell, for the chequer is not in that case that I can think it fit, (or if I doe) I am sure the Lord Treasurer will not think soe, that the king should pay the same sum twice; and yet I must confesse it falls very hard upon the poore men to bear the losse, but they should have been wiser in the choyce of their agent. Notwithstanding, if there can be any hope in this case to relieue them, I shall do my best; and for the future my lord hath promised me they shall be duly payed.

"Soe I leave you to the grace of God, and rest,
"Your Lordship's loving Friend and Brother,
"W. CANT.*
"Croyden, October 4, 1634."

In answer to an inquiry by Bellenden as to the plunder of the Chapel funds, Laud must have excited his surprise by naming Edward Kellie as the delinquent. Towards his correspondent the primate

* Wodrow MSS., folio, vol. lxvi., No. 17.

is, in his next letter, complimentary and reassuring:

"S. IN CHRISTO.

"My very good Lord,—I am very glad to heare your resolutions for the ordering of his Majesties Chappell Royall, and that you are resolved to wear your whites, notwithstanding the maliciousnes of foolish men. I know his Majestie will take your obedience and care very well; and being fully satisfied, both concerning your sermon and all thinges else committed to your trust, you may, as opportunity serues, expect from his Majestie all reasonable thinges; and I shall not be wanting to give you all the assistance that I can vpon all occasions, of which I heartily pray you not to doubt.

"My lord, the Earle of Traquare is now come, and I shall take the first opportunity I can to speake once more with him about the gentlemen of the Chappell, and shall showe him what your lordship writes concerning one Edward Kelly, whom you mention; and what answer soever I can gett, you shall receive from me.

"Soe in hast, I leave you to the grace of God, and rest,
"Your Lordship's very loving Friend and Brother,
"W. CANT.
"Lambeth, Jan. 12, 1634[5].

"I have spoken with my Lord Traquare, and he tells me (if I mistooke him not) that pay was made to Kelly with relation to the gentlemen of the Chappell, and that your oun hand, as well as others, is to some agreement that was made thereabout. The paper was not then about him, else he had showed it me. Your Lordship, therefore, shall doe very well to speak with him again about this particular. As for the time to come, he hath assumed to me they shall be duly paid."*

Prior to the 15th February 1634-5, Kellie was

* Wodrow MSS., folio, vol. lxvi., No. 14.

displaced, and "Mr Edward Millar, musician, residing in Edinburgh," appointed his successor.*

Bellenden's promotion at length arrived, but with it was accompanied the proviso that he was to become resident at Aberdeen. Should he accept, then the English primate made sure that the Scottish capital was ecclesiastically his own. In expression the following is abundantly fraternal:

"S. IN CHRISTO.

"My very good Lord,—The king hathe been acquainted with your care of the Chappell Royall, and is very well pleased with the conformity which hath been there at the late reception of the blessed Sacrament; and, for my part, I am heartyly glad to see in what a faire way the Church busynesses now are in those parts. I hope, if the bishops be pleased to continue theire good example and their care, all thinges will settle beyond expectation.

"The king hath declared his pleasure concerning the bishoprickes now void, and hath given yow the bishopricke of Aberdeen, as you will heare more at large by my Lord of Rosse. But being an Vniversity and a place of consequence, he will have you reside there, and relies much upon you for the well ordering of that place. I am very glad the kinge hath been soe mindful of you, and given you soe good a testimony vpon this occasion of your remove. So I leave you to the grace of God, and rest,

"Your Lordship's very loveinge Freind and Brother,

"W. CANT. †

"Lambeth, May 19, 1635."

As concerned Scotland, Laud's hopes had reached

---

* Register of Presentations, vii., fol. 24.
† Wodrow MSS., folio, vol. lxvi., No. 19.

a climax. David Lindsay, pliant and courtly, was Bishop of Edinburgh; and Bellenden, with his uncertainties, was residing in his distant diocese of Aberdeen.*

Lately constituted Lord Chancellor, Archbishop Spottiswoode, with his embarrassing assertion of Protestant doctrine, was virtually silenced. And above all, there was for the office of dean of the Chapel Royal an ecclesiastic in waiting whose obedience had been proved. It is here essential to place under review some recent occurrences. Desirous of assimilating the two national Churches, James VI. had sought, subsequent to the English accession, to accommodate the Scottish Church to the Anglican system in matters of ecclesiastical ritual, and clerical attire. Doctrinal considerations were at the outset deemed of less moment; but when Laud became king's chaplain, circumstances changed. James's resolution in 1617 to affix in the Chapel Royal certain carved figures, and his unwillingness to withdraw the order, were due to the perversity of Laud. On the withdrawal was substituted an order for the English Book of Common Prayer being used in daily service—an innovation which at this

---

* That Bellenden was translated to Aberdeen because Laud regarded him as an impediment to the execution of his plans was at the time well understood. In reference to the translation, Principal Robert Baillie thus writes to his correspondent, Mr William Spang :—"He was removed from the Chappell Royal to Aberdeen, as one who did not favour well enough Canterburie's new wayes" (Baillie's Letters, Edinb. 1841, i. 161).

time the king would not have ventured otherwise to propose.

Having introduced a liturgical service in the Chapel Royal, and then prescribed kneeling at the communion, the way for further innovation was opened up. Through Archbishop Spottiswoode of St Andrews, Laud in 1618 obtained for the celebrated "five articles" the sanction of the General Assembly. When these articles, sanctioned by the Estates of Parliament, became law, Laud urged the king to enforce their adoption. Partially this was done; but James, alarmed by his adviser's impetuosity on the one hand, and the defiant attitude of the Presbyterians on the other, somewhat hesitated. With the accession of Charles to the throne in 1625, ecclesiastical affairs assumed a new aspect. Having married Henrietta Maria of France, a Roman Catholic, Charles virtually adopted his consort's faith. Under his firm policy, Laud became a chief power in the state. With his approval, Charles made proclamation at Edinburgh that church lands and teinds, granted to members of the laity by his predecessors, were to be revoked. Obedience to the articles of Perth was exacted rigorously. Laud suggested the coronation visit; the religious ritual which attended it had his approval. In the Chapel Royal a liturgical service was, he maintained, to be observed daily. He had designs far more sweeping, and for fully accomplishing them the time seemed to have arrived.

As Bellenden's successor, Laud nominated Dr James Wedderburn, a churchman, of whose devotion to the king and attachment to himself he possessed ample experience. A native of Dundee, where his family had held some status, Wedderburn studied at Oxford,*; he was also a disciple of Isaac Casaubon. † Thereafter he became a professor in St Mary's College, St Andrews, where with his colleagues he, on receiving, in January 1624, the late king's commands to use the English Liturgy, yielded a ready compliance. ‡ Under Laud's recommendation, he soon afterwards was appointed prebendary of Ely; he subsequently held the living of Compton, Hants, and of Mildenhall, Suffolk. When appointed to the Chapel Royal and bishopric of Dunblane, he was prebendary of Whitchurch, in Wells.

With so many events conspiring to his ends, Laud, full of enterprise and hope, despatched Wedderburn to Edinburgh. The latter did not realise what he

* Russel's Keith's Bishops, Edinb. 1824, p. 182.

† Defending himself, in his autobiography, from the charge of recommending Bellenden and Wedderburn to the conjunct offices of dean and bishop as his "creatures" and "instruments," Laud writes:—"With the Bp. of Dunblane, Dr Wedderborne, I confess I had more and longer acquaintance; for he lived some years in England, and was recommended unto me as a man that had very good parts and learning in him. He lived long with Mr Isaac Casaubon, who was not like to teach him any Popery, and who certainly would not have retained him so long, or so near unto him, had he not found him a deserver. After I came acquainted with him, I wished him very well for his worth sake, and did what I could for him to live." It may here be added that Wedderburn nominated Laud as his executor (Archbishop Laud's Works, iii. 373, 374; vii. 591).

‡ Calderwood's History, vii. 569.

had expected, and was consequently discouraged.
This circumstance explains an observation made by
Laud at the commencement of the following extract
from a letter addressed by him to his confidential
adviser, John Maxwell, Bishop of Ross:

"I thanke you for your care of Dr Wedderbourne. He is very able to doe service, and will certainly doe it, if you can keepe up his heart. I was in good hope he had been consecrated, as well as my Lord of Brehen, but I perceive he is not. What the reason is [I know] not; but 'tis a thousand pityes that those uncertainties abide with him. I pray [commend] my love to him, and tell him I would not have him sticke att any thinge, for the kinge will not leave him long att Dunblane after he hath once settled the Chappell right, which I see will settle apace, if he keepe his footing. My letters are gone to the Bishop of Aberdene, by the king's command, to dissert his Protestation concerning the Chappell, [and] to leave the rents presently to Dr Wedderbourne. . . . Concerning that which you mension about fitting of the Chappell, both with silver vessels and other ornaments, upon the sale now to be made of some stuffe of the king's, I think my Lorde of St Andrewes will very shortly receive a letter, under the king's hand, to give power for all that yow desire; and then, if you do not see the Chappell well furnished, the blame for ever be yours." *

The letter from which we obtain the preceding
extract is dated at " Croydon, September 19, 1635."
Sufficiently characteristic, inasmuch as it conveys
counsel to his protégé that he would have him "not
to sticke att anythinge," it clearly shows that Wedder-

* Wodrow MSS., folio, vol. lxvi., No. 20.

burn was hesitating. One cause of discouragement is hinted at—his predecessor, Bishop Bellenden, had asserted his title to a portion of the chapel revenues. In the postscript of the letter a more costly decoration of the chapel is foreshadowed.*

From detached accounts of the High Treasurer, in the General Register House, we learn that, with the accession of Wedderburn to the deanery, certain repairs were carried out on his place of ministration. In these accounts are named two chapels, the new and "the auld," the former being described as having formed "the laich chalmeris vnder the Quenys chalmeris." This accommodation was probably selected by Wedderburn as being more suitable for his religious rites than that embraced in the older structure. A portion of the accounts follow:

"THE COMPT OF THE SCLATTERIS BEGYNNAND IN MENSE JULIJ IN ANNO, ETC., XXXV^{to}.

"Item, imprimis to Robert and Johne Blaris for iiij ruid iij quarteris ruid new theiking, with sclait and lyme vpon the auld chapell. Kichingis, weschelows, dresryis, and south toure. Ilk ruid xxxiij^s iiij^d. Summa, . vij^{llb} xviij^s iiij^d.

. . . .

* Those who have any misgiving as to Laud's secret intention in introducing the Book of Canons, should read the whole of his letter to the Bishop of Ross, from which we have made the preceding extract. In this letter he uses these words, "I am very glad your Canons are alsoe in so good a readiness, and that the true meaning of that ane Canone remains still *under the curtaine*. I hope you will tak care that it may be fully printed and passed with the rest." For a calm and lucid account of Laud's procedure in connection with the Scottish Church, see Dr Hill Burton's History of Scotland, 2d edit., vol. vi., pp. 104-206; also Prynne's "Hidden Workes of Darkenes," Lond. 1645, *passim.*

"Item, to the said Robert for the theiking of the lytill garding,
Chalmer beand ruiffit extending to —j rude, half ruid, and
quarter ruid, and to the foresaid Robert for new theiking,
with borit lath and Chathnes sclait and lyme, elekwys the
south syde of the new chapell, extending to —v ruid iij
quarteris ruid. Ilk ruid vt supra xxxiij^s iiij^d. Suma huius
—vij ruid half ruid is, . . . xij^{llb} x^s.

"SCLAITIS ENTERIT TO THE SAID WERK IN MENSE
JULIJ ANNO VT SUPRA.

"Item, to William Fynn for v^m Cathnes sclait. Ilk j^m iij^{llb}.,
Suma, ... xv^{llb}.

"Item, in ij south lychtis of the new chapell bewis the chancellary wall, ... j^{c}xx futtis half futt.
"Item, to the cartaris of the foresaid aikin tymmer of sindry
sortis brocht vp for the galre ruif, warping of the chapell
deskis, and chancelry wall xlij draucht. Ilk draucht fra
Leith to the abbay xvj^d. Suma, . . . lvj^s.

"THE EXPENSIS MAID APON IRNE WERK IN MENSE SEPTEMBRIS
ANNO UT SUPRA.

"Item, to Robert Monepenny for iij^c xl gret nalis to ruiffis for
the dowbill rynpannis of the fare entre and auld chapell,
extending to xx stane wecht.
"Item, to the said chapell gavill twa square lychtis vnder the
travys pece in bund, plet, and bosit Irne werk . .
. . . . . xxxvij stanis xv pund.
"Item, to the boys vyndo of the foresaid chapell gavill vnder
the laich travys pece in bosit maid Irne werk, xxx stane.
"Item, to the gret square lycht abone the bosit Irne windo and
travys pece twa plane plet windois contenand in maid Irne
werk, ... xxxiij stane.

"THE SCLATERIS EXPENSIS WITH SKAILZE IN

"Item, inprimis the north syde of the chapell extending to

vij ruid, half ruid, quarter ruid, and v elnis, wrocht be John Blayr.

"Item, to Robert Blayr for the new work of the fore entre elikwys, with skailze and fog theiking togiddir with the turpyk heid of the samyn, extending to —x ruidis, half ruid, vij elnis.

"And to the said Robert for j ruide xxxij elnis new theiking work, with skailze vpon ane part of the north syde of the chalmeris nixt the toure quhilk was the auld chapell, and for v ruid ij elnis new work elikwis apon the complete theiking of the inner syde of the saidis chalmeris fra the fare entre to the kirk stepill, and for vj elnis ane quarter new theiking werk upon the galre at the eist end of the new chapell.

Suma huius totalis ruidis skailze xxv ruidis, half ruid, vij elnis, price ilk ruid workmanschip furnysing of skailze thairto, with the haill carriage, vj^{lib}. Suma,

. . . . . j^c xxxiiij^{lib} iij^s iiij^d.

"Item, to Thomas Adeson, Allaster Campbell, and Andro Lokart, for v ruidis v elnis riging stane to the fore new werk, and to the samyn for vij ruid, half ruid, quarter ruid, v elnis riging stane to the chapell, and for iiij ruidis, iij elnis, riggin stane to the north chalmeris foresaid, extending in toto to xviij rude, v elnis, half eln, price ilk ruid xij^s. Suma, ... xj^{lib} vij^s vj^d.

"Item, for fog furnysing to the foresaid werk, . iij^{lib} x^s.

"Item, to Sir James Nichollson for certane sarking burd of Scotis ayk, and to John Brand for the fraucht thairof fra Striuiling hevyn to Leith, . . . viij^{lib} xj^s.

"IN MENSE AUGUSTJ ANNO, ETC., XXXV^{to}.

"Item, to Robert Days, pergeonar, for pergene of the laich chalmeris vnder the Quenys chalmeris, now the new chapell, with calk and glew of all costis, . . xxiiij^s.

"Item, to George Peblis for perginyng, harling, and beting of the glasin wyndois of the samyn without, . . vj^s.

Amidst his innovating precipitation, reminded that Wedderburn had not only not been consecrated, but had not even received his letters of presentation, Laud now attended to the latter formality. In an instrument of gift, dated at Royston, 14th October 1635, Wedderburn had granted to him over and above the ancient endowments and foundations made by the kings of Scotland, "all and whole that endowment and foundation annexed and made to the chapel, of the lands of the monastery and barony of Dundrennan, as contained in the gift thereof under the Privy Seal on 16th July 1621;" also "the annual rent of ten chalders of victual out of the lands of Markill and Traprane."*

Wedderburn was consecrated on the 11th February 1636, the event being followed up by new activities. For some time Laud had been occupied in framing his "Canons and Constitutions Ecclesiastical," a book, as we have seen, adroitly prepared, and intended to sap the foundations of Presbyterian government. Issued on the 23d May, by authority of a royal edict, and without any other sanction, it contained among other provisions, injunctions that each church should have its baptismal font, also a communion table at the upper end of the chancel; that the Sacrament of the Supper should be received kneeling, and that in the Communion service all should stand while repeating the Creed.

* Privy Seal Register, cvi., fol. 369.

However inoffensive some of these commands may seem, it must be remembered that they were thrust upon the Church by a sovereign who excited prejudice by cherishing Romish doctrine; also at the hands of an ecclesiastic whose Protestant professions were certainly insincere. It had been predicted by Dr Juxon, Bishop of London, in a letter to the Bishop of Ross, that the Book of Canons would "make more noise than all the cannons in Edinburgh Castle." * The demonstration attending the introduction was indeed less than might have been anticipated; for in these times intelligence travelled slowly, and a large proportion of the clergy had accepted the measures of the court. Prior to issuing his Book of Canons, Laud had, in April 1636, received from Charles a private warrant authorising him also to prepare a Scottish Liturgy or Service Book. On the day following the English primate addressed a lengthened communication to Dr Wedderburn, in which, after congratulating him on his being consecrated, he thanked him for some suggestions respecting the Service Book, and in the king's name offered others. With reference to the affairs of the Chapel Royal he proceeds:

"I have received other letters from you, by which I find you have written to his Majesty about the Communion in the Chapel Royal, concerning which the King holds his former resolution, that he would be very glad there should be a full communion at all solemn times, as is appointed. But because men

* Wodrow MSS., folio, vol. lxvi., No. 21.

doe not alwayes fit themselves as they ought for that great and holy worke, therefore his Majesty will be satisfied, if every one that is required to communicate there doe solemnly and conformably performe that action, once a year at least. And in conformity to this, you are to signifie once a yeare unto his sacred Majesty, who have communicated within the compasse of that year, and who not; and of this you must not faile." *

After some delay the Service Book was placed in the hands of Robert Young, the king's printer, who undertook to have it ready in autumn. Thereupon the Privy Council were enjoined to make proclamation that, under heavy penalties, the book should be used in every parish church. Hesitating to issue a work which might involve him in popular disfavour, Young moved tardily. At length the volume appeared in May 1637, when a royal edict provided that it should be first used in the churches of Edinburgh.

The Chapel Royal was situated within the precincts of the city, but in this connection no special arrangements had been made. It is probable that Wedderburn, who had early taken alarm, was content to leave the burden on his more venturous colleagues. That part of the cathedral of St Giles occupied by the congregation of the High Church was fixed on for giving public effect to the king's mandate.

An eagerly expectant crowd assembled early, and on the opening of the doors at once occupied the

* Prynne's "Hidden Workes of Darkenes," Lond. 1645, fol. 152, 154.

church. As the church bells ceased to ring, two dignitaries in white vestments entered—the Archbishop of St Andrews, Chancellor of the kingdom, who proceeded to occupy the throne, and Bishop Lindsay, who ascended the pulpit. Standing in the reading desk, Dr James Hannay, Dean of Edinburgh, commenced to read from the new Service Book. On every side arose murmurs, followed by angry ejaculations on the part of the more ardent. Near the pulpit a woman rose up, and cast towards it the small stool on which she had been seated. Confusion ensued, and after in vain attempting to restore order the archbishop and all the clergy withdrew.

Next day the Privy Council met at Holyroodhouse, seventeen members being present, among whom five were bishops.* On this occasion was passed the following minute :

"Apud Halyrudhous, 24 July 1637. Sederunt—Chancellar, Dumfreis, Bishop of Edinburgh, Bishop of Brechin, Thesaurar, Southesk, Bishop of Murray, Clerk Register, Glasgow, Lord Lorne, Bishop of Galloway, Justice Generall, Priuie Seale, Lord Alexander, Bishop of Ros, Depute Thesurer, Aduocat.

Forsamekle as the lords of secreit counsell having considderit the late turbulent and mutinous cariage of a number of base people, who vpon the Lords day, and in the Lords hous, in a rude, barbarous, and seditious way did with foule mouths and unpious hands appose themselffes to his divine seruice, to the dishonnour of God, disgrace of his majesteis governement, and disturbance of the publict peace of this citie of Edinburgh : and

* Bishop Wedderburn of the Chapel Royal was not of the number.

the saids lords being carefull in the dewtie of thair office to inquire for and make tryell of the authors and abbetters of this disorderlie tumult, and to preuent all further grouth of the same; The lords of secreit counsell ordains the Lyon herald, and his brethren heralds and pursevants with a trumpet, and displeyed coat of armes, to pas to the mercat croce of this citie, and there be opin proclamation to command and charge all and sindrie the inhabitants of the said citie of Edinburgh, als weill men as wemen, that they conteane themselffes in peace and quyetnes, and that nane of thame presoome nor take vpon hand to make anie gadderings or convocatiouns vpon the streit, or to haue anie meitings in priuat quhairby the publict peace of the citie may be disturbed: And in speciall that nane attempt to make disorder or raise anie tumult in the churches or churchyairds, nor to revile or belshe furth anie contumelious speeches or imprecations aganis anie of his majesteis servants, being of the ecclesiastick or civill estat, or of the inferior clergie, nor to offer violence or injurie to thame, or anie of thame be word or deid, nor to impugne nor traduce his majesteis governement, nor to raile and speeke aganis the seruice booke, whiche for the furtherance of Gods worship, hes beene warrantablie established, vnder the pane of death to be inflicted vpon thame as seditious persons and contemners of his majesteis religious and royall commandements, certifeing all and sindrie who sall doe or attempt anie thing in the contrare that the pane of death sall be execute vpon thame without favour or mercie, conforme to the lawes and acts of counsell provided in that behalfe: Lykeas the saids lords declares if anie servants, man or woman, sall offend in that kynde, or that anie of the inhabitants of this citie sall heare or see anie of the aforesaids misdemeanours and not reveale the names of the offenders, or apprehend and deliver thame to the magistrats of the said citie, or if anie of the rascall maisterlesse boyes committing anie suche disorder sall be ressett within anie hous of the said citie, that the maister of the servant, the hearer of the speeches and seer of the deid, and not doing diligence, as said is, and the ressetters of the saids persons sall be repute, haldin, and esteemed as persons guiltie, connivers, and favorers of the partie delinquent, and sall be accordinglie punished in thair persons and goods as the principall offender, and according to the merite and qualitie of his trespasse. Lykeas the saids lords finds and declares vpon good reason of state that the provest, bailleis, counsell, and communitie of the said citie of Edinburgh, ar and must be lyable and debtors for quhatsomever ryot, trouble, or wrong that sall be committed within thair citie, in maner foresaid: Commanding heirby the saids provest and bailleis of the said citie of Edinburgh to haue a speciall care and regard to see the premissis putt to dew and full execution in all points, and that they inquire for, apprehend, and committ to ward all and sindrie persons whome they sall leirne or deprehend to haue beene, or who hereafter sall be, guiltie of the bygane tumult, or after disorder as the saids provest and bailleis will answer vpon the dewtie of thair office at thair highest charge and parell." *

This proclamation served to whet popular indignation. From its centre to its extremities was the country aroused, and a storm swept abroad not less vehement than that which eighty years before had overthrown a Church and wrecked the cathedrals. At Edinburgh, Committees, or "Tables" as they were called, assembled daily. On the 1st March 1638, the National Covenant was renewed in the Greyfriars Church, many subscribing with their pens dipped in their own blood. Apprehensive of attack, members of the Privy Council left Edinburgh for Stirling. Their frequently repeated proclamations were received with scorn, or by uncompromising rejoinders. Laud and the king meditated revenge, but might not cope with the nation in arms. Charles at length offered

* Privy Council Register, *Acta*, May 1636; Nov. 1639, folio, 218*b*.

terms; on the 22d September 1638, the Service Book was recalled, and the infamous Court of High Commission suspended. Not only so, but the king consented to convene a Parliament and convoke a General Assembly. That Assembly, which met at Glasgow, among its many memorable enactments, deprived and excommunicated Bishops Bellenden and Wedderburn. To Bellenden Charles gave a small pension, which he received under an assumed name. Afterwards appointed Rector of Portlock in Somersetshire, he there died in 1647.* Laud had augured that Wedderburn would "settle the Chapel Royal if he kept his footing." A footing he did not attain. His history may be briefly summed up in his patron's words: " He came into England, and after he had been there about a twelvemonth, he fell sick and died."† His death took place on the 23d September 1639, and his remains were deposited in Canterbury Cathedral, where, in the chapel consecrated to the Virgin, a monument with a Latin inscription celebrates his virtues. One of the most scholarly of Scottish bishops, he unhappily identified himself with a despotic movement, and died in his fifty-fourth year the victim of regret. ‡

* Fasti Eccl. Scot., iii. 885.
† Russel's Keith's Bishops, 182; Fasti Eccl. Scot., ii. 840; Bishop Laud's Works, vii. 591.
‡ Bishop Wedderburn's brother John, M.D. of the University of St Andrews, attained reputation as a physician, and received the honour of knighthood. He became chief physician in the State of Moravia, and resided at Olmutz.

The Covenanters were not slow in improving their triumphs. Obtaining a general ascendancy in the north, where their cause at first was doubtful, they also got possession of the principal strongholds, and, under their military leader, General Leslie, became masters of the country. When the king, early in May 1639, sent a fleet into the Firth of Forth,* the Act was accepted as a declaration of war, and Leslie and his troops a few weeks later marched to the Border.

Intent on suppressing the Scottish malcontents, Charles had with an army reached Birks, seven miles beyond Berwick; but learning that twenty thousand troops were, under Leslie, entrenched at Dunse Hill, he procceded to offer terms. The treaty, known as the Pacification of Berwick, followed; it included permission to hold a General Assembly. That Assembly was summoned to meet at Edinburgh on the 12th August; a week previously Charles had by letter informed the bishops that they still enjoyed his support, which on fitting opportunity would be shown them. He also gave instructions that, in the carrying out of repairs at Holyroodhouse, the Chapel Royal should be placed in order, with a view to its future use in its former connection. Among other documents lately discovered in the General Register House are workmen's accounts in relation to the Chapel.

* Burton's History of Scotland, edit. 1873, vii. 273.

In August Clement Toweris, "glassen wright," was paid for glass work to the Chapel Royal, £66, 16s. 8d.; and in September "Jhonc Weir, maisoun, and his scruand," had 48 shillings as "ane oulkis [week's] wagis, for laying the pavement of the chapel." These charges also are ranged under August and September.

"Item, to George Wallace, spangeonar and his marrowis, spargeing the auld hall, the twa turnpykis, and pairts of the gallarie, the chapel, the twa chalmeris of the forewark, sett in task to thame, ... xxvj^{lib}.

Item, sett in task to George Hay, sclaitter, the poynting betterment of the bak chalmeris, and poynting and betten of the north syde of the chapell, with the stair, . . xij^{lib}.
Item, to twa women clengeing the chapell, . . ij^s.
Item, to George Tulloch, sawar, and his marrow, for v draucht of geistis to the chapell, ilk draucht ij^s; ij draucht of corbellis, ilk draucht xvj^d, . . . xij^s viij^d."

On a folio sheet, preserved in the Register House, is the following list:

"The names of ye ministeris within the diocie of Glasgow, who ar to be chaplanes to his Matie for service of ye Chapell Royall:
    1. Mr Wm. Annan, minister at Air.
    2. Doctor James Eliott, minister at Glasgow.
    3. Maister Jhone Lyndsay, att Carstaires.
    4. Mr Robert Hammilton, at Lesmahagow.
    5. Dr Theodor Hay, Archedeacon of Glasgow.
    6. Mr Jhone Hay, persone of Renfrow.
    7. Mr George Buchanan, persone of Kilpatrik.
    8. Mr Jhone Alexander, persone of Hoddom.

9. Mr Wm. Bennett, persone of Ancrum.
10. Mr Thomas Forrester, minister at Melros.
11. Mr Patrik Lyndsay, minister at Maxtoun.

These were named by the bishops as being suitable preachers in the Chapel Royal during the king's visit; they had severally adopted the Service Book, while some of them had lately been deprived of ministerial status.

The General Assembly, which met on the 12th August, abolished Episcopacy, rescinded the five articles of Perth, and condemned the Book of Canons and the Service Book,—all these acts being sanctioned by the Earl of Traquair, as king's commissioner. Parliament met on the 31st of August for the despatch of business; it was adjourned, as it had been several times previously. When it reassembled, on the 2d June 1640, an attempt was again made to arrest its deliberations. That attempt was resisted, and, in defiance of the royal will, its sittings were continued. Among its enactments were an adoption of the National Covenant, and a full ratification of the acts of the General Assembly. After appointing "the Committee of Estates" to act as a permanent body, Parliament adjourned till November. By his "Short" and his "Large" Declarations, Charles had sufficiently manifested what his real intentions were, and so abundantly justified that march into England, which terminated in the victory at Newburn and the capture of Newcastle. The negotiations which followed, commencing at Ripon on the 1st of October, were adjourned to London, and did not terminate till at the hands of the English Parliament Laud was committed to the Tower. On the 7th August 1641, a treaty was completed, and in one week thereafter Charles was at Holyrood.

During a brief period had occurred a marvellous transition. For attempting to crush liberty in his own portion of the kingdom Laud was a captive, charged with conspiracy and treason. At Edinburgh the new recipients of royal favour were those persons with whom Charles had lately been at war. The most conspicuous minister of the Presbyterian clergy was Mr Alexander Henderson. He had led opposition to the Service Book, drawn up the National Covenant, been a chief author of various Petitions and Protests, was Moderator of the General Assembly of 1638, and in August 1639 had preached at the opening of the adjourned Parliament; he was also one of the delegates from the Covenanting army which had conferred with the king at Berwick, and a commissioner in the recent treaty. When Charles arrived at Holyroodhouse on Saturday the 14th August, Mr Henderson was honoured by an interview, and named as royal chaplain. Next morning he preached before the king in the Abbey Church; he discoursed from Romans xi. and 13, on the subject of the Divine supremacy.* In

* Baillie's Letters and Journals, Edinb. 1841, i. 385, 386.

reality, as is stated by Baillie,* Mr Henderson was virtually appointed dean, and with the same endowments as had been enjoyed by Dr Wedderburn. The subjoined instrument of gift, printed for the first time, is not without interest, inasmuch that the reasons assigned for the appointment, and the nature of the appointment itself are set forth in measured language. The document proceeds:

"Ane Lettre maid making mentioun that his majestie considdering that it is necessar when his hienes or his sone, the Prince, shall come into this thair Kingdome of Scotland, that thair be some minister to attend thame for performing the dewties of divyne worshipe in thair famelies, and his majestie having now large prooff of the abilitie and faithfulnes of his hienes trustie and weilbelouit Maister Alexander Hendersoun, present minister at Edinburgh, for the said charge, hath maid choyse of him for performing of the aforsaid dewties in all tymes comeing, duiring the wholl tyme of the said Maister Alexander his lyfe, and thairfor in recompence of his seruice and attendance both bypast and to come, with advyse and consent of his hienes trustie counsallour Sir James Carmichaell, of that ilk, Knight, thesaurer depute, and of the remanent commissioneris of his hienes Exchequer of the said kingdome givand, grantand, and disponeand to the said Maister Alexander, for all the dayes of his lyftyme, All and haill the landis, monasterrie, and barony of Dundrennane, comprehending in the samen all and sundry tounes, landis, castellis, touris, fortalices, woodis, baronies, plaines, milnis, multuris, annualrentis, kirkis, kirklandis, teyndis, fishings, fruittis, rentis, proventis, emolumentis, seruices, and vtheris dewties of the samen quhatsumevir contenit in the lettre of donation, dispositioun, dotatioun, and mortificatioun of the same be his majesties vmquhill father, of worthie memorie, mortifeing

* Baillie's Letters and Journals, Edinb. 1841, i. 395.

the same to apperteane and belong to his hienes chappell royall within this kingdome: Quhilk mortificatioun is of the dait the sexteinth day of Julij j^m vj^c tuentie ane yeares: And als all and haill that annualrent or yearlie dewtie of ten chalderis victuall halff beir halff wheat yearlie, to be vplifted betuix Yule and Candlemes, furth of the landis of Markle and medow thairof videlicet, ane hundreth and tuentie bollis thairof furth of the saidis landis of Markle, tuentie four bollis thairof furth of the landis of Trapren, and sexteine bollis furth of the saidis landis of Medow of Markle, all lyand within the lordship of Hailles, Constabularie of Hadintoun and Sherefdome of Edinburgh: Quhilkis landis and vtheris particularlie abonewrittin comeing in our said Soverane lord, and his said vmquhill fatheris handes they did annex and mortifie the same to the bishoprik of Dumblane, and quhilkis ar now become agane in his hienes handis throw being of the functioun of bishops found vnlawfull within this kingdome: Beginand the said Maister Alexander, his entrie to the landis and vtheris abonwrittin, and to the vplifting of the mailles and dewties of the same of this instant cropt and year of God j^m vj^c and fourtie ane yeares, and so furth yerelie thairefter in tyme comeing duiring the said Maister Alexander his lyftyme, as said is. The said Maister Alexander alwayes paying to the minister present, and to come serving his cuir at the Kirk of Dundrennane, the yeirlie stipend vnderwrittin, videlicet: Tua chalderis ait meall, good and sufficient mercat stuff, and thrie hundreth merkis Scottis money yearlie, at the termes vsed and wont, and provyding the elementis for the celebratioun of the communion yearlie, als aft as the samyn shall happin to be celibrat at the said Kirk, and als relewing the saidis ministeris of all taxatiounes, impositiounes, and vtheris burdenis quhatsumevir that shall happin to be imposed vpon the teynd scheaves and vtheris teyndis of the forsaid Kirk of Dundrennane: And siclyk to best vphold and repair the samen kirk in tyme comeing duiring his lyftyme, as said is, with command thairin to the lordis of counsall and sessioune to grant and direct lettres and executoriallis necessar, at the instance of the said Maister Alexander for causing of him to be readily answerit and obeyit of the fruittis, rentis, and emolumentis of the landis and vtheris abonwrittin, of this instant cropt and yeir of God j^m vj^c and fourtie ane yeares, and in tyme comeing duiring his lyftyme, as said is: Lykas, his majestie promises in verbo principis to ratifie and approve the premissis in this or any vther subsequent parliament, and to doe every vther thing that shall be thought necessar to mak the said Maister Alexander to be readily ansuerit and obeyit of the fruittis, rentis, and emolumentis of the landis and vtheris abonwreittin dureing all the dayes of his lyftyme, as said is, without prejudice of any farder prouisioun to the ministeris serving the cuir within the forsaidis boundis. Givin at Halyrudhous, the first day of October j^m vj^c and fourtie ane yearis. Per Signaturam." *

At Holyroodhouse Mr Henderson at once commenced his duties as household chaplain, arranging as to those brethren who should preach before the king, and himself conducting morning and evening worship daily in the king's presence.† Publicly in Parliament Charles sanctioned the various proceedings of the General Assembly, bestowed offices and titles on the most prominent of his former opponents, and consented that the revenues of the several bishoprics should be devoted to the better endowment of the universities, and the augmentation of the stipends of the poorer clergy.

In 1642, certain feu-duties belonging to the Chapel Royal were conferred on James Livingston of the bedchamber (afterwards Baron Skirling), who subse-

---

* Privy Seal Register, cix., fol. 277.
† Baillie's Letters and Journals, i. 385, 386.

quently disposed of them to the Earl of Crawford; the transfer was, in 1647, confirmed by Parliament.

The emoluments of the prebendaryship, styled "Ayr primo," were conferred on Mr William Semple, Regent of Humanity at Glasgow, afterwards minister of Neilston; and in 1647 Parliament ratified the grant.* By a charter under the great seal, dated 3d November 1647, and which in the following year Parliament confirmed, the vicarage and parsonage teinds which had formerly belonged to the Chapel Royal were granted to the ministers of the churches of Ayr, Alloway, Coylton, Dalmellington, and Dalrymple. †

Andrew Ramsay, subdean of the Chapel Royal, claims special notice. Son of the proprietor of Balmain, he was sometime professor of divinity in the University of Saumur, was afterwards minister of Arbuthnott, and in 1614 was admitted to a charge at Edinburgh. In 1629 he was presented by Charles I. to the subdeanery. For maintaining the lawfulness of the expedition to England, he was, in 1649, deposed, but was restored in 1655. Retiring from the office of subdean in 1658, he spent his latter

* Fasti Eccl. Scot., ii. 840; Acta Parl. Scot., vi., i. 848.
† Acta Parl. Scot., vi., ii. 81. It would appear that a portion of the revenues of the Chapel Royal had been by Charles I. granted to the burgh of Elgin some time prior to the 29th October 1634, when the grant is referred to in two royal letters of that date, addressed to the Lords of Session and the Commissioners of Exchequer, in favour of Andrew Sinclair, one of the prebendaries appointed by James VI. (see Sir William Alexander's Register of Royal Letters, MS. in General Register House).

years on his estate of Abbotshall, where he died 30th December 1659, in his eighty-fifth year. He founded four bursaries in the University of Edinburgh, the patronage of which is vested in the Town Council of the city.*

In the office of subdean, Ramsay was succeeded by Archibald Turner, one of the ministers of Edinburgh, formerly of North Berwick. He retained the office from June 1663 till his death, which took place 30th March 1681. His brother was the cruel but gallant Sir James Turner. †

At Whitehall, on the 30th January 1649, Charles I. expiated with his blood his tergiversation and tyranny. His gallant lieutenant, the Marquis of Montrose, was executed at Edinburgh on the 25th of May. One week subsequent to the latter event, the Parliament, which met on the 1st of June, granted "full powers" to the Commissioners of the Treasury to remove the organs from the Chapel Royal, and to dispose of them. ‡ Not long afterwards the Commissioners for the Plantation of Kirks were recommended by Parliament to maintain a minister in the castle of Edinburgh, and with that view to secure "the reversion of the subdeanery of the Chapell Royall, now in the hands of Mr Andrew Ramsay." §
On the 23d June 1649, Parliament granted to the lately erected parish church of Glencross "sevine

---

* Fasti Eccl. Scot., i. 10, 394; iii. 855.   † *Ibid.*, i. 10.
‡ Acta Parl. Scot., vi., ii. 389.   § *Ibid.*, vi., ii. 720.

scoir marks zeirlie, payit of lait out of the landis of Castellaw, belonging to the erle of Roxburghe, for the mantinance of the organs and singers in the Chappell of Stirling, not onlie abolished bot now vacant, by deceas of vmq^{le} James Crichtoun and James Mouat, and by the demissioun of Johne Castellaw, last presentit thairto." *

On the 13th November 1650, Holyroodhouse was partially destroyed by fire, which seems to have been incidentally kindled by a company of Cromwell's soldiers, accommodated in the structure. The Protector did not occupy the palace during his visit in 1648, or during any portion of his sojourn in 1650-1. In 1659 he gave orders to restore the building, and in the course of the following year repairs were proceeded with. †

On the 8th August 1654, the Protector granted to the University of Glasgow, for its better endowment, the superiorities of lands which had belonged to the bishopric of Glasgow, exclusive of the superiority of the deanery of the Chapel Royal. ‡

During the early days of his adversity, Charles II.

* Acta Parl. Scot., vi., ii. 482. In the Register of Holyroodhouse parish, styled "The Buik of the Kirk off the Canageit, 1564-1567," occur these entries : "The 21 of Aprill, anno Domini 1565, Alexander Castellaw, in the Cowgait, ane child callit James, his witnes Thomas Hoge, James Patersoun, gott in merriage, and hes bene at the commonioun." "The viii of Novembre 1567, Alexander Castella, ane child callit Johne, witnes Johne Castella." Probably the children so baptized were the subsequent musicians.

† Nicoll's Diary, pp. 35, 224 ; Bannatyne Miscellany, ii. 404.

‡ Fasti Eccl. Scot., ii. 379, 840 ; Acta Parl. Scot., vi., ii. 831.

had sworn to uphold the Covenant and maintain the Presbyterian Church; but before he left Breda to occupy the throne in 1660, he consented that Episcopacy should be restored. Among those appointed to the bishoprics was Dr Robert Leighton, Principal of the University of Edinburgh, who was nominated to the diocese of Dunblane and deanery of the Chapel Royal. Justly reputed for his piety and learning, and withal moderate and conciliatory, his appointment was unexceptionable. But Leighton would not accede to a proposal, believed to have been made to him, to leave his diocese without supervision and discharge weekly duty in the Abbey Church, already a collegiate parochial charge. His resolution being inconvenient, he was, in 1669, after holding office in the Chapel Royal for eight years, appointed Commendator of the archdiocese of Glasgow. Thereby a way was opened up for other contemplated changes. Meanwhile the career of Dr Leighton may be summarised. He was appointed Archbishop of Glasgow in 1671; but, disgusted with regal despotism, and distressed by what he regarded as the indiscreet zeal of his Presbyterian brethren, he in 1674 relinquished his office. Retiring into private life, he died in London in June 1684. He bequeathed his important theological library to the clergy of the diocese of Dunblane, by whom it is preserved.

Among the more zealous promoters of the king's

restoration was Sir William Bruce, afterwards of Balcaskie, latterly of Kinross. Trained as an architect abroad, this ardent royalist there gained the intimacy of General Monk, to whom it is believed he suggested as a remedy for prevailing distractions the king's recall. He was privileged secretly to convey to Breda tidings of Monk's early efforts in the royal cause.* Charles did not forget this important service, and immediately on his restoration constituted his faithful adherent Clerk to the Bills in the Court of Session, then a lucrative office. In 1668 Bruce was created a baronet, and soon thereafter was appointed Surveyor-General of Royal Buildings. It was probably at this time that unknown to the Privy Council he was authorised by the king to prepare designs for the restoration of Holyroodhouse. Of these designs we are first informed in the summer of 1671, when the Commissioners of Exchequer received a royal warrant, dated at Windsor Castle 3d of June, in which they were enjoined to allow Sir William Bruce to proceed with the work of restoration, conformably with his designs, modified by certain "directions" sent along with them, and which, according to the Earl of Lauderdale, the king had personally prepared. Among these "directions" the following relative to the proposed renovation of the "new" and "auld" structures of the Chapel Royal are to be remarked specially :

* Douglas's Baronage, i. 245.

"In the Ground Plane, that which is designed for the low Chappell is to be made a large vaulted cellare; for His Majestie will have noe Chappell in this new house, but ane entire from the Guarde Chambre on the Royall Apartement towards the East into the Church, and his family prayers in or near the Presence as in Whitehall and his other houses here."

"The upper storie of the Chappell abone the Great Celler His Majestie intends for a Councell-Chamber with ane outer roome, and the Closets for Clerks."

Here we definitely learn the king's intention to dispense with his principal chapel within the palace, a resolution which implied that accommodation would be sought elsewhere. This soon became apparent. It may only be remarked that the change was not ventured upon till Leighton, relieved of the deanery, was established at Glasgow in his new office of commendator.*

The king's wishes could now be sanctioned without protest. So we find that on the 23d September 1672, the Privy Council and Commissioners of Exchequer passed an Act declaring that the Abbey Church belonged to the Crown, that it should be "His Majesteis Chapell Royeall in all tymes comeing," and that "the magistrates of Edinburgh or Cannongate" should be

---

* The date of Leighton's removal to Glasgow is not precisely known; it was certainly prior to the 6th April 1671, when he despatched from Glasgow a letter to the clergy of the diocese of Dunblane, which commences, "The superadded burden that I have here sits so hard upon me" ("Register of the Diocesan Synod of Dunblane," edited with an Introduction and Biographical Notes by John Wilson, D.D., minister of Dunning. Edinb. 1877, 4to).

discharged from longer using it as "ane paroch church."*

Whether owing to the royal visit, fixed for 1673, being postponed, or from financial or other considerations, the parishioners of the Canongate still continued in undisturbed possession of the Abbey Church. The cost of repairs on the palace proved not inconsiderable, and probably would have excited complaint, had not the joys of the restoration still lingered in Scottish hearts. Sir William's designs, which were chiefly executed by Robert Mylne, the king's mason, included the demolition of the five original courts and the removal of some works by Cromwell,† also the rebuilding of the entire palace, excepting that portion at the north-east corner, reared by James V. in 1528, and now known as Queen Mary's apartments. Commenced in 1671, the new palace was finished in 1574, but further repairs were proceeded with, which were not completed till 1679. The money which passed through the hands of the Surveyor-General from 1674 to 1679 was about £160,000 Scots, of which sum about four-fifths were spent on works at Holyrood.‡

* Privy Council Register, No. 2, p. 629.

† A portion of the king's "Directions" to the Privy Council accompanying his warrant of June 1671 proceeds thus : "Wee doe hereby order you to cause that pairt thereof which was built by the usurpers, and doth darken the court, to be taken down."

‡ See Papers by Dr Joseph Robertson and Mr David Marshall, in Proceedings of the Scottish Society of Antiquaries, vol. iii., 113-117, and vol. ii., new series, 324-337.

To the annals of the chapel we would return briefly. By a royal letter, dated 19th September 1662, James Hamilton, formerly minister at Dumfries and Edinburgh, was granted four hundred marks as "the yearly tack dewtie of the personage and vicarrage teinds of St Mary's kirk of the Lowes," described as "one of the kirkes founded and mortified to our Chapell Royal of Stirling now vacand in our hands by the deceis of Andro Sinclare, Johne Castellaw, or any others of the prebends or quiristers who had last right thereto."* Sometime agent to his uncle, Viscount Claneboy, James Hamilton was in 1625 ordained by Robert, Bishop of Down, minister of Ballywalter. Deprived for declining to use the Service Book, he was reponed by authority of Parliament. In 1638 he was chosen minister of Dumfries. Visiting by order of the General Assembly the Presbyterians in the north of Ireland, he was taken prisoner by Colkitto and committed to Mingary Castle, where he suffered irksome detention. Translated to Edinburgh in 1647, he was thereafter appointed by the Church, also by Parliament, to the discharge of important duties. In May 1650, he was commissioned to examine the Marquis of Montrose after his capture. While sitting with a Committee of the Estates at Alyth in August 1651, he was seized by the English army, carried to England, and there detained as a prisoner nineteen

---

* Privy Seal Register, new series, i., fol. 142.

months.* His pension from the Chapel Royal he received on account of his "constant affection and loyalty" to the king, and his "great losses and sufferings upon that accompt and imprisonment and otherwise during the late troubles."†

In 1673 James Ramsay, minister of Hamilton, was in succession to Archbishop Leighton appointed Bishop of Dunblane and Dean of the Chapel Royal. Having charged Francis Kinloch of Gilmerton to make payment to him as dean of eight and a half chalders of victual out of the lands of Markle, Kinloch sought a suspension on the ground that the annuity was originally granted by the Earl of Bothwell to Mr Thomas Craig, advocate, redeemable on the payment of 7000 marks. The lands afterwards came into the possession of Sir George Seton, who paid 7000 marks to the king, and thereupon obtained a grant of redemption. Much litigation supervened, attended with decisions for and against the complainant.‡

Bishop Ramsay was in 1684 translated to the bishopric of Ross, when Robert Douglas, Bishop of Brechin, was appointed to the conjunct offices. Deprived on the abolition of Episcopacy in 1689, Bishop Douglas retired to Dundee, where, in the enjoyment of a pension from William III., he

---

* Fasti Eccl. Scot., i. 14, 568.
† Privy Seal Register, new series, i., fol. 142.
‡ Lord Fountainhall's Historical Notices. Edinb. 1848, i. 105.

resided till his death, which took place in April 1716.*

John Hamilton, who was in succession a regent in the University of St Andrews and minister of Cramond and South Leith, was appointed subdean in 1681. He was promoted to the bishopric of Dunkeld in 1686, and died before the 24th February 1698.†

On the 6th February 1685, James, Duke of York, succeeded to the throne. Indiscreet, cruel, and overbearing, he was in his religious opinions strictly in earnest. Avowedly he was a member of the Romish Church. At his command the painter Verrio decorated St George's Chapel, Windsor, which otherwise he adapted for Catholic worship. But in matters ecclesiastical James bestowed on Scotland a chief attention. There was in the north a greater scope. Zealous Protestants as they were, the Scots were equally remarkable for an excessive loyalty. Allegiance to the throne they cherished with a passionate force, which might not be restrained even by injustice. Already, as heir-apparent, James had experienced on three occasions an abundant hospitality at Edinburgh, and there he had resolved to settle should his English subjects venture to dethrone him. Against this possible contingency some preparations were made even before the occurrence of the vacancy which

* Fasti Eccl. Scot., ii. 840.
† Ibid., i. 101, 133, 394.

made him king; for Hugh Wallace of Ingliston, the royal cash-keeper, had, during the two years preceding March 1686, disbursed to Mr James Smith, overseer at Holyroodhouse and Edinburgh Castle, for repairs chiefly on the former, the sum of £12,814, 10s. 10d. Scottish money. This amount, added to the £160,000 expended principally on the palace buildings a few years before, implied an outlay which in the then impoverished condition of the Scottish exchequer must be regarded as enormous. Among the items were payments to James Bane, wright, and John Callander, smith, for repairing at Holyrood the king's privy chamber and oratory.*

Having in the first instance resolved to traverse the late king's orders by causing the large apartment at Holyroodhouse, constructed as a council chamber, to be in terms of the original design adapted as a Chapel Royal, James despatched to the Scottish Privy Council the following mandate:

"JAMES, R.,—
"Right trusty and right welbeloved cousins and councellors, right trusty and entirely beloved cousin and councellor, and right trusty and welbeloved cousins and councellors, Wee greet you well. Whereas by our Letter (of the date of these presents) directed to the Duke of Hamilton, heretable Keeper of our Palace of Holyroodhouse, Wee have thought fit to require him to deliver up to our Chancellor, or any having his order, the Keys of that great Roome in our said Palace which formerly was designed to have been the Councell Chamber there; Which Wee have appointed to be made use of hereafter as our Chappell,

* Dr David Laing's MSS., University of Edinburgh.

and are now resolved that the same be fitted for that purpose with all possible diligence. It is now our Will and pleasure: and Wee doe hereby authorise and require you presently to give the necessary orders for fitting and preparing the said great Roome, so as it shalbe needfull for the same to be when made use of as our Chappell, according to such directions therein as shall be given by our said Chancellor, either for the Chappell it selfe or the closets and other conveniencies thereunto belonging, and at our charge to order the payment of all expenses needfull to be laid out upon this occasion, which shalbe allowed to you in your accompts. The performance whereof without any delay Wee doe hereby recommend to your particular care. And for your doing the same this shalbe your warrant. So wee bid you heartily ffarewell. Given at our Court at Windsor, the 25th day of September 1686, and of our Reigne the 2d year.

" By his Majesty's command.

"MELFORT."

The intended adaptation of the Great Room to the purpose for which it was originally designed may have been partly intended as a compliment to the architect, Sir William Bruce. Arrangements made progress, as appears from the following royal letter, dated 5th February 1687 :

"JAMES, R.,—

"Right trusty and right welbeloved cousins and councellors, right trusty and entirely beloved cousins and councellors, and right trusty and welbeloved cousins and councellors, Wee greet you well. Whereas by our Letter of the date of these presents to our right trusty and entirely beloved cousin and councellor William, Duke of Hamilton, Heretable Keeper of our Palace of Holyroodhouse, Wee haue signified our pleasure concerning the enlargement of our Chappell there, by allowing that wall to be taken downe which is upon the right hand in the passage that leads from the head of the great staire, to the round staires or turnpike that leads up to the third story, according to the directions of our Chancellor and our Almoner there. It is now our will and pleasure, and Wee doe hereby authorise and require you at our charge to cause the expenses of taking downe the said wall and making what other conveniencie is needfull for the enlargement aforesaid to be laid out, and to take care that the said expences be computed at reasonable rates to the workmen and others that shalbe imployed in making the said enlargement. For paying of which expences these presents together with the receipts of the workmen and others aforesaid, shalbe to you and to all others respectively who may be therein any way concerned, particularly to the Lords Auditors of your accompts for allowing the same a sufficient warrant. And so Wee bid you heartily ffarewell. Given at our Court at Whitehall, the 5th day of February 168$\frac{4}{5}$, and of our Reigne the 2d year.

" By his Majesty's command.

" MELFORT."

In view of a Roman Catholic Chapel being established at Holyroodhouse, the Lord Chancellor Perth, an attached friend of the king, had in 1685 made large purchases. Writes Lord Fountainhall : " He got from the king £8000 sterling, with which he bought altars, candlesticks, priests' garments, and other ornaments and popish gauds for erecting the Chappell in the Abbey and brought them home ; and tho ther be Acts of Parliament for seizing such trash, yet our customers past them." *

A counterpart to the conduct of Archbishop Laud at the court of Charles II. was at the court of James

* Lord Fountainhall's Historical Observes of Memorable Documents from October 1680 to April 1681. Edinb. 1840, 4to, p. 241.

enacted by the brothers James and John Drummond, Earls of Perth and Melfort. The Earl of Perth, the elder brother, who was now Lord Chancellor, had acquired an unenviable notoriety by inventing the thumbscrew, an instrument which, by producing exquisite torture, was found more efficacious in extorting confession than "the boot" of his royal master. Melfort, the younger brother, who as a principal secretary of state subscribes these earlier documents, possessed a literary aptitude which enabled him to indulge a lofty rodomontade that served momentarily to deceive.

From what had already occurred, the brothers Drummond well knew that any manifesto suddenly put forth to establish at Holyroodhouse a Catholic chapel would involve an unpleasant result, therefore they proceeded cautiously. There was a steady preparation secretly conducted. The king named, as Almoner of the Chapel Royal, Alexander Dunbar, a supposed Catholic, and in order to his maintenance granted the following letter:

"JAMES, R.,—
"Right trusty and right welbeloved cousins and councellors, right trusty and entirely beloved cousins and councellors, and right trusty and welbeloved cousins and councellors, Wee greet you well. Whereas Wee did formerly resolve to bestow the sume of one hundred pounds sterline money yearly for providing and furnishing Wine, Oyle, Bread, and other necessaries for the vse of our Chappell in our Palace of Holyroodhouse: and in regard the same was destinated by Us for the vse aforesaid

long before the terme of Mertimes last: It is now our will and pleasure, and Wee doe hereby authorise and require you to pay, or cause to be paid unto Mr Alexander Dunbar, our Almoner there (to be disposed of at the sight, and by the approbation of our right, trusty, and right welbeloved cousin and councellor James, Earle of Perth, our chancellor), the sume of fifty pounds sterline for the said terme of Mertimes last, with fifty pounds sterline more for the terme of Whitsunday, lately past in this present year of God, and fifty pounds sterline immediatly after the terme of Mertimes next ensuing the date of these presents, out of the first and readiest of our Rents, Revenues, Customes, and casualities whatsumever of that our ancient Kingdome: and so forth to continue yearly and termely thereafter during our Royall pleasure only. For doing whereof, these presents (together with our said Almoner, his receipts from time to time) shalbe to you, and all others respectively who may be therein any way concerned, particularly to the Lords Auditors of your accompts for allowing the same a sufficient warrant. And so Wee bid you heartily ffarewell. Given at our Court at Whitehall, the 19th day of May 1687, and of our Reigne the 3d year.
"By his Majesty's command.
"MELFORT."

Also on the 19th of May were the Privy Council enjoined to make payment of one hundred pounds for a musical service. The royal letter on this subject proceeds :

"JAMES, R.,—
"Right trusty and right welbeloved cousins and councellors, right trusty and entirely beloved cousins and councellors, and right trusty and welbeloved cousins and councellors, Wee greet you well. Whereas Wee did formerly resolve to bestow the sume of one hundred pounds sterline money yearly upon the Persones appointed for the service of the Musick imployed for the vse of our Chappell in our Palace of Holyrood-

house; and in regard the same was destinated by Us for them long before the terme of Whitsunday lately past in this present year of God: It is now our Will and pleasure, and Wee doe hereby authorise and require you to pay, or cause to be paid, unto Mr Alexander Dunbar, our Almoner there (to be disposed of at the sight and by the approbation of our right trusty and right welbeloved cousin and councellor, James, Earle of Perth, our Chancellor), the sume of fifty pounds sterline for the said terme of Whitsunday lately past in this present year of God, and fifty pounds sterline immediatly after the terme of Mertimes next ensuing the date of these presents, out of the first and readiest of our Rents, Revenues, Customes, and Casualities whatsoever of that our ancient Kingdome; and so forth to continue yearly and termely thereafter, during our Royall pleasure only. For doing whereof, these presents (together with our said Almoner his receipts from time to time) shalbe to you, and all others respectively who may be therein any way concerned, particularly to the Lords Auditors of your Accompts for allowing the same, a sufficient warrant. And so Wee bid you heartily ffarewell. Given at our Court at Whitehall, the 19th day of May 1687, and of Our Reigne the 3d year.

"By his Majesty's command.

"MELFORT."

Having nominated a Romish almoner, and made provision for a musical staff, James proceeded to fully constitute the Chapel Royal as a conventual church. As abbot he nominated Father Richard Augustin Hay, Canon of St Genevieve, Paris. On this subject we have Hay's own authority. "King James the seventh," he writes, "intended to bestow that place upon our Canons of Saint Genoveves. For that effect I began to trait with the Earle of Perth, the 29th of May 1687, att seven of the clock att night, and continued the 31st of May, the 2, 4, 13, 16 days of June."*

Under the guidance of Perth and Melfort, James had actually restored the Abbey Church as a Romish convent, when he publicly announced that he meant differently. It was his royal intention, he averred, to utilise the church as the chapel of an Order of Chivalry, which he had revived in honour of his ancient kingdom. To impress this upon the country, Melfort exercised his literary craft in framing the following warrant; it appeared in a Latin dress, but we present an English translation :

"JAMES, R.,—

"Our Sovereign Lord ordains a Letter Patent to be made and passed under the Great Seal of the ancient kingdom of Scotland, making mention that whereas his Majesty's royal predecessor, Achaius, King of Scots (of glorious memory), did institute the most ancient and most noble Order of the Thistle, consisting of the Sovereign and Twelve Knights Brethren, in allusion to our blessed Saviour and His Twelve Apostles, and that under the protection of our Blessed Lady and her holy Apostle, Saint Andrew, Patron of Scotland, the said Order being instituted for the defence of the Christian Religion, and in commemoration of a signal victory obtained by the said Achaius, King of Scots, over Athelstan, King of the Saxons, after a bloody battle, in the time of which there appeared in the heavens a White Cross, in form of that upon which the Apostle, Saint Andrew, suffered martyrdom, by which apparition the Scots, being encouraged, put their enemies to flight, killing the said Athelstan, with most of his followers. And it being most certain, by the general consent of ancient and modern historians,

* Father Hay, *Diplomatum Veterum Collectio*, i., p. 288, MS. Advocates Library.

and by several other authentic proofs and documents and records of that Kingdom, that the said most ancient and most noble Order of the Thistle continued in great glory and splendour for many hundreds of years, and that several Foreign Princes and Kings have been Knights of the said Order, and that the same was always had in great respect and honour in all places wherever Christian valour advanced the glory of the Cross, until the unfortunate Rebellion against His Majesty's Royal greatgrandmother, Mary Queen of Scots (of most pious and glorious memory), at which time the splendour both of Morals and Monarchy fell together into contempt, and the Most Noble Order, with all its ornaments and rites and ceremonies, was extinguished, some of the Brethren of that Order laying the the ensigns thereof aside, and out of a rebellious contempt to their then Sovereign Lady, His Majesty's said Royal Great Grandmother, and others of them, forced to fly into foreign countries for safety of their lives. And whereas the succeeding great disorders and dismal rebellions, in the reigns of His Majesty's Royal Predecessors since that time, hath hindered and diverted them from restoring the said Order to its former ancient lustre, His Majesty hath now thought fit, as a mark of Royal favour and esteem of that his ancient Kingdom, and of the desire he hath to restore it to its former splendour and reputation, considering the many and seasonable instances of duty and affection it has shown to His Royal person, both since his accession to the Crown and in times of his greatest difficulties, has, as a lasting mark of Royal favour, and in remembrance of the nation's duty and affection unto him, to all succeeding ages, thought fit at this time to revive the said Order, of which His Majesty is undoubted and rightful Sovereign; and doth hereby revive and restore the same to its full glory, lustre, and magnificence, as it heretofore was, with such change and additions as are already made, or shall hereafter be declared by His Majesty; hereby giving to it Twelve Knights, of which, with His Majesty as Sovereign, the Order above named is to consist in all time coming, all honours, dignities, titles, privileges, additions, and others, which either have in time past belonged to the Most

Noble Order of the Thistle, or what His Majesty shall declare to belong thereunto in time coming, as an evident proof that no dutiful or faithful service done by His people shall be passed over without suitable return of bounty, honour, and favour for him. And His Majesty ordains the said Letter patent to be passed under the Great Seal aforesaid *per saltum*, without passing any other Register or Seal; in order whereunto these presents shall be to the Director of His Majesty's Chancellary, and their Deputies for visiting of the same, and to the Lord High Chancellor, for causing the Great Seal to be appended thereunto, a sufficient Warrant. Given at the Court at Windsor, the 29th day of May 1687, and of His Majesty's reign the third year." *

The statements so put forth were wholly fictitious. The legend respecting Achaius and Athelstan is founded upon that other monastic legend connected with the conversion of the emperor Constantine. First assigned a place in history by John of Fordun, it was reproduced, with fresh colouring, by Bishop Leslie and others. Even though the narrative had rested on a probable foundation, it bears in its earlier details no relation to the establishment of a chivalric order. †

The figure of St Andrew the apostle was not used as a national symbol prior to the reign of Robert II. (1371-1390). In this reign was struck a gold coin exhibiting the apostle on his cross, and which was called the St Andrew. An effigy of the apostle was struck on

* Register of the Great Seal, lxxi. 128.
† See an exhaustive paper on the origin of the city of St Andrews and its early ecclesiastical settlement, by Mr William F. Skene, now Historiographer Royal. Proceedings of the Society of Antiquaries of Scotland, vol. iv., pp. 300-321.

gold coins of different sizes during the reigns of James II., III., and IV.* As an emblem the Thistle is unknown prior to the reign of James III. In an inventory of household articles belonging to the queen of that sovereign, dated 1488, a coverlet is described as embroidered with thistles. The words are, "A couering of variand purpir tartar, browdin with thrissillis and a vnicorne."† In his poem, "The Thistle and the Rose," composed in 1503 in honour of the betrothal of James IV. and the Princess Margaret, William Dunbar celebrates the king under the emblem of a Thistle. He chose this symbol apparently in contra-distinction to the Rose, under which emblem he designates the royal princess, who was descended from the joint stems of York and Lancaster. On his coin, the angel, James IV. had the thistle as a mint mark. And on a letter addressed by him to Ferdinand II., King of Aragon, dated at Edinburgh, the kalends of July 1512, the impression of his seal would seem to represent a collar of thistles and knots enclosing the royal shield.‡ A collar, formed of thistles of gold, to which was attached an oval badge, with the effigy of St Andrew, was by James V. worn as a decoration. Such a collar was displayed on the great seal of Queen Mary, and was also struck upon her coins.

* Cochran-Patrick's Coinage of Scotland, 1876, vol. ii., plate 2.
† Treasurer's Accounts, i. 85.
‡ Egerton MSS., in the British Museum, No. 616, p. 39.

The coins of James VI. displayed a thistle with leaves. The motto, *Nemo me impune lacesset*, which first appeared on the Scottish coinage in 1581, was, it is believed, suggested by Buchanan.

Up to this time we have in Scotland no trace of a chivalric order. The decoration of St Andrew on his cross and the symbol of the thistle were used by the sovereign only. So far as appears, the Order of St Andrew is first mentioned by Mennenius, in his *Deliciæ Equestrium sive Militarum Ordinum*, printed at Cologne in 1613. His authority was accepted by others, till at length Elias Ashmole, the heraldic antiquary, writing in 1672,* sets forth the Order of the Thistle in the manner described in James's warrant, though with details less copious. Ashmole chiefly depends on information derived from contemporaries. His informants are Sir Charles Erskine, Lyon King of Arms, and the Earl of Lauderdale. The latter assumed that "among his readings he had discovered that the knights were thirteen in number, corresponding with the numbers of the apostolic college." His acquaintance with the order, Sir Charles Erskine based on a MS. of Sir James Balfour, said to have been lost. But in Balfour's numerous writings which are extant, the order is unnamed!

That two gossiping and credulous writers such as

* The Institution, Laws, and Ceremonies of the Most Noble Order of the Garter, etc., by Elias Ashmole, Windsor Herald, Lond. 1672.

Sir George Mackenzie and Alexander Nisbet* should repeat the story of Achaius with modern additions may not excite surprise. After relating the legend in detail, Nisbet affects to doubt it. An accomplished scholar, Mackenzie was ready to assert anything which would gratify his sovereign's wishes. Both writers set forth that Achaius made a league with Charlemagne, and that in honour of the event the former instituted this knightly order. Among the ruins of the monastery at Sconé, writes Nisbet, Sir James Balfour found a MS., describing the coronation of Alexander III. in 1249, and in which it appeared that the coronation had been postponed till the sovereign, a child of nine years, became a knight of St Andrew. By Robert the Bruce the order, he asserts, was chivalrously restored. It was, he adds, splendidly renovated by James V., who added a collar of thyme and rue, and at a chapter at Linlithgow constituted George, Lord Seaton, one of the knight companions. Both Nisbet and Mackenzie allege that the knights, arrayed in their parliamentary robes, met yearly on St Andrew's Day. The latter describes them as convening in St Andrews cathedral, the former as assembling at St Andrews "in the ancient chapel of the order." But all this is fiction.

As in other conspiracies, everything had been arranged to strike at once. On the 29th May the

* Sir George Mackenzie's Observations upon the Laws and Customs of Nations as to Precedency. Edinb. 1680, pp. 99-101; Nisbet's System of Heraldry, ii. 104-122.

warrant was issued for the pretended revival of the order, and on the same day was prepared a patent for its restitution to be passed under the great seal. Such was the precipitation that the patent was exhibited even before the great seal had been appended. Other manifestoes followed. On the 31st May the statutes of the order were published, and Melfort's under-secretary, Sir Andrew Forrester, was appointed as its secretary.* Eight knights were created on the 8th June—all vigorous adherents of the royal policy.

On the 28th June James again communicated with the Council. Referring to his edict for reconstituting the Order of the Thistle, his Majesty reveals more plainly what his real intentions were. He desired that the Abbey Church might be recovered from the magistrates of Edinburgh, "not only as being most fit and convenient for accommodating the Knights of the Thistle," but as, to quote his own words, "also most proper for the performance of religious worship and exercise of our household, when we shall have occasion to be there, our present chapel in that palace not being large enough for the same." Therefore were the Council enjoined to call upon the civic authorities "to deliver up the keys of the church to the Earl of Perth, the Chancellor," in order that it might be adapted as "the chapel of the said Order."

* History of the Orders of Knighthood, by Sir Nicholas Harris Nicolas, iii. 18-20.

To compensate the parishioners of the Canongate, James proposed to grant to the Town Council for erecting a new church, money "long ago mortified by Thomas Moodie, sometime merchant in Edinburgh, of which the disposal was by Act of Parliament vested in the Crown. Private citizens who possessed lofts and galleries were to be accommodated with similar conveniences in the new church.*

The royal letter from which we have taken these extracts was on the 12th July laid on the Council table. Lord Fountainhall, who was present, thus describes the occurrence:

"July 12, 1687. At Privy Council, there is a letter read from the King, bearing, that the Abbay Church was the Chapel belonging to his Palace of Holy-roodhouse; and that the Knights of the noble Order of the Thistle, which he had now erected, could not meet in St Andrews church (being demolished in the Rebellion, as they called our Reformation), and so it was necessary for them to have this church; and the Provost of Edinburgh was ordained to see the keys of it given them. After a long silence, the Archbishop of Glasgow † told it was a mensal and

* Maitland's History of Edinburgh, 1753, fol., pp. 142, 143. In 1650 Thomas Moodie, or, as he is styled in Slezer's *Theatrum Scotiæ*, p. 7, Sir Thomas Moodie of Sachten-Hall, bequeathed the sum of twenty thousand marks to the Town Council, in trust, for building a church in the town, and which, after various projects for its application, was at length made use of in providing a church for the parishioners of the Canongate, on their ejection from the Abbey Church (Wilson's Memorials of Edinburgh, 1872, p. 428).

† A native of Aberdeenshire, Archbishop John Paterson, an early opponent of the Covenant, was promoted from Ellon to a charge at Edinburgh, in which diocese he became dean. He was afterwards in succession Bishop of Galloway and Edinburgh and Archbishop of Glasgow. He accumulated wealth, which he invested in estates in different parts of the country; he died in 1708.

patrimonial church of the Bishoprick of Edinburgh : And though he was now translated, and the See vacant, yet it belonged not to the Provost to deliver the keys; This was understood that he was seeking the compliment, to be employed himself, to keep some possession in Edinburgh, whereof he was seeking to be Commendator; however it was adjusted, that the keys should be immediately delivered to the Chancellor himself; and the inhabitants of the Canongate (whose parochial church, it was not of old before the Reformation, but belonged to the Convent there) were ordained to go to the Lady Yester's Church; and the French minister and congregation were put out of it to the High-school, or Common-hall. So this is the first Protestant church taken away from us." *

The preceding relation of Lord Fountainhall is confirmed and followed up by another contemporary, Father Richard Hay.—"Tewsday the 11th of July," writes this respected chronicler, "the keys of the church were given to my Lord Chancellar, who delivered them next morning to the Provost, and gave him fourteen days to take away the sets the bedler had care thereof. The Sunday following the Abbay parish was transferred to the Lady Esther's [Yester's] Church, and the minister thereof preached therein." †

The following minute of the Town Council of Edinburgh, dated 13th July 1687, proves that the surrender of the Abbey Church was promptly acceded to :

"Edinburgh, the thirteenth July j^m vj° eightie seven years.

"The which day the Councell considering the Kings Majestie

---

* Lord Fountainhall's Decisions, i. 466.
† Father Hay, *Diplomatum Veterum Collectio*, i., p. 288.

has appointed the inhabitants of the Canongate to remove from the Abbay Church in respect the said kirk is to be inlarged conforme to the draught therof approven by his Majestie, and that his Majestie by his Letter has appointed the parochiners and inhabitants to be accomodat in the Ladie Zester's kirk untill such tyme there be a kirk built for them: Therfor they recomend to the Dean of Gild to cause deliver the keyes of the said Ladie Zester's kirk befor ffryday next, and because the ffrench minister has this long tyme bygane preached in the said Ladie Zester's kirk, therfor they appoint him to preach in the comon hall of the Colledge quhich they think most fitt for accomodating the french congregation during the councells pleasure." *

The Privy Council moved tardily. Subservient as were the majority, neither the insignia of the Thistle, nor even the favour of the sovereign himself might induce them rashly to excite popular violence. Even Melfort hesitated. But Alexander Stewart, Earl of Moray, who had lately abjured Protestantism, proved equal to the occasion. As Lord High Commissioner he, in the following letter, bearing the king's superscription, charged and warned the Privy Council:

" JAMES, R.,—
" Right trusty and right welbeloved cousins and councellors, right trusty and entirely beloved cousins and councellors, and right trusty and welbeloved cousins and councellors, Wee greet you well. Whereas Wee haue resolved that our Chappell at Holyroodhouse (formerly made use of as the Parish Church of the Canongate) be repaired and put in order with all possible expedition, to the end it may be fitted in all things for being our own Catholick Chappell where divine service may be per-

* Burgh Records of Edinburgh, vol. xxxii., fol. 127.

formed, and likewise be made capable of the ceremonies and
solemnities of the most ancient and most Noble Order of the
Thistle: and whereas Wee doe well know that the much
greater part of the work and materialls needfull for this reparation can be had much better and cheaper at London than in
Scotland, and therefore haue ordered our right trusty and right
welbeloved cousin and councellor, John, Earle of Melfort, one of
our Principall Secretaries of State to engage Mr James Foulis,
merchant in London, to become bound to the carvers, joyners,
and other workmen here, to be employed in and about the said
work and reparation, who would not undertake the same without good security in our City of London for performance of the
conditions that are agreed on with them for that effect; in
order whereunto the said Earle of Melfort having by our expresse order and speciall command signed the severall Bills of
Exchange here undermentioned drawn by him upon
Maxwell of Kirkonnell, and John Drummond, two of our
Receivers and Paymasters, for the punctuall payment whereof
the said Earle has given his own private security to the said
Mr James Foulis, viz.: One Bill for nine hundred twenty two
pounds and six shillings sterline, payable here the 20th day of
January next: Item, a second Bill of Exchange for four hundred and seventy pounds and eight shillings sterline, payable
here the 20th of February next: Item, a third Bill for four
hundred and ten pounds sterline money, payable at Edinburgh
the first day of May next ensuing the date of these presents;
in which three Bills (all payable to the said Mr James Foulis or
his order) the exchange and other reasonable allowances being
already included: It is now our expresse Will and pleasure,
and Wee doe hereby authorise and strictly require you to make
or cause to be made exact and punctuall payments of the severall
sumes mentioned in the said Bills upon the respective dayes
aforesaid when they shall become due. Wherein you are not
(upon any consideration) to faile, not only for the reason of our
having obliged the said Earle of Melfort to engage his own
private credit for the punctuall performance of the same, but
also because Wee are obliged to pay interest to the said Mr

James Foulis, from and after the respective dayes aforesaid, so long as the said summes or any of them shall remaine unpaid; which Wee doe hereby recommend unto your speciall care to prevent, as that which will be very unacceptable unto Us. And in regard that for compleating the said works and reparations there wilbe a further charge and expence of moneys needfull for mason work, paving, glasing, sarking, and roofing, it is our further expresse will and pleasure that you pay or cause to be paid such summe or summes of money as shalbe from time to time needfull for the same, or for any other necessaries that wilbe requisite for that effect, so as the whole work and reparation may be fully compleated, and our own said Chappell be exactly put in order for the purposes already mentioned, before the first day of May next to come precisely—in failour of which Wee cannot but be highly displeased: And therefore doubt not but you wilbe most carefull to have the same fully performed. For all which, these presents shalbe to you, and all others respectively who may be therein any way concerned, particularly to the Lords Auditors of your accompts for allowing the payments of the severall summes, and the other charges and expences already mentioned, a sufficient warrant. And so Wee bid you heartily ffarewell. Given at our Court at Whitehall, the 3d day of December 1687, and of our Reigne the 3d year.
" By his Majesty's command.
" MORRAY."

Not as a mere act of despotism did James issue the command, whereby he demanded of the Privy Council to make payment of bills of exchange, in the executing of which they had expressed no concurrence. There were hidden causes. James had committed himself to purchases of an illegal character, a revelation of which would have excited insurrection. On his behalf the Lord Chancellor Perth had, in 1685, expended £8000 sterling in procuring Romish "gauds" for Holyrood Chapel, in contravention of the Acts of Parliament.* And, according to Lord Fountainhall, a further importation had lately been effected. His lordship writes: " 23 Novembris 1686.—The King's Yaught arrived from London at Leith, with the Popish altar, vestements, images, Priests, and other dependers, for the Popish Chapell in the Abbey."† This cargo was no doubt the product of "the carvers, joyners, and other workmen," engaged by Mr James Foulis, and for which were drawn Melfort's bills. The charge of £1802, 14s. sterling, being made in three bills, it was hoped that the small amount payable on each would avert complaint. Doubtless the cause of the debt, disguised in the king's letter, was patent to the Council; but under the recollection of the serious disturbance which occurred in 1680, when the Pope's effigy was burned at Edinburgh, they maintained a prudent silence. In the second portion of his letter, James enjoins the Council to at once employ skilled workmen, in order to the restoration of the church, so that, under his Majesty's highest displeasure, it might be completed before the following May.

A brief outline of the early history of the Abbey Church is now essential. Founded by David I. in 1128, and by him dedicated to the honour of the Holy Cross, the Virgin, and All Saints, the Abbey

* See *supra*, p. ccxxi.
† Lord Fountainhall's Historical Notices, ii. 763.

was planted with canons regular of the Augustine order. Within the structure John Baliol held a Parliament in 1296, and in the adjacent chapel was a Council convened in 1303 by his son Edward. In the abbey hospitality was, in 1381, extended to John of Gaunt. Burned in 1385 by Richard II., the fabric was subsequently repaired. The occasional resort of Robert III. and James I., it was the birthplace of James II., the place of his coronation, also of his sepulture. In the abbey was James III. married in 1469 to Margaret of Denmark. Preparatory to his marriage with Margaret, the English princess, in 1503, James IV. constructed a palace at the spot, which, afterwards extended by the regent John, Duke of Albany, and James V., forms the older portion of that royal residence which exists now. After several dilapidations, the church of the abbey was, about 1460, restored by the abbot, Archibald Campbell; it was, along with the palace, partially burned by the English army in 1544; and again in 1547. The palace was further dilapidated, and a portion of the furniture seized and scattered, by the Reformers in 1559; yet it was found sufficient to accommodate Queen Mary and her court on her return to Scotland in 1561.*

* At the Reformation the revenues of the abbey were set down at £2926, 8s. 6d. money, and 116 chalders of victual. For further authentic details respecting the history of Holyroodhouse, see Historia Miraculose Fundationis Monasterii Sancte Crucis, prope Edinburgh; Inventarium Iocalium, etc., Magni Altaris ejusdem monasterii, MCCCCLXXXIII., Bannatyne Miscel-

The prevailing belief that Queen Mary was married to Lord Darnley in the Abbey Church rests, we think, on insufficient evidence. At the time of the marriage the church seems to have been used for worship by the parishioners of the Canongate. Mr John Brand, minister of the Canongate, published the queen's banns, and a record of the event in the Kirk Session Minute Book of that parish proceeds thus :

"The 21 of Julij Anno Domini 1565.—The quhilk day Johne Brand, mynister, presentit to ye Kirk ane writting, written be ye Justice Clark hand, desyring ye Kirk of ye Cannogait and mynister thairof, to proclame Harie, Duk of Abbynye, erle of Rois, etc., on ye one part, and Marie, be ye grace of God quene souerane of this realme, on ye vthair part. The q^{lk} ye Kirk ordanis ye mynister so to do with inwocation of ye name of God."

In the Marriage Register of the Canongate is the following entry : "Henry, Duk of Albany, erll of Rois, Marie, be the grace of God, quen souerane of this realme, 1, 2, ℞." In continuation of this entry are these words : "Married in the chappell."*

lany, vol. ii., p. 11 ; Chronicon Cœnobii Sanctae Crucis Edinburgensis, edited by Mr Robert Pitcairn, Bannatyne Club, 1828, 4to; also Liber Cartarum Sancte Crucis ; Munimenta Ecclesie Sancte Crucis de Edwinesburg, with a preface by Professor Cosmo Innes, Bannatyne Club, 1841.

* *Buik of the Kirk of the Canagait*, 1564-67. The entry in the Marriage Register is in these words : "The 29 day of Julij anno 1565. Henry and Marie, Kyng and qwene of Scottis." It will be remarked in the entry of proclamation that the banns had been proclaimed twice only, the figure 3 being deleted by the registrar. In the same Register appear under the heading of " The persons that has communicat the time of their deceis day and zeir beginning anno 1565," these two remarkable entries, which are totally unconnected with the preamble—" Monsr Singnior Dauid ves slane in Halyrudhous the ix day of Merche anno 1565 ;" " The Kyng's grace blaven vp v^t buder in ye Kirk of Feild the x of Februar 1566."

In naming the locality of Queen Mary's marriage, Lord Herries, a contemporary, remarks that it was solemnised "by Mr John Sinkclare, persone of Restelrigg, in the Chappell Royal of Hallirudhous, at mass."* And Sir James Melville describes the ceremony as being performed in the "Palace of Halyroodhouse uithin the Queen's Chappel at the Mass."† Now the place in which Mary had mass performed on her arrival from France was certainly not the Abbey Church, but a chapel *within* the Palace. Such a chapel is described in the report of Sir Robert Drummond in 1583,‡ and to it, we conceive, does Lord Herries allude when he refers to Lord Glencairn's procedure at Holyroodhouse in June 1567, after Mary's imprisonment at Lochleven. His statement is :

"The Earle of Glencairne, with his domestick servants onlie in his companie, went to the Chappell of Halliroodhous, and with great noyse broake doune the altar, and defaced everie thing that pertained to the ornaments therof; which was much commended by the ministrie, for an act of pietie and zeale; but the nobilitie did not approve it, for they reprehended him for acting without a publick order." §

Further, the General Assembly of 1569 having charged Adam Bothwell, commendator of Holyrood,

* Lord Herries' " Historie of the Reigne of Marie Queen of Scots." Abbotsford Club, 1834, pp. 70, 71.
† Sir James Melvil's " Memoires." Lond. 1683, p. 57.
‡ See *supra*, p. xciv.
§ Lord Herries's " Historie," p. 97. In his History of Edinburgh, Mait-

with allowing some churches to fall into decay, he in defence pleaded that with respect to the Abbey Church it had been ruinous "these twenty years bygane," and accordingly he proposed and was permitted by the Assembly to dispose of the materials forming the choir and transept in order to procure funds for repairing the nave, so that it might be in comfortable use by the parishioners of the Canongate.* Within the restored nave was crowned, in 1590, Anne of Denmark, Queen of James VI.† From this period up to the accession of James VII. the chief events connected with the Abbey Church have been detailed.

By the Privy Council the injunction of the 3d December 1687 was fully obeyed. Under their sanction was introduced daily service according to the Romish ritual. In reference to this arrangement Lord Fountainhall has the following :

"6 Februarij 1688.—In the evening and next morning many Litanies and Masses are said in the Abbey, by the Popish Priests, for the soul of King Charles the 2d, to bring him out of Purgatory, he having died on that day now three years agoe." ‡

land remarks that there was a Chapel at Holyrood adjoining the Dean's House in St Aune's Yard, of which the remains existed in his time (Maitland's History of Edinburgh, 1753, p. 153). As confirmatory of our view as to the Queen's Chapel in the Palace being the scene of her marriage with Lord Darnley, we may refer to a case of discipline in the Canongate Register. Therein it appears that, on the 12th July 1565, Symon Lokart acknowledged his offence in having "abusit" the sacrament of baptism, by having "his barne baptizet in Papestrie in the chappell."

* Booke of the Universall Kirk, Bannatyne Club, pp. 163, 167.

† Papers relative to the Marriage of King James VI., Bannatyne Club, 1828, p. 39.

‡ Lord Fountainhall's Historical Notices, p. 852.

Having actively pushed forward his monastic preparations, Father Hay was enabled on the 22d March to issue the printed rules of a Catholic College which he had established at Holyrood, and in which was offered gratuitous instruction.* Riots in the city which attended these innovations were rigorously suppressed, two of the rioters being executed and others publicly flogged.†

In the Town Council minute of the 13th July 1687, the ground stated for surrendering the Abbey Church is, that it was "to be inlarged conforme to the draught thereof approven by his Majestie." That "draught," prepared by Sir William Bruce, embraced an accommodation for the Knights of the Thistle, quaintly described by Father Hay as "a curious work of timber."‡ Sir William's design, elegantly engraved in folio, is presented in *Vitruvius Scoticus*, an architectural work of much rarity.§ Entitled "The Interior of the Chapel Royal," the plate represents the Knights stalls, six on each side with the throne of the sovereign at the western extremity. Resting on a dais approached by six

* Lord Fountainhall's Historical Notices, p. 860.
† Dr Daniel Wilson's Memorials of Edinburgh, 1872, p. 105.
‡ *Diplomatum Veterum Collectio*, i. 288, 289, Advocates Library.
§ *Vitruvius Scoticus* is a collection of plans and elevations of public buildings, engraved chiefly from designs by the celebrated architect Mr William Adam, who died in 1748. Several of the designs relating to Holyroodhouse are described as having been executed by Sir William Bruce. The work was published early in the century, and contains one hundred and sixty plates. A perfect copy is in the Edinburgh University Library; that in the Advocates Library is imperfect.

steps fenced right and left by carved representations of the lion and unicorn, the throne is topped by a canopy, displaying the royal escutcheon and other appropriate emblems. The stalls, which are separated from the side aisles by a screen, are formed by elegant Corinthian columns, supporting an architrave over each stall on which are displayed each knight's heraldic insignia, with his helmet and weapons. The general effect is imposing, notwithstanding the incongruity of Greek architecture in combination with a structure wholly Gothic.

In course of operations the royal vault containing the ancient tombs was restored, while the less offensive portion of "the gauds" or ornaments of 1685 and 1686 was utilised and displayed. Among these ornaments Nisbet refers to figures of the Saviour and Twelve Apostles, and other well-executed pieces of sculpture.* There was a large and magnificent organ, and the flooring was of marble.†

Insurrection was imminent, hence, by order of the Privy Council, Captain John Wallace (probably of the family of Craigie) was stationed in the Palace, with a military guard. The precaution had become especially essential under the now universal unpopularity of the king. On the 11th December 1688 —the day on which James escaped from Whitehall,

---

* Nisbet's Heraldry, ii. 120.
† Maitland's History of Edinburgh, p. 153 ; Journey through Scotland, Lond. 1729, p. 61 ; Arnot's History of Edinburgh, pp. 252-255.

the Town Council of Edinburgh assembled at the Council Chambers, and passed the following minute :

"At Edinburgh, the eleventh of December j^m vj^c
"eightie eight years.

"The which day, the Lord Provost produced two orders of his Majestie's privy councell in relation to the unhappie tumult that has arisen this day of ane rable of all sorts of people quhich is signed by his Majestie's privy councell, quhich the councell appoints the same to be recorded, quhairof the tennor ffollowes: Edinburgh, the tenth of December j^m vj^c eightie eight—These are requireing the provost and baillies of Edinburgh upon sight hereof, with the Traine bands and Militia, and to besiege the place quhair Captain Wallace is, and to take care that none escape, except such as shall render themselves prissoners, and to make search for and apprehend Captain Wallace himself and the officers of his companie, and to keep thame strict untill they be brought to judgement, and secure all other posts about the town for apprehending all others that are guiltie. This yow shall doe without farder delay, as yow will be answerable. Sic subscribitur—Atholl, Breadalbane, Tarbat, Jo. Dalrymple.

"ffollowes the order of his Majesties privie councell ordaineing Captain Wallace to deliver himself prissoner.

"Edinburgh, the said Tenth December j^m vj^c eightie eight.

"These are ordering yow Captain Wallace to deliver up your persone to the provost of Edinburgh or any of the baillies therof, under all highest paines. Sic subscribitur—Atholl, Breadalbane, Tarbat, Jo. Dalrymple.

"After receipt of the quhich orders the Lord Provost and remanent Magistrats issued forth a proclamation commanding all the Iuhabitants belonging to the Train bands of this Cittie to attend their respective captains' colloures, with their armes, imediatly, that conforme to the abovewrittin order the persone of Captain Wallace might be seized upon, and made certification to them conforme to the said order, and the Magistrats haveing gone upon the head of the Train bands, and Livetenant Colonell Grahame's Companie and the Militia of this Cittie, and Henry Frazer, Rosse herauld, and James [Guthrie], Dingwall pursevant, haveing with trumpeters gone to the entrie of the abbay closse, the said herauld and pursevant haveing their coats displayed, did require Captain Wallace to give obedience to the orders of his Majestie's privy councell, and upon his refuseall they gave into the Magistrats their execution upon the back of the said last order, quhich execution the councell appointed to be recorded, quhairof the tennor ffollowes: Wpon the tenth day of December j^m vj^c eightie eight years Wee, Henry Frazer, Rosse herauld, and James Guthrie, Dingwall pursevant, be vertue of the abovewrittin orders, past with the baillies of Edinburgh to the foot of the Cannogate and there they stopped and ordered us to goe forward with our coats of armes displayed and sound of trumpet, to Captain Wallace and require him conforme to the saids abovewrittin orders, and his Company being standing at the innerside of the Strand near the entrie to the Abbay, with all their armes presented: The comanding officer of the said Company called to us to stand off for none should enter, and the said Captain Wallace was standing a litle back amongst his souldiers, and cryed for one of us to enter; and I, the said Henry Frazer, went foreward to him and told him that the Lords of his Majestie's privy councell had ordered him to deliver up his persone to the baillies of Edinburgh, who was there readie to receive him. He gave no ansuer, but called his Livetenant and whispered to him, and went imediatly away backward behind his owne Companie, and the said Livetenant came to the front of the said companie and comanded us to be gone, and we told him that we thought the Captain wold be so discreet as to give ane ansuer to the Lords of the privy councells orders, and wee was waiting for it, and he againe comanded us to be gone, for we should have no more ansuer nor we had gotten already, and if we stayed any longer we should have ane ansuer by and by: And I, the said Henry Frazer, came back to the saids baillies and told them what had been said to us, and they ordered me to goe back and wait upon ane ansuer, quhich accordingly I did, and being befor the said company I saw ane serjeant come and asked the Livetenant if the rabble was gone, he ansuered not: The said serjeant said yee are ordered to make your post good, and imediatly the said Livetenant fired ane gun that was in his hand, and then all the souldiers of the said companie fired likewayes. This wee did conforme to the saids orders, with our coats of armes displayed and sound of trumpet, befor thir witnesses, Alexander Bonner and William Eckford, town officers in Edinburgh, and John Wightman, officer there, with severall other witnesses to the premisses: And for the verification hereof wee and the said witnesses have subscrived the samen with our hands: Sic subscribitur, Henry ffrazer, herauld ; James Guthrie, pursevant; Alexr. Bonner, witnes; John Wightman, witnes; Wm. Eckford, witnes: Sic subscribitur, Magnus Prince, pro."*

Captain Wallace was compelled to surrender soon afterwards. In Appendix VII. will be found a narrative of the circumstances attending the event, also of the devastation of the church. With that devastation terminated a scheme for restoring under royal sanction the Roman Catholic faith—a scheme which, formulated by Laud, had been advanced by Lauderdale, and all but enforced by Moray and Perth and Melfort.

In reviewing the history of the Chapel Royal certain points stand out prominently. Seeking by his own authority to transform his Chapel Royal into a musical college, James III. excited among his nobles that wide discontent which resulted in their rebellion and in his own discomfiture and death. Moved by

* Burgh Records of Edinburgh, vol. xxxii., fol. 270, 271.

despotic counsels, James VII. sought to constitute as his Chapel Royal a structure which would accommodate a Roman Catholic college, and wherein might be practised those rites calculated to attract an interest in the old creed. The new despotic movement was like the old, checked by insurrection, with this important difference that subsequent to the second overthrow absolutism perished. As from the ashes of the Pre-Reformation martyrs sprung up the seeds of religious freedom—so the odour of that conflagration which consumed the adornments of the Abbey Church has been felt ever since in the enjoyment of civil liberty and constitutional government.

Reckoning from 1120, the probable year in which was reared at Stirling Castle the earliest semblance of a royal fane to the devastation of the church of Holyrood in 1688, a Chapel Royal may be held to have been connected with the headquarters of the sovereign for 568 years. And if, as we have found, the Chapel Royal at Stirling had only a covering of thatch four centuries and a half after it was reared, it may be concluded that the original erection was primitive in the extreme. In a condition the reverse of superb was that chapel in Holyrood Palace * in which Queen Mary attended the celebration of mass. The Abbey Church, a noble pile not inferior in the magnificence of its Gothic architecture to any of the cathedrals, was the Chapel Royal at the last. At

* *Supra*, p. lxxxvi.-xciv.

the last, indeed; for if we date from the probable commencement of repairs in December 1687 to the devastation in December of the following year, it is most doubtful whether in its new connection religious service was performed in it even once!

With the popular insurrection in December 1688 terminated the last effort put forth in this country for the re-establishment of the Romish Church. By the destruction of the knights' stalls, James's Order of chivalry also fell into abeyance, and so remained for fifteen years.

Revived by Queen Anne, in a patent passed under the Great Seal, 31st December 1703, the Order of the Thistle has been held in respect and honour ever since. On the 8th May 1827, George IV. increased the number of the Knights from twelve to sixteen. The Star of the Order consists of a St Andrew's cross of silver embroidery, with rays emanating from between the points of the cross, in the centre of which, on a gold field, is a Thistle of green, heightened with gold, the flower being of its natural colour, the whole surrounded by a circle of green, bearing the motto, *Nemo me impune lacessit*, in golden characters. The Badge, worn attached to a green ribbon, is an oval plate entirely of gold, bearing St Andrew with his cross within a circle containing the motto of the Order, the whole being surrounded by rays of light in the form of a glory. The collar is composed of golden Thistles and sprigs of rue, enamelled proper. A Dean of the Order was first appointed by George III., on the 7th January 1763.* The other officers are the Lyon King of Arms, a Secretary, and the Gentleman Usher of the Green Rod.

By the mob of December 1688, the Abbey Church was not only deprived of its ornaments and elegant fittings, but other vandalisms were perpetrated. The royal vault was opened, and leaden coffins enclosing the remains of members of the royal house were rudely broken up. On the 20th May 1689, or six months after the occurrence of this tumult, James, fourth Duke of Hamilton, remarks in a letter to the Earl of Melville, Secretary of State, that the entire building had been seriously despoiled.† It would not appear that any considerable restoration was attempted till half a century later.

On a representation by James, sixth Duke of Hamilton, as hereditary keeper, addressed to the Barons of Exchequer, these consulted an architect and a builder, who recommended that the church should have a roofing of flagstones; they also presented an estimate for the work which amounted to £1003. The recommendation and estimate were, on the 7th August 1758, both approved. When these repairs were carried out, it became evident that the walls were very much overweighted. To this effect a

---

* For List of the Deans of the Order of the Thistle from the first appointment in 1763 till 1845, see Fasti Eccl. Scot., i. 398.

† Leven and Melville Papers, Bannatyne Club, 1843, p. 27.

report was made to the Barons in 1766, but no action supervened. The anticipated result followed, for on the 2d December 1768, the roof fell into the interior, destroying in its descent the more considerable mouldings. In 1776 Hugo Arnot remarked the exposed remains of James V. and other royal personages, but three years later when he composed his History these coffins had been rifled.*

Among the skulls seized by the populace were those of Queen Magdalene and Lord Darnley. The former at once disappeared, but Darnley's skull fell into the possession of Mr James Cummyng of the Lyon Office, at whose death it was included in a collection of statuary at Edinburgh. It has not latterly been traced.

The last subdean of the Chapel Royal prior to the Revolution was Mr John Mackqueene, one of the ministers of Edinburgh, who was appointed by James VII. in 1688. Deprived in April 1689, by the Convention of Estates, for refusing to submit to the Revolution settlement, he visited the exiled king at St Germains, and subsequently ministered in England. His habits were eccentric and unclerical. He died in 1733, having attained about the age of ninety.†

* Arnot's History of Edinburgh, 1779, pp. 252-255; Dr D. Wilson's Memorials of Edinburgh, 1872, p. 409. For a detailed account of the monuments and tombstones in the Abbey Church and churchyard of Holyrood, see Gordon's Monasticon, vol. i., pp. 184-202, and Rogers' Monuments and Monumental Inscriptions, voL i., 99-116.
† Fasti Eccl. Scot., i. 36, 394.

The revenues of the deanery, subsequent to the abolition of Episcopacy at the Revolution, having reverted to the Crown, William III. conferred them on his vigorous adherent and private chaplain, Dr William Carstairs.

With the approval of the General Assembly, the funds connected with the office of dean were in 1737 divided into three parts, each being conferred on a clergyman selected by the Crown, who was described as one of the deans of the Chapel Royal. The original apportionment to each dean was about £84.*

Prior to 1841, certain leases of teinds belonging to the Chapel Royal having expired, the aggregate yearly rental greatly increased. To effectually utilise the augmented revenues, a chair of Biblical Criticism was established in the University of Edinburgh. The revenues were further disposed by the Scottish Universities' Commissioners as set forth in their Report issued in 1863. From that document we make the following extract:

"In view of the difficulty of obtaining farther grants of public money for the support of the Theological Chairs in the Faculties of Divinity, the attention of the Commissioners has been directed to a source which has already partly been made use of for the object in question. That source is the income of the deanery of the Chapel Royal. This deanery, which, before the abolition of Episcopacy in Scotland, had been attached to the See of Dunblane, fell on that event to the Crown, and the revenues have

* For a list of Deans and Subdeans of the Chapel Royal, also of Chaplains in Ordinary to the Sovereign, and of Royal Almoners, see Fasti Eccl. Scot., i. 393-399.

since been bestowed by grants on three of the Crown chaplains, who are commonly called Deans of the Chapel Royal, and who divide the revenues equally among them. The practice which is now followed is, that, when one of the three deans dies, a new gift is made out in favour of the two surviving deans and the new dean. The last gift was on 11th December 1846, 'in favour of Dr John Lee, so long as he shall hold the office of Principal of the University of Edinburgh, of Dr Norman M'Leod during our pleasure, and of Dr Robert Lee, so long as he shall hold the office of Professor of Biblical Criticism and Biblical Antiquities in the University of Edinburgh, and to his successors in office, and to each of them as aforesaid, equally.' The gift to Dr Robert Lee attaches one-third of the revenues of the deanery to the Chair in the University of Edinburgh, now held by him; and the Commissioners would respectfully submit that, were the principle extended to the remaining two-thirds of the revenues, with the view of benefiting the Faculties of Divinity in the several Universities of Scotland generally, than which a more fitting object for this Royal bounty could not be found, a gracious act would be done to the Church and the Universities, and the Government would be saved the difficulty of seeking public money for the purpose.

"The manner in which it seems to the Commissioners that the portion of the revenues of the deanery to which they refer could with the greatest advantage be used for the benefit of the Theological Chairs in the Universities is as follows: The present average amount of the whole divisible revenues of the deanery, which vary to a certain extent from year to year, but which are now not likely permanently to alter much in value, is £2018 a year. The Commissioners propose that, leaving out of view the one-third now attached to the Chair of Biblical Criticism in the University of Edinburgh, each of the remaining two-thirds of the revenues should, as it becomes vacant, be divided into two, and each of the sixth parts so obtained (£336 a year on the average) should be given to one of four deans, who should be certain theological professors in the four universities, and that this scheme should be carried out in the following order, viz.,—

there being now one-third vacant by the death of the late Dr John Lee, Principal of the University of Edinburgh, one-half of this to be given to the person who shall be appointed Professor of Divinity in that university, the person so appointed giving up the amount of the present endowment of his Chair, to increase the income of the Chair of Ecclesiastical History in the same university, and the other half to be given to found a Chair of Biblical Criticism in the University of Aberdeen; and, on the remaining third becoming vacant by the death of Dr M'Leod, one-half to be given as an endowment for a Chair of Biblical Criticism in the University of Glasgow, and the other half to be attached to the Chair of Church History in St Mary's College, St Andrews, the salary from the Woods and Forests of that Chair (£150) being then given as an assistance to the Principal, and the college endowment of the same Chair (£106) being added to the Chair of Biblical Criticism, now the second professorship of divinity in that college.

"With regard to the one-third of the revenues of the deanery at present attached to the Chair of Biblical Criticism in the University of Edinburgh, it will be for Her Majesty to consider, when it becomes vacant, whether it may be advisable that the whole should continue attached to that Chair, so as to provide an independent endowment to the professor, irrespective of class fees, or whether it may be advantageous and practicable that part of it should be applied for the benefit of the other Theological Chairs in that university, or in the universities generally." *

According to the preceding scheme the Universities' Commissioners distributed the Deanery revenues in this manner. They granted to the University of Edinburgh for the Professorship of Divinity,

* General Report of Universities' Commissioners, Scotland, p. 173. The Commissioners, in their ordinances, were subsequently enabled to give effect to the main principle on which these suggestions proceeded; though, in carrying them out, they saw occasion to introduce alterations as to some of the details.

£336, and for the Professorship of Biblical Criticism, £672; to the University of Glasgow for the Professorship of Biblical Criticism, £336; to St Mary's College, St Andrews, for the Professorship of Church History, £336; and to the University of Aberdeen for the Professorship of Biblical Criticism, £336. The Deanery revenues are derived from lands in the counties of Wigtown, Kirkcudbright, Ayr, and Perth; also from teinds on the lands of Shaws, Helmburn, and Balliades, in the parishes of Ettrick and Kirkhope, in the county of Selkirk.

The teinds of the Selkirkshire estates were in 1647 valued at £210 Scots, and in 1863 the deans raised an action in the Court of Teinds, setting forth that the valuation so made was effected without the requisite sanction, and that it should consequently be rescinded. The Court of Teinds, also the Second Division of the Court of Session, held otherwise, whereupon the deans appealed to the House of Lords, which, on the 18th March 1869, affirmed with costs the judgments of the courts below.

REGISTRUM
CAPELLÆ REGIÆ STRIVELINENSIS.

REGISTRUM
CAPELLÆ REGIÆ STRIVELINENSIS.

1. PROCESSUS SUPER ERECCIONE ECCLESIE COLLEGIATE   Maria.
DE STRIUELING.

VNIUERSIS et singulis Christi fidelibus et presertim Scoticane nacionis, omnibusque aliis et singulis quorum interest, intererit, seu interesse quousque infrascriptum tangit negocium seu tangere poterit quomodolibet infuturum, quibuscunque nominibus censeantur aut quacunque prefulgeant dignitate, Jacobus Abercrumby, permissione diuina abbas monasterii de Scona ordinis Sancti Augustini Sancti Andree diocesis, et Dauid Arnote, archidiaconus Laudonie in ecclesia sancti Andree, iudices et executores ad infrascripta, vna cum nostro in hac parte collega, cum illa clausula—Quatenus uos vel duo aut unus uestrum etc.—a sede apostolica specialiter deputati, salutem in Domino, et presentibus fidem indubiam inhibere nostrisque huiusmodi ymmouerius apostolicis firmiter obedire mandatis: LITERAS sanctissimi in Christo patris et domini nostri domini, Alexandri diuina prouidencia Pape Sexti, eius vera bulla plumbea cum cordula canapis more Romane curie impendente, bullatas, sanas, siquidem et integras, non viciatas, non cancellatas, nec in aliqua sui parte suspectas, sed omni prorsus vicio et suspicione carentes vt in eis prima facie apparebat, nobis per illustrissimum et serenissimum principem et dominum, dominum Jacobum diuina fauente clemencia Scotorum regem Quartum, principalem in eis-

A

dem litteris apostolicis principaliter nominatum, coram notario publico et testibus infrascriptis presentatas, nos cum ea qua decuit reuerencia noueritis recepisse huiusmodi sub tenore :

ALEXANDER, Episcopus Seruus seruorum Dei, dilectis filiis Sancte Crucis et de Scona, Sanctiandree diocesis, monasteriorum abbatibus, ac archidiacono Laudonie in ecclesia Sanctiandree, salutem et apostolicam benedictionem. Inter cetera cordis nostri desiderabilia illa intensis desideramus affectibus ut ubique locorum maiestas Altissimi in graciarum benedictionibus collaudetur et cultus sui nominis gloriosi amplietur; ac pia Christi fidelium presertim Catholicorum regum vota, ex quibus eiusdem diuini nominis exaltacio ipsorumque regum et aliorum Christi fidelium animarum salus prouenire et persone quelibet diuinorum officiorum decantacioni et celebracioni in singulis ecclesiis presertim collegiatis de nouo erigendis cum animi quiete et tranquillitate insistere possint, ad exaudicionis graciam libenter admittimus; ac ea, prout in domino conspicimus, salubriter expedire fauoribus prosequimur oportunis. Exhibita siquidem nobis nuper pro parte carissimi in Christo filii nostri, Jacobi Scotorum Regis illustris, peticio continebat quod, licet in Capella Regia nuncupata Beate Marie et Sancti Michaelis, infra palacium ipsius Jacobi regis opidi de Striueling Sanctiandree diocesis sita, vnus decanus nuncupatus ac plures alij cantores et capellani ac clerici missas et alia diuina officia singulis diebus ad libitum prefati Jacobi Regis ammouibiles celebrent, ipseque Jacobus Rex predictam capellam suis expensis reformari fecerit, ac libris, calicibus, et aliis ornamentis ecclesiasticis pro diuino cultu in eadem capella necessariis honorifice munuerit et ornauerit, ac eciam nonnulla bona immobilia ad eum legittime pertinencia eidem capelle pro illius dote assignauerit : Tamen si dicta capella in collegiatam ecclesiam, et prepositura Ecclesie beate Marie de Rupe Sanctiandree, que inibi dignitas principalis et de iure patronatus prefati Jacobi et pro tempore existentis Scotorum Regis, ex priuilegio apostolico cui hactenus derogatum non est, existit, et ad eius meram collacionem ex simili priuilegio apostolico pertinet, cciam in decanatum eiusdem erigende ecclesie qui Nota. inibi dignitas eciam principalis existeret,—pro vno decano qui aliis eiusdem erigende ecclesie personis preesset cuique cura animarum dicti Jacobi et pro tempore existentis regis et regine Scotorum et eorum officialium et familiarium continuorum conmensalium et eorumdem familiarium familiarum et seruitorum imminerit, quique omnimodam jurisdictionem in omnes personas dicte erigende ecclesie pro tempore existentes haberet, et qui, dum in ecclesia eadem beate Marie in illa prepositus, dum uero in erigenda ecclesia residerit in illa decanus foret, ita ut non due dignitates existant sed vnica dumtaxat in qualibet dictarum ecclesiarum preeminenciam habens existeret; et vnus subdecanus qui in eadem erigenda ecclesia dignitas secunda,—pro vno subdecano qui dicti decani, cum absens uel impeditus fuerit aut alias in ecclesia Beate Marie residerit, in omnibus vices exerceat et suppleat; ac vna sacristia que inibi officium seu administracio existerent,—pro vno sacrista, qui iocalium et ornamentorum dicte erigende ecclesie curam haberet; necnon sedecim canonicatus et totidem prebende,—pro sedecim canonicis in cantu et alias sufficienter instructis; ac sex pueri clerici similiter in cantu competenter instructi seu vt instruerentur apti et ydonei, qui in eadem erigenda ecclesia diuina officia diurna, pariter et nocturna, prout in aliis ecclesiis collegiatis regni Scocie celebrantur seu ad libitum et voluntatem prefati Jacobi et pro tempore existentis regis Scotorum, secundum morem et consuetudinem Romane ecclesie, prout magis prefato Jacobo et pro tempore existenti regi Scotorum placeret, ita quod ad alium morem seu consuetudinem in ipsa erigenda ecclesia nisi prout rex uoluerit in illis celebrandis obseruare non tenerentur, ad Dei laudem et [pro] ipsius Jacobi Regis eiusque antecessorum et successorum animarum salute decantare et celebrare, et alias eidem erigende ecclesie in diuinis iuxta prouidam ipsius Jacobi Regis ordinacionem faciendam, deseruire tenerentur, erigerentur et instruerentur: Et cum in prioratu de Rostnot, ordinis Sancti Augustini, dicte diocesis, duo dumtaxat canonici residere consueuerint, quamuis illius fructus, redditus, et prouentus centum viginti librarum Sterlingorum secundum communem existimacionem valeant annuatim et sufficientes sint ad sustentacionem sex ac eciam plurium canonicorum dicti ordinis; ac in ecclesia

✠ Vide nota de jurisdictione subdecani in absentia episcopi.

nota penes sex pueros.

Nota de prioratu de Rostnot fructus eiusdem valent annuatim 120 lib Stirling.

de Dunbar, eiusdem diocesis, illius canonici pro maiori parte non per se, sed prout in multis aliis collegiatis ecclesiis regni Scocie iuxta consuetudinem hactenus obseruatam fieri consueuerint per substitutos deseruiant ; si, reseruata congrua porcione ex fructibus dicti prioratus pro sex canonicis dicti ordinis, quorum prior dicti prioratus pro tempore existens vnus existeret, residuum fructuum dicti prioratus decanatui et aliis inibi erigendis, subdecanatui et sacristie ac canonicatibus et prebendis, pro decano, subdecano, sacrista, canonicis, et aliis personis dicte erigende ecclesie pro tempore existentibus, iuxta huiusmodo prouidam ordinacionem prefati Jacobi Regis perpetuo applicarentur ac canonicatus et prebende dicte ecclesie de Dunbar, qui de iure patronatus ipsius regis existunt, ac alia beneficia ecclesiastica cum cura et sine cura in ciuitate uel dicta diocesi Sanctiandree seu alias vbilibet consistencia et de iure patronatus ipsius regis seu aliorum laicorum existencia, quorum fructus, redditus, et prouentus ad valorem duarum millium librarum monete Scocie, quingintas libras sterlingorum, uel circa constituencium, dumtaxat ascenderint annuatim, de quibus eidem Jacobo Regi videbitur, de ipsius Jacobi Regis et aliorum laicorum patronorum respectiue consensu, dicte erigende ecclesie, reseruata ex fructibus curatorum beneficiorum pro vicariis perpetuis eorumdem beneficiorum curatorum congrua porcione, ex qua ipsi vicarii se comode sustentari, jura episcopalia persoluere, et alia onera sibi racione curatorum beneficiorum huiusmodi incumbencia supportare, possint, perpetuo vnirentur, annecterentur, et incorporarentur, ita quod eciam congrua porcio presbytris ydoneis ad hoc deputandis, qui canonicatibus et prebendis et aliis vniendis sine cura beneficiis in diuinis officiis deseruirent, per eos ex canonicatuum et prebendarum ac sine cura vniendorum beneficiorum huiusmodi fructibus, quamdiu illis deseruierint, percipienda, assignaretur, et residuum fructuum vniendorum beneficiorum huiusmodi, deductis porcionibus predictis, inter decanum, subdecanum, sacristam, et canonicos predictos, ac alias personas dicte erigende ecclesie, iuxta prouidam ordinacionem ipsius Jacobi Regis desuper faciendam, distribuerentur: PROFECTO ex hoc, non solum in ipsa capella postquam in collegiatam ecclesiam ac in ea digni-

tates ac canonicatus et prebende ac alia officia huiusmodi erecta
seu instituta et pueri huiusmodi instituti fuerint, sed eciam in
de Dunbar et aliis ecclesiis et beneficiis vniendis ac prioratu
huiusmodi, diuinus cultus augmentum susciperet et eciam ad
decorem dicte capelle cederet : Et ipse Jacobus Rex, vltra bona
predicta per eum dicte capelle assignata, alia bona patrimonialia
valoris annui quingintarum librarum, uel circa, monete Scocie,
huiusmodi pro premissis assignaret : Quare pro parte dicti
Jacobi Regis nobis fuit humiliter supplicatum vt eandem capellam sub eadem inuocacione in collegiatam ecclesiam, cum communi archa, sigillo, capitulo, et aliis collegialibus insigniis, et in
ea dictam preposituram eciam in decanatum qui inibi eciam
dignitas principalis, ut prefertur, existat, pro moderno et pro Nota.
tempore existente preposito dicte ecclesie Beate Marie, qui eciam
decanus in dicta erigenda ecclesia sit, et aliis eiusdem erigende
ecclesie presit, cuique cura animarum dicti Jacobi et pro tempore
existentis regis et regine Scotorum et aliorum predictorum
immineat, quique omnimodam iurisdictionem et preeminenciam
predictas habeat ; et vnum subdiaconum, qui in eadem erigenda
ecclesia dignitas secunda, pro vno subdecano qui vices dicti
decani ut prefertur suppleat ; ac vnam sacristiam, que inibi officium seu administracio existant, pro vno sacrista qui dictorum
iocalium et ornamentorum dicte ecclesie curam habeat ; necnon
sedecim canonicatus et totidem prebendas, pro sexdecim canonicis in cantu et alias sufficienter instructis ; ac sex pueros clericos
similiter in cantu competenter instructos, seu ut instruantur aptos
et ydoneos, qui in eadem erigenda ecclesia diuina officia diurna,
pariter et nocturna, prout in ecclesiis collegiatis dicti Regni
Scocie celebrantur seu ad libitum et voluntatem prefati Jacobi et
pro tempore existentis Regis Scotorum, secundum morem et consuetudinem Romane ecclesie huiusmodi, prout magis prefato
Jacobo et pro tempore existenti Regi Scotorum placuerit, ad Dei
laudem et pro ipsius Jacobi Regis eiusque antecessorum et successorum animarum salute decantare et celebrare, et alias eidem
erigende ecclesie in diuinis iuxta huiusmodi prouidam ipsius
Jacobi Regis ordinacionem faciendum deseruire teneantur, erigere et instituere, ac eidem ecclesie dicta beneficia vnire, an-

necterc, et incorporare, aliasque in permissis oportune prouidere de benignitate apostolica, diguaremur: Nos IGITUR, qui dudum inter alia volumus quod semper in vnionibus commissio fieret ad partes, uocatis quorum interesset, quique ecclesiarum omnium decorem et uenustatem ac in illis diuini cultus augmentum nostris potissime temporibus supremis desideramus affectibus, fructuum, reddituum, et prouentuum dictorum beneficiorum per dictum Jacobum Regem assignatorum verum ualorem annuum presentibus pro expresso haberi volentes, piumque et laudabile ipsius Jacobi Regis in hoc propositum plurimum in Domino commendantes, ac alias de premissis certam noticiam non habentes,

Nota. huiusmodi supplicacionibus inclinati, etc., MANDAMUS quatenus vos, uel duo, aut vnus uestrum, si est ita, eandem capellam, postquam prefatus Jacobus Rex alia bona valoris annui quingintarum librarum monete Scocie huiusmodi, uel circa, realiter et cum effectu pro premissis assignauerit, sub eadem inuocacione in collegiatam ecclesiam cum communi archa, sigillo, capitulo et aliis collegialibus insigniis, et in ea dictam preposituram in decanatum qui inibi eciam dignitas principalis existat, pro moderno et pro tempore existente preposito dicte ecclesie beate Marie, qui eciam decanus in dicta erigenda ecclesia existat ac aliis [personis] eiusdem erigende ecclesie presit, cuique cura animarum dicti Jacobi et pro tempore existentis regis et regine Scotorum et eius officialium et familiarium continuorum conmensalium et eorumdem famuliarium famuliarium et seruitorum et pro tempore existencium immineat, quique omnimodam iurisdictionem in omnes personas dicte erigende ecclesie pro tempore existentes habeat, et qui, dum in ecclesia beate Marie resederit seu fuerit in illa prepositus, dum vero in erigenda ecclesia in illa decanus existat, ita ut non sint due dignitates sed vnica dumtaxat in qualibet dictarum ecclesiarum preeminenciam habens existat;

Vide et vnum subdecanatum qui in eadem erigenda ecclesia dignitas secunda, pro vno subdecano qui vices dicti decani, cum absens uel impeditus fuerit aut alias in ecclesia Beate Marie residerit, in omnibus exerceat et suppleat; ac vnam sacristiam que inibi officium seu administracio existant, pro vno sacrista qui iocalium et aliorum ornamentorum dicte ecclesie erigende curam habeat;

necnon sexdecim canonicatus et totidem prebendas, pro sedecim
canonicis in cantu peritis et alias sufficienter instructis; ac sex
pueros clericos similiter in cantu competenter instructos seu ut
instruantur aptos et ydoneos, qui in eadem erigenda ecclesia
diuina officia diurna, pariter et nocturna, prout in aliis ecclesiis
collegiatis predicti regni Scocie celebrantur, seu ad libitum et
voluntatem prefati Jacobi et pro tempore existentis regis
Scotorum, secundum morem et consuetudinem Romane ecclesie
huiusmodi, prout magis prefato Jacobo et pro tempore existenti
regi Scotorum placuerit, ita quod ad alium morem seu consuetudinem in ipsa ecclesia erigenda, nisi prout rex voluerit, in illis
celebrandis obseruare non teneantur, ad Dei laudem et eciam
pro ipsius Jacobi Regis eiusque antecessorum et successorum animarum salute decantare et celebrare, et alias eidem erigende
ecclesie in diuinis iuxta prouidam ipsius Jacobi Regis ordinacionem faciendam, deseruire teneantur, erigere et instituere:
Necnon predicta iam per ipsum regem assignata et in posterum
assignanda bona, mobilia et immobilia, pro ipsius capelle in collegiatam erigende ecclesie, ac decanatus, subdecanatus, sacristie, canonicatuum, et prebendarum, ac clericorum predictorum
dote, et eorumdem decani, subdecani, sacriste, ac canonicorum, et puerorum, et aliorum eiusdem ecclesie personarum
sustentacione; ac, reseruata congrua porcione pro sex canonicis
dicti ordinis qui in eodem prioratu in diuinis deseruire
et vacare habeant, et ex quibus dicti prioratus prior pro
tempore existens vnus existat, ex bonis et fructibus dicti prioratus, residuum quod dein ex bonis et fructibus dicti prioratus
superfuerit, decanatui, subdeca[na]tui, sacristie, ac canonicatibus,
et prebendis predictis, pro decani, subdecani, sacriste, ac canonicorum predictorum, et aliarum personarum dicte ecclesie sustentacione, iuxta huiusmodi dicti Jacobi Regis ordinacionem, perpetuo applicare assignare et appropriare; ac dicte ecclesie
erigende, postquam erecta fuerit, dicte de Dunbar et aliarum *fructus ac*
collegiatarum ecclesiarum dicte seu aliarum diocesium, canoni- *redditus capellæ*
catus, et prebendas, ac perrochiales ecclesias, et alia beneficia *valent an-*
ecclesiastica cum cura vel sine cura, iurispatronatus ipsius regis *nuatim duo millia*
seu aliorum laicorum, quorum fructus redditus et prouentus *librarum monetæ Scotiæ.*

duo millia librarum monete predicte Scocie dumtaxat secundum communem extimacionem valeant annuatim, si ad hoc prefati regis et aliorum laicorum de quorum iure patronatus beneficia vnienda huiusmodi fuerint respectiue expressus accesserit assensus, perpetuo vnire, annectere, et incorporare; ac qualiter fructus canonicatuum et prebendarum ac aliorum beneficiorum vnitorum huiusmodi ac aliorum bonorum per dictum regem assignatorum seu assignandorum inter singulas personas dicte erigende ecclesie distribui debeant, de ipsius Jacobi Regis consensu statuere et ordinare; ac ex fructibus curatorum beneficiorum huiusmodi vniendorum congruam porcionem pro vicariis perpetuis, ex qua ipsi vicarij se commode sustentare et iura episcopalia persoluere ac alia onera sibi racione vicariarum perpetuarum huiusmodi incumbencia supportare possint, reseruare; ac eciam porciones pro presbiteris ydoneis qui in de Dunbar ac aliis collegiatis ecclesiis, quorum canonicatus et prebende, ac aliis ecclesiis siue beneficiis sine cura que dicte erigende ecclesie vnientur, in diuinis deseruiant et alia illis incumbencia onera supportent, quique huiusmodi porcionem, quamdiu canonicatibus et prebendis ac sine cura beneficiis vnitis huiusmodi de seruierint, percipiant, alioquin illorum loco alij substituantur, assignare; ac singula que pro felici statu et directione ecclesie predicte erigende, et personarum in ea diuinis officiis huiusmodi insistencium, salubria et vtilia esse cognoueritis ac alias licita et honesta et sacris canonibus non contraria, statuere et ordinare; ac ius patronatus et presentandi personas ydoneas predicto decano et pro tempore existenti ad subdecanatum, sacristiam, ac canonicatus, et prebendas erigendos predictos, tam hac prima vice quam quociens vacabunt, prefato Jacobo et pro tempore existenti regi Scotorum, et illorum institucionem eidem decano, jus vero instituendi et destituendi dictos sex pueros, tam hac prima vice quam quociens placuerit, similiter eidem Jacobo et pro tempore existenti regi Scotorum, perpetuo reseruare et concedere auctoritate nostra curetis. Nos enim, si erectionem huiusmodi et alia premissa per vos aut aliquem ex vobis vigore presencium fieri contigerit, vt prefertur, dictam erigendam ecclesiam, priusquam in collegiatam erecta fuerit, et illius decanum, subdecanum,

sacristam, canonicos, capitulum, clericos pueros, et singulares exempcio
personas eiusdem, cum omnibus bonis predictis, assignatis et personarum in
assignandis, et que ad dictam erigendam ecclesiam et illius per- ecclesia
sonas in posterum quomodolibet pertinebunt, ab omni visitacione, residencollegiata
correctione, jurisdictione, superioritate, dominio, et potestate tium ab
moderni et pro tempore existentis archiepiscopi Sanctiandree iurisdic-omni alia
aliorumque ordinariorum quorumcunque eiusque officialium et tione nisi
vicariorum similiter pro tempore existencium, penitus et omnino papœ.decani et
perpetuo auctoritate apostolica tenore presencium eximimus
totaliter et liberamus; ac ecclesiam, subdecanum, sacristam,
canonicos, capitulum, clericos seu pueros, et alias personas
eiusdem ecclesie pro tempore existentes, visitacioni, correctioni,
et superioritati ac omnimode jurisdictioni dicti decani pro tempore existentis, decanum vero predictum sedi apostolice et illius
ac beati Petri apostoli protectioni immediate subicimus; ita ut
archiepiscopus, ordinarij, officiales, et vicarii predicti, eciam
racione delicti aut contractus seu rei de qua agetur, vbicumque
committatur delictum, iniatur contractus, aut res ipsa consistat,
nullam iurisdictionem, superioritatem, potestatem, aut dominium
in ecclesiam, decanum, subdecanum, sacristam, canonicos, capitulum, pueros, et personas predictas, aut eorum bona predicta
assignata et assignanda et ad ipsam ecclesiam eciam racione
vnitorum beneficiorum quomodolibet pertinencia, exercere possint; sed teneantur decanus coram nobis vel sede predicta aut
legatis uel subdelegatis eius, subdecanus uero, sacrista, et
canonici, ac pueri predicti, et alie eiusdem erigende ecclesie pro
tempore existentes persone, de se conquerentibus coram dicto
decano vel eius locum tenente in iusticia respondere; aut quos- decretum
cunque processus quos in contrarium haberi, ac eciam sentencias irritans.
quas proferri, necnon quicquid in contrarium attemptari contigerit, irrita et inania nulliusque roboris vel momenti existere
decernimus: Ac eidem erigende ecclesie, et illius decano, sub- nota bene.
decano, sacriste, capitulo, canonicis, pueris, et personis predictis
pro tempore existentibus, quod omnibus et singulis priuilegiis,
immunitatibus exempcionibus, fauoribus, graciis, et indultis
aliis collegiatis ecclesiis regni Scocie huiusmodi quomodolibet
concessis, et quibus ille et illarum persone eciam dignitates ac

canonicatus et prebendas in eis obtinentes de jure vel consuetudine vtuntur, potiuntur, et gaudent, seu vti, potiri, et gaudere poterunt quomodolibet in futurum, vti, potiri, et gaudere possint, eadem auctoritate apostolica eciam presencium tenore indulgemus: Ac dicto decano pro tempore existenti, absoluendi regem et reginam Scotorum pro tempore existentes eorumque liberos, in casibus sedi predicte reseruatis, preterquam offense ecclesiastice libertatis criminum, heresis et rebellionis aut conspiracionis in personam vel statum Romani pontificis seu sedem predictam, falsitatis litterarum apostolicarum, supplicacionum et commissionum, inuasionis, depredacionis, occupacionis, aut deuastacionis terrarum et maris Romane ecclesie mediate vel immediate subiectorum, offense personalis in episcopum vel alium prelatum, prohibicionis deuolucionis causarum ad Romanam curiam, delacionis armorum, et aliorum prohibitorum ad partes infidelium, semel dumtaxat in uita; in aliis uero quociens fuerit oportunum, confessione eorum diligenter audita pro commissis, absoluendi, et iniungendi eis penitenciam salutarem, ac omnium peccatorum suorum, de quibus corde contriti et ore confessi fuerint, eciam semel in vita et in mortis articulo, quociens mortis articulus huiusmodi euenerit, plenam remissionem eis in sinceritate fidei, vnitate dicte Romane ecclesie ac obediencia et deuocione nostra et successorum nostrorum Romanorum pontificum canonice intrancium persistentibus, auctoritate apostolica concedendi, eadem auctoritate apostolica tenore presencium facultatem concedimus; Sic tamen quod idem confessor de hiis de quibus fuerit alteri satisfactio impendenda, dictus decanus eam illis per eos superuixerit vel per alios, si forte tunc transierint, faciendam iniungat, qua rex et regina ac filii predicti uel illi facere teneantur; et ut, quod absit, propter huiusmodi graciam vel concessionem rex et regina ac eorum filij predicti reddantur procliuiores ad illicita in posterum committenda, volumus quod si a sinceritate fidei, vnitate Romane ecclesie, ac obediencia et deuocione nostra et successorum nostrorum predictorum canonice intrancium destiterint, aut ex confidencia concessionis uel remissionis predictarum, aliqua forsan commiserint, concessio et remissio ac quo ad illas presentes littere huiusmodi eis nullatenus suffragentur, non obstantibus felicis recordacionis Innocencij pape quarti predecessoris nostri circa exemptos edita que incipit—Volentes,—ac aliis apostolicis necnon in prouincialibus et synodalibus conciliis editis, generalibus uel specialibus constitucionibus et ordinacionibus, ac de Dumbar et aliarum ecclesiarum predictarum necnon monasterij seu regularis loci a quo dictus prioratus forsan dependet, et ipsius ordinis iuramento, confirmacione apostolica, uel quauis firmitate alia roboratis statutis et consuetudinibus ceterisque contrariis quibuscumque: Prouiso quod canonicatus et prebende ac alia beneficia cum cura et sine cura vigore presencium vnienda, ut prefertur, debitis propterea non fraudentur obsequijs et animarum cura in beneficiis curatis huiusmodi nullatenus necligatur, sed illorum ac canonicatuum et prebendarum ac aliorum vniendorum sine cura beneficiorum huiusmodi congrue support- *Decretum* entur onera consueta. Nos enim ex nunc irritum decernimus et *irritans.* inane, si secus super hiis a quoquam quauis auctoritate scienter vel ignoranter contigerit attemptari. Datum Rome apud Sanctum Petrum, anno Incarnacionis Dominice millesimo quingentesimo primo, sexto nonas Maij, pontificatus nostri anno nono.

POST QUARUM quidem litterarum apostolicarum presentacionem et recepcionem nobis et per nos, ut premittitur, factas, productis premitus coram nobis per prefatum illustrissimum dominum Jacobum Regem, ad informandum animum nostrum de et super contentis et narratis in preinsertis litteris apostolicis, nonnullis testibus fidedignis, ipsisque rite et legittime per nos receptis et ad iurandum admissis juratisque et diligenter examinatis, de et *bona immobilia* super omnibus et singulis in eisdem literis contentis nos infor- *valoris* mauimus: Consequenter vero prefatus illustrissimus dominus *quingentarum* Jacobus Rex, vltra bona Capelle Regie nuncupate Beate Marie *Librarum Scotiæ per* et Sancti Michaelis intra palacium ipsius illustrissimi domini *regem* Jacobi Regis, opidi de Striueling, Sanctiandree diocesis, per eum, *Capellæ Sanctæ* vt in dictis litteris assignata continetur, nonnulla bona patri- *Mariæ assignata* monialia valoris annui quingentarum librarum uel circa monete *eaque ex* Scocie, pro erectione et aliis in eisdem litteris contentis, videlicet, *ipsius patrimonio.* de firmis et fructibus terrarum de Castellaw nonaginta tres libras *Castellaw.* sex solidos et octo denarios, in vicecomitatu de Edinburgh; de *Streichbraun de* Streichbrawne, de Glenche, de Auchtnabaid, nonaginta quatuor *glenche.* libras tresdecim solidos et quatuor denarios, in vicecomitatu de *Kyntair Lochaber.*

Perth; de Kynteir et de Lochabbir trescentas duodecim libras, in vicecomitatibus de Tervert, et de Elgyn et Fores iacencium, realiter et cum effectu assignauit. Subsequenter fuimus per prefatum illustrissimum dominum Jacobum Regem debita cum instancia requisiti quatenus ad execucionem dictarum litterarum apostolicarum et contentorum in eisdem procedere dignaremur, iuxta traditam seu directam per eas a sede apostolica nobis for-

execucio judicum.

mam. NOS IGITUR, Jacobus abbas dicti monasterij de Scona et Dauid archidiaconus, iudices et executores prefati, attendentes requisitionem huiusmodi fore iustam et racioni consonam, volentesque mandatum apostolicum supradictum nobis in hac parte directum reuerenter exequi, vt tenemur, et quia per informacionem legittimam et diligenter a dictis testibus per nos, ut premittitur, factam et receptam examinationem, omnia et singula in dictis litteris narrata et expressa veritate fulciri

ERECTIO.

inuenimus; idcirco, auctoritate apostolica nobis commissa et qua fungimur in hac parte, eandem capellam in collegiatam ecclesiam, cum communi archa, sigillo, capitulo, et aliis collegialibus insignijs; et in ea preposituram ecclesie Beate Marie de Rupe Sanctiandree in preinsertis litteris apostolicis mentionatam, que inibi dignitas principalis existit, in decanatum qui eciam in ipsa per nos eadem auctoritate apostolica erecta ecclesia dignitas principalis existat, pro moderno et pro tempore existente preposito dicte ecclesie beate Marie, qui eciam decanus in dicta erecta ecclesia existat, ac aliis eiusdem ecclesie erecte presit, cuique cura animarum dicti illustrissimi domini Jacobi et pro tempore existentis regis et regine Scotorum et eorum officialium, familiarium, continuorum commensalium, et eorumdem familiarium familiarium et seruitorum existencium habeat, et qui, dum in ecclesia beate Marie fuerit in illa prepositus, dum vero in erecta ecclesia huiusmodi fuerit, in illa decanus existat, ita ut non due dignitates sed vnica dumtaxat in qualibet dictarum eccles-

✠ *nota de Jurisdictione subdecani in absentia decani.*

iarum preeminenciam habens existat; et vnum subdecanatum, qui in eadem erecta ecclesia dignitas secunda, pro vno subdecano, qui vices dicti decani, cum absens vel impeditus fuerit aut alias in ecclesia Beate Marie resederit, in omnibus exerceat et suppleat; ac vnam sacristiam, que in dicta ecclesia erecta officium seu administracio existunt, pro vno sacrista qui iocalium et ornamentorum dicte ecclesie curam habeat; necnon sexdecim canonicatus et totidem prebendas, pro sexdecim canonicis in cantu peritis et alias sufficienter instructis; ac sex pueros clericos similiter in cantu competenter instructos seu ut instruantur aptos et ydoneos, qui in eadem ecclesia erecta diuina officia diurna, pariter et nocturna, prout in alijs ecclesiis collegiatis regni Scocie celebrantur seu ad libitum et uoluntatem prefati illustrissimi domini Jacobi et pro tempore existentis regis Scotorum, secundum morem et consuetudinem Romane ecclesie prout magis prefato illustrissimo domino Jacobo et pro tempore existenti regi Scotorum placuerit, ita quod ad alium morem seu consuetudinem in ipsa erecta ecclesia, nisi prout dictus illustrissimus dominus Jacobus Rex voluerit in illis celebrandis, obseruare non teneantur, ad Dei laudem et eciam pro ipsius illustrissimi domini Jacobi Regis eiusque antecessorum et successorum animarum salute decantare et celebrare, et alias eidem erecte ecclesie in diuinis iuxta prouidam ipsius illustrissimi domini Jacobi Regis ordinacionem faciendum deseruire teneantur, EREXIMUS ET INSTITUIMUS. Necnon predicta, tam per ipsum illustrissimum dominum Jacobum Regem dudum, quam nunc, coram nobis, ut premittitur, assignata bona, mobilia et immobilia, pro ipsius capelle in collegiatam erecte, ac decanatus, subdecanatus, sacristie, canonicatuum, et prebendarum, ac clericorum predictorum dote, et eorumdem decani, subdecani, sacriste, et canonicorum, ac puerorum, et aliarum eiusdem ecclesie personarum sustentacione; ac nonnulla bona et fructus, videlicet, in terris, domibus, ortis, pratis, annuis redditibus, oblacionibus, decimis, aliisque obuencionibus, ad valorem quadringentarum marcarum prefate monete Scocie, pro sex canonicis ordinis Sancti Augustini qui prioratui de Rostinot, ordinis et diocesis predictorum, in diuinis deseruire et vacare habeant, et ex quibus dicti prioratus prior pro tempore existens vnus existat, ex bonis et fructibus dicti prioratus pro congrua porcione reseruauimus; reseruataque huiusmodi congrua porcione, residuum uero quod ex bonis et fructibus dicti prioratus superfuit ac superest decanatui, subdecanatui, sacristie, ac canonicatibus, et prebendis predictis, pro decani, subdecani, sacriste, et canonicorum predictorum ac aliarum personarum dicte ecclesie sustentacione, iuxta infrascriptam

Rostinot. redditus prioratus deRostinot residuus deducendo 400 marcas ecclesiæ Stirlin ordinatur.

prouidam dicti illustrissimi domini Jacobi Regis ordinacionem, perpetuo APPLICAUIMUS, ASSIGNAUIMUS, ET APPROPRIAUIMUS; ac infrascriptos canonicatus et prebendas de Spot, de Beltone, de Dunse, de Pyncartone, infra ecclesiam collegiatam de Dunbar, vnacum archipresbiteratu et rectoria eiusdem ecclesie de Dunbar, Sanctiandree diocesis, de Ayr cum sua capella, de Dampnellytone, infra ecclesiam Glasgwensem, de Crieff infra ecclesiam Dunkelddensem, de Kyncardyne cum suis capellis annexis infra ecclesiam Abordenensem, de Pettebrawchle et de Duthell infra ecclesias Morauienses, insuper ecclesias perochiales de Kyrkandris, de Balmaclellane, de Kellis, Candedicase diocesis, de Forrest, de Glenquhoome, de Sutheke, Glasguensis diocesis, de Butt, Sodorensis diocesis, de Ellam et Cranschawis, dicte Sanctiandree diocesis,— quiquidem Canonicatus et prebende ac perochiales ecclesie antedicte de jure patronatus dicti illustrissimi domini Jacobi Regis existunt, et illorum canonicatuum et prebendarum ac ipsarum ecclesiarum perochialium fructus ad summam duarum millium librarum monete predicte Scocie non ascendunt, de ipsius illustrissimi domini Jacobi Regis ibidem presentis et id fieri petentis expresso consensu et assensu, seruatis tamen premitus legittime iuris ordine, modo, et forma, ac singulis aliis in premissis necessariis et requisitis seruandis, perpetuo VNIUIMUS, ANNEXIMUS, ET INCORPORAUIMUS. Statuimus insuper et ordinauimus, de ipsius illustrissimi domini Jacobi Regis ibidem, ut premittitur, presentis et id fieri petentis expresso consensu et assensu, fructus canonicatuum et prebendarum ac aliorum beneficiorum vnitorum et bonorum per dictum illustrissimum dominum Jacobum Regem assignatorum huiusmodi, inter singulas personas dicte erecte ecclesie in hunc qui sequitur modum distribui debere et distribuimus: decano, videlicet, quingentas marcas, fructus tamen et eorumdem valores dicte prepositure ecclesie collegiate Beate Marie de Rupe in Sanctoandrea in huiusmodi summa includendo; subdecano ducentas quadraginta marcas; sacriste ducentas quadragenta marcas; vni canonico de dictis sexdecim canonicis quem prefatus illustrissimus dominus Jacobus Rex assumere uoluerit, centum libras; ac septem canonicis de dicto numero canonicorum vnicuique illorum centum marcas; reliquis vero octo canonicis singulis

eorumdem viginti libras, vnacum distribucionibus quotidianis ex quibus
competentibus; sex autem pueris octogenta decem marcas ecclesiis sumenda.
dicte monete; ac ex fructibus curatorum beneficiorum predic- de pueris.
torum ut prefertur per nos vnitorum congruam porcionem, de
ecclesiis de Kyrkandris viginti quatuor marcas, de Balmak-
lellane vigenti quatuor, de Kellis viginti quator, de Glen-
quhome vigenti quatuor, de Suthleke vigenti quatuor, de Butt
viginti quatuor, de Forest vigenti sex, de Cranschawis viginti, de
Ellam viginti, et vnicuique de quatuor capellis de Kynkardyn
quindecim marcas in pecunia numerata dicte monete Scocie,
dictarum diocesium, vnacum competenti mansione ad quamlibet vide bene.
ecclesiam perochialem de predictis, pro vicariis perpetuis, ex
qua ipsi vicarij se commode sustentare et iura episcopalia persoluere ac alia onera sibi racione vicariarum perpetuarum huiusmodi incumbencia supportare possint, reseruamus; insuper et
porcionem de prouentibus canonicatuum et prebendarum, de
Pyncartone vigenti, de Spot vigenti, de Beltone vigenti, de Dunse
vigenti, de Rectoria dicte ecclesie collegiate de Dunbar vigenti, et
de illius archipresbiteratu vigenti quatuor, dicte Sanctiandree diocesis, infra huiusmodi ecclesiam collegiatam de Dumbar, de Creiff
infra Dunkeldensem decem marcas, preterea de Ayr infra Glasguensem, de Kyncardyne infra Abberdonensem, de Pettebrawchly et
de Duthel infra Morauiensem ecclesias, tantam et talem quantam
presbiteri seu alij clerici remouibiles qui seruierunt in huiusmodi
quatuor canonicatibus et prebendis iam immediate predictis percipere consueuerunt seu de presenti percipiunt, insuper et vnicuique
illorum quatuor vnam marcam sepefate monete pro presbiteris
seu alijs ydoneis seruientibus clericis qui in ecclesiis siue beneficiis sine cura predictis sic, vt premittitur, vnitis, in diuinis
deseruiant, et alia illis incumbencia onera supportent, quique
huiusmodi porcionem, quam diu canonicatibus et prebendis ac
sine cura beneficiis vnitis huiusmodi deseruierint, percipiant,
alioquin aliis illorum loco substituendis, assignamus. Volumus
eciam et ordinamus quod decanus, subdecanus, canonici, et ceteri vide bene.
ministrantes in dicta erecta ecclesia, choros aliaque ornamenta
summis altaribus pertinencia et rectoribus dictarum ecclesiarum
vnitarum de consuetudine incumbencia episcopalibus tamen
iuribus demptis, suis sumptibus et expensis sustentent con-

gruenter et reforment. Ac dicto illustrissimo domino Jacobo Regi, pro felici statu et directione dicte erecte ecclesie et personarum in ea diuinis officiis insistencium, salubria vtilia et honesta ac sacris canonibus non contraria edendi statuta quantum sue regie maiestati placuerit, auctoritate apostolica facultatem impertimur; ac ius patronatus et presentandi personas ydoneas predicto decano et pro tempore existenti ad subdecanatum, sacristiam, ac canonicatus, et prebendas erectos predictos, tam de pueris. hac prima vice quam quociens vacabunt prefato illustrissimo domino Jacobo et pro tempore existenti Scotorum regi, et illorum institucionem, eidem decano jus vero instituendi et distituendi dictos sex pueros, tam hac prima vice quam quociens placuerit, similiter eidem illustrissimo domino Jacobo et pro tempore existenti regi Scotorum perpetuo reseruamus et concessimus, prout erigimus, et instituimus, applicamus, assignamus, appropriamus, vnimus, annectimus, incorporamus, statuimus, ordinamus, reseruamus, et concedimus, per presentes; Nota bene. oblaciones uero et alias obuenciones in dicta erecta ecclesia racione cure animarum prouenientes, decano eiusdem ecclesie si inibi residenciam personalem fecerit et huiusmodi curam animarum regis, regine, et suorum officialium et familiarium exercuerit, alioquin, eo absente et residenciam personalem ibi minime faciente, subdecano eiusdem collegij erecti qui decani vices supplere habeat, de supremi domini nostri Regis predicti consensu et assensu, pro perpetuo pertinere decernimus.—QUE OMNIA et singula necnon litteras apostolicas huiusmodi, et hunc nostrum processum, ac omnia et singula in eis contenta, vobis omnibus et singulis supradictis, communiter uel diuisim, quibus presens noster processus dirigitur, intimamus, insinuamus, et notificamus, ac ad vestram et cuiuslibet uestrum noticiam deducimus et deduci volumus, presencium per tenorem. In quorum omnium et singulorum fidem et testimonium premissorum, presentes litteras siue presens publicum instrumentum processum nostrum huiusmodi in se continentes siue continens, exinde fieri et per notarios publicos infrascriptos subscribi et publicari mandauimus nostrorumque sigillorum iussimus et fecimus appensionem communiri; et in signum consensus et assensus dicti serenissimi domini nostri regis, ad perpetue firmitatis corroboracionem omnium et singulorum premissorum, suum magnum sigillum presentibus est appensum. Acta fuerunt hec quoad presentacionem dictarum litterarum apostolicarum per prefatum dominum nostrum regem iudicibus prescriptis, apud palacium suum de Falklande, primo die mensis Septembris, hora decima, aut eo circa, ante meridiem ; quo vero ad alia premissa per prefatos iudices dicta, erecta, et publicata, apud castrum de Streuyling sexto die mensis antedicti hora vndecima ante meridiem, anno Incarnacionis Dominice millesimo quingentesimo primo, indictione quarta, pontificatus sanctissimi in Christo patris et domini domini Alexandri diuina prouidencia Pape sexti anno decimo, presentibus ibidem venerabilibus in Christo patribus Andrea abbate monasterij de Lundoris, Andrea priore de Mayo ac prothonotario apostolico, nobili et potenti domino Alexandro domino Hvme magno camerario Scocie, honorabilibus viris Archbaldo Edmonstone de Duntreith, Johanne Ramsay, militibus, venerandis viris magistris Johanne Hepburne preposito de Lynclowdane, Willelmo Bailzhe rectore de Kerretone, Thoma Halkarstone preposito de Creichtoune, Roberto Schaw, clericis, Necnon prouidis viris Roberto Coluile de Hyltoune, Petro Creichtoune, Dauid Betone, Willelmo Sympsone, et Adam Reid, laicis, testibus ad premissa successiue rogatis, pariter et requisitis.

JAMES R.

Et ego Henricus Alani, archidiaconus Dunblanensis, publicus auctoritatibus imperiali et regia notarius, quia predictarum litterarum apostolicarum presentacioni, recepcioni, processus huiusmodi decreti interpositioni, erectionis publicacioni, ceterisque premissis successiue gestis et narratis, dum, vt premittitur, dicerentur et fierent, vnacum notario publico subscripto et testibus prenominatis, presens interfui, eaque sic dici et fieri vidi, sciui et audiui ac in notam cepi, ex qua presentem processum manu alterius scriptum in duabus membranis, quarum vltima linea prime sic desinit—Immediate subicimus,—et prima secunde sic incipit—Ita ut archiepiscopus,—filo consutis, meis nomine et subscripcione, vnacum corroboracione sigillorum de quibus superius est facta mentio,

B

Henricus
Alani.

signaui in fidem et testimonium omnium et singulorum
premissorum, requisitus et rogatus.

Et ego Thomas Allani, presbiter Glasguensis diocesis, sacris
apostolica imperiali et regia auctoritatibus notarius publicus, quia predictarum litterarum apostolicarum presentacioni, recepcioni, processus huiusmodi decreti interposicioni, erectionis publicacioni, ceterisque premissis
successiue gestis et narratis, dum, ut premittitur, dicerentur et fierent, vnacum domino notario publico et
testibus suprascriptis, presens interfui, eaque sic dici et
fieri vidi et sciui ac in notam cepi, ex qua presentem
processum alterius manu scriptum in duabus membranis
quarum vltima linea prime sic desinit—Inmediate subicimus,—et prima secunde sic incipit—Ita ut archiepiscopus,—filo consutis, meis nomine et subscripcione
solitis, cum corroboracione sigillorum superius expressorum, signaui in testimonium veritatis premissorum,

Thomas
Allani.

requisitus.

2. CONFIRMACIO ERECCIONIS ECCLESIE COLLEGIATE DE
STRIUELING CUM ERECCIONE CANTORIE.

ALEXANDER episcopus, seruus seruorum Dei, ad perpetuam rei
memoriam. Apostolice nobis desuper meritis licet insufficientibus iniuncte seruitutis officium mentem nostram excitat, et inducit ut ea que eciam de mandato nostro pro statu prospero
ecclesiarum ecclesiasticorumque beneficiorum ac personarum in
illis diuinis laudibus insistencium et eciam ad diuini cultus augmentum et perseueranciam prouide facta dicuntur apostolico
munimine roboremus, vt eo firmius illibata persistant quo magis
nostro fuerint presidio communita, ac alias in hijs eiusdem officii
partes fauorabiliter impendamus prout in domino conspicimus
salubriter expedire : Dudum siquidem pro parte carissimi in
Christo filii nostri Jacobi Scotorum Regis illustris nobis exposito
quod, licet in Capella Regia nuncupata Beate Marie et Sancti
Michaelis intra palacium ipsius Jacobi Regis, opidi de Sterling,

Sanctiandree diocesis, sita, vnus decanus nuncupatus ac quamplures alii cantores et capellani ac clerici missas et alia diuina officia singulis diebus ad libitum prefati Jacobi Regis ammouibiles celebrarent, ipseque Jacobus Rex predictam Capellam suis expensis reformari fecisset, ac libris, calicibus, et aliis ornamentis ecclesiasticis pro diuino cultu in eadem capella necessariis honorifice muniuisset et ornasset, ac eciam nonnulla bona immobilia ad eum legittime pertinencia eidem capelle pro illius dote assignasset : Tamen si dicta capella in collegiatam ecclesiam, et prepositura ecclesie Beate Marie de Rupe Sanctiandree, que inibi dignitas principalis et de jure patronatus prefati Jacobi et pro tempore existentis Scotorum regis, ex priuilegio apostolico cui eatenus derogatum non erat, existebat, et ad eius meram collacionem ex simili priuilegio apostolico pertinebat, eciam in decanatum eiusdem erigende ecclesie qui inibi dignitas eciam principalis existeret,—pro vno decano qui alijs eiusdem erigende ecclesie personis presset cuique cura animarum dicti Jacobi et pro tempore existentis regis et regine Scotorum et eorum officialium et familiarium continuorum conmensalium et eorumdem familiarium familiarum et seruitorum imineret, quique omnimodam iurisdictionem in omnes personas dicte erigende ecclesie pro tempore existentes haberet, et qui, dum in eadem ecclesia beate Marie de Rupe in illa prepositus, dum uero in erigenda ecclesia resideret in illa decanus foret, ita ut non due dignitates existerent sed vnica dumtaxat in qualibet dictarum ecclesiarum preeminenciam habens existeret; et vnus subdecanatus qui in *vide* eadem erigenda ecclesia dignitas secunda,—pro vno subdecano qui dicti decani, cum absens uel impeditus foret aut alias in ecclesia Beate Marie resideret, in omnibus vices exerceret et suppleret; ac vna sacristia que inibi officium seu administracio existerent,—pro vno sacrista qui iocalium et ornamentorum dicte erigende ecclesie curam haberet; necnon sedecim canonicatus et totidem prebende,—pro sedecim canonicis in cantu et De canonialijs sufficienter instructis; ac sex pueri clerici similiter in cantu cis et competenter instructi seu ut instruerentur apti et ydonei, qui in pueris. eadem erigenda ecclesia diuina officia diurna, pariter et nocturna, prout in alijs ecclesiis collegiatis regni Scocie celebrabantur seu ad libitum et uoluntatem prefati Jacobi et pro tempore existentis regis Scotorum, secundum morem et consuetudines Romane ecclesie, prout magis prefato Jacobo et pro tempore existenti regi Scotorum placeret, ita quod ad alium morem seu consuetudinem in ipsa erigenda ecclesia nisi prout Rex uellet in illis celebrandis obseruare non tenerentur, ad Dei laudem et pro ipsius Jacobi Regis eiusque antecessorum et successorum animarum salute decantare et celebrare et alias eidem erigende ecclesie in diuinis

vide iuxta prouidam ipsius Jacobi Regis ordinacionem faciendam deseruire tenerentur, erigerentur et instituerentur: Et cum in prioratu de Rosnot, ordinis Sancti Augustini, dicti diocesis, duo dumtaxat canonici residere consueuissent, quamuis illius fructus, redditus, et prouentus. Centum uiginti libras Stirlingorum secundum communem extimacionem ualerent annuatim et sufficientes essent ad sustentacionem sex ac eciam plurium canonicorum dicti ordinis; ac in ecclesia de Dumbar, eiusdem diocesis, illius canonici pro maiori parte non per se, sed prout in multis alijs collegiatis ecclesijs regni Scocie iuxta consuetudinem eatenus obseruatam fieri consuetum erat per substitutos deseruirent; si, reseruata congrua porcione ex fructibus dicti prioratus pro sex canonicis dicti ordinis, quorum prior dicti prioratus pro tempore existens vnus existeret, residuum fructuum dicti prioratus decanatui et aliis inibi erigendis, subdecanatui et sacristie ac canonicatibus et prebendis, pro decano, subdecano, et sacrista, canonicis, et aliis personis dicte erigende ecclesie pro tempore existentibus, iuxta huiusmodi prouidam ordinacionem prefati Jacobi Regis perpetuo applicarentur, ac canonicatus et prebende dicte ecclesie de Dunbar, qui de iure patronatus ipsius regis existebant, ac alia beneficia ecclesiastica cum cura et sine cura in ciuitate vel dicta diocesi Sanctiandree seu alias vbilibet consistencia et de jure patronatus ipsius regis seu aliorum laicorum existencia, quorum fructus, redditus, et prouentus ad valorem duarum millium librarum monete Scocie, quingentas libras Stirlingorum, uel circa constituencium, dumtaxat ascenderent annuatim, de quibus eidem Jacobo Regi videretur, de ipsius Jacobi regis et aliorum laicorum

Nota. patronorum respectiue consensu, dicte erigende ecclesie, reseruata ex fructibus curatorum beneficiorum pro vicariis perpetuis eorum-

dem beneficiorum curatorum congrua porcione, ex qua ipsi vicarii
se commode sustentare, iura episcopalia persoluere, et alia onera
sibi racione curatorum beneficiorum huiusmodi incumbencia
supportare, possent, perpetuo vnirentur, annecterentur, et incorporarentur, ita quod eciam congrua porcio presbiteris ydoneis ad
hoc deputandis, qui canonicatibus et prebendis et aliis vniendis
sine cura beneficiis in diuinis officiis deseruirent, per eos ex
canonicatuum et prebendarum ac sine cura vniendorum beneficiorum huiusmodi fructibus, quamdiu illis deseruirent, percipienda, assignaretur, et residuum fructuum vniendorum beneficiorum huiusmodi, deductis porcionibus predictis, inter decanum,
subdecanum, sacristam, et canonicos predictos, et alias personas
dicte erigende ecclesie, iuxta prouidam ordinacionem ipsius
Jacobi Regis desuper faciendam, distribuerentur : EX HOC, non
solum in ipsa capella postquam in collegiatam ecclesiam ac in ea
dignitates ac canonicatus et prebende et alia officia huiusmodi
erecta seu instituta et pueri huiusmodi instituti forent, sed eciam
in de Dunbar et aliis ecclesiis et beneficiis vniendis ac prioratu
huiusmodi, diuinus cultus augmentum susciperet et eciam ad
decorem dicte capelle cederet : Et ipse Jacobus Rex, ultra bona
predicta per eum dicte capelle assignata alia bona patrimonialia
valoris annui quingentarum librarum uel circa monete Scocie
huiusmodi pro premissis assignaret ; ac pro parte dicti Jacobi
Regis nobis humiliter supplicato vt in premissis oportune prouidere de benignitate apostolica dignaremur: Nos tunc, de premissis certam noticiam non habentes, eiusdem Jacobi Regis in ea
parte supplicacionibus inclinati, Sancte Crucis et de Scona, dicte
diocesis, monasteriorum abbatibus, ac archidiacono Laudonie, in
ecclesia Sanctiandree, eorum propriis nominibus non expressis,
alijs nostris litteris dedimus in mandatis quatenus ipsi, uel duo,
aut vnus eorum, si erat ita, eandem capellam postquam prefatus
Jacobus Rex, alia bona valoris annui quingentarum librarum
monete Scocie huiusmodi, uel circa, realiter et cum effectu pro
premissis assignasset, sub eadem inuocacione in collegiatam ecclesiam cum communi archa, sigillo, capitulo et alijs collegialibus
insignijs, et in ea dictam prepositaram in decanatum qui inibi
eciam dignitas principalis existeret, pro tunc et pro tempore

existente preposito dicte ecclesie Beate Marie, qui eciam decanus
in dicta erigenda ecclesia existeret, ac alijs personis eiusdem
erigende ecclesie preesset cuique cura animarum dicti Jacobi et
pro tempore existentis regis et regine Scotorum et eorum officialium et familiarium continuorum conmensalium et eorumdem
familiarium familiarium et seruitorum pro tempore existencium
immineret quique omnimodam iurisdictionem in omnes personas
dicte erigende ecclesie pro tempore existentes haberet, et qui
dum in ecclesia beate Marie resideret seu foret in illa prepositus,
dum uero in erigenda ecclesia in illa decanus existeret, ita quod
non essent due dignitates sed vnica dumtaxat in qualibet dic-
vide bene. tarum ecclesiarum preeminenciam habens existeret ; et vnum
subdecanatum qui in eadem erigenda ecclesia dignitas secunda,
pro vno subdecano qui vices dicti decani, cum absens uel impeditus foret aut alias in ecclesia Beate Marie resideret, in omnibus
exerceret et suppleret; ac vnam sacristiam que inibi officium
seu administracio existeret, pro uno sacrista qui iocalium et
aliorum ornamentorum dicte ecclesie erigende curam haberet ;
necnon sedecim canonicatus et totidem prebendas, pro sedecim
canonicis in cantu peritis et alias sufficienter instructis; ac sex
de pueris. pueros clericos similiter in cantu competenter instructos seu ut
instruerentur aptos et ydoneos, qui in eadem erigenda ecclesia
diuina officia diurna, pariter et nocturna, prout in ecclesiis aliis
collegiatis predicti regni Scocie celebrabantur seu ad libitum et
voluntatem prefati Jacobi et pro tempore existentis regis
Scotorum, secundum morem et consuetudinem Romane ecclesie
huiusmodi, prout magis prefato Jacobo et pro tempore existenti
Regi Scotorum placeret, ita quod ad alium morem seu consuetudinem in ipsa erigenda ecclesia, nisi prout Rex uellet, in illis
celebrandis obseruare non tenerentur, ad Dei laudem et eciam
pro ipsius Jacobi Regis eiusque antecessorum et successorum
animarum salute decantare et celebrare, et alias eidem erigende
ecclesie in diuinis iuxta prouidam ipsius Jacobi Regis ordinacionem faciendam, deseruire tenerentur, erigere et instituere :
Necnon predicta per ipsum regem tunc assignata et in posterum
assignanda bona, mobilia et immobilia, pro ipsius capelle in collegiatam erigende ecclesie, ac decanatus, subdecanatus, sacristie,

canonicatuum, et prebendarum, ac clericorum predictorum dote,
et eorumdem decani subdecani, sacriste, ac canonicorum, et puerorum, et aliarum eiusdem erigende ecclesie personarum sustentacione; ac, reseruata congrua porcione pro sex canonicis dicti
ordinis qui in eodem prioratu in diuinis deseruire et uacare
haberent, et ex quibus dicti prioratus prior pro tempore existens
vnus existeret, ex bonis et fructibus dicti prioratus, residuum
quod ex bonis et fructibus dicti prioratus superesset, decanatui,
subdecanatui, sacristie, ac canonicatibus, et prebendis predictis,
pro decani, subdecani, sacriste, ac canonicorum predictorum, et
aliarum personarum dicte ecclesie sustentacione, iuxta huiusmodi dicti Jacobi Regis ordinacionem, perpetuo applicare assignare et appropriare; ac dicte erigende ecclesie, postquam erecta
foret, dicte de Dumbar et aliarum collegiatarum ecclesiarum
dicte seu aliarum diocesium, canonicatus, et prebendas, ac perrochiales ecclesias, et alia beneficia ecclesiastica cum cura et sine
cura, iuris patronatus ipsius regis seu aliorum laicorum, quorum
fructus, redditus, et prouentus duo millia librarum monete Scocie
dumtaxat secundum communem extimacionem ualerent annuatim, si ad hoc prefati Regis et aliorum laicorum de quorum iure
patronatus beneficia unienda huiusmodi forent respectiue expressus accederet assensus, perpetuo unire, annectere, et incorporare;
ac qualiter fructus canonicatuum et prebendarum ac aliorum
beneficiorum unitorum huiusmodi et aliorum bonorum per dictum
regem assignatorum uel assignandorum inter singulas personas
dicte erigende ecclesie distribui deberent, de ipsius Jacobi Regis
consensu statuere et ordinare; ac ex fructibus curatorum beneficiorum huiusmodi uniendorum congruam porcionem pro vicariis
perpetuis, ex qua ipsi vicarii se commode sustentare et iura
episcopalia persoluere ac alia onera sibi racione vicariarum perpetuarum huiusmodi incumbencia supportare possent, reseruare;
ac eciam porcionem pro presbiteris ydoneis qui in de Dunbar et
aliis collegiatis ecclesiis siue beneficiis sine cura, que dicte erigende ecclesie unirentur, in diuiuis deseruirent et alia illis
incumbencia onera supportarent, quique huiusmodi porcionem,
quamdiu canonicatibus et prebendis ac sine cura beneficiis unitis
huiusmodi deseruirent, preciperent, alioquin eorum loco alij

de statutis substituerentur, assignare; ac singula que pro felici statu ac
dicte ca- directione ecclesie predicte erigende, et personarum in ea diuinis
pelle. officiis huiusmodi insistencium, salubria et vtilia esse cognosce-
rent et alias licita et honesta et sacris canonibus non contraria,
statuere et ordinare; ac ius patronatus et presentandi personas
ydoneas predicto decano eciam pro tempore existenti ad subdecanatum, sacristiam, ac canonicatus, et prebendas erigendos
predictos, tam ea prima vice quam quociens vacarent, prefato
Jacobo et pro tempore existenti regi Scotorum, et illorum insti-
tuciones eidem decano, ius vero instituendi et destituendi dictos
sex pueros, tam ea prima vice quam quociens placeret, similiter
eidem Jacobo et pro tempore existenti Regi Scotorum, perpetuo
De cura reseruare et concedere auctoritate nostra curarent. Nos, si
animarum
regis et erectionem huiusmodi et alia premissa per eos aut aliquem ex eis
regine et earumdem litterarum nostrarum uigore fieri contingeret, ut pre-
priuilegiis
eiis con- fertur, dicto decano pro tempore existenti, absoluendi regem et
sessis. reginam Scotorum pro tempore existentes eorumque liberos in
casibus sedi predicte reseruatis, de casibus* non consessis preterquam offense ecclesiastice libertatis criminum, heresis et
rebellionis aut conspiracionis in personam uel statum Romani
pontificis seu sedem predictam, falsitatis litterarum apostolicarum, supplicacionum et commissionum, inuasionis, depredacionis, occupacionis, aut deuastacionis terrarum et maris Romane
ecclesie mediate uel immediate subiectorum, offense personalis in
episcopum uel alium prelatum, prohibicionis deuolucionis causarum ad Romanam curiam, delacionis armorum, et aliorum prohibitorum ad partes infidelium, semel dumtaxat in uita; in aliis uero
quociens foret oportunum, confessione eorum diligenter audita
pro commissis, absoluendi, et iniungendi eis penitenciam salutarem, ac omnium peccatorum suorum, de quibus corde contriti
et ore confessi forent, eciam semel in uita et in mortis articulo,
quociens articulus mortis huiusmodi eueniret, plenam remissionem eis in sinceritate fidei, vnitate dicte Romane ecclesie ac
obediencia et deuocione nostra et successorum nostrorum
Romanorum Pontificum canonice intrantium persistentibus,

* The words "de casibus non consessis" are written on the margin, and in
another hand than that of the text.

auctoritate apostolica concedendi, eadem auctoritate facultatem concessimus. Et DEINDE, sicut exhibita nobis nuper pro parte prefati Jacobi Regis et dilectorum filiorum decani et capituli dicte erecte ecclesie peticio continebat, tunc abbas monasterii de Scona et archidiaconus Laudonie huiusmodi ad execucionem earumdem litterarum, alias illarum forma seruata, procedentes, quia ita esse repericrunt, dictam capellam, postquam prefatus Jacobus Rex de suis bonis patrimonialibus, certa bona immobilia tunc expressa, valoris annui quingentarum librarum monete Scocie, pro dote dicte erigende ecclesie et alias iuxta dictarum litterarum tenorem assignauerat, in collegiatam ecclesiam, ac in ea dictam preposituram in decanatum dignitatem principalem, subdecanatum, sacristiam, et sedecim canonicatus, et totidem prebendas, ac sex pueros clericos, alias iuxta tenorem dictarum litterarum erexerunt et instituerunt ; ac, reseruatis ex fructibus dicti prioratus pro priore et aliis quinque canonicis regularibus dicti ordinis quadringentis marchis monete Scocie huiusmodi, residuum fructuum dicti prioratus dicte ecclesie erecte perpetuo applicarunt et appropriarunt ; ac rectoriam et archipresbiteratum nuncupatos et certos alios tunc expressos canonicatus et prebendas dicte ecclesie de Dunbar, ac de Kyrkandris, et de Balmaclellane, et de Kellis, ac de Glenquhoome, necnon de Swythtyk, et de Butt, ac de Foresta, necnon de Cranschawis, et de Ellam predicte, et Glasguensis ac Candidecase diocesium perrochiales ecclesias, que, ac rectoria et archipresbiteratus nuncupati ac singuli alii canonicatus et prebende predicti, iurispatronatus prefati Regis existebant et quorum omnium insimul fructus, redditus, et prouentus duarum millium librarum monete Scocie secundum communem extimacionem ualorem annuum non excedunt, de ipsius Jacobi consensu, eidem erecte ecclesie pro illius dote et ministris seu personis eius, perpetuo vnierunt, annexerunt, et incorporauerunt, ita quod, cedentibus uel decedentibus rectoriam archpresbiteratum et alios canonicatus et prebendas ac perrochiales ecclesias huiusmodi obtinentibus, liceret eisdem decano et capitulo dicte ecclesie erecte illorum corporalem possessionem propria auctoritate apprehendere et perpetuo retinere, et ex dictis fructibus inclusis in eis fructibus, dicte prepositure

_{peticio regis decani et capituli.}

26 REGISTRUM

Nota.—
Prima institucio cantoris.

distribuciones quotidianæ.
Nota.—De pueris.
De porcionibus puerorum.

Beate Marie de Rupe decano quingentas; et subdecano ducentas et quadraginta marchas; et totidem sacriste; ac vni canonico ex dictis sedecim canonicis quem rex assumere seu nominare uoluerit, ita quod cantor dicte ecclesie collegiate erecte existat, centum libras dicte monete; ac singulis ex septem centum marchas; reliquis uero singulis octo canonicis viginti libras vnacum distribucionibus quottidianis; pro omnibus uero sex pueris predictis nonaginta marcas dicte monete; et ex fructibus singularum de Kyrkandris, et de Balmaclellane, ac de Kellis, et de Glenquhoome, necnon de Swythtyk, et de Buytt, viginti quatuor, et de Foresta viginti sex, de Cranschawis viginti, et de Ellam, perrochialium ecclesiarum predictarum pro singulis illarum perpetuis vicariis viginti marchas similes in pecunia numerata, cum mansione seu habitacione competenti ad quamlibet perrochialium ecclesiarum predictarum pertinente pro congrua porcione singulorum illorum vicariorum perpetuorum pro tempore existencium, ac eciam congruam porcionem ecclesie de Dunbar, uidelicet, rectorie, viginti, archipresbiteratui viginti quatuor, de Pyncartone viginti, de Spot viginti, de Beltone viginti, de Dunsque nuncupatis canonicatibus et prebendis viginti marchas similes, ac aliis beneficiis sine cura predictis eciam dicte erecte ecclesie vnitis seu illorum fructibus pro presbiteris ydoneis qui illis, alias iuxta tenorem dictarum litterarum, deseruire haberent, congruas porciones reseruarunt, et assignarunt, et tantum percipere habeant deseruiendo: Ac eciam quod

De oblacionibus.
Nota bene.

oblaciones in dicta erecta ecclesia racione cure animarum prouenientes, decano eiusdem ecclesie cum inibi residenciam fecerit, alioquin, eo absente, subdecano pro tempore existenti pertineant,

De statutis.

de prefati regis consensu ordinarunt: Ac eidem Jacobo et pro tempore existenti regi Scotorum, pro felici statu dicte erecte ecclesie, racionabilia ac licita et honesta statuta faciendi et edendi facultatem concesserunt, ac jus patronatus et presentandi subdecanum, sacristam, ac canonicos ad subdecanatum, sacristiam, ac canonicatus, et prebendas, tam ea vice quam quociens uacabunt, et ius instituendi dictos pueros prefato Jacobo Regi et successoribus suis; ius uero instituendi ad subdecanatum, sacristiam, ac canonicatus, et prebendas predictos, tam ea prima uice quam eciam quociens uacabunt, pro tempore presentatos, decano predicto eciam pro tempore existenti perpetuo reseruarunt et concesserunt : Et alia sibi commissa fecerunt prout in litteris predictis continetur ac processu seu quodam instrumento publico desuper habito et confecto dicitur plenius contineri. CUM AUTEM sicut eadem peticio subiungebat dictus Jacobus Rex cupiat quod unus ex dictis canonicis nominandis, pro quo est reseruata porcio centum librarum dicte monete Scocie, sit cantor in dicta ecclesia, sic in collegiatam erecta, et si in illa erigeretur vna cantoria que inibi dignitas et similiter de iure patronatus dicti Jacobi et pro tempore existentis Regis Scotorum existeret, et per dictum canonicum cantorem canonicatum et prebendam predictos pro quibus dicta porcio centum librarum reseruata est pro tempore obtinentem obtineatur, erigeretur et institueretur in eadem ecclesia, dignitatum numerus augeretur ad Dei laudem et ipsius ecclesie decorem ; pro parte Jacobi Regis ac decani et capituli predictorum nobis fuit humiliter supplicatum vt premissis omnibus et singulis, per dictos abbatem de Scona et archidiaconum litterarum dictarum vigore factis et executis, pro illorum subsistencia firmiori robur apostolice confirmacionis adicere, ac in dicta erecta ecclesia vnam cantoriam, que inibi dignitas eciam de iure patronatus dicti Regis sit, erigere, ac alias in premissis oportune prouidere de benignitate apostolica dignaremur, NOS IGITUR, qui dudum inter alia uolumus quod petentes beneficia ecclesiastica alijs uniri tenerentur exprimere uerum valorem secundum extimacionem predictam, eciam beneficii cui aliud uniri peteretur, alioquin vnio non ualeret, et semper in vnionibus commissio fieret ad partes, uocatis quorum interesset, et idem obseruaretur in confirmacionibus vnionum iam factarum, decanum et capitulum prefatos ac ipsius capituli singulares personas a quibuscunque excommunicacionis suspensionis et inter dicti aliisque ecclesiasticis sentenciis censuris et penis a iure uel ab homine quauis occasione uel causa latis si quibus quomodolibet innodati existunt ad effectum presencium dumtaxat consequendum harum serie absoluentes et absolutos fore censentes ac fructuum reddituum et prouentuum mense capitularis dicte erecte ecclesie uerum

Erectio cantoris.

Cantoria.

Nota.— Exemptio personarum decani subdecani sacriste et aliarum personarum capelle regie Striuilengensis.

valorem annuum presentibus pro expresso habentes, huiusmodi
supplicacionibus inclinati, dicte capelle in collegiatam ecclesiam
Nota. et in ea decanatus subdecanatus sacristie sedecim canonicatuum
et totidem prebendarum necnon sex puerorum predictorum
erectionem et institucionem ac eidem ecclesie pro eius ac
decanatus subdecanatus sacristie canonicatuum et prebendarum
dote et decani subdecani sacriste canonicorum et puerorum et
aliarum personarum dicte ecclesie sustentacione applicacionem
bonorum et dicti prioratus fructuum necnon Rectorie et Archipresbiteratus nuncapatorum et singulorum aliorum canonicatuum et prebendarum dicte ecclesie de Dunbar ac aliorum
beneficiorum curatorum et non curatorum vnionem annexionem
et incorporacionem ac reseruacionem seu assignacionem con-
gruarum porcionum pro vicarijs perpetuis curatorum beneficiorum
et presbitris qui Rectorie et Archipresbiteratui nuncupatis ac aliis
canonicatibus et prebendis et sine cura vnitis beneficiis huiusmodi deseruire habeant necnon ordinacionem et facultatem ac
reseruacionem tam iuris patronatus quam institucionis et desti-
tucionis predictarum tam Regi quam decano predictis respectiue
Nota bene. factas predictas et alia premissa omnia et singula per dictos
Abbatem de Scona et Archidiaconum ut prefertur statuta et
ordinata et facta et executa auctoritate apostolica tenore presencium approbamus et confirmamus supplentes omnes singulos
defectus si qui forsan interuenerint in eisdem, premissaque
omnia perpetue firmitatis robur obtinere debere decernimus,
necnon facultatem absoluendi Regem et Reginam et alios predictos
in casibus predictis eidem decano per dictas litteras concessam
ad subdecanum eiusdem ecclesie pro tempore existentem per se
uel alium seu alios presbiteros ydoneos seculares vel cuiusuis
ordinis regulares, dicto decano absente et eciam eo presente
exercendam, extendimus, seu dicto subdecano ut prefertur concedimus; ac in eadem erecta ecclesia vnam cantoriam que inibi
dignitas ante dictam sacristiam et similiter de iure patronatus
dicti Regis eciam pro tempore existentis existat, pro uno cantore,
qui similiter ex dictis sedecim canonicis per dictum Regem
nominandus existat, et ad illam prefato decano presentetur
et per cum instituatur, eisdem auctoritate et tenore absque

alicuius preiudicio erigimus et instituimus, non obstantibus uoluntate nostra predicta et alijs constitucionibus et ordinacionibus apostolicis ac dicte ecclesie iuramento confirmacione apostolica uel quauis firmitate alia roboratis statutis et consuetudinibus ceterisque contrariis quibuscunque: Nulli ergo omnino hominum liceat hanc paginam nostre absolucionis approbacionis confirmacionis suppletionis decreti extensionis concessionis erectionis et institucionis infringere uel ei ausutemerario contraire: Si quis antem hoc attemptare presumpserit, indignacionem omnipotentis Dei ac beatorum Petri et Pauli apostolorum eius se nouerit incursurum. Datum Rome apud Sanctum Petrum anno incarnacionis dominice Millesimo quingentesimo secundo sextodecimo Kalendas Maij Pontificatus nostri anno decimo.

3. Conseruatoria Ecclesie Collegiate de Striueling.

Alexander episcopus Seruus seruorum Dei Dilectis filijs Sancte crucis et Cambusthinet ac de Pasleto Sanctiandree et Glasguensis diocesium monasteriorum abbatibus, salutem et apostolicam benedictionem: Militanti ecclesie licet inmeriti disponente domino presidentes circa curam ecclesiarum omnium solercia reddimur indefessa solliciti ut iuxta debitum pastoralis officii earum occuramus dispendijs et profectibus diuina cooperante clemencia salubriter intendamus. Sane pro parte dilectorum filiorum Decani subdecani sacriste canonicorum puerorum clericorum et aliarum personarum ecclesie Capelle Regie nuncupate beate Marie et Sancti Michaelis, intra palacium opidi de Stirlyng Sancte Andree diocesis site, conquestione percepimus quod ipsi dubitant ne aliqui archiepiscopi et episcopi alijque ecclesiarum prelati et clerici ac ecclesiastice persone tam religiose quam seculares, necnon Duces Marchiones Comites Barones Nobiles Milites et laici, communia ciuitatum vniuersitates opidorum Castrorum villarum et aliorum locorum, ac alie singulares persone ciuitatum et diocesium et aliarum partium diuersarum occupent et occupari faciant Castra villas et alia

loca terras domos possessiones iura et iurisdictiones necnon
fructus census redditus et prouentus dicte ecclesie, et nonnulla
alia bona mobilia et immobilia spiritualia et temporalia, ad decanum subdecanum sacristam canonicos pueros et alias personas
et ecclesiam predictos spectancia, et ea detineant indebite occupata
seu ea detinentibus prestent auxilium consilium uel fauorem, ac
eciam nonnulli ciuitatum et diocesium ac parcium predictarum
qui nomen domini inuanum recipere, non formidabunt eisdem
decano subdecano sacriste canonicis pueris et personis necnon
cantori eiusdem ecclesie nunc et pro tempore existentibus, super
predictis castris villis et locis alijs terris domibus possessionibus
iuribus et iurisdictionibus priuilegiis indultis exempcionibus
immunitatibus ac fructibus censibus redditibus et prouentibus
eorumdem, et quibuscumque aliis bonis mobilibus et immobilibus
spiritualibus et temporalibus et alijs rebus ad eosdem decanum
subdecanum sacristam cantorem canonicos pueros et personas ac
ecclesiam predictos communiter uel diuisim nunc et pro tempore spectantibus, multiplices molestias et iniurias inferant et
iacturas: Quare dicti decanus subdecanus sacrista canonici et
persone nobis humiliter supplicarunt, ut cum eis et eciam decano
eiusdem ecclesie pro tempore existenti ualde redderetur difficile
pro singulis querelis ad apostolicam sedem habere recursum
prouidere ipsis super hoc paterna diligencia curaremus. Nos
IGITUR, qui hodie in eadem ecclesia vnam cantoriam que inibi
dignitas existeret pro uno cantore qui vnus ex canonicis eiusdem
ecclesie existeret, per alias litteras nostras ereximus, aduersus
occupatores detentores presumptores molestatores et iniuriatores
huiusmodi illo volentes eisdem decano subdecano sacriste cantori
canonicis pueris et personis remedio subuenire, per quod ipsorum
compescatur temeritas, et aliis aditus committendi similia pre-
cludatur, discretioni nostre per apostolica scripta mandamus,
quatenus uos uel duo aut vnus uestrum per uos uel alium seu
alios eciam si sint extra loca in quibus deputati estis conseruatores et iudices prefatis decano subdecano sacriste cantori
canonicis pueris et personis nunc et pro tempore existentibus
efficacis defensionis presidio assistentes, non permittatis eosdem
super hijs et quibuslibet aliis bonis ac iuribus ad decanum sub-

decanum sacristam cantorem canonicos pueros et personas nec- Cantoria.
non ecclesiam predictos communiter uel diuisim nunc et pro
tempore existentibus super priuilegijs indultis exempcionibus et
immunitatibus predictis ab eisdem uel quibusuis alijs indebite
molestari uel eis grauamina uel dampna seu iniurias irrogari
facturi, dictis decano subdecano sacriste cantori canonicis personis et pueris cum ab eis uel procuratoribus suis aut eorum de robore
aliquo fueritis requisiti de predictis et alijs personis quibuslibet conseruatorie.
super restitucione dictorum castrorum villarum terrarum et
aliorum locorum iurisdictionem iurium et bonorum mobilium
et immobilium reddituum quoque et prouentuum et aliorum
quorumcunque bonorum necnon de quibuslibet molestiis
iniuriis atque damnis presentibus et futuris in illis videlicet
qui iudicialem requirunt indaginem summarie et de plano sine
strepitu et figura iudicij in alijs uero prout qualitas eorum
exegerit iusticie complementum occupatores seu detentores presumptores molestatores et iniuriatores huiusmodi necnon contradictores quoslibet et rebelles eciam exemptos eciam ordinum
quorumcunque eciam quascumque similes uel dissimiles conser-
uatorias habentes et quibuscumque priuilegiis munitos cuiuscumque dignitatis status gradus ordinis uel condicionis extiterint
quandocumque et quocienscumque expedierit auctoritate nostra
per censuram ecclesiasticam appellatione postposita compescendo Nota.—De
inuocato ad hoc si opus fuerit auxilio brachij secularis Ita quod appellatione.
ipsi decanus subdecanus sacrista cantor canonici pueri et alie
persone dicte ecclesie nunc et pro tempore existentes ne a diuinis Nota.—
retrahantur extra locum dicte ecclesie eciam pretextu quarum- Ne retrahantur a
cumque aliarum conseruatoriarum ad iudicium euocari non pos- diuinis extra locum.
sint sed teneantur dumtaxat coram uobis aut aliquo uestrum
seu deputatis a uobis de iusticia respondere ceterum si per
summariam informacionem super hiis per uos habendam uobis
constiterit quod ad loca in quibus occupatores detentores presumptores molestatores et iniuriatores huiusmodi ac alios quos
presentes littere concernunt pro tempore moneri contigerit. pro
monicionibus ipsis et citacionibus de eis faciendis tutus non
pateat accessus seu eorum copia commode haberi non possit nos
uobis citaciones et moniciones quaslibet per edita publica locis

affigenda publicis et partibus illis uicinis de quibus sit uerisimilis coniectura quod ad noticiam citatorum et monitorum huiusmodi peruenire valeant faciendi ac quibuscumque alijs conseruatoribus quibusuis alijs personis ecclesiis monasterijs locis et ordinibus eciam per litteras apostolicas sub quibuscumque tenoribus deputatis et deputandis eciam sub censuris ecclesiasticis inhibendi plenam et liberam concedimus tenore presencium facultatem, ac uolumus et predicta auctoritate decernimus quod moniciones et citaciones huiusmodi sic facte perinde citatos et monitos arctent ac si eis personaliter insinuate et intimate extitissent, non obstantibus tam felicis recordacionis Bonifacij pape octaui predecessoris nostri, in quibus cauetur ne aliquis extra suam ciuitatem et diocesim nisi in certis exceptis casibus et in illis ultra unam dietam a fine sue diocesis ad iudicium euocetur: Seu ne iudices et conseruatores prefati a sede deputati predicta extra ciuitatem et diocesim in quibus deputati fuerint contra quoscumque procedere seu alij uel alijs uices suas committere aut aliquos ultra unam dietam a fine diocesis eorum trahere presumant et de duabus dietis in consilio generali edita dummodo ultra quatuor dietas aliquis auctoritate presencium non trahatur, seu quod de alijs quam manifestis iniurijs et uiolentiis ac alijs que iudicialem requirunt indaginem penis in eos si secus egerint ad id procurantes adiectis Conseruatores se nullatenus intromittant quam aliis quibuscumque constitucionibus a predecessoribus nostris Romanis pontificibus tam de iudicibus delegatis et conseruatoribus quam personis ultra certum numerum ad iudicium non uocandis aut alijs editis que uestre possent in hac parte iurisdictioni aut potestati eiusque libero exercicio quomodolibet obuiare necnon quibusuis priuilegijs et indultis alijs ecclesiis monasterijs et locis ac illorum personis et ordinibus quibuscumque eciam Cluniacensis uel Cisterciensis sub quibuscumque tenoribus concessis eciam si in illis caueatur expresse quod pretextu quarumcumque aliarum conseruatoriarum et litterarum apostolicarum extra loca eorum coram quibusuis iudicibus et conseruatoribus apostolicis ad iudicium euocari non possiut sed teneantur coram eorum conseruatoribus et delegatis ab eis dumtaxat respondere et queuis citaciones et inhibiciones inde pro

tempore secute nullius sint roboris uel momenti quibus illis
alias in suo robore permansuris quoad premissa hac uice dumtaxat harum serie specialiter et expresse derogamus contrariis
quibuscumque seu si aliquibus communiter uel diuisim a predicta sit sede indultum quod interdici suspendi uel excommunicari seu extra uel ultra certa loca ad iudicium euocari non
possint per litteras apostolicas non facientes plenam et expressam
ac de uerbo ad uerbum de indulto huiusmodi et eorum personis
locis ordinibus et nominibus propriis mencionibus et qualibet
alia dicte sedis indulgencia generali uel speciali cuiuscumque
tenoris existat per quam presentibus non expressam uel totaliter
non insertam uestre iurisdictionis explicacio in hac parte ualeat
quomodolibet impediri et de qua cuiusque toto tenore habenda
sit de uerbo ad uerbum in nostris litteris mencio specialis. Et
insuper uolumus et apostolica auctoritate decernimus quod
quilibet uestrum prosequi ualeat articulum eciam per alium
inchoatum quamuis idem inchoans nullo fuerit impedimento
canonico prepeditus quodque a dato presencium sit uobis et
unicuique uestrum in premissis et eorum singulis ceptis et non
ceptis presentibus et futuris perpetuata potestas et iurisdictio
attributa ut eo uigore eaque firmitate possitis in premissis
omnibus ceptis et non ceptis presentibus et futuris ac pro predictis procedere ac si predicta omnia et singula coram uobis
cepta fuissent et iurisdictio uestra et cuiuslibet vestrum in predictis omnibus et singulis per citacionem uel modum alium
perpetuata legittime extitisset constitucione predicta super conseruatoribus et alia qualibet in contrarium edita non obstantibus
presentibus perpetuis futuris temporibus ualituris. Datum
Rome apud Sanctum Petrum anno incarnacionis Dominice
millesimo quingentesimo secundo sextodecimo kalendas Maij
Pontificatus nostri anno decimo.

4. Vnio ecclesie de Kirkynner.

GEORGIUS MISERACIONE DIUINA EPISCOPUS Candidecase Omnibus
et singulis dominis Abbatibus Prioribus Archidiaconis Decanis

Cantoribus Sacristis ecclesiarum perrochialium Rectoribus vicariis perpetuis alteristis presbiteris curatis et non curatis ceterisque Christi fidelibus clericis et laicis per regnum Scocie ubilibet constitutis ad quorum noticias presentes littere peruenerint salutem cum benedictione diuina Iniunctum nobis pastorale officium mentem nostram excitat et inducit ut ad ea per que ecclesiarum presertim collegiatarum necnon personarum in illis altissimo famulancium necessitatibus consulatur operosis studiis et remediis fauorabiliter intendamus Sane pro parte venerabilium et religiosorum nostrorum Prioris et capituli nostri ecclesie nostre Candidecase ordinis premonstratensis nobis nuper exhibita peticio continebat quod excellentissimus ac metuendissimus princeps et dominus noster dominus Jacobus Rex quartus Scotorum illustrissimus modernus ecclesiam perrochialem de Kyrkandris nostre diocesis de ipsius iure patronatus hereditarie pertinentem cum omnibus iuribus et pertinenciis suis dictis priori et capitulo eorumque successoribus in perpetua elimosina concessit et in proprietate donauit cuius donacionis uigore eorum necessitatibus prouidetur utiliter ac laudabiliter subuenitur et cum ecclesia perrochialis de Kyrkynnire eciam nostre diocesis ad quam dum pro tempore uacat presentacio persone ydonee ad dictos priorem pro tempore existentem et capitulum nostrum pertinere dinoscitur si eadem ecclesia de Kyrkynnere cum omnibus iuribus et pertinenciis suis mense capitulari ecclesie collegiate beate Marie et Sancti Michaelis alias Capelle Regie site infra palacium Opidi de Stirlyng Sanctiandree diocesis que per dictum regem nostrum illustrissimum de nouo fundata extitit perpetuo vniretur annectaretur et incorporaretur decani et capituli dicte ecclesie de Sterlyng commoditatibus non parum consularet maxime ex eo quia prefatus Rex noster illustrissimus dictam ecclesiam de Kyrkandris motiuo et occasione huiusmodi unionis fiende prefatis priori et capitulo nostro prauitate et dolo cessante ut premittitur proinde concessit Quaré pro parte prioris et capituli prefatorum nobis fuit humiliter supplicatum ut consensum nostrum dictis donacioni et concessioni per dictum Regem factis prebere et concedere ac ecclesiam perrochialem predictam

de Kyrkynner cum omnibus iuribus et pertinenciis suis ad
dictam ecclesiam collegiatam alias Capellam Regiam de Stirlyng
et ad eius mensam capitularem perpetuo ut prefertur vnire
annectere et incorporare aliasque in premissis oportune prouidere
auctoritate nostra ordinaria benigniter dignaremur Nos igitur
Georgius episcopus antedictus huiusmodi supplicacionibus in ea
parte inclinati necnon consideracione prefati illustrissimi domini
nostri Regis super hoc humiliter supplicantis volentes tamen in
premissis nostris ordinem in omnibus obseruare dictos priorem
et capitulum nostrum ac venerabilem uirum magistrum Jacobum
Betoune rectorem prefate ecclesie de Kyrkynnere omnesque
alios et singulos in premissis interesse habentes ad comparendum coram nobis certis die et hora sibi limitatis infra locum
capitularem ecclesie nostre Candidecase predicto ad uidendum
et audiendum nos ex nostra auctoritate ordinaria dictam ecclesiam de Kyrkynnere cum omnibus iuribus et pertinenciis
suis ad prefatam ecclesiam collegiatam de Stirlyng et eius
mensam capitularem perpetuo unire annectere et incorporare
uel ad allegandum causam racionabilem si quam habent quare
huiusmodi vnio et incorporacio fieri non deberent cum intima-
cione debita ut moris est legittime citari fecimus Unde dicte
citacionis termino adueniente nobis in loco capitulari dicte
ecclesie nostre Candidecase pro tribunali sedentibus priore et
capitulo nostro prefatis capitulariter ac venerabili uiro magistro
Dauid Abyrcrumby subdecano ecclesie Dunkeldensis pro cura-
tore et eo nomine dicti magistri Jacobi Betoune rectoris dicte
ecclesie perrochialis de Kyrkynnere ad hoc ab eo specialiter
constituto coram nobis uigore dicte citacionis in iudicio legittime comparentibus et consensum nostrum ac vnionem annexionem et incorporacionem predictas cum instancia diligenter fieri
petentibus Nos UERO ut in premissis calumpniantibus uiam
penitus excludamus cartam quandam domini nostri Regis
predicti super prefata donacione ecclesie perrochialis de Kyrkandris confectam et coram nobis in iudicio productam diligenter
inspeximus ex cuius tenore de et super omnibus et singulis
narratis premissis animum nostrum summarie informauimus
habitisque super huiusmodi narratis et petitis cum priore et

capitulo nostro predictis ad hoc capitulariter ut premittitur
congregatis diligenti et sollenni tractatu et deliberacione pre-
cedenciis in talibus debitis et consuetis: Suadentes eciam
eorumdem prioris et capituli perpetua utilitate euidenter in
omnibus preuisa et undique considerata seruatis insuper cause
cognicione iuris ordine modo et forma debitis ac singulis aliis
in premissis necessariis et requisitis seruandis dictas donacionem
et concessionem per dominum nostrum Regem illustrissimum
de ecclesia perrochiali de Kyrkandris ut predicitur factas admittimus recipimus et approbamus et eisdem nostrum consensum damus et concedimus ac ecclesiam predictam de Kyrkynnere que est de iure patronatus predictorum prioris et capituli
nostri cum omnibus iuribus et pertinenciis suis ad prefatam
ecclesiam collegiatam alias capellam regiam de Stirlyng et
eius mensam capitularem de expresso et unanimi consensu et
assensu prioris et capituli nostri predictorum ac procuratoris et
eo nomine ad hoc speciale mandatum habentis omnibus melioribus uia et iure quibus melius et efficacius poterimus auctoritate
nostra ordinaria saluis iuribus episcopalibus perpetuo vniuimus
anneximus et incorporauimus prout tenore presencium eadem
auctoritate admittimus recipimus approbamus damus concedimus vnimus annectimus incorporamus applicamus et appropriamus imperpetuum. Ita quod cedente uel decedente moderno
ipsius perrochialis ecclesie unite rectore seu illam alias quomodolibet dimittente liceat eisdem decano et capitulo dicte ecclesie
de Stirlynge per se uel alium seu alios corporalem perrochialis
ecclesie de Kyrkynnyre predicte iuriumque et pertinenciarum
predictorum eiusdem possessionem propria auctoritate libere
apprehendere et perpetuo retinere illiusque fructus redditus et
prouentus in suos ac mense capitularis ecclesie de Stirlyng
predictorum usus et utilitatem conuertere: Pariformiter eciam
cedente uel decedente moderno ipsius perrochialis ecclesie de
Kyrkandris rectore seu illam alias dimittente liceat dictis
priori et capitulo nostro per se uel alium seu alios corporalem
huiusmodi ecclesie de Kyrkandris juriumque et pertinenciarum
predictorum eiusdem possessionem propria auctoritate libere
apprehendere et perpetuo retinere illiusque fructus redditus et

prouentus in suos usus et utilitatem conuertere Nostra et successorum nostrorum ac cuiusuis alterius licencia super hijs minime requisita: Et quod dictus Rex noster illustrissimus fructus redditus et prouentus prefate ecclesie unite inter personas ecclesie collegiate de Stirlyng pro earundem sustentacione iuxta suam prouidam ordinacionem eciam perpetuo duraturam faciendam in prebendas seu porciones unam ve plures diuidere ualeat et disponere ac cum reliquis prouentibus huiusmodi ecclesie de Stirlyng in prouisionibus et alijs predicti fructus uniti naturam penitus sorciantur eandem: Prouiso quod propter unionem annexionem incorporacionem donacionem et concessionem huiusmodi dicte ecclesie perrochiales de Kyrkynnyre et Kyrkandris debitis propterea non fraudentur obsequijs et animarum cura in illis nullatenus necligatur sed earum congrua supportentur onera consueta dictis autem vnione annexione et incorporacione per nos ut premittitur factis prior et capitulum nostrum ac procurator predicti huiusmodi unionem annexionem incorporacionem applicacionem et appropriacionem admiserunt receperunt approbauerunt ratum gratum firmum atque stabile habuerunt perpetuo. Et ne de carta Regia predicta aliquibus dubitandi occasio forsitan tribuatur illius tenorem sub presentibus de verbo in uerbum integraliter inserere fecimus in hac forma:

JACOBUS DEI GRACIA Rex Scotorum omnibus probis hominibus tocius terre sue clericis et laicis salutem Sciatis quia nos considerantes et perpendentes quod venerabilis in Christo pater et religiosi uiri nostri oratores Prior et conuentus moderni ecclesie cathedralis Candidecase gratuiti et beniuoli extiterunt et existunt in eorum unanimi consensu et assensu datis et exhibitis annexioni unioni et incorporacioni faciendis per Reuerendum in Christo patrem eorumque ordinarium Georgium episcopum Candidecase ecclesie nostre collegiate nuncupate capelle Regie situate infra castrum nostrum de Stirlynge de et super ecclesia de Kyrkynnyre tam rectoria quam uicaria Candidecase diocesis cum omnibus et singulis decimis fructibus et prouentibus eiusdem cum pertinenciis que ad dictorum prioris et conuentus iuspatronatus spectabat: Nolentes igitur ipsos priorem et conuentum seu ecclesiam Candidecase predictam inde grauari seu aliquod dampnum sustinere ymmopocius per nos aliusmodi ad eorum euidentem vtilitatem et proficuum provideri dedimus ob id concessimus, admortizauimus et confirmauimus et hac presenti carta nostra damus concedimus admortizamus et pro nobis et successoribus nostris ad manum mortuam pro perpetuo confirmamus predicte ecclesie Candidecase ac Priori et conuentui eiusdem modernis eorumque successoribus inibi Deo seruituris imperpetuum diuini cultus augmentum et pro specialibus oracionum suffragiis per ipsos pro nobis nostrisque successoribus celebrantibus, ecclesiam de Kyrkandris tam rectoriam quam uicariam Candidecase diocesis predicte, cum omnibus et singulis decimis fructibus et prouentibus eiusdem cum pertinenciis ad nostrum iuspatronatus spectantibus et pertinentibus. Tenendam et habendam ac cum ipsis priore et conuentu et eorum successoribus in proprietate et in puram et perpetuam elimosinam ac ad manum mortuam imperpetuum remanendam libere quiete bene et in pace sine aliquo retenemento aut reuocacione quacumque faciendo ei. Celebrando inde annuatim dicti prior et conuentus et eorum successores in predicta ecclesia pro perpetuo Deo seruituri pro nobis nostrisque predecessoribus et successoribus specialia oracionum suffragia deuotarum tantum ut premittitur: In cuius rei testimonium presenti carte nostre magnum sigillum nostrum apponi precipimus. Testibus reuerendissimo in Christo patre nostroque carissimo fratre Jacobo Sanctiandree Archiepiscopo duce Rossie etc. cancellario nostro, reuerendo in Christo patre Willelmo episcopo Abberdenensi nostri secreti sigilli custode dilectis consanguineis nostris Archibaldo Comite de Ergyle domino Campbell et Lorne magistro hospicii nostri, Patricio comite de Bothuile domino Halys etc. Matheo comite de Lennax domino Dernle Alexandro domino Hume magno camerario nostro Andrea domino Gray iusticiario nostro et dilecto clerico nostro magistro Gauino Dumbar decano Morauiensi nostrorum rotulorum et registri ac consilij clerico apud Edinburgh octauo die mensis Decembris anno Domini millesimo quingentesimo tercio et regni nostri decimo sexto.

QUE OMNIA et singula et hunc processum nostrum atque

omnia et singula in eo contenta uobis omnibus et singulis supradictis communiter uel diuisim insinuamus et notificamus et ad uestram et cuiuslibet uestrum noticiam deducimus et deduci uolumus presencium per tenorem. In quorum omnium et singulorum fidem et testimonium premissorum presentes litteras siue presens publicum instrumentum processum nostrum huiusmodi in se continentes seu continens exinde fieri et per notarios publicos infrascriptos subscribi et publicari sigilli nostri auctentici ac sigilli dicti capituli nostri iussimus et fecimus appensione communiri ad perpetue firmitatis corroboracionem omnium et singulorum premissorum. Insuper autem nos Georgius episcopus et singulares persone capituli nostri predicti presentes litteras siue presens publicum instrumentum subscripsimus et subscripserunt Acta fuerunt hec in loco capitulari predicto quarto die mensis Januarij hora undecima ante meridiem uel ea circa anno incarnacionis dominice millesimo quingentesimo tercio indiccione septima pontificatus sanctissimi in Christo patris et domini nostri domini Juliani diuina prouidencia pape secundi anno primo Presentibus ibidem venerabilibus uiris magistris Fergusio Makdowel officiali generali Candidecase Willelmo Magarwe uicario perpetuo ecclesie perrochialis de Penneghame dicte Candidecase diocesis dominis Johanne Makcrekane Johanne Makneile presbyteris prouidis cciam uiris Patricio Wause de Berynberyth Duncano Murraw et Cuthberto Conynghaim laicis testibus ad premissa uocatis pariter et rogatis.

Nos Georgius episcopus Candidecase manu nostra subscripsimus hunc processum et eundem approbamus et ratificamus, etc.

Nos Patricius prior dicte ecclesie Candidecase manu nostra propria subscripsimus.

Ego Johannes canonicus et supprior dicte ecclesie manu mea propria subscripsi.

Ego Willelmus canonicus dicte ecclesie manu propria subscripsi.

Ego Henricus Makkynnel canonicus dicte ecclesie manu propria subscripsi.

Ego Rollandus Makclaouthan canonicus dicte ecclesie manu propria subscripsi.
Ego Andreas Melygam canonicus dicte ecclesie manu propria subscripsi.
Ego Nycholayus Walcar canonicus dicte ecclesie manu propria subscripsi.
Ego Jacobus Conynghaim canonicus dicte ecclesie manu propria subscripsi.
Ego Andreas Steuynson manu propria canonicus dicte ecclesie subscripsi.
Ego Dauid Cartar canonicus dicte ecclesie manu propria subscripsi.
Ego Alexander Kynneir canonicus dicte ecclesie manu propria subscripsi.
Ego Alexander Waus canonicus dicte ecclesie manu propria subscripsi.
Ego Andreas Ferny canonicus dicte ecclesie manu mea propria subscripsi.

Et ego Johannes Makcrekane presbiter Candidecase diocesis uicariusque perpetuus ecclesie perrochialis Insule eiusdem diocesis imperiali et regali auctoritatibus notarius publicus dictis peticioni supplicacioni citacionis decreto carte Regie productioni procuratoris comparicioni et sui mandati productioni prioris et capituli consensus prestacioni tractatui deliberacioni unioni annexioni incorporacioni reseruacioni recepcioni approbacioni ratihabicioni processus huiusmodi decreti interposicioni ceterisque premissis gestis et narratis dum ut premittitur dicerentur et fierent unacum notariis publicis subscriptis et testibus prenominatis presens interfui eaque sic dici et fieri uidi sciui et audiui ac in notam cepi. Ex qua presentem processum manu propria scriptum meis nomine et subscripcione una cum corroboracione sigillorum et subscripcionum de quibus superius est facta mencio signaui in fidem et testimonium omnium et singulorum premissorum rogatus specialiter et requisitus.

Et ego Willelmus Makgarwe artium magister ac presbiter

Johannes. Makcrekane notarius.

Candidecase diocesis uicariusque perpetuus ecclesie perrochialis de Pennyghaim publicus imperiali et regali auctoritatibus notarius dictis peticioni supplicacioni citacionis decreto carte regie productioni procuratoris comparicioni et sui mandati productioni prioris et capituli consensus prestacioni tractatui deliberacioni unioni annexioni incorporacioni rescruacioni recepcioni approbacioni ratihabicioni processus huiusmodi decreti interposicioni ceterisque premissis gestis et narratis dum ut premittitur dicerentur et fierent unacum notariis suprascripto et subscriptis ac testibus prenominatis presens interfui eaque sic dici et fieri vidi sciui et audiui ac in notam cepi. Ex qua presentem processum manu suprascripti notarii scriptum meis nomine signo et subscripcione unacum corroboracione sigillorum et subscripcionum de quibus superius est facta mencio signaui in fidem et testimonium omnium et singulorum premissorum rogatus specialiter et requisitus. *Willelmus Makgarwe notarius.*

Et ego Johannes Makcrekane presbiter Candidecase diocesis publicus imperiali ac regali auctoritatibus notarius dictis peticioni supplicacioni citacionis decreto carte regie productioni procuratoris comparicioni et sui mandati productioni prioris et capituli consensus prestacioni tractatui deliberacioni vnioni annexioni incorporacioni reseruacioni recepcioni approbacioni ratihabicioni processus huiusmodi decreti interposicioni ceterisque premissis gestis et narratis dum ut premittitur dicerentur et fierent unacum notariis subscriptis et testibus prenominatis presens interfui eaque sic dici et fieri uidi sciui et audiui ac in notam cepi. Ex qua presentem processum manu suprascripti notarij primo subscribentis scriptum meis nomine signo et subscripcione una cum corroboracione sigillorum et subscripcionum de quibus superius est facta mencio signaui in fidem et testimonium omnium et singulorum premissorum rogatus specialiter et requisitus. *Johannes Makcrekane notarius.*

5. Secunda applicacio siue vnio fructuum de Creif et
quarumdem prebendarum de Dunbar ac ecclesiarum de
Ellam Bute et Balmaclellane.

Julius episcopus seruus seruorum Dei ad perpetuam rei
memoriam iniunctum nobis desuper apostolice seruitutis officium
nos inducit ut uotis illis per que singularum ecclesiarum et
personarum in illis diuinis officijs insistencium inde unitatibus
ac commoditatibus salubriter consulatur libenter animamus ac
prout expedit nostri pastoralis officij partes fauorabiliter impendamus Dudum siquidem postquam felicis recordacionis
Alexandro Papa sexto predecessori nostro pro parte carissimi
in Christo filij nostri tunc sui Jacobi Scotorum Regis illustris
inter alia expositum fuerat quod licet in Capella Regia nuncupata
beate Marie et Sancti Michaelis intra palacium ipsius Jacobi
Regis opidi de Sterlyng Sanctiandree diocesis sita vnus decanus
nuncupatus et plures alij cantores et cappellani ac clerici missas
et alia diuina officia singulis diebus ad libitum ipsius Jacobi
Regis ammouibiles celebrarent ipseque Jacobus Rex predictam
capellam suis sumptibus reformari fecisset ac libris calicibus et
aliis ornamentis ecclesiasticis pro diuino cultu in eadem capella
necessarijs honorifice muniuisset et ornasset ac eciam nonnulla
bona immobilia ad eum legittime pertinencia eidem capelle pro
illius dote assignauisset tamen si dicta capella in collegiatam
ecclesiam et prepositura ecclesie beate Marie de Rupe Sanctiandree que inibi dignitas principalis et de iure patronatus prefati
Jacobi et pro tempore existentis Scotorum Regis ex priuilegio
apostolico existebat et ad eius meram collacionem ex simili
priuilegio pertinebat eciam in decanatum eiusdem erigende
ecclesie qui inibi dignitas eciam principalis existeret pro uno
decano qui alijs eiusdem erigende ecclesie personis preesset et
certam tunc expressam iurisdictionem in omnes personas dicte
erigende ecclesie haberet et dum in eadem beate Marie in illa
prepositus dum uero in erigenda ecclesia resideret in illa decanus
foret et unus subdecanatus qui in eadem erigenda ecclesia
dignitas secunda pro uno subdecano qui dicti decani certo modo

tunc expresso uices suppleret ac una sacristia que inibi officium
seu administracio existeret pro uno sacrista qui curam iocalium
dicte ecclesie haberet necnon sedecim canonicatus et totidem
prebende pro sedecim canonicis in cantu et aliis sufficienter
instructis ac sex pueri clerici similiter in cantu competenter
instructi seu ut instruerentur apti et ydonei qui in eadem
erigenda ecclesia diuina officia diurna pariter et nocturna certo
modo tunc expresso ad Dei laudem et pro ipsius Jacobi Regis
eiusque antecessorum et successorum animarum salute decantare
et celebrare et alias eidem erigende ecclesie in diuinis iuxta
prouidam ipsius Jacobi Regis ordinacionem faciendam deseruire
tenerentur. Et cum in ecclesia de Dunbar eiusdem diocesis
illius canonici pro maiori parte non per se set prout in multis
alijs collegiatis ecclesijs regni Scocie iuxta consuetudinem
eatenus obseruatam per substitutos deseruirent si canonicatus
et prebende dicte ecclesie de Dunbar qui de iure patronatus
ipsius regis existebant et alia beneficia ecclesiastica cum cura et
sine cura iuris patronatus ipsius regis seu aliorum laicorum
existencia quorum fructus redditus et prouentus ad ualorem
duarum millium librarum monete Scocie quingentas libras
Sterlingorum uel circa constituencium dumtaxat ascenderent
annuatim et de quibus ipsi Jacobo Regi uideretur de eius et
aliorum laicorum patronorum respectiue consensu dicte erigende
ecclesie reseruata ex fructibus curatorum beneficiorum pro
uicariis perpetuis earumdem congrua porcione ex qua se commode sustentare iura episcopalia persoluere et alia onera sibi
racione curatorum beneficiorum huiusmodi incumbencia supportare possent perpetuo vnirentur annecterentur et incorporarentur. Ita quod eciam congrua porcio presbiteris ydoneis
qui canonicatibus et prebendis et alijs vniendis sine cura beneficiorum huiusmodi quamdiu illis deseruirent percipienda assignaretur et residuum deductis huiusmodi porcionibus inter
decanum subdecanum sacristam et canonicos predictos ac alias
personas dicte erigende ecclesie certo modo tunc expresso dis-
tribueretur. Ex hoc non solum in capella postquam in collegiatam ecclesiam ac in ea dignitates et canonicatus et prebende
et alia officia huiusmodi erecta seu instituta et dicti sex pueri

et instituti forent sed eciam in de Dunbar ac alijs ecclesijs
et beneficiis uniendis predictis diuinus cultus augmentum
susciperet et ipse Jacobus Rex eciam alia bona patrimonialia
ualoris annui quingentarum librarum uel circa monete Scocie
pro premissis assignaret ac pro parte dicti Jacobi Regis eidem
predecessori humiliter supplicato ut in premissis oportune
prouidere de benignitate apostolica dignaretur et dictus predecessor eiusdem Jacobi Regis in ea parte supplicacionibus
tunc inclinatus Sancte crucis et de Scona Sanctiandree diocesis
monasteriorum abbatibus ac archidiacono Laudonie in ecclesia
Sanctiandree eorum propriis nominibus non expressis suis
litteris dederat in mandatis quatenus si erat ita eandem capellam
postquam prefatus Jacobus Rex alia bona immobilia ualoris
quingentarum librarum monete Scocie huiusmodi cum effectu
pro premissis assignasset in collegiatam ecclesiam cum communi archa sigillo capitulo et aliis insigniis collegialibus et
in ea dictam preposituram in decanatum dignitatem principalem
pro tunc et pro tempore existente preposito dicte ecclesie beate
Marie qui eciam decanus in eadem erigenda ecclesia existeret
et vnum subdecanatum pro uno subdecano qui uices eiusdem
decani eciam modo et forma tunc expressis suppleret ac sacristiam et sedecim canonicatus et prebendas et sex pueros clericos
qui eciam certo modo tunc expresso diuina officia celebrarent
et decantarent erigerent et instituerent ac dicte ecclesie erigende
postquam erecta foret dicte de Dunbar et aliarum collegiatarum
ecclesiarum predicte seu aliarum diocesium canonicatus et
prebendas ac perrochiales ecclesias et alia beneficia ecclesiastica
cum cura et sine cura iuris patronatus ipsius Regis seu aliorum
laicorum ualoris annui duarum millium librarum monete predicte de consensu Jacobi Regis et aliorum laicorum predictorum
respectiue unirent annecterent et incorporarent ac congruam
porcionem tam pro uicarijs curatorum beneficiorum quam pro
presbiteris ydoneis qui canonicatibus et prebendis ac aliis
beneficiis sine cura vniendis deseruirent assignarent sub certis
modo et forma eciam tunc expressis pro parte Jacobi Regis
prefati ac dilectorum filiorum decani et capituli dicte erecte
ecclesie eidem predecessori eciam exposito quod tunc abbas

monasterij de Scona et Archidiaconus Laudonie huiusmodi ad execucionem earumdem litterarum alias illorum forma seruata procedentes quia ita esse repererant dictam capellam postquam prefatus Jacobus Rex de suis bonis patrimonialibus certa bona immobilia tunc expressa ualoris annui quingentarum librarum monete Socie pro dote dicte erigende ecclesie et alias iuxta dictarum litterarum tenorem assignauerat in collegiatam ecclesiam et in ea dictam preposituram in decanatum dignitatem principalem subdecanatum sacristiam et sedecim canonicatus et totidem prebendas ac sex pueros clericos alias iuxta tenorem earumdem litterarum erexerant et instituerant ac inter alia de Balmaclellane et de Foresta ac de Buytt necnon de Ellam Glasguensis ac Sodorensis et dicte Sanctiandree diocesium perrochiales ecclesias necnon Rectoriam et Archipresbiteratum et de Dunse ac de Beltoun et de Spott necnon de Pynkartoun nuncupatos dicte ecclesie Dunbar canonicatus et prebendas qui iuris patronatus prefati Regis existebant de ipsius Jacobi Regis consensu eidem erecte ecclesie pro illius dote et ministris seu personis eius perpetuo unierant annexerant et incorporauerant ac quod fructus redditus et prouentus canonicatus et de Creyff nuncupate prebende ecclesie Dunkeldensis quinquaginta libras Sterlingorum ualebant annuatim et si reseruatis ex fructibus canonicatus et prebende de Creiff huiusmodi triginta marchis monete Scocie pro obtinente pro tempore eosdem canonicatum et prebendam de Creiff residuum fructuum eorumdem dicte erecte ecclesie perpetuo applicaretur et appropriaretur profecto ex hoc canonicorum numerus in dicta ecclesia Dunkeldense non minueretur et eciam huiusmodi canonicatum et prebendam de Creyff pro tempore obtinens ex residuo fructuum qui ei remanerent se commode sustentare posset ac eciam decanus subdecanus sacrista et cantor ac alie persone dicte erecte ecclesie aliquod subuencionis auxilium pro eorum commodiori sustentacione reciperet dictus predecessor ipsorum Jacobi Regis ac decani et capituli in ea parte supplicacionibus tunc inclinatus dicte capelle in collegiatam ecclesiam et in ea decanatus subdecanatus sacriste sedecim canonicatuum et totidem prebendarum necnon sex puerorum predictorum erectionem et instituci-

Foresta.

onem ac eidem ecclesie pro eius ac decanatus subdecanatus
sacristie canonicatuum et prebendarum huiusmodi dote et
decani subdecani sacriste canonicorum et puerorum ac aliarum
personarum dicte ecclesie sustentacione applicacionem bonorum
et Rectorie et Archipresbiteratus nuncupatorum ac singulorum
aliorum canonicatuum et prebendarum dicte ecclesie de Dunbar
ac aliorum beneficiorum curatorum et non curatorum unionem
annexionem et incorporacionem factas predictas et alia per
dictos Abbatem de Scona et Archidiaconum statuta ordinata
facta et executa auctoritate apostolica per quasdem approbauit
et confirmauit ac per alias suas litteras in dicta erecta ecclesia
unam cantoriam que inibi dignitas ante sacristiam et similiter
de iure patronatus ipsius Regis eciam pro tempore existentis
existeret pro uno cantore qui similiter ex dictis sedecim canonicis
esset et ad illam prefato decano per dictum Regem nominaretur
et per eum institueretur eadem auctoritate apostolica sine alicuius
preiudicio erexit et reseruatis pro canonico dictos canonicatum
et prebendam de Creyff obtinente triginta marchis eiusdem
monete Scocie residuos fructus redditus et prouentus dictorum
canonicatus et prebende de Creyff, eidem erecte ecclesie seu
illius mense capitulari eadem auctoritate perpetuo applicauit
et appropriauit ac residuos huiusmodi fructus ab eisdem canoni-
catu et prebenda de Creyff perpetuo dimembrauit et separauit.
Ita que exceptis triginta marchis pro obtinente canonicatum et
prebendam de Creiff huiusmodi reseruatis liceret decano et
capitulo prefatis cedente uel decedente canonicatum et prebendam de Creiff huiusmodi obtinente residuum fructuum
reddituum et prouentuum canonicatus et prebende de Creyff
huiusmodi propria auctoritate libere apprehendere et in suos
et ecclesie erecte huiusmodi usus et utilitatem conuertere
diocesani loci et cuiusuis alterius licencia super hoc minime
requisita certis desuper executoribus prout in singulis litteris
predictis desuper respectiue confectis plenius continetur. Cum
autem sicut exhibita nobis nuper pro parte Jacobi Regis ac
decani et capituli predictorum petitio continebat unio predicta
quoad canonicatus et prebendas dicte ecclesie de Dunbar et
quoad de Balmaclellane et de Foresta ac de Buytt necnon de

Ellam ecclesias perrochiales ac eciam applicacio residui fructuum canonicatus et prebende de Creiff huiusmodi non dum effectum sortite fuerint et pro eo quia reuocaciones unionum et incorporacionum effectum non sortitarum tam a pie memorie Pio Papa III. eciam predecessore nostro quam eciam postmodum a nobis ad summum apostolicatus apicem assumptis emanauerint Et propterea decanus et capitulum prefati dubitent effectu unionis annexionis et incorporacionis ac applicacionis et appropriacionis predictorum frustrari posse. Pro parte eorumdem Jacobi Regis ac decani et capituli nobis fuit humiliter supplicatum ut in premissis oportune prouidere de benignitate apostolica dignaremur. Nos qui dudum inter alia uolumus quod petentes beneficia ecclesiastica alijs uniri tenerentur exprimere uerum annuum ualorem secundum communem extimacionem tam beneficij uniti quam eius cui aliud uniri peteretur alioquin unio non ualeret et semper in unionibus commissio fieret ad partes uocatis quorum interesse decanum et capitulum prefatos ac ipsius capituli singulares personas a quibuscunque excommunicacionis suspensionis et interdicti alijsque ecclesiasticis sentenciis censuris et penis a iure uel ab homine quauis occasione uel causalitatis si quibus quomodolibet innodati existunt ad effectum presencium dumtaxat consequendum harum serie absoluentes et absolutos fore censentes ac fructuum reddituum et prouentuum mense capitularis necnon canonicatuum et prebendarum ecclesie de Dunbar ac de Balmaclellane et de Buytt necnon de Foresta et Ellam perrochialium ecclesiarum ac residui canonicatus et prebende de Creyff predictorum ueros ualores annuos presentibus pro expressis habentes huiusmodi supplicacionibus inclinati priores litteras predictas quoad, unionem annexionem et incorporacionem predictas quoad canonicatus et prebendas dicte ecclesie de Dunbar ac de Balmaclellane et Foresta necnon de Buytt et Ellam perrochiales ecclesias necnon applicacionem residui fructuum dictorum canonicatus et prebende de Creiff dicte erecte ecclesie ac desuper confectas litteras cum omnibus et singulis in eis contentis clausulis. Ipsosque decanum et capitulum quoad illarum consequendum effectum in pristinum et cum statum in quo antequam reuocaciones huiusmodi unionum

effectum non sortitarum ab eodem pio predecessore et a nobis
emanarent quomodolibet existebant eadem auctoritate apostolica
tenore presentium restituimus reponimus et plenarie reintegramus
ac pro pociori cautela ipsos canonicatus et prebendas dicte
ecclesie de Dunbar ac easdem de Balmaclellane et de Foresta ac
de Buytt necnon de Ellam perrochiales ecclesias alias sub modo
et forma in prioribus litteris contentis eidem erecte ecclesie
auctoritate et tenore predictis de nouo perpetuo unimus annectimus et incorporamus ac residuum fructuum dictorum canonicatus
et prebende de Creyff eidem eciam erecte ecclesie applicatum et
appropriatum eciam perpetuo applicamus et appropriamus.
Itaque cedentibus uel decedentibus dicte ecclesie de Dunbar
canonicis et de Creiff unitos canonicatus et prebendas ac uni-
tarum ecclesiarum rectoribus perrochiales ecclesias huiusmodi
respectiue obtinentibus liceat eisdem decano et capitulo corporalem possessionem vnitorum canonicatuum et prebendarum
ac perrochialium ecclesiarum et residuum fructuum applicati et
appropriati huiusmodi alias iuxta tenorem litterarum predictarum propria auctoritate libere apprehendere et perpetuo
retinere ac iuxta tenorem litterarum earumdem in suos et
erecte ecclesie huiusmodi usus et utilitatem conuertere non
obstantibus uoluntate nostra predicta et alijs apostolicis
constitucionibus ac Dunkeldensis et de Dunbar necnon erecte
ecclesiarum predictarum iuramento confirmacione apostolica uel
quauis firmitate alia roboratis statutis et consuetudinibus ac
omnibus illis que dictus Alexander predecessor in prefatis
litteris uoluit non obstare ceterisque contrarijs quibuscumque.
Nulli ergo omnino hominum liceat hanc paginam nostre absolucionis restitucionis reposicionis reintegracionis unionis annexionis
incorporacionis applicacionis et appropriacionis infringere uel ei
ausu temerario contraire. Si quis autem hoc attemptare presumpserit indignacionem omnipotentis Dei ac beatorum Petri et
Pauli apostolorum eius se nouerit incursurum. Datum Rome
apud Sanctum Petrum anno incarnacionis dominice millesimo
quingentesimo quarto Pridie nonas Junij Pontificatus nostri
anno primo.

6. Constitucio procuratorum ad prestandum consensum
rectoris vnioni de Kirkynner et ad resignandum post
vnionem factam.

In dei nomine Amen. Per hoc presens publicum instrumentum cunctis pateat euidenter Quod anno incarnacionis dominice millesimo quingentesimo tercio mensis uero Decembris die nona indictione septima Pontificatus Sanctissimi in Christo patris et domini nostri domini Julij diuina prouidencia Pape secundi anno primo in mei notarij publici et testium subscriptorum presencia personaliter constitutus egregius uir Magister Jacobus Betounc Rector de Kyrkynnere Candidecase diocesis dixit et asseruit quod perrochialis ecclesia de Kyrkynnere ad presentacionem siue ius patronatus venerabilium et religiosorum nostrorum prioris et conuentus ecclesie Candidecase ac ad institucionem siue collacionem episcopi ordinarij eiusdem pro tempore existentis pertinere dinoscitur et pertinet Et cum Reuerendus in Christo pater et dominus dominus Georgeus miseracione diuina episcopus Candidecase modernus ex certis causis racionabilibus animum suum ad hoc moventibus dictam ecclesiam perrochialem de Kyrkynnere cum suis iuribus et uniuersis pertinenciis de consensu et assensu sui capituli uidelicet dictorum Prioris et conuentus ecclesie collegiate beate Marie et Sancti Michaelis alias capelle regie situate infra castrum de Striuelyng Sanctiandree diocesis sub certis modo et forma pro perpetuo unire annectere et incorporare nuper intendit Ideoque idem magister Jacobus non vi aut metu ductus nec errore lapsus sed sua mera pura et spontanea uoluntate ut asseruit omnibus melioribus modo uia et forma quibus melius et efficacius potuit et debuit fecit constituit creauit nominauit et solenniter ordinauit ac tenore presentis publici instrumenti facit constituit creat nominat et solempniter ordinat venerabiles et circumspectos uiros magistros Dauid Abircrommye subdecanum ecclesie cathedralis Dunkeldensis Fergusium Makdowel officialem Candidecase Jacobum Akynheide et Johannem Abercrommye et eorum quemlibet in solidum suos ueros legittimos et indubitatos procuratores actores

factores et negociorum suorum gestores ac nuncios speciales et
generales Dans et concedens dictis suis procuratoribus et eorum
cuilibet insolidum suam ueram liberam puram et expressam potestatem ac mandatum speciale et generale pro se et nomine suo
citato uel non citato coram dicto reuerendo in Christo patre et
domino quibuscumque diebus et locis comparendum ad uidendum
et audiendum dictas annexionem unionem et incorporacionem
prefate ecclesie perrochialis cum suis iuribus fructibus et pertinenciis per dictum reuerendum patrem de sua ordinaria potestate de
consensu et assensu dictorum Prioris et conuentus ecclesie collegiate alias capelle regie de Striuelyng fieri et compleri ac eciam
ad dandum et prestandum ex certa sciencia pro se et nomine
suo suum liberum et purum consensum et assensum eciam in
suum preiudicium dictis annectioni vnioni et incorporacioni et
ipsas annectionem unionem et incorporacionem approbandum
recipiendum et ratificandum Et postquam huiusmodi unio annec-
tacio et incorporacio ut predicitur iure ordinario facta fuerit ad
dictam perrochialem ecclesiam de Kyrkynner ac omne ius et
iuris titulum quod habet in eadem aut habere poterit in futurum
tam in petitorio quam in possessorio in presencia dicti reuerendi
patris aut extra suam presenciam seu coram notario et testibus
prout melius videbitur expedire simpliciter dimittendum et
renunciandum necnon ad iurandum in animam dicti domini
constituentis quod in dictis suis consensu et assensu approba-
cione ratificacione recepcione dimissione seu renunciacione non
interuenit neque interueniet fraus dolus decepcio Symoniaca
labes seu queuis alia pactio illicita Processus litteras instrumentum seu instrumenta desuper petendum levandum et optinendum.
Et generaliter omnia alia et singula faciendum gerendum et
exercendum que in premissis et circa ea necessaria fuerint seu
oportuna et que ipsemet dominus constituens faceret seu facere
posset si in premissis omnibus et singulis presens personaliter
interesset. Promisit insuper idem dominus constituens michi
notario publico subscripto stipulanti et recipienti uice et nomine
omnium et singulorum quorum interest intererit aut interesse
poterit se ratum gratum firmum atque stabile habendum et
habiturum totum id et quicquid dicti sui procuratores plures

aut unus in premissis seu premissorum aliquo duxerint seu duxerit faciendum sub ypotheca et obligacione omnium bonorum suorum presencium et futurorum. Super quibus omnibus et singulis prefatus dominus constituens a me notario publico subscripto sibi fieri petiit hoc presens publicum instrumentum seu publica instrumenta Acta erant hec in ecclesia beati Egidij de Edinburgh hora undecima ante meridiem aut eo circa sub anno die mense indictione et pontificatu quibus supra Presentibus ibidem prouidis uiris Roberto Wardlaw Johanne Maxwall et Jacobo Lermonthe cum diuersis alijs testibus ad premissa uocatis pariter et rogatis.

Et ego Georgeus Newtoune presbiter Glasguensis diocesis publicus auctoritatibus imperiali et regali notarius quia dictorum procuratorum constitucioni nominacioni potestatis dacioni et ratihabicioni ceterisque premissis omnibus et singulis dum sic ut premittitur dicerentur agerentur et fierent una cum prenominatis testibus presens interfui eaque omnia et singula sic fieri et dici vidi et audiui ac in notam recepi Ideoque hoc presens publicum instrumentum manu aliena scriptum exinde confeci et in hanc publicam formam redegi signoque et nomine meis solitis et consuetis signaui rogatus et requisitus in fidem et testimonium premissorum.   Georgeus Neutoun.

7. INSTRUMENTUM PUBLICUM SUPER RESIGNACIONE DE KYRKYNNER.

IN DEI NOMINE AMEN. Per hoc presens publicum instrumentum cunctis pateat euidenter quod anno incarnacionis dominice millesimo quingentesimo tercio mensis uero Januarij die duodecima pontificatus Sanctissimi in Christo patris et domini nostri domini Julij diuina prouidencia Pape secundi anno primo in mei notarij publici et testium subscriptorum presencia personaliter constitutus venerabilis vir magister David Abircrummy subdecanus ecclesie Dunkeldensis procurator et eo nomine ad infrascripta eciam venerabilis uiri magistri Jacobi Betoune Rectoris ecclesie perrochialis de Kyrkynuere Candidecase diocesis tenens manualiter quoddam instrumentum publicum manu discreti uiri Georgei Newtoune presbitri ac notarij publici Glasguensis diocesis super dicto mandato procuratorio confectum et subscriptum Idem dominus procurator et eo nomine dixit et asseruit quod reuerendus in Christo pater et dominus dominus Georgeus episcopus ecclesie Candidecase de consensu et assensu capituli sui scilicet prioris et conuentus eiusdem ecclesie Candidecase ac prefati magistri Jacobi Betoune dictam ecclesiam perrochialem de Kyrkynner cum suis iuribus et vniuersis pertinenciis ad dictam ecclesiam collegiatam beate Marie et Sancti Michaelis alias Capelle Regie situate infra castrum de Striuelyng Sanctiandree diocesis ex causis racionabilibus animum suum ad hoc mouentibus sub certis modo et forma iure ordinario uniuit et perpetuo incorporauit prout in processibus et euidenciis desuper confectis ad plenum continetur Ideoque idem dominus procurator procuratorio nomine prefati magistri Jacobi Betoune uigore dicti instrumenti publici sufficientem potestatem habens prout michi notario publico luculenter constabat omnibus melioribus via iure et modo quibus potuit dictam ecclesiam perrochialem de Kyrkynner coram me notario publico et testibus subscriptis pure et simpliciter dimisit ac omni iuri et iuris titulo tam in possessorio quam petitorio per eundem magistrum Jacobum Betoun in huiusmodi ecclesia de Kyrkynnere habitis in manu eciam mei notarij publici uoluntarie renunciauit Super quibus omnibus et singulis prefatis magister Dauid Abircrummye a me notario publico subscripto sibi fieri petiit vnum aut plura publicum seu publica instrumentum aut instrumenta Acta erant hec in hospicio Alexandri Leuingstoune infra Burgum de Striuelyng hora prima post meridiem aut eacirca sub anno die mense indictione et pontificatu quibus supra. Presentibus ibidem prouidis viris Alexandro Leuyngstoune Jacobo Watsone Dauid Braide Johanne Abircrummye et dominis Jacobo Fransche Johanne Gourlay capellanis cum diuersis alijs testibus ad premissa uocatis specialiter atque rogatis.

 Et Ego Thomas Kyrkaldy presbiter Sancti andree diocesis sacra autoritate apostolica notarius dictum mandatum procuratorium vidi tenui et diligenter consideraui ac prefati procuratoris assercioni dimissioni renunciacioni ceterisque omnibus et singulis dum sic ut premittitur agerentur dicerentur et fierent una cum prenominatis testibus presens interfui eaque omnia et singula sic fieri vidi sciui et audiui ac in notam recepi Indeque presens publicum instrumentum manu mea propria scriptum in hanc publicam formam redegi signoque ac nomine meis solitis et consuetis signaui Rogatus et requisitus in fidem ac testimonium omnium et singulorum premissorum.   Thomas Kyrkaldye.

8. COMMISSIO AD ERIGENDUM THESAURARIAM ET DECEM CANONICATUS ET PREBENDAS.

JULIUS EPISCOPUS SERUUS SERUORUM DEI dilectis filiis de Dunfermlyne et de Scona ac de Cambuskynneth Sanctiandree diocesis monasteriorum abbatibus salutem et apostolicam benedictionem Admonet nos suscepti cura regiminis ut uotis singulorum Christi fidelium presertim catholicorum regum per que diuinus cultus et ministrorum numerus in ecclesiis quibuslibet augmentum suscipiant libenter annuamus ac ea fauoribus prosequamur oportunus exhibita siquidem nobis nuper pro parte carissimi in Christo filij nostri Jacobi Scotorum regis illustris ac dilectorum filiorum decani et capituli ecclesie beate Marie et Sancti Michaelis opidi de Stirlyng Sanctiandree diocesis peticio continebat quod cum alias auctoritate quarumdem litterarum felicis recordacionis Alexandri Pape VI. predecessoris nostri dicta ecclesia tunc capella regia nuncupata in collegiatam ecclesiam et prepositura ecclesie beate Marie de rupe Sanctiandree que inibi dignitas principalis et de iure patronatus prefati Jacobi et pro tempore existentis Scotorum Regis ex priuilegio apostolico existebat et ad eius meram collacionem ex simili priuilegio pertinebat eciam in decanatum eiusdem erecte ecclesie qui inibi dignitas eciam principalis existeret pro vno decano qui alijs eiusdem erigende ecclesie personis preesset et dum in eadem beate Marie in illa prepositus dum uero in erecta ecclesia resideret in illa decanus existat et vnus subdecanus qui inibi dignitas secunda pro uno subdecano qui dicti decani certo modo tunc expresso uices suppleret ac vna cantoria que inibi tercia dignitas ac vna sacristia que inibi officium seu administracio existant pro vno sacrista qui curam iocalium dicte ecclesie habeat necnon sedecim canonicatus et totidem prebende pro sedecim canonicis in cantu et alijs sufficienter instructis ac sex pueri clerici similiter in cantu competenter instructi seu ut instruerentur apti et ydonei qui in eadem erigenda ecclesia diuina officia diurna pariter et nocturna certo modo tunc expresso ad Dei laudem et pro ipsius Jacobi Regis eiusque antecessorum et successorum animarum salute decantare et celebrare et alias eidem ecclesie in diuinis iuxta prouidam ipsius Jacobi regis ordinacionem desuper apostolica auctoritate factam deseruire tenentur erecti et instituti fuerint et certi redditus annui certorum beneficiorum ecclesiasticorum ac alia beneficia ecclesiastica cum cura iuris patronatus ipsius regis seu aliorum laicorum quorum fructus redditus et prouentus ad valorem duarum millium librarum monete Scocie quingentas libras sterlingorum uel circa constituentium dumtaxat ascendunt annuatim de consensu dicti Jacobi Regis eidem erecte ecclesie pro illius dote ac decani subdecani cantoris sacriste canonicorum et puerorum predictorum sustentacione sub certis modo et forma vnita annexa et incorporata ac applicati et appropriati fuerint et ipse Jacobus Rex eciam alia bona patrimonialia valoris annui quingentarum librarum uel circa monete Scocie pro premissis assignauerit ac ius patronatus et presentacio decano dicte erecte ecclesie pro tempore existenti de personis ydoneis ad subdecanatum cantoriam sacristiam canonicatus et prebendas predictas tam ea uice a primeua eorum erectione quam quociens uacarent per dictum decanum instituendas eidem Jacobo et pro tempore existenti Regi Scotorum litterarum predictarum uigore reseruatum et concessum fuerit et postmodum perrochialis ecclesia de Kyrkynner Candidecase diocesis que ad presentacionem dilectorum filiorum Prioris et capituli ecclesie Candidecase Premonstratensis ordinis pertinebat de consensu prioris et capituli ecclesie Candidecase predictorum eidem erecte ecclesie ordinaria auctoritate perpetuo vnita annexa et incor-

porata ac huiusmodi vnio effectum sortita fuerint et prefatus
Jacobus Rex in recompensam dicte perrochialis ecclesie de
Kyrkynner perrochialem ecclesiam de Kyrkandris dicte Candidecase diocesis que iuris patronatus ipsius regis existebat et que
prius dicte ecclesie collegiate unita fuerat licet huiusmodi vnio
ex certis causis effectum sortita non fuit prefatis priori et
capitulo ecclesie Candidecase in perpetuam elimosinam conces-
serit et huiusmodi concessio dicta ordinaria auctoritate appro-
bata et confirmata fuerit. Et si in dicta erecta ecclesia vna
thesauraria que inibi dignitas postdictam cantoriam existeret thesau-
pro uno Thesaurario et decem alij seu pauciores canonicatus et raria.
totidem prebende pro totidem canonicis qui vnacum decano nota.
cantore sacrista et alijs canonicis prefatis iuxta modum et
formam in prioribus litteris traditas et contentas in eadem
erecta ecclesia in diuinis deseruire tenerentur. Et ipse thesau- thesaurari-
rarius pro prebenda sua qualem cantor seu aliam porcionem per portionem
decanum et capitulum prefatos de consensu regis prefati statu- qualem
endam seu ordinandam et similiter alij decem seu pauciores cantor.
canonici instituendi equales prebendas seu porciones quales alij
sedecim canonici percipiunt seu per decanum et capitulum prefatos de consensu ipsius regis statuendam perciperent profecto
ex hoc in ipsa erecta ecclesia dignitatum et canonicorum ac
ministrorum numerus augeretur ad ipsius erecte ecclesie decorem
et diuini cultus augmentum ac eciam fructus dicte ecclesie de
Kyrkynnere unacum aliis bonis per dictum regem assignatis et
alijs fructibus predictis eidem ecclesie applicatis sufficerent ut
Thesaurarius et alij decem seu pauciores canonici predicti
equalem porcionem cum cantore et aliis canonicis predictis
respectiue seu aliam congruentem porcionem per regem et
capitulum prefatos prouide statuendam et ordinandam percipere
posent. Quare pro parte Jacobi regis ac decani et capituli
predictorum nobis fuit humiliter supplicatum ut in dicta erecta
ecclesia vnam thesaurariam que inibi quarta dignitas existat pro
uno thesaurario et alios decem seu pauciores prout Jacobus
rex ac decanus et capitulum prefati expedire cognouerint canonicatus et totidem prebendas qui et dicta thesauraria similiter de
jure patronatus Jacobi prefati et pro tempore existentis Scotorum

regis existant erigere et instituere ac alias in premissis oportune
prouidere de benignitate apostolica dignaremur Nos igitur qui
ecclesiarum quarumlibet decorem sinceris desideramus affectibus de premissis certam noticiam non habentes ac decanum et
capitulum prefatos ipsiusque capituli singulares personas a
quibuscumque excommunicacionis suspensionis et interdicti
alijsque ecclesiasticis sentenciis censuris et penis a iure vel ab
homine quauis occasione uel causa latis si quibus quomodolibet
innodati existunt ad effectum presentium dumtaxat consequendum harum serie absoluentes et absolutos fore censentes
huiusmodi supplicacionibus inclinati discrecioni vestre per
apostolica scripta mandamus quatenus si est ita in dicta erecta
vnam thesaurariam que inibi quarta dignitas existat pro uno
thesaurario et alios decem seu pauciores prout Jacobus Rex et
decanus et capitulum prefati expedire cognouerint canonicatus
et totidem prebendas qui et dicta thesauraria tam hac vice primeua ab eorum erectione quam quociens uacabunt similiter de
iure patronatus Jacobi prefati et pro tempore existentis regis
Scotorum existant pro totidem canonicis qui thesaurarius et
canonici equalem quoad thesaurariam qualem cantor et decem
canonici aliorum decem canonicatuum et prebendarum erigen-
dorum huiusmodi quales alij sedecim canonici predicti percipiunt aut alias congruentes per eosdem decanum et capitulum
de consensu prefati Jacobi regis statuendas et ordinandas seu
limitandas prebendas seu porciones ex fructibus redditibus
et prouentibus mense capitularis dicte erecte ecclesie seu illi
vnitorum beneficiorum percipiant ac eciam eisdem prerogatiuis
immunitatibus exempcionibus et priuilegiis vtantur pociantur et
gaudeant quibus alij dignitates ac canonicatus et prebendas in
eadem erecta ecclesia obtinentes vtantur pociuntur et gaudent
ac vti potiri et gaudere poterunt quomodolibet in futurum
erigere instituere sine alicuius preiudicio auctoritate nostra
curetis non obstantibus constitucionibus et ordinacionibus
apostolicis ac dicte erecte ecclesie iuramento confirmacione
apostolica uel quauis firmitate alia roboratis statutis et consuetudinibus ceterisque contrariis quibuscumque Datum Rome
Apud Sanctum Petrum anno incarnacionis dominice millesimo

quingentesimo quarto pridie nonas Junij Pontificatus nostri
anno primo.

9. Confirmacio Vnionis ecclesie de Kirkynner.

Julius episcopus seruus seruorum Dei Ad perpetuam rei
memoriam exposcit iniunctum nobis desuper apostolice seruitutis
officium ut eaque pro ecclesiarum quarumlibet presertim collegiatarum insignium et personarum in illis diuinis officiis Domino
psallentium commoditatibus et utilitate facta fuisse dicuntur
ut in sua ualiditate persistant cum a nobis petitur apostolico
munimine roboremus exhibita siquidem nobis nuper pro parte
carissimi in Christo filii nostri Jacobi Scotorum Regis illustris
ac dilectorum filiorum decani et capituli ecclesie beate Marie
et Sancte Michaelis opidi de Sterlyng Sanctiandree diocesis
peticio continebat quod cum ipse Jacobus perrochialem ecclesiam
de Kyrkandris Candidecase diocesis que de jure patronatus
ipsius Jacobi Regis existebat et alias dicte ecclesie de Stirlyng
vnita fuerat licet ipsa unio effectum sortita non fuerit delectis
filiis priori et capitulo candide case ecclesie premonstratensis
ordinis in perpetuam elimosinam concessisset et proprietatem
ac huiusmodi concessio ordinaria auctoritate confirmata fuisset
venerabilis frater noster Georgeus episcopus Candidecase perrochialem ecclesiam de Kyrkynner dicte Candidecase diocesis que
dum pro tempore uacabat presentacionem prioris capitulique
predictorum pertinebat de eorumdem Prioris et capituli ac dilecti
filij Jacobi Betone tunc dicte ecclesie de Kyrkynner rectoris
consensu dicte ecclesie de Sterlyng seu eius mense capitulari
perpetuo uniuit annexuit et incorporauit Ita quod dicto Jacobo
Betone cedente uel decedente seu alias dictam ecclesiam de
Kyrkynner quomodolibet dimittente liceret eisdem decano et
capitulo prefate ecclesie de Sterlyng per se uel alium seu alios
corporalem possessionem dicte ecclesie de Kyrkynner propria
auctoritate libere apprehendere et retinere. Et cum postmodum
ipse Jacobus Betoun ad effectum unionis huiusmodi dictam
ecclesiam de Kyrkynner sponte et libere extra romanam curiam

dimississet ipsi decanus et capitulum possessionem dicte ecclesie
de Kyrkynner assecuti fuerint. Quare pro parte eorumdem
Jacobi Regis ac decani et capituli dicte ecclesie de Stirlyng
asserentium fructus redditus et prouentus dicte ecclesie de
Kyrkynnere octuaginta librarum Sterlingorum secundum communem extimacionem ualorem annuum non excedere nobis fuit
humiliter supplicatum vt vnioni annexioni et incorporacioni
predictis pro illarum subsistencia firmiori robore apostolice
confirmacionis adicere aliasque in premissis oportune prouidere
de benignitate apostolica dignaremur. Nos igitur qui dudum
inter alia volumus quod petentes beneficia ecclesiastica alijs
uniri tenerentur exprimere uerum annuum ualorem secundum
extimacionem predictam eciam beneficij cui aliud uniri peteretur
alioquin unio non ualeret et semper in vnionibus commissio
fieret ad partes uocatis quorum interesset et idem obseruaretur
in confirmacionibus unionum iam factarum decanum et capitulum
ecclesie de Sterlyng huiusmodi ipsiusque capituli singulares
personas a quibuscumque excommunicacionis suspensionis et
interdicti aliisque ecclesiasticis sentenciis censuris et penis a
iure uel ab homine quauis occasione uel causa latis si quibus
quomodolibet innodati existunt ad effectum presentium dumtaxat consequendum harum serie absoluentes et absolutos fore
censentes necnon fructuum reddituum et prouentuum mense
capitularis dicte ecclesie de Sterlyng uerum annuum ualorem
presentibus pro expresso habentes huiusmodi supplicacionibus
inclinati unionem annexionem et incorporacionem ecclesie de
Kyrkynner huiusmodi auctoritate apostolica tenore presentium
approbamus et confirmamus supplemusque omnes et singulos
defectus si qui forsan interuenerint in eisdem. Et nichilominus
pro pociori cautela eandem ecclesiam de Kyrkynnere siue ut
premittitur siue alias quouismodo aut ex alterius cuiuscumque
persona seu per liberam resignacionem dicti Jacobi Betoun uel
cuiusuis alterius de illa extra dictam curiam eciam coram notario
publico et testibus sponte factam aut constitucionem felicis
recordacionis Johannis Pape XXII. eciam predecessoris nostri que
incipit—Execrabilis—uel assecucionem alterius beneficii eccle-
siastici dicta ordinaria auctoritate collati uacet eciam si tanto

tempore uacauerit quod eius collacio iuxta Lateranensis statuta concilii ad sedem apostolicam legittime denoluta ipsaque ecclesia de Kyrkynner disposicioni apostolice specialiter reseruata existat et super ea inter aliquos lis cuius statum presentibus haberi uolumus pro expresso pendeat indecisa dummodo tempore datum presencium non sit in ea alicui specialiter ius quesitum cum omnibus iuribus et pertinenciis suis eidem ecclesie de Stirlyng de nouo perpetuo unimus annectimus et incorporamus. Ita quod liceat eisdem decano et capitulo eiusdem ecclesie de Stirlyng per se uel alium seu alios corporalem possessionem ecclesie de Kyrkynnere iuriumque et pertinenciarum predictorum libere continuare seu de nouo propria auctoritate apprehendere et perpetuo retinere ac illius fructus redditus et prouentus in suos ac de Sterlyng necnon de Kyrkynnere ecclesiarum usus et utilitatem conuertere diocesam loci et cuiusuis alterius licencia super hoc minime requisita non obstantibus uoluntate nostra predicta ac pie memorie Bonifacii Pape VIII. similiter predecessoris nostri et alijs apostolicis constitucionibus necnon ecclesie Candidecase et ordinis predictorum iuramento confirmacione apostolica uel quauis firmitate alia roboratis statutis et consuetudinibus ac priuilegiis et indultis eidem ordini sub quibuscumque tenoribus concessis quibus illorum tenores pro sufficienter expressis habentes hac uice dumtaxat specialiter et expresse derogamus contrariis quibuscumque Aut si aliqui super prouisionibus sibi faciendis de huiusmodi uel aliis beneficiis ecclesiasticis in illis partibus speciales uel generales dicte sedis uel legatorum eius litteras impetrauerint eciam si per eas ad inhibicionem reseruacionem et decretum uel alias quomodolibet sit processum quas quidem litteras et processus habitos per easdem et inde secuta quecumque ad dictam ecclesiam de Kyrkynner uolumus non extendi sed nullum per hoc eis quoad assecucionem beneficiorum aliorum preiudicium generari et quibuslibet alijs indulgenciis et litteris apostolicis generalibus uel specialibus quorumcumque tenorum existant per que presentibus non expressa uel totaliter non inserta effectus earum impediri ualeat quomodolibet uel differri de quibus quorumque totis tenoribus de uerbo ad uerbum habenda sit in nostris litteris mencio specialis

Prouiso quod dicta ecclesia de Kyrkynnere debitis propterea non fraudetur obsequiis et animarum cura in ea nullatenus necligatur sed eius congrue supportentur onera consueta. Nos enim exnunc irritum decernimus et inane si secus super hijs a quo quam quauis auctoritate scienter uel ignoranter contigerit attemptari Nulli ergo omnino hominum liceat hanc paginam nostre absolucionis approbacionis confirmacionis supplecionis vnionis annexionis incorporacionis voluntatis derogacionis et constitucionis infringere uel ei ausu temerario contraire Si quis autem hoc attemptare presumpserit indignacionem omnipotentis Dei ac beatorum Petri et Pauli apostolorum eius se nouerit incursurum Datum Rome apud Sanctum Petrum anno incarnacionis Dominice millesimo quingentesimo quarto pridie nonas Junii pontificatus nostri anno primo.

10. Applicacio prima fructuum de Aire Kincardin Creif et Petty Brachlee.

ALEXANDER episcopus seruus seruorum Dei ad perpetuam rei memoriam ad ea ex iniuncto nobis desuper apostolice seruitutis officio libenter intendimus per que dignitatibus personisque ecclesiasticis de oportune prouisionis auxilio ualeat salubriter prouideri Dudum siquidem pro parte nobis carissimi in Christo filij nostri Jacobi Scotorum Regis illustris exposito quod licet in capella regia nuncupata beate Marie et Sancti Michaelis intra palacium ipsius Jacobi regis opidi de Stirlyng Sanctiandree diocesis sita vnus decanus nuncupatus et plures alij cantores et capellani ac clerici missas et alia diuina officia singulis diebus ad libitum ipsius Jacobi Regis ammouibiles celebrarent Ipseque rex predictam capellam suis sumptibus reformari fecisset ac ornamentis ecclesiasticis pro diuino cultu in eadem necessariis honorifice ornasset et nonnulla bona immobilia pro dote dicte capelle assignasset tamen si dicta capella in collegiatam ecclesiam et prepositura ecclesie beate Marie de Rupe Sanctiandree que inibi dignitas principalis et de iure patronatus prefati Jacobi et pro tempore existentis Scotorum Regis ex priuilegio apostolico existebat et ad eius meram collacionem ex simili priuilegio pertinebat eciam in decanatum eiusdem erigende ecclesie qui inibi dignitas eciam principalis existeret pro uno decano qui alijs eiusdem erigende ecclesie personis preesset et certam tunc expressam iurisdictionem in omnes personas dicte erigende ecclesie haberet et dum in eadem beate Marie in illa prepositus dum uero in erigenda ecclesia resideret in illa decanus foret et vnus subdecanatus qui in eadem erigenda ecclesia dignitas secunda pro uno subdecano qui dicti decani certo modo tunc expresso uices suppleret ac vna sacristia que inibi officium seu administracio existerent pro uno sacrista qui curam iocalium dicte ecclesie haberet necnon sedecim canonicatus et totidem prebende pro sedecim canonicis in cantu et aliis sufficienter instructis ac sex pueri clerici similiter in cantu competenter instructi seu ut instruerentur apti et ydonei qui in eadem erigenda ecclesia diuina officia diurna pariter et nocturna certo modo tunc expresso ad Dei laudem et pro ipsius Jacobi regis eiusque antecessorum et successorum animarum salute decantare et celebrare et alias eidem erigende ecclesie in diuinis iuxta prouidam ipsius regis ordinacionem faciendam deseruire tenerentur erigerentur et instituerentur et cum in prioratu de Rostinot ordinis sancti Augustini dicte diocesis duo canonici residere consueuissent quamuis illius fructus centum uiginti libras sterlingorum secundum communem exstimacionem ualerent annuatim et sufficientes essent ad sustentacionem sex et eciam plurium canonicorum dicti ordinis ac in ecclesia de Dunbar eiusdem diocesis canonici pro maiori parte non per se sed prout in multis aliis collegiatis ecclesiis regni Scocie iuxta consuetudinem eatenus obseruatam per substitutos deseruirent si reseruata congrua porcione ex fructibus dicti prioratus pro sex canonicis dicti ordinis quorum prior dicti prioratus pro tempore existens unus existeret residuum fructuum dicti prioratus decanatui et aliis inibi erigendis Subdecanatui et Sacristie ac canonicatibus et prebendis pro decano subdecano sacrista canonicis et alijs personis dicte erigende ecclesie iuxta ordinacionem prefati Jacobi Regis perpetuo applicaretur ac canonicus et prebende dicte ecclesie de Dunbar qui de iure patronatus ipsius

Prioratus de Rostinot.

Regis existebant et alia beneficia ecclesiastica cum cura et sine
cura in ciuitate uel dicta diocesi Sanctiandree seu alias ubilibet
consistencia et de iure patronatus ipsius regis seu aliorum
laicorum existencia quorum fructus redditus et prouentus ad
ualorem duarum millium librarum monete Scocie quingentas
libras Sterlingorum uel circa constituencium dumtaxat ascenderent annuatim et de quibus ipsi Jacobi Regi uideretur de
eius et aliorum laicorum patronorum respectiue consensu dicte

Reseruata portio pro vicariis perpetuis.

erigende ecclesie reseruata ex fructibus curatorum beneficiorum
pro uicariis perpetuis eorumdem congrua porcione ex qua se
commode sustentare iura episcopalia persoluere et alia onera
sibi racione beneficiorum curatorum huiusmodi incumbencia
supportare possent perpetuo vnirentur annecterentur et incorporarentur ita quod eciam congrua porcio presbiteris ydoneis qui
canonicatibus et prebendis et aliis uniendis sine cura beneficiis
in diuinis deseruirent ex fructibus redditibus et prouentibus
canonicatuum et prebendarum et sine cura beneficiorum huiusmodi quamdiu illis deseruirent percipienda assignaretur et residuum deductis huiusmodi porcionibus inter decanum subdecanum
sacristam et canonicos predictos ac alias personas dicte erigende
ecclesie certo modo tunc expresso distribuerentur ex hoc non
solum in capella postquam in collegiatam ecclesiam ac in ea
dignitates ac canonicatus et prebende et alia officia huiusmodi
erecta seu instituta et dicti sex pueri instituti forent sed eciam
inde Dumbar ac aliis ecclesiis et beneficiis uniendis ac prioratu
predictis diuinus cultus augmentum susciperet et ipse Jacobus
rex eciam alia bona patrimonialia ualoris annui quingentarum
librarum uel circa monete Scocie pro premissis assignaret ac pro
parte dicti Jacobi regis nobis tunc humiliter supplicati ut in
premissis oportune prouidere de benignitate apostolica dignaremur Nos tunc de premissis certam noticiam non habentes eiusdem Jacobi regis in ea parte supplicacionibus inclinati Sancte
Crucis et de Scona Sanctiandree diocesis monasteriorum abbatibus
ac archidiacono Laudonie in ecclesie Sanctiandree eorum propriis
nominibus non expressis aliis nostris litteris dedimus in mandatis quatenus si erat ita eandem capellam postquam prefatus
Jacobus Rex alia bona immobilia ualoris annui quingentarum

librarum monete Scocie huiusmodi cum effectu pro premissis assignasset in collegiatam ecclesiam cum communi archa sigillo capitulo et alijs insigniis collegialibus et in ea dictam prepesituram in decanatum dignitatem principalem pro tunc et pro tempore existente preposito dicte ecclesie beate Marie qui eciam decanus in eadem erigenda ecclesia existeret et unum subdecanatum pro uno sub decano qui uices eiusdem decani eciam modo et forma tunc expressis haberet ac sacristiam et sedecim canonicatus et prebendas et sex pueros clericos qui eciam certo modo tunc expresso diuina officia celebrarent et decantarent erigerent et instituerent ac reseruata congrua porcione pro sex canonicis dicti ordinis qui in eodem prioratu in diuinis deseruirent et quorum vnus dictus prior existeret ex bonis et fructibus dicti prioratus residuum quod superesset decanatui subdecanatui sacristie ac canonicatibus et prebendis predictis perpetuo applicarent et appropriarent ac dicte erigende ecclesie postquam erecta foret dicte de Dunbar et aliarum collegiatarum ecclesiarum predicte seu aliarum diocesium canonicatus et prebendas ac perrochiales ecclesias et alia beneficia ecclesiastica cum cura et sine cura iuris patronatus ipsius Regis seu aliorum laicorum ualoris annui duarum millium librarum monete predicte de consensu Jacobi Regis et aliorum laicorum predictorum respectiue vnirent et incorporarent ac congruam porcionem tam pro uicariis curatorum beneficiorum quam pro presbitris ydoneis qui canonicatibus et prebendis et aliis beneficiis sine cura uniendis deseruirent assignarent sub certis modo et forma eciam tunc expressis Et deinde sicut exhibita nobis nuper pro parte prefati Jacobi regis ac dilectorum filiorum decani et capituli dicte erecte ecclesie peticio continebat tunc abbas monasterij de Scona et archidiaconus Laudonie huiusmodi ad execucionem dictarum litterarum alias illarum forma seruata procedentes quia ita esse reperierunt dictam capellam postquam prefatus Jacobus Rex de suis bonis patrimonialibus certa bona immobilia tunc expressa ualoris annui quingentarum librarum monete Scocie assignauerat in collegiatam ecclesiam ac in ea dictam prepesituram in decanatum dignitatem principalem subdecanatum sacristiam et sedecim canonicatus et totidem prebendas ac sex pueros clericos

congrua porcio pro vicariis.

alias iuxta tenorem dictarum litterarum crexerunt et instituerunt ac reseruatis ex fructibus dicti prioratus pro priore et aliis quinque canonicis regularibus dicti ordinis quadringentis marchis monete Scocie Residuum fructuum dicti prioratus dicte ecclesie erecte perpetuo applicarunt et appropriarunt ac certas tunc expressas perrochiales ecclesias necnon rectoriam et archipresbiteratum nuncupatos et certos alios tunc expressos dicte ecclesie de Dunbare et quamuis de facto de Ayre Glasguensis cum suis pertinenciis seu annexis et de Creiff Dun-

Kyncardin. keldensis ac de Kyncardyne Abbordenensis cum capellis annexis necnon de Pettybrachele et de Duchel nuncupatos Morauiensis ecclesiarum canonicatus et prebendas qui iuris patronatus prefati Regis existunt et quorum omnium insimul fructus redditus et prouentus duarum millium librarum monete Scocie secundum communem extimacionem ualorem annuum non excedunt de ipsius Jacobi Regis consensu eidem erecte ecclesie pro illius dote et ministris seu personis eius perpetuo unierunt annexuerunt et incorporauerunt Ita quod cedentibus uel decedentibus prioratum rectoriam et Archipresbiteratum nuncupatos ac alios canonicatus et prebendas huiusmodi obtinentibus liceat capitulo dicte ecclesie erecte illorum corporalem possessionem apprehendere prout in litteris predictis plenius continetur et quodam instrumento publico seu processu desuper habito et confecto dicitur plenius contineri cum autem sicut eadem peticio subiungebat fructus redditus et prouentus singulorum canonicatuum et prebendarum metropolitane et aliarum ecclesiarum predictarum satis uberes existant cum de Ayre Glasguensis octuaginta et de Kyncardyne Abordenensis centum ac de Creiff Dunkeldensis quinquaginta et de Petty Brachlye et de Duchel Morauiensis ecclesiarum canonicatuum et prebendarum huiusmodi quadraginta libras Sterlingorum ualeant annuatim et si reseruatis pro Glasguensis quinquaginta et Abordenensis eciam quinquaginta ac pro singulis Dunkeldensis et Morauiensis ecclesiarum canonicatibus et prebendis huiusmodi et illos pro tempore obtinentibus triginta marchis monete regni Scocie residuum fructuum earumdem dicte erecte ecclesie perpetuo applicaretur et appropriaretur profecto ex hoc canonico-

rum numerus in dictis cathedralibus ecclesiis non minueretur et
eciam huiusmodi canonicatus et prebendas earumdem metropolitane et cathedralium ecclesiarum pro tempore obtinentes ex
residuo fructuum qui eis remanerent se commode sustentare
possent ac eciam decanus subdecanus cantor sacrista canonici
pueri ac alie persone dicte erecte ecclesie aliquod subuencionis
auxilium pro eorum commodiori sustentacione susciperent pro
parte Jacobi Regis ac decani et capituli predictorum nobis fuit
humiliter supplicatum ut in premissis oportune prouidere de
benignitate apostolica dignaremur Nos igitur qui hodie vnam Cantoria.
cantoriam que inibi dignitas existeret et per vnum ex sedecim
canonicis obtineretur in eadem erecta ecclesia per alias nostras
litteras ereximus quique ecclesiarum et personarum ecclesiasticarum quarumlibet statui et commoditatibus quantum cum Deo
possumus libenter consulimus decanum et capitulum prefatos
ipsiusque capituli singulares personas a quibuscumque excom-
unicacionis suspensionis et interdicti aliisque ecclesiasticis sentenciis censuris et penis a iure uel ab homine quauis occasione
uel causa latis si quibus quomodolibet innodati existunt ad
effectum presencium dumtaxat consequendum harum serie absoluentes et absolutos fore censentes ac fructus redditus et
prouentus mense capitularis dicte erecte ecclesie presentibus
pro expressis habentes huiusmodi supplicacionibus Jacobi Regis
ac decani et capituli predictorum inclinati reseruatis pro singulis
de Ayre Glasguensis quinquaginta et de Kynkardyne Abor- Kyncar-
denensis eciam quinquaginta ac de Creiff Dunkeldensis triginta et dyne.
de Pettybrachlye et Duchel nuncupatis canonicatibus et prebendis Morauiensis ecclesiarum predictarum triginta marchis
eiusdem monete Scocie residuos fructus redditus et prouentus
canonicatuum et prebendarum Glasguensis et Abordenensis ac
Dunkeldensis et Morauiensis ecclesiarum predictarum qui insimul
ducentarum librarum Stirlingorum similium secundum communem extimacionem ualorem annuum ut asseritur non excedunt eidem erecte ecclesie seu eius mense capitulari auctoritate
apostolica tenore presencium perpetuo applicamus et appropriamus et residuos huiusmodi fructus ab eisdem canonicatibus
et prebendis dictarum Glasguensis et Abordenensis et Dunkeld-

E

ensis et Morauiensis ecclesiarum perpetuo dimembramus et separamus Ita quod exceptis quinquaginta pro singulis Glasguensis et Abordenensis et triginta marchis pro singulis Dunkeldensis et Morauiensis ecclesiarum canonicatuum et prebendarum huiusmodi reseruatis liceat decano et capitulo prefatis cedentibus uel decedentibus canonicatus et prebendas Glasguensis et Aberdonensis ac Dunkeldensis et Morauiensis ecclesiarum huiusmodi obtinentibus Residuum fructuum redituum et prouentuum huiusmodi quatuor canonicatuum et prebendarum propria auctoritate libere apprehendere et in suos et ecclesie erecte huiusmodi vsus et vtilitatem conuertere diocesanorum locorum et quorumuis aliorum licencia super hoc minime requisita Non obstantibus constitucionibus et ordinacionibus Apostolicis et Glasguensis Dunkeldensis Aberdonensis et Morauiensis ecclesiarum predictarum iuramento confirmacione apostolica uel quauis firmitate alia roboratis statutis et consuetudinibus ceterisque contrariis quibuscumque Nulli ergo omnino hominum liceat hanc paginam nostre absolucionis appropriacionis applicacionis dimembracionis et separacionis infringere uel ei ausu temerario contraire Si quis autem hoc attemptare presumpserit indignacionem omnipotentis Dei ac beatorum Petri et Pauli Apostolorum eius se nouerit incursurum Datum Rome apud Sanctum Petrum anno incarnacionis dominice Millesimo quingentesimo secundo sexto decimo Kalendas Maij Pontificatus nostri anno decimo.

11. BULLA SI IN EUIDENTEM.

ALEXANDER EPISCOPUS SERUUS SERUORUM Dei dilectis filiis Abbati Monasterij Sancte Crucis Sanctiandree diocesis et Archidiacono Laudonie in ecclesia Sanctiandree salutem et apostolicam benedictionem Ex iniuncto nobis desuper apostolice seruitutis officio ad ea libenter intendimus per que ecclesiarum omnium ac personarum in eis diuinis laudibus deditarum vtilitas procuratur illaque fauoribus prosequimur oportunus Dudum siquidem a felicis recordacionis Paulo Pape II. predecessore nostro emanarunt littere tenoris subsequentis:

Paulus episcopus seruus seruorum Dei ad perpetuam rei memoriam cum in omnibus iudiciis sit rectitudo iusticie et consciencie puritas obseruanda id multo magis in commissionibus alienacionum rerum ecclesiasticarum conuenit obseruari in quibus de Christi patrimonio et dispensacione pauperum non de proprio cuiusque peculio agitur aut tractatur Qua propter oportet ut in examinandis huiusmodi alienacionum causis que a sede apostolica in forma SI IN EUIDENTEM utilitatem cedant oneratis ecclesiasticorum iudicum consciencijs delegantur nichil fauor usurpet nichil timor extorqueat nulla expectacio pecunij iusticiam consciencie que subuertat Monemus igitur et sub interminacione diuini iudicij omnibus commissarijs et delegatis huiusmodi districte precipimus ut caute et diligenter attendant causas in litteris apostolicis per supplicantes expressas illasque sollicite examinent atque discuciant testes et probaciones super narratorum ueritate recipiant et solum Deum pre oculis habentes omni timore aut fauore deposito ecclesiarum indemnitatibus consulant nec in lesionem aut detrimentum earum decretum quomodolibet interponant Si quis autem commissarius aut delegatus consciencie sue prodigus in grauamen et detrimentum ecclesie per graciam timorem uel sordes alienacioni consenserit aut decretum uel auctoritatem interposuerit inferior quidem episcopo sentenciam excommunicacionis incurrat Episcopus uero aut superior ab execucione officij per annum nouerit se suspensum ad extimacionem detrimenti ecclesie illati nichilominus condemnandus sciturus quod si suspensione durante damnabiliter ingesserit se in diuinis irregularitatis laqueo se inuoluet a quo nisi per summum pontificem poterit liberari. Is uero qui dolo uel fraude aut scienter in detrimentum ecclesiarum alienacionem fieri procurauerit aut per sordes uel inpressionem alienacionis decretum extorserit similem sentenciam excommunicacionis incurrat a qua nisi per Romanum pontificem possit absolui ad restitucionem nichilominus rerum alienarum cum fructibus quandocumque de premissis constiterit condemnandus. Volumus autem quod delegati et commissarij predicti de penis constitucionis nostre specifice moneantur et in quibuscumque litteris commissionum huiusmodi hoc statutum nostrum inseratur Nulli ergo omnino hominum liceat hanc paginam nostre monicionis precepti et uoluntatis infringere uel et ausu temerario contraire Si quis autem hoc attemptare presumpserit indignacionem omnipotentis Dei ac beatorum Petri et Pauli apostolorum eius se nouerit incursurum Datum Rome apud Sanctum Petrum anno incarnacionis dominice Millesimo quadringentesimo sexagesimo quinto quinto Idus Maij Pontificatus nostri anno primo.

Et deiude sicut exhibita nobis pro parte dilectorum filiorum decani et capituli ecclesie capelle regie nuncupate beate Marie et Sancti'Michaelis intra palacium carissimi in Christo filij nostri Jacobi Scotorum regis illustris opidi de Stirling Sanctiandree

nota bene. diocesis peticio continebat: Cum nos nuper alias dicti Jacobi Regis in ea parte supplicacionibus inclinati eandem capellam in collegiatam et in ea vnum decanum et vnum subdecanum dignitates ac unam sacristiam officium necnon certos canonicatus et prebendas pro totidem canonicis et alias certas personas postquam dictus Jacobus Rex certa bona immobilia ualoris annui tunc expressi pro dote ipsius ecclesie assignasset exigi et institui per alias nostras litteras mandauissemus postquam ipse Jacobus Rex iuxta dictarum litterarum nostrarum tenorem bona predicta assignauerat earumdem litterarum nostrarum vigore dicta capella in collegiatam ecclesiam et in illa dignitates ac canonicatus et prebende huiusmodi erecti et persone institute fuerint; cum autem sicut eadem peticio subiungebat inter certa bona per dictum Regem assignata prefatus Jacobus Rex de Kyntire et de Lochabire possessiones et bona immobilia Lesmorensis et Morauiensis siue Rossensis diocesium ualoris annui septuaginta librarum Stirlingorum uel circa eidem ecclesie assignauerit et si illa cum alijs bonis immobilibus utilioribus per eumdem Regem in cambium assignandis permutarentur seu loco bonorum assignatorum ut prefertur certe ecclesie iuris patronatus ipsius regis ex quorum fructibus redditibus et prouentibus annuis octuaginta libre similes uel circa singulis annis peruenirent et perciperentur mense capitulari dicte ecclesie perpetuo vnirentur annecterentur et incorporarentur permutacio seu unio huiusmodi si fierent in euidentem utilitatem dicte mense capitularis cederent; pro parte dictorum decani et capituli nobis fuit humiliter supplicatum ut in premissis prouidere de benignitate apostolica dignaremur: Nos igitur qui dudum inter alia uolumus quod petentes beneficia ecclesiastica alijs uniri tenerentur exprimere uerum ualorem annuum secundum communem extimacionem eciam beneficii cui vnio fieri peteretur alioquin unio non ualeret et semper in unionibus commissio fieret ad partes uocatis quorum interest de premissis certam noticiam non habentes et capituli singulares personas a quibusuis excommunicacionis suspensionis et interdicti aliisque ecclesiasticis sentenciis censuris et penis a iure uel ab homine quauis occasione uel causa si quibus quomodolibet innodate existunt ad effectum presencium dumtaxat consequendum harum serie absoluentes et absolutas fore censentes necnon possessionum et bonorum predictorum assignatorum et assignandorum situs et confines ac fructuum reddituum et prouentuum dicte mense ueros ualores annuos presentibus pro expressis habentes huiusmodi, suplicacionibus inclinati, discrecioni uestre per apostolica scripta mandamus quatenus possessionibus et bonis predictis tam assignatis quam assignandis coram uobis insimul procedentibus specificatis prius ac seruata forma litterarum preinsertarum huiusmodi coniunctim procedentes de premissis nos diligenter informetis et per informacionem huiusmodi ita esse et permutacionem seu vnionem aliquarum ecclesiarum que de iure patronatus dicti Regis existant quarumque fructus redditus et prouentus ad minus octuaginta libras ualeant annuatim eidem ecclesie seu illius mense capitulari SI FIENT IN EUIDENTEM utilitatem dicte ecclesie cedere reppereritis eisdem decano et capitulo recipiendi alia bona immobilia utiliora si illa prefatus Jacobus Rex pro prefatis possessionibus et bonis per eum assignatis assignare seu in excambium dare uoluerit licenciam et facultatem concedere seu alias ecclesias que de iure patronatus dicti regis existant et quarum fructus redditus et prouentus ad ualorem octuaginta librarum similium ad minus ascendant annuatim cum omnibus iuribus et pertinenciis suis si ad hoc prefati Regis accesserit assensus eidem mense perpetuo

vnire annectere et incorporare auctoritate nostra curetis, ita quod
cedentibus uel decedentibus dictarum uniendarum ecclesiarum
tunc rectoribus seu ecclesias ipsas uniendas alias quomodolibet
dimittentibus liceat decano et capitulo prefatis per se uel alium
seu alios corporalem possessionem ecclesiarum uniendarum
iuriumque et pertinenciarum predictorum propria auctoritate
apprehendere et perpetuo retinere ac illarum fructus redditus et
prouentus predictos in suos et dicte mense usus et utilitatem
conuertere diocesani loci et cuiusuis alterius licencia super hoc
minime requisita, non obstantibus uoluntate nostra predicta et
aliis apostolicis constitucionibus et ordinacionibus necnon dicte
ecclesie erecte iuramento confirmacione apostolica uel quauis
alia firmitate roboratis statutis et consuetudinibus contrarijs
quibuscumque aut si aliqui super prouisionibus sibi faciendis de
huiusmodi uel aliis beneficiis ecclesiasticis in illis partibus
speciales uel generales dicte sedis uel legatorum eius litteras
impetrauerit eciam si per eas ad inhibicionem reseruacionem et
decretum uel alias quomodolibet sit processum quasquidem
litteras et processus habitos per easdem et inde secuta quecumque ad dictas uniendas ecclesias uolumus non extendi sed
nullum per hoc eis quo ad assecucionem beneficiorum aliorum
preiudicium generari et quibuslibet priuilegiis indulgenciis et
litteris apostolicis generalibus uel specialibus quorumcumque
tenorum existant per que presentibus non expressa uel totaliter
non inserta effectus earum impediri ualeat quomodolibet uel
differri et de quibus quorumque totis tenoribus de uerbo ad
uerbum habenda sit in nostris litteris mencio specialis : Volumus autem quod propter unionem annexionem et incorporacionem predictas si eas uigore presencium fieri contingat dicte
ecclesie uniende debitis non fraudentur obsequiis et animarum
cura in quibus illa imminet nullatenus necligatur sed illarum
congrue supportentur onera consueta : et insuper quoad unionem
huiusmodi si illam uigore presencium fieri contingat exnunc irritum decernimus et inane si secus super hiis a quoquam quauis
auctoritate scienter uel ignoranter contigerit attemptari. Datum
Rome apud Sanctum Petrum anno incarnacionis dominice

Millesimo quingentesimo primo quarto decimo kalendas Aprilis
Pontificatus nostri anno Decimo.

12. CONSERUATORIA PENES APPLICACIONEM FRUCTUUM DE AIR KINCARDIN CREIF ET PETTYBRACHLIE.

ALEXANDER EPISCOPUS SERUUS SERUORUM Dei Dilectis filiis de
Cambuskynneth et Pasleto Sanctiandree et Glasguensis diocesium monasteriorum abbatibus ac archidiacono ecclesie Sanctiandree salutem et apostolicam benedictionem Hodie ex certis
causis ac sub certis modo et forma tunc expressis reseruatis
pro de Ayre Glasguensis quinquaginta et de Kyncardyne Abordenensis eciam quinquaginta ac de Crieff Dunkeldensis triginta et de Pettybrachlye et Duchel nuncupatis canonicatibus et
prebendis Morauiensis ecclesiarum similiter triginta marchis
monete Scocie Residuos fructus redditus et prouentus singulorum
eorumdem canonicatuum et prebendarum ecclesie capelle regie
nuncupate beate Marie et Sancti Michaelis intra palacium opidi
de Stirlyng Sanctiandree diocesis site seu illius mense capitulari apostolica auctoritate perpetuo applicauimus et appropriauimus ac residuos fructus huiusmodi ab eisdem canonicatibus
et prebendis eadem auctoritate perpetuo dimembrauimus et sep-
arauimus prout in nostris inde confectis litteris plenius continetur Quocirca discrecioni uestre per apostolica scripta mandamus quatenus uos uel duo aut unus uestrum si et postquam
dicte littere uobis presentate fuerint per uos uel alium seu
alios litteras ipsas et in eis contenta quecumque ubi et
quando ac quocienscumque opus fuerit ac pro parte decani
pro tempore existentis et dilectorum filiorum capituli dicte
ecclesie seu alicuius eorum desuper requisiti fueritis publicantes ac eis in premissis efficacis defensionis presidio assistentes faciatis eos auctoritate nostra pacifica possessione uel
quasi applicacionis appropriacionis dimembracionis et separacionis ac aliorum in eisdem litteris contentorum gaudere non
permittentes eosdem decanum et capitulum per venerabiles
fratres nostros Glasguensem Archiepiscopum et Abordenensem
ac Dunkeldensem et Morauiensem episcopos necnon dilectos

filios singularum Glasguensis Abordonensis Dunkeldensis et Morauiensis ecclesiarum predictarum capitula seu per quoscumque alios contra applicacionis appropriacionis dimembracionis et separacionis ac litterarum predictarum tenorem quomodolibet indebite molestari contradictores quoslibet et rebelles auctoritate nostra per censuram ecclesiasticam appellacione postposita compescendo inuocato eciam ad hoc si opus fuerit auxilio brachii secularis Non obstantibus felicis recordacionis Bonifacij Pape VIII predecessoris nostri qua inter alia cauuetur expresse ne aliquis extra suam ciuitatem uel diocesim nisi in certis exceptis casibus et in illis ultra unam dictam a fine sue diocesis ad iudicium euocetur Seu ne iudices et conseruatores a sede apostolica deputati extra ciuitatem et diocesim in quibus deputati fuerint contra quoscumque procedere aut alij uel aliis uices suas committere presumant et de duabus dictis in concilio generali edita dummodo ultra quatuor dictas aliquis auctoritate presencium non trahatur ac aliis constitucionibus et ordinacionibus apostolicis ac omnibus illis que in dictis litteris uolumus non obstare. Aut si archiepiscopo episcopis et capitulis prefatis uel quibusuis aliis communiter uel diuisim ab eadem sit sede indultum quod interdici suspendi uel excommunicari aut extra uel vltra certa loca ad iudicium euocari non possint per litteras apostolicas non facientes plenam expressam ac de uerbo in uerbum huiusmodi mencionem. Datum Rome apud Sanctum Petrum anno incarnacionis dominice Millesimo quingentesimo secundo sextodecimo Kalendas Maii Pontificatus nostri anno decimo.

13. HEC sunt ornamenta iocalia et volumina que habentur in ecclesia collegiata beate Marie et Sancti Michaelis de Striueling et ponuntur sub firma custodia discreti uiri magistri Dauid Traile sacriste dicte ecclesie quarto die mensis Nouembris de anno Domini millesimo quingentesimo quinto.

De colore nigro.

In primis vna casula una stola unus manipulus cum ly parrus

pro vna alba et uno amictu de ly satene nigri coloris habenti duplicaturam de ly bucram nigri coloris et hec casula habet ly orphus de vellus eciam nigri coloris. Item tres cape de ly vellus eciam nigri coloris noue et preciose portantes arma domini Regis de quibus una earum est consuta cum filis aureis ad modum stellarum splendencium. Item una casula et due tunice de vellus nigri coloris consute cum filis aureis due stole tres manipuli cum ly parrus pro tribus albis et tribus amictibus eiusdem coloris et substancie. Item unum pendiculum de uellus nigri coloris consutum cum filis aureis ad modum stellarum splendencium pro summo altari ordinatum et habet duplicaturam de bucram blodij coloris. Item unus paruus et longus pannus de vellus nigri coloris super quem consuta sunt cum filis aureis hec uerba—Misericordia eius super omnia opera eius—et habet duplicaturam de bucram blodij coloris. Item vua capa de ly dammes nigri coloris habens ly orphus de vellus subrubij coloris. Item vna casula de dammes nigri coloris habens ly orphus de vellus subrubii coloris. Item vnum pendiculum de dammes nigri coloris pro summo altari. Item vna parua et curta capa serica antiqua nigri et rubei coloris mixtim plus tamen participat de nigro colore. Item una casula tres stole tres manipuli cum ly parrus pro tribus albis et tribus amictibus de cameleto nigri coloris cum dupplicatura de bucram eiusdem coloris et hec casula habet ly parrus de dammes nigri coloris cum quibusdem lineis rubei coloris.

De blodio colore.

In primis due cape de dammes blodij seu celestis coloris cum filis aureis consute ad modum radiorum solis et sunt large et preciose habentes capucia sua et ly orphus de panno precioso auri et habent pannum lineum ad illas conseruandas. Item una casula due tunice vna stola tres manipuli cum ly parrus pro tribus albis et uno amictu de dammes eiusdem coloris bonitatis et substancie cum duabus capis inmediate predictis et hec due tunice habent ly orphus de precioso panno auri. Et cum istis tunicis habentur vna stola et ly parrus pro uno amictu de auro ualde precioso. Item unum pendiculum pro summo altari de dammes blodij coloris cum filis aureis consutum ad modum radiorum solis portans pulcherime salutacionem nostre domine. Item vnum aliud pendiculum pro summo altari de dammes eiusdem coloris et bonitatis cum pendiculo inmediate precedente portans honestissime ymaginem Dei patris et nostre Domine ac ymagines quorumdam angelorum et hoc pendiculum habet in se multas margaritas ad eius decorem et hec duo pendicula habent pannum lineum ad eorum conseruacionem. Item duo alia pendicula minora de vellus celestis seu blodij coloris contexta cum filis aureis et vnum illorum portat ymaginem Sancte Trinitatis in auro contextam. Item vna casula due tunice due stole tres manipuli et cum ly parrus et tribus albis et tribus amictibus de vellus subuellus blodij coloris et habent ly orphus de panno auri. Item duo pendicula pro summo altari de ly taffate blodij coloris quorum vnum portat in eius medio ymaginem crucifixi consutam cum filis aureis et hec duo pendicula duplicaturam habent de ly fustiane albi coloris.

De colore rubio.

Item due cape de panno precioso auri habentes capucia et ly orphus eciam de panno auri rubij coloris et habent pannum lineum ad earum conseruacionem et sunt meliores cape in ecclesia et magni precii. Item due cape de panno auri et vellus subuellus rubei coloris et habent pannum lineum ad earum conseruacionem. Item due cape de panno auri et de vellus commixtim rubei coloris cum ly orphus de panno auri et habent ly frenzeis de filis cericis in earum circumferencijs et cum panno lineo ad earum conseruacionem. Item due cape vna casula due tunice vna stola unus manipulus cum ly parrus pro una alba et vno amictu de satene rubij coloris contexta cum filis aureis ad modum ramorum arborum et hec due cape habent pannum lineum ad earum conseruacionem. Item unus pannus preciosus de auro rubij coloris ad honorem eucharistie ordinatus quando deportatur extra ecclesiam et habet pannum lineum ad eius conseruacionem. Item quatuor haste lignie rubij coloris ad portandum in alto dictum pannum super eucharistiam. Item vnum paruum frontale preciosum de auro et cum filis aureis pendentibus portans arma Regis et diuersa alia arma et certas ymagines sanctorum et habet in se multas margaritas ad eius decorem. Item una capa de vellus rubij coloris cum ly orphus de vellus nigri coloris. Item vna capa de Sateyne crammasy rubij coloris cum ly orphus de dammes viridis coloris. Item una casula de sateyne crammasy rudii coloris cum ly parrus de sateyne uiridis coloris. Item una capsula serica figure quadrangularis rubii coloris exterius et albi coloris interius pro corporalibus seruandis. Et ibi includitur unum co-opertorium pro calice sub figura quadrangulari de auro consutum cum multis margaritis sumptuose fabricatum. Item una casula noua una stola unus manipulus cum ly parrus pro una alba et uno amictu de panno auri preciosi rubij coloris sumptuose consute et fabricate habente duplicaturam de sateyne blodij coloris et hec casula habet ly orphus de panno auri cum filis aureis consutum et est res magni precii. Item unum antiquum ly orphus de panno auri conueniens pro una capa. Item unum aliud antiquum ly orphus de panno auri pro una capa et hec duo ly orphus sunt rubii coloris. Item unum antiquum frontale de serico diuersorum colorum portans diuersa arma desuper contexta et est modici ualoris.

De subalbo colore alias ly dunne coloure.

Item vna casula due tunice due stole tres manipuli cum ly parrus pro tribus albis et tribus amictibus de dammes de ly dwne colore habentibus ly orphus de panno auri. Item duo panni cerici antiqui cum filis aureis contexti ly dwne coloris. Item vnus paruus pannus sericus antiquus cum filis aureis contextus ly dwne coloris. Item unus antiquus de vellus de ly dwne colore pro ambone ut apparet ordinatus.

De colore viridi.

Item vna casula antiqua vna stola vnus manipulus portans arma regis et regine que uenit de Dacia de dammes uiridis coloris et cum ly parrus pro una alba et uno amictu eiusdem coloris et substancie. Item vnus pannus de ly verdoure diuersorum colorum plus tamen declinans ad colorem uiridem. Item duo panni de ly burdalexander habentes duplicaturam de panneo lineo pro duobus ambobus co-operiendis. Item vna casula cum armis domini regis due tunice due stole tres manipuli cum ly parrus pro tribus albis et tribus amictibus de dammes uiridis coloris. Item vna casula portans arma regis una stola unus manipulus cum ly parrus pro una alba de dammes uiridis coloris et hec casula habet ly orphus de vellus nigri coloris.

De colore albo.

Item due cape de panno auri albi coloris et habent pannum lyneum ad earum conseruacionem. Item una capa de dammes albi coloris cum filis aureis consuta ad modum solis splendentis et ly orphus de panno auri. Item due casule due stole duo manipuli cum ly parrus pro duabus albis et duobus amictibus de dammes albi coloris Et dicte casule habent ly orphus de uellus nigri coloris. Item una casula due tunice due stole tres manipuli cum ly parrus pro tribus albis et tribus amictibus de dammes albi coloris et habent ly orphus de panno auri et duplicaturam de bucram rubij coloris et sunt noue et preciose et dicte tunice habent cordas sericas pendentes retro et portant arma Regis abante et regis ac regine filic regis Anglie commixtim retro.

De colore purpureo.

Item due casule de vellus purpurei coloris cum ly orphus de panno auri due stole duo manipuli et cum ly parrus pro duabus albis et duobus amictibus eiusdem coloris et substancie.

ITEM duo candelabra erea aliquantulum magna. Item octo fiole de stanno. Item una parua campana pendens ante fores ecclesie. Item tres magne campane que uenerunt ex ciuitate Lundoniarum ibi empte per dominum Regem fundatorem ecclesie. Item unum pulcrum horecudium completum per dominum Jacobum Pettygrew fabricatum. Item duo ly flacottis de stanno. Item crux de stanno de aurato portans ymaginem crucifixi. Item tria tintinabula. Item una crux lignea rubij coloris habens hastam longam. Item una hasta longa ad portandum ymaginem crucifixi extra ecclesiam. Item duo magni ambones de lignis stantes in choro. Item tria paria organorum quorum unum est de lignis et duo alia de stanno siue de plumbo. Item tria scruicalia ad supponendum missalibus in altari. Item vna tabula cum tribus folijs ubi depinguntur ymago Domine nostre gerentis Filium suum in ulnis suis et duo angeli portantes instrumenta musicalia. Item una tabula in qua scribitur qui pridie etc. Item vna magna archa clausa cum duabus feris pro ornamentis ecclesie seruandis. Item ly Judas bellis et ly traditor pro officio tenebrarum in septimana dominice passionis. Item boxa correa apta ad seruandum euidencias ecclesie. Item habentur in pictura multa arma regis et regine pro obsequiis celebrandis. Item una habens tria folia ubi depinguntur sub uitro ymago crucifixi et quatuor sanctorum eciam sub uitro in lateribus. Item una tabula portans formam uultus nostri Saluatoris et uocatur ly vernakill. Item una tabula in qua depingitur ymago nostre domine. Item una capsula pro crismate de stanno.

Et sequitur de jocalibus.

In primis una magna capsula de argento pro eucharistia portanda et iocale magni ponderis ac sumptuose fabricatum et portat in eius summitate ymaginem crucifixi. Item due fiole de argento et sunt deaurate circa earum summitates. Item tria candelabra de argento et sunt ponderis notabilis. Item unus thuribulus cum naui et cocleari de argento pro incenso. Item ly teistyr de argento deaurato portans ymaginem crucifixi ac nostre domine et Johannis euuangeliste habet eciam multas gemmas diuersorum colorum in se fixas et est notabile iocale. Item unum iocale de argento deaurato fabricatum ad modum habens campanile in eius summitate una locatur una particula siue pecia ligni crucis sancte et ornatur illud iocale cum multis margaritis et includuntur in eodem ut ueraciter creditur multe reliquie sanctorum. Item unum paruum iocale de argento deaurato habens ymaginem crucifixi in eius summitate et protenditur aliquantulum in altum. Item unus circulus de puro auro habens formam capitis beati Johannis Baptiste. Item quatuor calices et quatuor patene de argento deaurato et bene ponderantes. Item una parua capsula de argento deaurato rotunde figure pro eucharistia seruanda. Item unum magnum et preciosum iocale de puro auro portans ymaginem nostre domine gerentis Filium suum mortuum super genua eius et diuersas alias ymagines et hoc iocale habet in eius summitate ymaginem crucifixi et est artificiose fabricatum portat eciam multas gemmas diuersorum et margaritas et includitur in una boxa de correo ad eius conseruacionem. Item tria parua candelabra de argento deaurato portantia arma regis Anglie et deportata fuerunt ad partes Scoticanas cum Regina nostra que est filia Regis Anglie.

Et sequitur de Voluminibus.

In primis duo missalia in papiro de littera impressa. Item duo missalia in pergamino de littera impressa. Item unum antiquum missale in pergamino cum penna scriptum. Item liber euuangeliorum in pergamino cum penna scriptus. Item liber epistolarum in pergamino cum penna scriptus. Item duo psalteria antiqua in pergamino cum penna scripta. Item quatuor magna antiphonaria in pergamino cum penna scripta et habent diuersas litteras capitales deauratas. Item duo magna breuiaria in pergamino de littera impressa. Item vnum magnum breuiarium in papiro in littera impressa et est ruptum in multis foliis. Item duo volumina in pergamino cum notis de ly faburdone. Item due legende in pergamino cum penna scripte quarum vna est de temporali et altera de proprietatibus sanctorum. Item decem processionalia in pergamino cum penna scripta et notata. Item tria gradalia in pergamino cum penna scripta. Item unum alterum gradale magnum et nouum in pergamino cum penna scriptum datum domino regi per abbatem Insule sancte Columbe defunctum. Item unum breuiarium magnum in papiro de littera impressa. Item unum paruum breuiarium in papiro de littera impressa. Item unum uolumen uocatum ordinarium secundum vsum Sarum in pergamino cum penna scriptum. Item vnum paruum missale in papiro de littera impressa. Item velum templi et est diuisum in duas partes pro quadragesima. Item septem parui panni linei ornati cum crucibus et ordinantur ad co-operiendum ymagines sanctorum tempore quadragesimali. Item octo manitergia pro manibus lauandis in missa de quibus sunt quatuor de ly dornyke. Item quatuor corporalia pro missis celebrandis.

[*In the MS. there is a blank space here of two leaves and half a page.*]

14. Preuilegium Familiarium Regis et Regine.

Julius episcopus seruus seruorum Dei ad perpetuam rei memoriam. Honestis omnium fidelium uotis et apostolice sedis deuotarum personarum presertim Catholicorum principum desideriis per que persone quelibet eorum obsequiis insistentes sublatis uexationibus et inquietacionibus vniuersis in pacis et quietis dulcedine ualeant eis debitum prestare famulatum libenter annuimus eaque quantum cum Deo possumus fauoribus prosequimur oportunis sane pro parte carissimi filii nostri Jacobi Scotorum Regis et carissime in Christo filie nostre Margarete Regine Scotorum illustrium nobis nuper exhibita peticio continebat quod cum sepe contingat quod familiares continui commensales eorundem Regis et Regine et eorum obsequiis insistentes ad instanciam diuersarum personarum coram diuersis iudicibus et forsan non ordinariis suis in diuersis causis et quandoque ciuilibus ad iudicium euocenter quamuis ipsi familiares in obsequiis huiusmodi insistentes parati essent coram iudice ordinario ubi resident pro tempore de se querelantibus in iusticia respondere et ex huiusmodi euocacione eorundem familiarium et obsequiis insistencium coram diuersis iudicibus ipsi familiares et obsequiis insistentes diuersa damna et incomoda quandoque paciuntur impedianturque eciam ne in hiis que ad obsequium Regis et Regine predictorum pertinent cum illa diligencia et assiduitate intendere possint Conueniensque uideretur et tam pro eorum quiete quam eciam ut circa obsequia Regis et Regine predictorum congruis temporibus insistere valeant ut aliquis iudex deputetur coram quo commode conueniri possint Quare pro parte Regis et Regine predictorum nobis fuit humiliter supplicatum ut omnes et singulos eorum et pro tempore existencium Regis et Regine Scotorum nunc et pro tempore existentes familiares continuos commensales eorumque et cuiuslibet eorum obsequiis insistentes et actu seruientes. Et qui per sex menses seruiuerint eisdem a quorumcunque Episcoporum et Archiepiscoporum aliorumque ordinariorum eorumque officialium presencium et futurorum jurisdictione correccione dominio et potestate penitus eximere et totaliter liberare aliasque in premissis oportune prouidere de benignitate apostolica dignaremur Nos igitur qui personarum singularum presertim seruiciis Regum et Reginarum insistencium pacem et quietem summis desideriis exoptamus huiusmodi supplicacionibus inclinati omnes et singulos Jacobi et Margarite predictorum et pro tempore existencium Regis et Regine Scotorum familiares continuos commensales eorumque et cuiuslibet eorum obsequiis insistentes ac actu seruientes et qui per sex menses continuos seruiuerint eisdem a quorumcunque Episcoporum Archiepiscoporum aliorumque ordinariorum eorumque officialium presencium et futurorum iurisdictione correccione dominio et potestate preterquam racione uel causa quorumcunque beneficiorum ecclesiasticorum secularium uel regularium obtentorum uel optinendorum pro tempore eximimus et totaliter liberamus Ita quod Episcopi Archiepiscopi aliique ordinarii et officiales prefati seu eorum aliquis nullam eciam racione delicti aut rei de qua ageretur ubicunque committatur delictum aut res ipsa consistat correccionem superioritatem aut dominium et potestatem in familiares et obsequiis prefatos presentes et futuros aut eorum aliquem exercere possint Sed teneantur ipsi familiares in obsequiis insistentes presentes et futuri de se querelantibus tam laicis quam ecclesiasticis coram dilecto filio decano ecclesie beate Marie et Sancti Michaelis Capelle Regie nuncupate opidi de Sterlyng Sancti Andree diocesis nunc et pro tempore existente in iusticia respondere possintque ipsi familiares et obsequiis insistentes presentes et futuri Coram prefato decano in iusticia respondere; decernentes ex nunc omnes et singulos processus

qui censentur exempti familiares.

Nota.—Familiares actu seriuentes per sex menses continuos.

sentencias quos et quas contra familiares et obsequiis insistentes
prefatos presencium tenorem exempcionis et liberacionis huiusmodi haberi et promulgari contigerit nullius roboris uel momenti
existere ac irritum et inane quicquid secus super hiis a quoquam
quauis autoritate scienter uel ignoranter contra tenorem presencium fieri uel attemptari contigerit et quecunque pro tempore
inde secuta nulla irrita et inania nulliusque roboris uel momenti
Quocirca dilectis filiis de Dunfermlyn et Cambuskynneth Sancti- Quocirca
andree diocesis monasteriorum Abbatibus ac preposito ecclesie filiis de
Fesulan per apostolica scripta mandamus quatinus ipsi uel duo Dunferm-
aut vnus eorum eisdem familiaribus et obsequiis insistentibus Cambus-
in premissis efficacis defensionis auxilio assistentes faciant eos kynnet ac
exempcione et liberacione predictis pacifice frui et gaudere non ecclesie
permittentes eos per episcopos archiepiscopos ordinarios et Fesulan
officiales predictos aut quoscunque alios contra tenorem ex- lica scripta
empcionis et liberacionis huiusmodi quomodolibet molestari manda-
contradictores autoritate nostra appellacione postposita compescendo Non obstantibus felicis recordacionis Innocencij Pape
IIII. predecessoris nostri circa exemptos que incipit—Volentes—
etaliis constitucionibus et ordinacionibus apostolicis necnon statutis et consuetudinibus dicte ecclesie beate Marie iuramento
confirmacione apostolica uel quauis firmitate alia roboratis contrariis quibuscunque Seu si archiepiscopis episcopis ordinariis Nota.—
et officialibus prefatis uel quibusuis aliis communiter uel diuisim Priuilegia
ab eadem sit sede indultum quod interdici suspendi uel excom- cassabuun-
municari non possint per litteras apostolicas non facientes ex speciali
plenam et expressam ac de uerbo ad uerbum de indulto huius- autoritate
modi mencionem Nulli ergo omnino hominum liceat hanc pagi- tolica et
nam nostre exempcionis liberacionis decreti et mandati infringere hoc ex-
uel ei ausu temerario contraire Si quis autem hoc attemptare
presumpserit indignacione omnipotentis Dei ac beatorum Petri
et Pauli apostolorum eius se nouerit incursurum Datum Rome
apud Sanctum Petrum anno Incarnacionis diuinice Millesimo
quingentesimo quarto Quinto nonas Julij.

15. Mutacio Decani Ecclesie Collegiate de Sterlyng.

Julius episcopus Seruus seruorum dei ad rei perpetuam memoriam. Romani Pontificis prouidencia circumspecta nonnunquam per sedem apostolicam ordinata commutat prout ecclesiarum commoditatibus et Catholicorum regum uotis attentis id in domino conspicit salubriter expedire sane pro parte Carissimi in Christo filii nostri Jacobi Scotorum Regis illustris nobis nuper exhibita peticio continebat quod alias ad supplicacionem prefati regis capella Regia nuncupata beate Marie et Sancti Michaelis intra palacium ipsius Regis opidi de Sterlyng Sanctiandree dyocesis in collegiatam ecclesiam et in ea inter alias dignitates et beneficia ecclesiastica inibi erecta Prepositura beate Marie de Rupe Sanctiandree que inibi dignitas principalis et de iure patronatus prefati Jacobi et pro tempore existentis Scotorum regis et preuilegio apostolico existit et ad eius meram collacionem ex eodem preuiligio pertinet in decanatum dignitatem inibi principalem pro uno decano qui aliis eiusdem tunc erigende ecclesie presset personis cuique cura animarum dicti Jacobi et pro tempore existentis Regis et Regine Scotorum et eorum officialium et familiarium continuorum commensalium et familiarium eorumdem familiarium et seruorum immineret quodque omnimodam jurisdictionem in omnes personas dicte erigende ecclesie pro tempore existentes haberet et dum in eadem beate Marie de Rupe in illa prepositus dum uero in erecta ecclesiis huiusmodi resideret in ea decanus foret Ita ut non due dignitates existerent sed una dumtaxat in qualibet dictarum ecclesiarum preeminenciam habens existeret apostolica autoritate erecta fuit. Et quia prepositus dicte ecclesie de Rupe commode circa curam animarum utriusque dictarum ecclesiarum in quibus respectiue Prepositus et Decanus existit intendere non potest et decanus pro tempore existens curam animarum Regis et Regine predictorum habere, conueniens uidetur quod persona magis qualificata quam ipse decanus sit existat; et propterea si statueretur et ordinaretur quod dictus prepositus dicte ecclesie de Rupe nunc et pro tempore existens de cetero decanus in dicta ecclesia de Sterlyng non esset, sed venerabilis frater noster modernus et pro tempore existens Episcopus Candicase Episcopus decanus eiusdem ecclesie beate Marie existeret, profecto ex hoc decori et uenustati dicte ecclesie de Sterlyng magis consuleretur : Quare pro parte eiusdem Jacobi Regis nobis sunt humiliter supplicatum vt in premissis oportune prouidere de benignitate apostolica dignaremur :—Nos IGITUR huiusmodi supplicationibus inclinati quod de cetero perpetuis futuris temporibus prefatus Prepositus dicte ecclesie de Rupe non decanus eiusdem ecclesie de Sterling sed solum prout ante huiusmodi erectionem Prepositus prefate ecclesie de Rupe ut prius remaneat, et ipse Episcopus Candidecase nunc et pro tempore existens Decanus eiusdem ecclesie de Sterling existat eandemque preheminentiam et superioritatem in dicta ecclesia de Sterling habeat et curam animarum Regis et Regine ac aliarum predictorum exerceat prout Prepositus dicte ecclesie de Rupe dum in ipsa ecclesia de Sterling residebat iuxta tenorem litterarum apostolicarum super huiusmodi erectione confectarum habebat et exercebat et habere et exercere poterat ac eadem emolumenta ex fructibus dicte ecclesie erecte prout ipse prepositus percipiebat etiam vnacum ecclesia sua Candidecase percipere possit auctoritate apostolica tenore presencium statuimus et ordinamus Non obstantibus premissis ac constitutionibus et ordinationibus apostolicis necnon ecclesiarum predictarum iuramento confirmatione apostolica vel quauis firmitate alia roboratis statutis et consuetudinibus ceterisque contrariis quibuscunque Nulli ergo omnino hominum liceat hanc paginam nostrorum statuti et ordinationis infringere vel ei ausu temerario contraire Siquis autem hoc attemptare presumpserit indignationem omnipotentis Dei ac beatorum Petri et Pauli apostolorum eius se venerit incursurum Datum Rome apud Sanctum Petrum anno Incarnationis dominice Millesimo quingentesimo quarto Quinto nonas Julii Pontificatus nostri anno primo.

[*Here in the original MS. occurs a blank of two pages.*]

16. CONFIRMACIO BULLE SUPER FUNERALIA JURA ECCLESIASTICA ET JURISDICTIONE ECCLESIARUM VNITARUM.

JULIUS EPISCOPUS SERUUS SERUORUM DEI Venerabili fratri Archiepiscopo Sipontini et dilectis filiis de Cambuskynnet et Lowndoris Sanctiandree diocesis Monasteriorum Abbatibus salutem et apostolicam benedictionem hodie emanarunt a nobis littere tenoris subsequentis :

Julius episcopus seruus seruorum Dei ad perpetuam rei memoriam Romani pontificis prouidencia circumspecta ad ea libenter intendit per que litibus obuietur et sue prouisionis * adminiculo que in concessis per eum graciis suboriri possent dubia sopiantur sane pro parte Carissimi in Christo filij nostri Jacobi Scotorum Regis illustris ac dilecti filii Jacobi electi Candidecase nobis nuper exhibita peticio continebat quod alias felicis recordacionis Alexander Pape VI.† predecessor noster ad supplicationem dicti Jacobi Regis Capellam Regiam beate Marie et Sancti Michaelis intra palacium‡ in opido de Sterling Sanctiandree diocesis in collegiatam ecclesiam et in ea decanatum principalem et subdecanatum ac sacristiam § dignitates necnon certos ‖ canonicatus et prebendas tunc expressos erigi ac certa beneficia ecclesiastica usque ¶ ad certam summam tunc expressam cum cura et sine cura que de iure patronatus ipsius Regis et aliorum laicorum erant de consensu regis et patronorum predictorum respectiue per quasdam uniri annecti et incorporari

* *Et sua provisionis et ordinacions,* in No. 17. † *Sextus* for VI., in No. 17.
‡ *Palacium situm,* in No. 17. § *Sacristam,* in No. 17.
‖ *Certa,* in No. 17. ¶ *Vsque,* in No. 17.

mandauit ac decanatum subdecanatum sacristiam * et canonicos
ac clericos et alias personas dicte ecclesie tunc erigenda † et
ipsam ecclesiam postquam erecta foret necnon bona omnia eidem
ecclesie tunc unita et imposterum unienda ab Archiepiscopi Nota de
et ‡ quorumcunque aliorum ordinariorum eorumque officialium exempcione ab
tunc et pro tempore existentium iurisdictione superioritate archiepiscopo
dominio ac uisitatione et correctione penitus et omnino exeunt Sancti-
et totaliter liberauit ita ut decanus coram sede apostolica uel andree.
delegatis § eius subdecanus uero sacrista ac canonici et persone
ecclesie huiusmodi coram ipso decano pro tempore existente
tenerentur de se querelantibus in iusticia respondere ac irritum
et inane quicquid secus super hiis a quaquam ‖ quauis auctoritate scienter uel ignoranter contingeret attemptari decreuit. Et
deinde per alias suas statuit et ordinauit quod prepositus ecclesie
de Rupe ¶ Sanctiandree diocesis dum in ipsa ecclesia tunc
[e]recta inibi decanus et dum in ipsa ecclesia de Ruppe resideret
inibi prepositus existeret ac successiue nos per reliquas omnes
et singulos dicti Jacobi et pro tempore existentis Regis ac eciam
Regine Scotorum similiter pro tempore existentis famuliares Nota.—
Familiares
continuos commensales et eorumdem familiarum familiares ** et
seruitores a iurisdictione dominio et superioritate quorumcunque
Archiepiscoporum et episcoporum ordinariorum et †† officialium
suorum pro tempore existentium eximimus et totaliter liber-
auimus ac iurisdictioni dicti decani pro tempore existentis sub-
misimus ac statuimus et ordinauimus quod ex tunc de cetero
dictus prepositus prefate ecclesie de Ruppe non esset decanus
dicte erecte ecclesie sed episcopus Candidecase tunc et pro tempore existens esset decanus dicte ecclesie erecte et curam animarum Regis et Regine et eorum officialium ac familiarium
seruitorum ‡‡ predictorum haberet prout prepositus dicte ecclesie
de Ruppe dum in ipsa ecclesia erecta §§ residebat juxta tenorem
litterarum Alexandri predecessoris habebat ac exercere poterat

* *Sacristam*, in No. 17.   † *Erigende*, in No. 17.
‡ *Archiepiscopi Sanctiandree ac*, in No. 17.   § *Delegatus*, in No. 17.
‖ *Quoquam*, in No. 17.   ¶ *Ruppe*, in No. 17.
** *Famuliares*, in No. 17.   †† *Et*, omitted in No. 17.
‡‡ *Et seruitorum*, in No. 17.   §§ *In ipsa erecta ecclesia*, in No. 17.

eademque emolumenta ex fructibus dicte ecclesie erecte prout ipse Prepositus percipiebat eciam* vnacum ecclesia Candidecase recipere † posset et nouissime per alias nostras litteras de fratrum nostrorum consilio eciam ad requisicionem prefati Regis statuimus et ordinauimus quod ipse Episcopus Candidecase ‡ pro tempore existens denominetur Episcopus Capelle Regie Sterlingensis et gaudeat omnibus priuilegiis jurisdictionibus et indultis quibus ipse Episcopus Candidecase vt decanus dicte ecclesie Capelle Regie iuxta priuilegia desuper concessa gaudere posset prout in singulis litteris predictis dicitur plenius contineri cum autem sicut eadem peticio subiungebat licet per prefatum Alexandrum predecessorem omnia et singula bona dicte erecte ecclesie a jurisdictione ordinaria exempta et perrochiales § ecclesie de jure patronatus ipsius Regis et aliorum laicorum patronorum de illorum consensu respectiue eidem erecte ecclesie uigore litterarum Alexandri predecessoris cum omnibus iuribus et pertinenciis suis unite fuerunt ipsaque vnio effectum sortita extiterit ad ipsumque Episcopum cura animarum Regis et Regine ac famuliarum ‖ et aliorum predictorum pertineat Tamen ab aliquibus reuocatur indubium an ipse episcopus Candidecase et capelle regie jurisdictionem ordinariam super ecclesias parrochiales et illarum parrochianos exercere et iura ordinaria eciam funeralia a perochianis ¶ et famuliaribus ac aliis predictis cure ipsius Episcopi vt decano dicte ecclesie erecte vt prefertur commissis illis pro tempore decedentibus habere possit pro parte Jacobi regis et Jacobi electi predictorum asserencium equum uideri ab eodem episcopo ab illis temporalia recipi deberi ** quibus spiritualia ministrant ipsosque Regem et Reginam pro tempore eorumque famuliares †† et seruitores ac parrochialium ecclesiarum parrochianos ad temporalia per eas ante erectionem ac vnionem parrochialium ecclesiarum huiusmodi solui solita post erectionem et vnionem huiusmodi eidem episcopo soluendi ‡‡ teneri nobis fuit humiliter supplicatum vt in premissis et ad tollendas

Episcopus Candidecasie denominetur Episcopus capelle regie Striuilingensis

* *Eciam*, omitted in No. 17. † *Percipere*, in No. 17.
‡ *Candidecasie*, in No. 17. § *Parrochiales*, in No. 17.
‖ *Familiarum*, in No. 17. ¶ *Parrochianis*, in No. 17.
** *Debere*, in No. 17. †† *Familiares*, in No. 17. ‡‡ *Soluendam*, in No. 17.

contenciones que premissorum occasione inter prefatum Episcopum Candidecase et capelle Regie nunc et pro tempore existentem et * alios locorum ordinarios seu parrochialium ecclesiarum Rectores exoriri possent oportune prouidere de benignitate apostolica dignaremur Nos igitur prefatum Jacobum Electum a quibuscunque excommunicacionis suspensionis et interdicti aliisque ecclesiasticis sentenciis censuris † et penis a iure vel ab homine quauis occasione vel causa latis siquibus quomodolibet innodatos existit ad effectum presencium dumtaxat consequendum harum serie absoluentes et absolutum fore censentes huiusmodi supplicacionibus inclinati auctoritate apostolica tenore presencium decernimus et declaramus quod prefatus Jacobus Electus et pro tempore existens Episcopus Candidecase ‡ Capelle Regie omnia et singula predicta ac alia iura quacumque eciam funeralia in parrochiales ecclesias unitas et alias predictas ac illarum parrochianos officiales famuliares et seruitores prefatos que rectores predictarum eidem erecte ecclesie vnitarum et aliarum ecclesiarum infra quarum parrochias Regem et Reginam ac eorum officiales famulares § et seruitores cure et iurisdictioni dicti Episcopi Candidecase et Capelle Regie commissas ‖ vt prefertur pro tempore decedere contigerit vt alii ordinarii locorum ab eisdem Regeet Regina et eorum ¶ officialibus et familiarum ** familiaribus et seruitoribus predictis ac si ipsi sub cura et iurisdictione dicti Episcopi Candidecase et Capelle Regie et ipse parrochiales ecclesie eidem erecte ecclesie vnite non essent petere et exigere possent recipere que et habere ac exigere et omnimodam iurisdictionem in parrochiales ecclesias vnitas et alias predictas ac parrochianos †† officiales familiares et seruitores prefatos exercere possit et debeat Non obstantibus premissis ac apostolicis necnon in prouincialibus et sinodalibus Conciliis editis generalibus uel specialibus constitucionibus et ordinacionibus necnon omnibus illis que in nostris volumus ac Alexander predecessor prefatus in suis litteris predictis uoluit non

Nota.— De interdictione

Nota.—De funeralibus.

de funeralibus.

Episcopus Candidecase habet omnimodam jurisdictionem dicte capelle et aliarum ecclesiarum vnitarum quando presens est.

* *Ac*, in No. 17.   † *Censuris*, omitted in No. 17.   ‡ *Candidecase et*, in No. 17.
§ *Familiares*, in No. 17.   ‖ *Commissos*, in No. 17.
¶ *Eorum*, omitted in No. 17.   ** *Ac familiarium*, in No. 17.
†† *Par*—at this point No. 17 stops, one folio of the original wanting.

obstare ceterisque contrariis quibuscunque Nulli ergo omnino hominum liceat hanc paginam nostre absolucionis decreti et declaracionis infringere uel ei ausu temerario contraire Siquis autem hoc attemptare presumpserit indignacionem omnipotentis Dei ac beatorum Petri et Pauli Apostolorum eius se nouerit incursurum Datum Rome apud Sanctum petrum Anno Incarnacionis dominice Millesimo quingentesimo octauo sexto Idus Septembris pontificatus nostri Anno quinto.

Quocirca discrecioni uestre per apostolica scripta mandamus quatinus uos uel duo aut vnum uestrum per uos vel alium seu alios litteras predictas ac omnia et singula in eis contenta ubi et quando expedierit ac quociens pro parte Jacobi Regis et Jacobi Electi seu pro tempore Episcopi Candidecase et capelle Regie predictorum super hoc fueritis requisiti solemniter publicantes ac eisdem Jacobo Regi et Jacobo electo ac pro tempore Episcopo Candidecase et capelle Regie in premissis efficacis defensionis presidio assistentes faciatis litteras et in eis contenta huiusmodi inuiolabiliter obseruari non permittentes eundem Jacobum electum et pro tempore Episcopi Candidecase et capelle regie existente super illis per quoscumque cuiuscunque status uel condictionis fuerint contra tenorem litterarum predictarum quomodolibet molestari Contradictores per censuram ecclesiasticam appellacione postposita compescendo non obstantibus pie memorie Bonifacii Pape vni eciam predecessoris nostri quo inter alia cauetur ne quis extra suas ciuitatem et diocesim nisi in certis exceptis casibus et in illis ultra vnam dietam a fine sue diocesis ad iudicium reuocetur seu ne iudices a sede predicta deputati fuerint contra quoscunque procedere aut alii vel aliis uices suas committere presumunt et duabus dietis in consilio generali edita dummodo ultra tres dietas aliquis auctoritate presencium non trahitur ac aliis constitucionibus et ordinacionibus apostolicis necnon omnibus supradictis aut si aliquibus communiter uel diuisim ab eadem sit sede indultum quod interdici suspendi vel excommunicari non possint per litteras apostolicas non facientes plenam et expressam ac de verbo ad uerbum de indulto huiusmodi mencionem Datum Rome apud Sanctum petrum Anno Incarnacionis dominice Millesimo quingentesimo octauo sexto idus Septembris Pontificatus nostri anno quinto.

[*A blank of one page and a half in original.*]

17. BULLA SUPER FUNERALIA JURA ECCLESIASTICA ET IURISDICTIONEM ECCLESIARUM VNITARUM, ETC.

JULIUS EPISCOPUS SERWS SERVORUM DEI ad perpetuam rei memoriam Romani Pontificis prouidencia circumspecta [etc. as incorporated in No. 16, under which the variations are noted.

No. 17 is imperfect, through the loss of one folio of the original MS., and closes with " *ac par-*," as noted in No. 16.]

18. SUBSEQUITUR tenor erectionis vicarie ecclesie de Creyf per Fol. 50. lecte audite et postea judicialiter et recongnite ac per dominum Ninianum Spotiswoid archidiaconum capelle Regie Striuelingensis et dominum Willelmum Aitoune Rectorem de Banue testes in scriptis huiusmodi erectione insertos legittime probate. Qui vero testes tempore promulgacionis iudicialis dicte erectionis per quondam Magistrum Dauid Abercumbby iudicem ac eiusdem capelle Regie subdicanum pro tribunali sedentem sentencialiter late presentes fuerunt ac tenorem continenciam dicte erectionis sufficienter, probauerunt verum eciam Magistrum Willelmum Dennestoun notarium et scribam tunc temporis memorati quon-

dam judicis in dicta erectione recongnouerunt. Propterea Reuerendus in Christo pater Henricus miseratione diuina prenominate capelle et Candidecase Episcopus pro tribunali sedens confratrum suorum consilio canonicorum aut saltem maiorum partis eorum capitulariter in loco capitulari capitulariter congregati et imperpetue rei memoriam eandem erectionem per dominum Johannem Lambert prebendarum prelibate capelle ac scribam predicti capituli regestrari et in libris regestrorum sepedicte capelle inscribi et imponi mandauit ordinauit et decreuit primo die mensis Decembris Anno Domini Millesimo quingentesimo tricesimo septimo.

In Dei Nomine Amen Per hoc presens publicum Instrumentum cunctis pateat euidenter quod anno Incarnacionis dominice Millesimo quingentesimo vndecimo mensis vero Mercii die quinto indictione decima quinta pontificatus Sanctissimi in Christo patris et domini nostri domini Julij diuina prouidencia pape secundi anno nono In mei notarii publici et testium subscriptorum presencia sedente pro tribunali venerabili et egregio viro Magistro Dauid Abbercrummy officiali principali Candidecase et Capelle Regie Struelingensis ac eiusdem capelle regie subdicano comparuerunt personaliter in iudicio discretus vir dominus Johannes Broune vicarius pensionarius perpetuus ecclesie parrochialis de Creyf in Stratherne actor ab vna Et domini Willelmus Sterheid et Johannes Goldsmyth canonici dicte capelle Regie ac prebendarij eiusdem ecclesie de Creyf rei partibus ab altera dictis prebendariis prius ad hoc legitime citatis tanquam in termino per dictum Judicem assignato ad augmentandam pensionem annuam dicti vicarij Quequid pensio vt idem vicarius asseruit erat nimie exigua perua et exilis sic quod de eadem commode se sustentari non valuit. Idem vero vicarius ad suam intencionem roborandam duas in iudicio produxit scripturas vnam videlicet subscriptam manu propria excellentissimi principis et domini nostri domini Jacobi quarti Scotorum regis illustrissimi ac in margine eiusdem cum illo uerbo—Rex. Alteram vero manu propria reuerendi in Christo patris et domini domini Dauid miseracioni diuina Candidecase et capelle Regie Struelingensis Episcopi subscriptam Duarum quidem scripturarum tenores sequuntur et sunt tales:—Rex.—We as patrone of the kyrk of Creyf gyffis ouyr full consent and assent be thir ouyr lettres that the bischop of ouyr chapel rial erec and mak the vicar pensione of the sayd kyrk equauilent to the vtheris vicaris pensionarys of the kyrkys of Balmaclellene Suthwyth and Kellys vnit erectit to ouyr sayd chapel wyth ane manse zard and gleyb of twa akaris of the kyrk land of Creyf callyt for nixt adiacent to the sayd kyrk to the sustentacione of the vicar therof to serue the cuyr payand procuragis and synnagis and mak the dene Rurale expensys in visitacion as efferys and ordanys that this be done be the bischop of ouyr chapel Ryel and official tharof be tharis dyscrecionys the quantyte of the cuyr beyng consyderit. Subscriuit wyth our hand at Edynbrugh the xxv daye of September and of our reng the xxiiij^{or} zeir Et sequitur subscripcio manualis. Rex James. Schyr officiale forsamekyll as the vicarage of the kyrk of Creyf is nocht contenyt in the erectioun of our souerane lordis chapel riale as the layf of the vicaragis that ar incorporat tharto is tharfor that ze assyngne and mak our vicar of Creyf als mekyll zeyrly to his pensioun of the fructis o the said vicarage to sustene hym and serue the cuyr as ony of the vicaragis of Balmaclelen Suchwych or Kellis has wyth ane manse zard and gleib and tua akaris of the kyrk land callyt For nixt adiacent to the sayd kyrk wyth certane gress sovmes for gudyng of the said gleib accordyng to the extent of the said kyrkland he payand of the samyn zerly procurage and synage aucht and wount and makand the deyne rurale expense quhen he vesiis the sayd kyrk alanerlye for our souerane lordys patroun of the sayd kyrk of Creyf has consentyt heirto and commendit ws to hys writtingis to do the samyn keip this our mandment for zour warand and cause the samyn to be fulfyllyt sa that we heir na complant tharof in tymys cuming. Subscriuit wyth our hand at Edinbrugh the v day of March the zer of God 1^m v^c xi yeris. Et sequitur subscripcio manualis dicti Episcopi D. Candidecase et capelle Regie Striuelingensis Episcopus. Quibusquidem scripturis in iudicio coram partibus publice perlectis et ostensis dictus vicarius instanter a Iudice postulauit vt augmentacionem sue annue pensionis dicte vicarie perpetue secundum tenorem dictarum duarum scripturarum procedere dignaretur attenta maxime quod per dictos prebendarios nulla racionabilis tam fuerat in iudicio alligata quare huiusmodi augmentacio fieri non deberet Dominus vero Iudex antedictus inspectis deligenter dictis duabus scripturis et fundacione prefate capelle Regie Striuelingensis in illo presertim posse vbi agitur de ereccione vicariarum perpetuarum et eorumdem pencionibus annuis ecclesiarum parrochialium de Suchwich Kellis et Balmᶜlellane pertinencium ad dictam capellam regiam pensionem annuam dicte vicarie perpetue de Creif in modo qui sequitur Augmentauit et ordinauit videlicet quod vicarius perpetuus eiusdem ecclesie de Creif in Stratherne qui pro tempore fuerit deinceps habeat annuatim pro perpetuis temporibus futuris de fructibus ipsius ecclesie de Creif pro sua sustentacione et omnibus supportandis vnde commode viuere valeat viginti quatuor marcas vsualis monete Regni Scocie et duas acras arrabiles viciniores dicte ecclesie de villa que For nuncupatur pertinentes ad eandem ecclesiam ortumque et domos edificatas vna cum pastura animalium suorum secundum congruenciam earundem dictarum acrarum et cum focalibus competentibus in moris et marresiis eiusdem ville. Et preterea quod prefatus vicarius qui pro tempore fuit sic deinceps perpetuus temporibus futuris astrictus ad soluendum annuatim Episcopo ordinario loci procuraciones debitas et consuetas pro dicta ecclesia pecunias sinodales et expensas ordinarias decano christianitatis qui pro tempore dictam ecclesiam de Creif in Strathern et eius parrochia annuatim visitauerit. Et quod solucio pensionis quo ad prefatas xxiiij^{or} marcas fieri deberet dicto vicario de Creif qui pro tempore fuerit ad quatuor anni terminos vsuales porciones equales annuatim leuandas ex fructibus dicte ecclesie de Creif videlicet in festiuitatibus Inuencionis Sancte Crucis Sancti Petri qui ad uincula dicitur Omnium Sanctorum et Purificacionis nostre domine. Super quibus omnibus et singulis premissis prefatus dominus Johannes Brovn vicarius pensionarius perpetuus dicte ecclesie parrochialis de Creif in Stratherne a me notario publico subscripto sibi fieri peciit presens publicum Instrumentum seu publica Instrumenta vnum vel plura. Acta erant hec in capella regia prope opidum de Edinburgh sita in loco consistoriali eiusdem hora quasi duodecima ante meridiem vel eo circa sub anno die mense Indictione et pontificatu quibus supra presentibus ibidem discretis viris et dominis Niniano Spottiswode archidiacono prefate capelle regie Striuelingensis Johanne Tod Alexandro Painter Willelmo Atkyn Nycholaio Buchane capellanis. Jacobo Aikman burgensi de Edinbrugh Johanne Abercrumby et Alexandro Ramsay cum diuersis aliis testibus ad premissa vocatis pariter et rogatis.

(Sd.) J. PRYMROIS.

19. ANE INDEX OF RIGHTS OF THE CHAPPELL AND OF THEIR BULLS OR PATENTS.

1. Processus super erectione ecclesiæ collegiatæ de Sterling. The erection of the Chappell, ... Fol. 1.
2. Confirmatio erectionis. A confirmation theirof . Fol. 9.
3. Conseruatoria ecclesiæ collegiatæ de Sterling. A conservatorie Bull theirof, ... Fol. 14.
4. Vnio ecclesiæ de Kirkinner. The vnion of Kirkinner to the Chappell, ... Fol. 16.
 Constitutio procuratorum ad præstandum consensum rectoris vnioni de Kirkinner et ad resignandum post vnionem factam, ... Fol. 23.
 Confirmatio erectionis de Kirkinner, . . . Fol. 27.
5. Vnio fructuum de Creiff Dunbar Ellam, Bute Balmaclellan, etc., ... Fol. 19.
6. Commissio ad erigendam Thesaurariam et decem canonicatus et præbendas. Commission for erection of the thesaurer and mo præbenderis, ... Fol. 25.
7. Applicatio fructuum de Air, Kincardin Creiff and Pettie Brachley, ... Fol. 28.
8. Bulla si in euidentem, ... Fol. 32.
9. Conseruatoria de Air, Kincardin Creiff, etc., . Fol. 34.

10. A registre of ornaments and books perteining to the Chappell, ... Fol. 35.
11. Priuelegium familiarium regis et reginæ, . . Fol. 41.
12. Mutatio decani. The transferring of the Deanrie to the Bishop of Galloway.
13. A patent of the Deanes iurisdiction ouer all the vnited kirks, Fol. 47. Confirmation of it, . . Fol. 44.
14. Erectio vicariæ ecclesia de Creiff.
   Besyde these conteined in this registre there are eleuen Bulles.

I . R . 6 . 5 .
T H ·
C V M ° M A N V
P R O P R I A

APPENDIX.

I.

Grant to the Chapel Royal by the Regent, Duke of Albany.

Pp. xi., xii.—In the text we have omitted to refer to a grant to the Chapel Royal by the Regent Albany. On the 26th June 1407, the Regent granted half an annual rent of twenty marks of the lands of Craggroth for the sustenance of a chaplain in the Chapel of Michael the Archangel at Stirling Castle, where masses might be said for his own soul, the souls of his two wives, Margaret and Muriel, and their children, and also for the souls of the kings of Scotland, since King Robert the Bruce. We subjoin the original instrument, from the Register of the Great Seal:

"Carta pro capellano fundato in Castro de Striuelyne.

"Robertus, dux Albanie, comes de Fyfe et de Menteth, ac gubernator regni Scocie omnibus probis hominibus tocius regni predicti clericis et laicis salutem. Sciatis nos dedisse concessisse et hac presenti carta nostra confirmasse pro salute animarum excellentissimorum principum bone memorie Roberti et David de Bruys Roberti senescalli progenitoris nostri et Roberti senescalli fratris nostri quondam regum Scocie ac eciam pro salute anime nostre et animarum Margarete et Murielle uxorum nostrarum et prolum nostrarum ac antecessorum et successorum nostrorum ac omnium fidelium defunctorum Deo et beate Marie virgini et beato Michali Archangelo ac uni capellano divina celebraturi et imperpetuum celebraturo in capella beati Michaelis Archangeli infra castrum de Striuelyne situata decem marcas annualis redditus annuatim levandas et recipiendas de annuo redditu viginti marcarum exeunte de terris de Cragortht cum pertinenciis jacentibus infra vicecomitatum de Striuelyne per manus tenencium et inhabitancium earundem: Tenendas et habendas ac percipiendas dictas decem marcas annuatim ad duos anni terminos penthecostes videlicet et Santi Martini in yeme per porciones equales predicto capellano et successoribus suis qui pro tempore fuerint in liberam puram et perpetuam elemosinam ad manum mortuam imperpetuam cum omnibus libertatibus commoditatibus et aysiamentis ac iustis pertinenciis quibuscunque ad dictum annuum redditum spectantibus seu iuste spectare valentibus in futurum adeo libere et quiete plenarie integre honorifice bene et in pace in omnibus et per omnia sicut aliqua elemosina infra regnum Scocie per aliquem conceditur siue datur. Volumus eciam et concedimus quod quandocunque et quocienscunque dictum capellanum qui pro tempore fuerit decedere contigerit seu ex aliqua causa racionalibi (*sic*) a dicta capellania ammoveri extunc nos vel heredes nostri qui pro tempore fuerint infra mensem a tempore vacacionis huiusmodi alium capellanum ydoneum domino episcopo Sanctiandree vel eius vicario generali sede vacante debite presentent admittendum pro salute omnium animarum predictarum in capella beati Michaelis supradicta pro perpetuo celebratarum. Et quandocunque dictum capellanum qui pro tempore fuerit ad aliquod aliud beneficium ecclesiasticum contigerit promoveri statim postquam illud perceperit seu obtinuerit dicta capellania vacabit Insuper volumus et per presentes ordinamus quod si dictus annuus redditus decem marcarum dicto capellano qui pro tempore fuerit ad dictos terminos bene et prompte annuatim non soluant, licet extunc eidem capellano sine licencia alicuius ministri predictas terras de Craggrotht distringere et namare quousque de dicte animá redditu plenarie fuerit satisfactum nichil inde faciendo dictus capellanus et successores sui nobis et heredibus nostris qui pro tempore fuerint nisi missam cotidie cum dispositi fuerint in capella supradicta et oracionum suffragia devotarum pro omni alio servicio seculari exaccione seu demanda que de dicti annuo redditu decem marcarum aliqualiter exigi poterunt vel requiri. In cuius rei testimonium presenti carte nostre sigillum officii nostri apponi fecimus : Testibus reverendo in Christo patre Gilberto episcopo Abirdonensi cancellario Scocie Roberto senescallo primogenito carissimi filii nostri et heredis Murdaci senescalli militis Johanne Senescallo filio nostro domino Buchanie Alexandro Senescallo comite de Marr et de Garvyach nepote nostro Johanne Senescallo domino de Lorne Willelmo de Ertht militibus domino Donaldo de Bute decano Dunblanensi et Andrea de Hawyk secretario nostro apud Perth vicesimi sexti Die mensis Junii anno domini millesimo cccc^{mo} septimo et gubernacionis nostre anno secundo." *

II.

PRESENTATION BY JAMES V. OF TREASURERSHIP OF THE CHAPEL ROYAL TO MR ANDREW DURIE.

P. liv.—We here find the celebrated John Mair or Major in 1518-22 holding the offices of canon and treasurer of the Chapel Royal of Stirling. Since the text was printed we have fallen upon an entry in the Register of the Privy Seal, which shows that in prospect of his demission Mr Andrew Dury or Durie was by James V. presented to the treasurership. The instrument of gift, dated at Glasgow on the 1st June 1520, is directed to David [Arnot], Bishop of Galloway, and of the Chapel Royal, who is instructed to confer on the presentee ordinary collation. It proceeds thus :

"Presentacio magistri Andree Dury directa reuerendo in Christo patri David episcopo Candidecase et capelle regie Striuelingensis, ad conferendum collacionem ordinariam super thesauraria dicte capelle regie cum eam vacare contigerit per resignacionem seu dimissionem magistri Johannis Mair theologie professoris vltimi thesaurarii et possessoris eiusdem ad preseutacionem supremi domini nostri regis ac dispositionem reuerendi in Christo patris, etc., ac collacionem ordinariam dicti reuerendi patris spectante, etc. Apud Glasgow primo die mensis Junii anno

* Reg. Mag. Sig. Rot., xi. 22.

etc., xx et regni regis septimo. Gratis domino cancellario. Per signaturam manu dicti domini cancellarii subscriptam.*

Dury or Durie was appointed Abbot of Melrose in 1526; he obtained the bishopric of Galloway and Deanery of the Chapel Royal in 1541. When on the 3d July 1541 he was recommended to the Pope as successor to Bishop Wemyss in the see of Galloway, the king's letter stipulates, "that according to ancient custom, the Deanery of the Chapel Royal and the Abbey of Tungland should continue united to the bishoprick, but that Durie should resign Melrose, retaining a pension of 1000 marks from its rents, and the usufruct of Mauchline and the surrounding fields." Consequent on the mob breaking the image of St Giles during a procession in honour of that saint, which took place at Edinburgh on the 1st September 1558, Durie became so overwhelmed that he died soon afterwards. By Knox and Calderwood he is denounced as profane and licentious, and is further described as having asserted that the Gospel would not be preached in Scotland so long as he and his Episcopal colleagues survived (Knox's History, 105; Calderwood, i. 332). Bishop Dury was son of John Dury of that Ilk, in the county of Fife, and brother of George Dury, Archdeacon of St Andrews, a canonised saint of the Church of Rome. To their uncle, Archbishop James Beaton, both brothers owed their preferments (Chalmers' History of Dunfermline, i. 198; Brunton and Haig's Senators of the College of Justice, pp. 67, 68).

III.

APPOINTMENT OF JAMES CAMPBELL AS A MUSICIAN IN THE CHAPEL ROYAL.

Pp. liv., v.—A contemporary of Alexander Paterson, the sacristan, and of Roland Carmichael, musician in the Chapel, has yet to be named. In the Register of the Privy Seal (vii., fol. 57), under the year 1527, is the following entry:

"Ane lettre to James Campbell makand him singar in the

* Reg. Sec. Sig., lib. v., fol. 144.

kingis chapell riall, and to haue for his seruice thairin xx^{lib}, to be pait be the thesaurar for his lyftyme, or quhill he be promovit to j^{e} ^{lib} of benefice, etc. At Edinburgh, the first day of Maij and of the Kingis regne the xiiij [zeir].

"Per Signaturam, etc."

IV.

JOHN TAYLOR, THE WATER POET'S VISIT TO EDINBURGH.

Pp. cxxviii., cxxix.—John Taylor was at Edinburgh in the autumn of 1618, the year subsequent to the restoration of the Abbey Church, on the occasion of King James's visit. "I was," he writes, "at his Majesty's Palace, a stately and princely seat, wherein I saw a sumptuous chapel, most nobly adorned with all the appurtenances belonging to so sacred a place, or so royal an owner. In the inner court I saw the king's arms cunningly carved in stone, and fixed over a door aloft on the wall, the red lion being in the crest, over which was written this inscription in Latin, '*Nobis hæc invicta miserunt*, 106 *proavi*.' I inquired what the English of it was? It was told me as followeth: '106 *forefathers have left this to us, unconquered*.' The poet then indulges in some poetical reflections on the virtues of a nation which could boast such honours. (See "The Penniless Pilgrimage," in Taylor's Works, 1872, pp. 31, 32.)

V.

LETTER OF LORD BINNING TO JAMES VI.

Pp. cxxvi.-cxxix.—Thomas Hamilton, created in 1613 Lord Binning and Byres, afterwards Earl of Melrose, and latterly Earl of Haddington, became President of the Privy Council in 1616. The following extract from a letter, addressed by him to the king, on the 4th February 1618, would seem to show how (doubtless under Laud's counsel) James VI. had already determined that members of the Privy Council should give compulsory attendance on episcopal service in the Chapel Royal:

"Most Sacred Souerane, . . . I signified to the counsell

your maiesties pleasour anent their repairing to sermon vpoun the Soundayes to your maiesties chapell of Halyrudhows, which they ar uilling to do, and wald haue done alreddie, if the Bischop of Gallowayes heavie seiknes had not hindered him to preache this tyme bygane. He promeisis to aduerteis the counscil when his recouerie sall enable him to preache, and they to resort to it as your maiestie hes commanded. . . .

"BINNING." *

VI.

MR JAMES LAW'S MISSION TO LONDON.

Pp. cxlviii.-cl.—The following letter, addressed "To the King, his most excellent Maiestie," is No. 104 of a volume of the Balfour MSS. in the Advocates Library, with the press mark, 33, 3, 12. Written by Mr James Law, treasurer of the Chapel Royal, and representative at court of its dean and chapter, the letter refers to a proposal of the king "touching another purpose" made in the royal audience chamber, and respecting which the writer had subsequently received a vague and mysterious mission. In imitation of the court, Law expresses himself mysteriously; but in the light of past resolutions and occurrences, it is obvious that James was willing to grant the prayer of his memorial, on the condition that his constituents gave effect to the court views, by introducing into the chapel Anglican rites. Law's request for a further interview would doubtless be granted, unless apprehension was entertained by the impecunious sovereign that the treasurer would insist on immediate payment of his travelling costs. Mr Law's letter proceeds:

* As the members of the Privy Council and Officers of State were directly amenable to the sovereign, they were selected as the first victims of despotic power. To Laud, as the son of a Berkshire silk mercer, it must have been intensely gratifying, that, in his capacity of domestic chaplain to the weakest prince in Europe, he could, with some hope of success, command the nobles of an ancient and unconquered kingdom to submit to his authority. Extravagantly loyal as the Scots are, it is to be remarked that in religious concerns they have not since the Reformation stooped to despotic rule.—(State Papers of Thomas, Earl of Melros, Abbotsford Club, 1837, ii. 626.)

"Most Sacred and Gratious Soveraigne,—In your maiesties audience at Windsore, vpon the sext day of Julij last bypast, wher I wes gratiouslie hard in the effairs of your maiesties Chapell Royall some litle twiching ane other purpose wes expressed, and vpon the morne by wreat supplied, yet not so cleerlie, bot that it is more then neidfull some farder wer hard for detecting that which is evill, and proponing that which no doubt may prove proffitable for pace in the church, and perpetuall strenthning your sacred maiestie and most hopefull successioun; so that now I most hairtilie wisch and desyre yet once again on my bended knees to offer vp old mit, new stampt, wnto your heighnesse grave consideration, that the same being put to tryell may (efter your maiesties princelie censure) prove no les fyned from impuritie then offerred with sinceritie. Not doubting bot when your maiestie will be pleased to call for me to court, ordour will be takin that I receave some reasonable supplie for my better addresse ther.

"Efter my dispatch in the effairs of your maiesties Royall Chapell, for expeding the same, I reteired my selff home, to my no small expenss, wher wee receave a vehement opposition of some to whom ar trusted the manadging of your maiesties rents, who, vpon plausible reasones and weak pretences (bot fra ther own privat respects), labour in the very cradill to extinguisch that laudable work. In which case I can sufficientlie verefie against them all that these proceidings do least tend to the hurt of the crown rent or lieges; and will not be infeebled, bot think my self more then happie, if your maiestie, considdering the equitie of the caus, by your own sacred hand erecting that Godlie work, winn to your maiestie immortall gloir. So creaveing pardon for that wherin I may haue offended, I beseech Almichtie God to blisse your maiestie with all maner of happiness.

"Your maiesties most humble and obedient servand,
(Signed)   "Mr JAMES LAW.

"Edinburgh,
  "14 August 1623."

VII.

THE RIOT AT HOLYROODHOUSE ON THE 10TH DECEMBER 1688, AND SUBSEQUENT PROCEEDINGS IN RELATION TO CAPTAIN JOHN WALLACE.

Pp. ccxliii.—The wrecking of the Abbey Church in December 1688, attended as it was with a bold defence by Captain Wallace, who, on behalf of the Government of James VII., held Holyroodhouse by an armed force, forms a not unimportant episode in the national history. As the subject has not hitherto been referred to fully in any connected narrative, we have thought of supplementing what is stated in the text by a detailed relation. It is convenient to adduce, in the first instance, an account of the occurrence drawn up by Colin, Earl of Balcarres, and transmitted by that nobleman to the dethroned sovereign at St Germains. His lordship writes:

"The night after he [the Earl of Perth] left Edinburgh, the rabble met in great numbers in the streets; George Stirling, an apothecary, and Mr Menzies, a merchant, to inflame them, made drums beat through all quarters of the town; the inhabitants came running out of their houses to know the cause of so sudden an alarm, were met by those posted by Mr Stirling and Menzies, who told them they had good reasons to believe the Papists designed that night to burn the town—that therefore all good Protestants should arm and meet for their own defence. After they had assembled all they could, and seeing no appearance of any danger, they began to tire; one of them proposed that it was a pity so many honest men should meet without doing something worthy of themselves, and that it would please and satisfy all good Protestants if they should go and pull down the Popish chapel of the abbey. The proposal took, and, as ever in such tumultuous meetings, all cried 'Agreed;' men and boys mingled together in confusion. Captain John Wallace was then in your Majesty's palace, with 120 men, raised by the Council to defend it. When he saw them approaching he sent a sergeant to desire them to retire—that otherwise he should be obliged to do his duty, and fire upon them. This they did not regard, so he gave them a volley of firelocks, which killed about a dozen and wounded others. Upon the first fire they ran, and the noise was industriously spread by the Lords and Gentlemen, sitting at the same time at their meetings, that Captain Wallace had made a butchery of the inhabitants; and, to inflame the more, it was asserted that few of any consideration in the town but had children killed; this brought all to meet, and they were joined by the discontented Lords and Gentlemen, who resolved to go altogether to attack Captain Wallace. One of them proposed, since what they were going to do might afterwards be challenged, and they brought to trouble, that some of their number should be sent to the Marquis of Atholl, to desire him to give them a warrant for what they intended, and likewise that he, with some other Councillors, might order the Magistrates' concurrence.

"At their desire his Lordship, Viscount of Tarbat,* and the Earl of Breadalbane, signed them a warrant, and ordered the heralds and pursuivants to attend them, to summon Captain Wallace, in the King's name, to deliver up the palace. The town company, commanded by Captain Graham, marched first; next the discontented Gentlemen (the chief of them were Sir James Montgomery, William Lockhart, Riccarton, Drummond, Lord Mersington, William Drummond, Clerk to the Artillery, Livingstone); next the Provost and all the magistrates in their robes, accompanied by a mob of several thousands. When they came near the Abbey, the Magistrates sent the heralds and trumpets with the Marquis's warrant and order to Captain Wallace to quit the place, which he positively refused, as the order was not from a full quorum of the Council. Upon his refusal, they began to fire at each other, and the Gentlemen and Magistrates got behind cover, and left Captain Graham with the trained bands and rabble to dispute the matter. Captain Graham left them, and got into the court by a back way, which, when Captain Wallace knew, and saw himself like to be attacked before and behind, he retired and forsook his post. When his men missed him, they threw down their arms and begged quarter. The Gentle-

* Afterwards Earl of Cromarty.

men and rabble, when they saw all danger over, rushed in upon them, killed some and put the rest in prison, where many of them died of their wounds and hunger. The rabble, having nothing to resist them, entered the house, pulled down all they could find in the private chapel, demolished all things within the Abbey Church, which had been finished some days before they entered, and plundered the house the Jesuits had lived in. When their work was over, they opened the Chancellor's cellars and wines, and made themselves as drunk with wine as before they had been with zeal."*

So far Lord Balcarres, writing as a partisan of the dethroned sovereign. Wodrow, who presents the next version, quotes as his authorities "a reverend minister since the revolution, then a student in Edinburgh, who was engaged in the attack and wounded very sore;" also "some letters writ at this time." He writes:

"Upon Sabbath, December 9th [1688], some idle people walking in the Park and St Anthony's Yards, seeking to come through the Abbey as their nearest road, found all the gates shut, and cannons placed at every gate, and were discharged by the sentinels to come near. This, with the addition that the court was full of armed men, when reported in the town, heightened the jealousies of the populace, and the fears of more thinking persons, that evil was designed. And in the evening a few young lads accidentally got together, after some conversation upon the present danger, began to huzza, and there was soon a vast gathering of students at the college, and apprentices. The magistrates caused shut all the ports, and the keys were brought to the Provost, Magnus Prince, his house at the foot of Libberton's Wynd, and the rest of the magistrates absconded. The youths gathered about his lodgings, which were inaccessible, calling for the keys, and upon his refusal, threatened to burn his house, but did no hurt. From thence they came to the Cross, and having forced up the door with forehammers, they proclaimed an offer of four hundred pounds sterling to any who

* Memoirs touching the Revolution in Scotland, 1688-1690, by Colin Earl of Balcarres, presented to King James II. at St Germains, 1690. Edinb., Bannatyne Club, 1841, pp. 15-17.

should bring Perth or Melford dead or alive. No more happened this night.

"Next day, in the forenoon, the Town Council met, and emitted a proclamation 'discharging tumults, and ordering parents and masters to keep their servants and children within doors.' This proclamation was torn as soon as it was read, and the officers and drummer stopped when going through the town. This day the Chancellor and his family saw good to retire from the Abbey and go out of town. Matters continued quiet till twilight, and then a multitude began to gather at the head of the Cowgate, and after they had provided themselves in staves and torches, they came up the Bow, where they knew of two drums, and seized them; one of them soon broke, and with the other, their numbers still increasing, they went down the town to the Netherbow. In the Canongate they stopped a little, seeing the Guard drawing out, and upon sending to inquire what the matter was, they found the Captain friendly, and that he only drew out his men to put respect upon them. They desired he should call them in; which was presently done, and they went forward. At the Canongate Cross they took down the Earl of Perth's picture and carried it with them to the Abbey. There Captain Wallace was advanced with some soldiers beyond the strand. Whereupon they stopped, and sent to demand access to the court; which, he refusing, they beat their drum, and with a cry run in upon him. He ordered his men to fire, which did abundance of hurt; severals were killed upon the spot, and many wounded, to the number of 36 or 38, whereof not a few died afterward. After the fire the apprentices and youths fell in upon the Captain with great fury, forced him and his men off the street, and killed two of them outright before they could enter the Abbey gate; that being presently shut, they could get no further in the pursuit. Upon this they retired a little, and ordered some of their number to carry off the dead, and to help up the wounded to the town, and require assistance; and then lodged themselves in houses and closses the best way they could. Meanwhile Captain Wallace and his men continued, from this time about nine till eleven, firing up the street. Those who went up to the town carried up with them some of the arms and hands of the dead and maimed, and hearing of a number of gentlemen and others in a vintner's, went to them and showed how they had been treated. The gentlemen applied to the Town Council then sitting for assistance; which they refused, and the commissioners from the apprentices and others threatened to burn the town. The gentlemen went and got a quorum of the Privy Council, who ordered the magistrates to raise the trained bands, and sent down two heralds with them in their coats displayed before them, to require Captain Wallace to surrender, and the trained bands were ordered to force him if he did not. When the heralds came down, they summoned Captain Wallace to surrender the Abbey in the council's name; this he refused. Then the town-guards, and trained bands, commanded by Captains M'Gill and Graham, came up, and some firing was on both sides, without any great hurt, but some slight wounds. The Captain would have defended the Abbey against them all, having a vast advantage of the ground; but Captain Graham, with a part of his men, broke in by a back entry not so well guarded, which the party in the Abbey observing, fled, and about thirty-six were taken prisoners, but Wallace and a good many escaped. The youths observing this, broke into the court, and killed all the soldiers they met with. It was said about fourteen soldiers were killed. Whether they got liberty, as some of my accounts say, from the town captains I know not, but they fell presently to rifle the chapel and schools, and brought the timber work, and library, with everything that came in their way, to the closs, and burnt them. It was some time before they could fall upon the images, to destroy which was their end in making the attack. At length they found them in an oven, with an old press set before it to cover its mouth. Those they took out, and carried them up to the town in procession through the streets, and back again to the Abbey Closs, and there burned them. They entered the church, rased the new work there, and turned up the marble pavement, and rifled the chancellor's lodgings, and some others in the Abbey; but none of the youths and apprentices laid their hands on anything to carry it off, but all was burned."*

* Wodrow's History. Glasgow, 1830, iv. 473, 474.

On his surrender, Captain Wallace was sent as a prisoner to the Bass, where we find him detained on the 4th January 1689, when an order was made by the city authorities that his personal effects should be delivered to Craufurd of Craufurdstoun, probably a relation. The order proceeds thus:

"Edinburgh, the fourth January J^m vj^c eightie nyne.

"The said day the Councell, considering that there was severall goods in trunks pertaineing to Captain John Wallace, who is now prissoner in the Bass, sequestrat in Captain Patrick Steill and Captain Dumbar their hands, by order of the Lord provost, they appoint the goods to be inventured at the sight of baillie John Charters, and the whole goods, excepting armes, to be delivered therafter to Robert Craufurd of Craufurdstoun, upon his receipt therof, for the saids persones exoneration." *

Wallace was subsequently transferred to the Tolbooth of Edinburgh, then crowded with political offenders.' After he had been a captive fourteen months, the Privy Council proceeded to consider a memorial presented by him, detailing the circumstances under which he was arrested, and entreating liberation. In the following minute of Council, of the 5th February 1691, the memorial is quoted:

"Att Edinburgh, the ffifth day of ffebruary
"J^m vj^c nyntie one yearis.

"Anent a petition given in to the Lords of their Majesties privy councell be Captain John Wallace, prisoner in the tolbooth of Edinburgh, Shewing that the petitioner, being in the year J^m vi^c eightie eight commanded by the privy Councell to goe with his company to Lochaber for suppressing some Insurection among the highlanders, And having returned, he was therafter comanded to goe to Ailison Bank to convoy and bring back some Cannon and Amunition from thence to the Castle of Edinburgh, All which comands the petitioner did punctually execute

* Burgh Records of Edinburgh, vol. xxxii., fol. 281.

to the satisfaction of the privy councell, from whom he receaved his commands. After which the petitioner was comanded to augment the number of the company, and to keep guard within the precinct of the pallace of Hollyroodhouse, and to defend the King's house and court from all violence and attempts, as he should be ansuerable at his highest perrill: And he having applyed himself accordingly, and used all imaginable moderation therin, Truc it is that, when he was upon his deuty, he and his company were invaded and assaulted, and their very lifes putt in hazard, by ane numerous and disordorly rabble; and they having keeped themselves within the bounds of *moderamen inculpate tutele* ther was some blood happned to be shed on aither syde, upon which the petitioner was shortly therafter apprehended, and hath been keept prisoner these five months bygone: And seing the petitioner had parliament ordours from the privy councell in wryte sufficient to vindicat him and justifie all his behaviour in the premissis; and that, in case the petitioner had omitted to doe what he did, he might justly have been in hazard of being shott to death, upon ane sentence of ane court martiall, for not obeying and executing these peremptar ordors, which were given to him not by ane privat persone or single officer of state, but by the privy councell, solemnly mett together, and subscribit by their clerk, conforme their oune warrand in presentia: And the petitioner being assaulted and invaded, and he and his company putt in hazard of their lives, under cloud and silence of night, he humbly conceaves that by the Law of all nationes, alse well as by the martiall Law, he is altogither secure and unquestionable ffor any accident that fell out and hapned upon that occasion: And seing the petitioners small fortune and meanes is exhausted by this long expensive imprisonment, and that for freeing himself of any longer imprisonment he is content to accept of and undergoe voluntar banishment out of the kingdome: And therfore, craving their Lordships to take the premissis to their consideration, and ordaine him to be sett att liberty, upon enacting himself to goe abroad out of the kingdome, within such a competent tyme as their Lordships shall think fitt, and never to returne againe therto without their Lordships speciall warrand for that effect, under such paines and penalties as their Lordships shall think fitt, as the said petition bears. THE SAIDS LORDS of their majesties privy councell having considered the above petition, they heirby give ordor and warrand to Sir William Lockhart, their majesties sollicitor, with assistance of Sir Patrick Hume and Mr Hugh Dallrymple, advocatts, to intent and follow furth a criminall pursuite before the Lords of Justiciary against the petitioner, conforme to the former ordor of Councell, given to his Majesties advocat or his deputes for that effect." *

The Privy Council's order was not carried out, and in the summer of 1692 we find Wallace again pleading for his liberation. The minute of Council thereanent, dated 14th June, is in these terms:

"Att Edinburgh, the ffourteint day of Junij
"J^m vj^c and nyntie tuo years.

" Anent the petition given in to the Lords of there Majesties privie Councill be Captain John Wallace, prisoner in the tolbooth of Edinburgh, Shewing that wheras the petitioner hes continowed upwards of three years in a severe imprisonment in the Bass and tolbooth of Edinburgh, whereby his health is impaired, his bodie weakned, and his small fortune intirely ruined, and that be frequent applicationes made be the petitioner himself to the saids Lords, he wes severall tymes remitted to the sollicitor and assessouris, and his speedie tryall recomended to them, at his oune earnest desyre, yet hitherto there hes been no process intended againest him; and sieing the petitioner hes alreadie suffered verie considerably by a tedious imprisonement, equallie hurtfull to his persone and small fortune, notwithstanding whereof he is heartily willing for farder satisfactione to signe a voluntar banishment from all his majesties dominiones for ever; And therefore humbly craveing that the saids Lords would be pleased to take the premissis to there consideratione, and in respect of the petitioner's long imprisonement, and the great

* Privy Council Register, Acta, Jan. 1691-2, p. 68.

prejudice he hes sustained both in his persone and small fortune therethrough, as also of the voluntar banishment the petitioner is willing to undertake from all his majestyes dominions, under what penalty shall be thought fitt to allow the petitioner to be dismissed upon signeing the same. And he shall never ceass to pray that God may bless the natione with ane lasting peace, off [which] he shall never be a disturber. As also that the saids Lords would be pleased to recomend the maister of the prisone to the Lords of theasurie for what Jayll fies shall bee due be the petitioner, as the said petitione bears. THE SAIDS LORDS of there Majestyes privie councill, haveing considered this petition given in to them be the above Captain John Wallace, they hereby give order and warrand to Sir William Lockhart, there majestyes sollicitor, to raise a Lybell againest the petitioner befor the Lords Comissioners of there Majestyes Justiciare, and to cause cite the petitioner thereon betuixt and the ffourth day of Jully next." *

With respect to this further resolution, Sir William Lockhart, as Solicitor General, reported to the Council, that without their special authority he could not enter upon proceedings. The next minute proceeds :

" Att Edinburgh, the Threttie day of Junij.

There Majestyes Sollicitour haveing moved to the councill that the warrand direct to him for persewing of Captain John Wallace who comanded the guaird in the Abbay in winter j^m vj^o and eightie eight when severall persones were killed, docs not bear the cryme of treasone, and that he could not persew for treasone without a speciall warrand to that effect: And therefore desyred to know if they would ordor him to persew for treasone or not: The same haveing gone to a vote wes carryed in the negative, and appoynted the Interloquitor to stand as formerly pronounced." †

* Privy Council Register, Acta, February 1692 to March 1693.
† Ibid.

On the 6th August 1692 and two following days, Captain Wallace, charged with manslaughter, was subjected to trial in the Justiciary Court at Edinburgh, the judges being Robert, Earl of Lothian, Justiciary-General, Sir Colin Campbell of Aberuchill, Mr David Home of Crossrig, Sir John Lauder of Fountainhall, Mr Archibald Hope of Rankeillour, and Mr James Falconer of Pheasdo, Commissioners. Captain Wallace was "indyted and accused for the slaughter of William Lourie, John Insch, and David Auchterlonie, and others, in maner mentioned in his Indytement." On behalf of the Privy Council, the "persewers" were "Sir William Lockhart, there majesties sollicitor, Sir Patrick Home, and Mr Hugh Dalrymple." For the defence appeared as " procurators Sir James Ogilvie, Sir Robert Colt, Sir David Thoirs, James Stewart, and Mr Thomas Skein." There was a prolonged discussion on the relevancy, when the Court found that " when some boys and others were at the foot of the Canongate the panell caused fire upon them, whereby the abovenamed were killed or received wounds from which they died, and that the panell was art and part thereof." They also found relevant the defence "that a rabble met and declared to John Paterson that they would trouble the soldiers and pillage the abbey;" also "that the said rabble came down the Canongate with swords and firearms, and beat some of the sentinels and advanced within speaking distance." Further " that Captain Wallace caused his men to fire after having been visited by a Herald and Pursuivant, with some of the bailies." After Mr Thomas Skein and Sir James Ogilvie had been heard on behalf of the prisoner, and Sir Patrick Home in reply, James Smith, ensign in the castle of Dumbarton, deponed, " that being one of the artillery and master gunner he was ordered to the abbey to receive commands from Captain Wallace: that he accordingly pointed and directed the cannons: that while in Laurens Orr's house he heard firing by the soldiers: that before the firing he saw a multitude of people at the Nether Cross near the Watergate, who had neither firearms nor other weapons, and that they dispersed after the first firing: that having left the house he heard a second firing, but on what provocation knows not, nor who ordered the firing: thereafter heard the sounding of a trumpet and saw a great multitude, but knows not if armed; that Mr Bruce, lieutenant to Captain Wallace, came near and asked for the captain, and when told that he had gone, cursed him for leaving him in that condition: that the lieutenant desired him to go to the commanding officer of the multitude to request him to desist encroaching on that which they had undertaken to defend: that he refused, but would send one of his men: did not hear any volley except from the soldiers: heard a granade fired and break before leaving Orr's house, and found none of the cannons had been fired: thinks that the granade must have been thrown by Captain Wallace's company, as no others had any of them: but did not see the same fired." David Robertson, gunner in the castle of Edinburgh, deponed, that "he heard firing by Captain Wallace's company, but did not see any killed or wounded: heard a trumpet and the noise of a multitude, and heard a second firing, but knows not whether from the soldiers or multitude: knows no more, being beside the cannons within the pend, till dismissed by Captain Grahame.

Alexander Adamson, son to the deceased Andrew Adamson, indweller in Edinburgh, deponed, that "there was a rumour in the streets on Sabbath night of a designed massacre, whereupon a number of boys and girls gathered together and paraded the streets, but did no harm: had some swords, and offered to break up the door of the Cross, but did not do so: that the next day being 10th December, a number of boys and others with sticks and staves again gathered together, and that they had no other weapons excepting one boy who had a stick in one hand and a pistol in the other, and some with swords hanging by their sides, and a drum beating: that they took down the Earl of Perth's picture on the new land at the back of the Canongate Cross, and proposed to burn it at the Cross of Edinburgh, but that immediately thereafter they proceeded to the foot of the Canongate, near the Abbey, where Captain Wallace was with part of his company: that one of the boys went near to the Captain and spoke to him: that the Captain having his sword drawn wagged the same and said, 'Stand off, Doges,' but did not hear other discourse that passed betwixt them: that there was a firing by the Captain's company, and one fell down before him wounded, but did not see any blood, it being dark: that the people gathered together by sound of Drum near the Chapel door at the Water Yett, where he heard some say, 'Run in upon him:' again heard firing."

Thomas Litlejohn, son to the deceased Thomas Litlejohn, tailor in Edinburgh, gave similar evidence.

John Wightman, town officer of Edinburgh, accompanied Bailies Graham and Pattoun with the heralds. He deponed, that "more than a dozen shots were fired up the Canongate: that in going down with the Magistrates and heralds he met at the Nether Bow the deceased William Lourie, servant to John Inch, stabler, and heard him moaning of a shot in his hand, which he afterwards learned was all shattered."

Further evidence for the prosecution was given by William Eckford and Alexander Bonner, town officers, John Inch, stabler, Henry Fraser, Ross Herald, James Guthrie, Dingwall Pursuivant, and James Grahame and William Patton, late Bailies of Edinburgh.

For the defence the witnesses were William Carmichael, prisoner in the Tolbooth of Edinburgh, who deponed that he heard a number of the multitude express their purpose of going to the Abbey to destroy the pictures and images there: Captain Paterson, in the Links of Leith; David Robertson, vintner; William Pratt, servitor to Saughtounhall, younger; Henry Pitcairn of Pitlour; Captain James Cuninghame, late in Glencairn's regiment, and James Horne, smith in the Abbey. These generally testified to the forbearance of Captain Wallace before the firing took place. Thereupon the jury returned as verdict—"The assyse haveing chosen Peter Wedderburn of Gosford there Chancellar, and haveing considered the lybell and the Lords there interloquitor, and the wholl depositiones of the witnessis adduced thereanent, they all in one voyce, by the mouth of the said Chancellour ffind the lybell against the said Captain John Wallace not proven, but ffinds the exculpation conform to the Lords interloquitor sufficiently proven. In witnes whereof, thir presents are subscryved by there said Chancellour and James Livingstoun there wreitter hereof. Att Edinburgh, the sixt day of August $j^m\ vj^c$ and ffourscore tuelve yearis. Sic subscribitur, Pet. Wedderburn, Cau^{ler}, Ja. Livingstoun, cl^k."

" Upon the opening and reading of the which verdict of Assyse Captain John Wallace and his procurators abovenamed asked and took Instrumentis." * The subsequent history of Captain Wallace has not been ascertained.

* Book of Adjournal, 1690-1693, being the Records of the Justiciary Court, preserved in the General Register House.

INDEX.

ABBOT, George, Archbishop of Canterbury, cxxiv.
Abbotshall, estate of, ccx.
Abercromby, Mr David, subdean of Dunkeld, xl, xlii; official of Whithorn, etc., lvi, 35, 49, 51, 52, 89, 90.
James, Abbot of Scone, xxxi, 1, 2.
John, xli; 49, 52, 93.
Aberdeen, William, Bishop of, 38.
Aberdeen, Diocese of, xxxvi; church of, 14, 15, etc.
Bishop of, xxxviii, cxxiii, cxci.
new church of, xcvi.
University of, ccliii, ccliv.
Abernethy, Nicolas, a singer, liii.
Achaius, King of Scots, ccxxv, ccxxxvii, ccxxx.
Adam, Mr William, architect, ccxlii.
son of Thomas, x, xi.
Adamson, Alexander, 112.
Andrew, 112.
Adesone, John, valet, lxiii.
Thomas, cxciv.
Aikman, James, burgess of Edinburgh, 93.
Ailison Bank, 107.
Aitkine, John, cxlviii.
Aitoune, Sir William, rector of Banue (Benve), 89.
Akynheid, James, xl, 49.
Alan, son of the steward, x. xi.
Alanson, Henry, Archdean of Dunblane, 17, 18.
Thomas, presbyter, 18.
Albany, Duke of, xi, xix, xxi.
Henry (Darnley), Duke of, ccxxxix.
John, Duke of, ccxxxviii.
Robert, Duke of, 95, 96.
Alexander I., King of Scots, vii, viii.
III., King of Scots, ccxxx.
IV., Pope, xl.
VI., Pope, xxxi, xxxvi, cxxxi, cxliii, cxliv, 1, 2.
a harper, xxix.
Mr John, minister of Hoddom, cciii.
Sir William, clxxx.
Alexandria, cloth from, xlviii.
Allan, river, v, lxxxvi.

Allardyce, James, provost of Kirkheugh, xxxviii, xxxix.
Alloway, vicarage of, lxxviii, cix, cxv, ccix.
parson of, cxxxii.
Alyth, committee of estates at, ccxvi.
Anderson, Grissell, relict of William, Bishop of Galloway, cxlii, cxliii.
Angus, Earl of, xx, xxiii.
Annan, Mr William, minister at Ayr, cciii.
Anne, Queen, lxxxix; revives the Order of the Thistle, ccxlviii.
of Denmark, Queen of James VI., ccxl.
Antonio Maria dal Monte, Archbishop of Siponto, xliii.
Antony, Grand Penitentiary of the Pope, lv.
Arbroath, xcvii, ci.
Arbuthnott, Andrew Ramsay, minister of, ccix.
Argyle, Countess of, lxvii, lxviii, lxix.
Earl of, xxiv, lxii.
Archibald, Earl of, lxx, 38.
Arnot, David, Archdean of Lothian, xxxi; Dean of Chapel Royal and Bishop of Galloway, xliv, 1, 2, 97.
Hugo, historian, ccl.
Sir John, of that ilk, xxxi.
Sir John, of Birswick, cx.
Arran, James, Earl of, clxxv.
Ashmole, Elias, heraldic antiquary, ccxxix.
Athelstan, King of the Saxons, ccxxv, ccxxvii.
Athole, Earl of, lxviii, lxx.
Atholl, Marquis of, 102.
Atkyn, William, chaplain, 93.
Auchtnabaid, lands of, xxxiii, 11.
Avenel, Robert, justiciar, x, xi.
Ayr, Chapel of, xxxiv, xxxvi, xxxviii, cix, cxxxii, cxliv, cxlvi, ccix;
united to Chapel Royal, 60-66.
lands in shire of, belonging to Chapel Royal, ccliv.
Aytoun, James, artificer, of Culross, cxxi.

INDEX.

Baillie, Principal Robert, clxxxviii.
  Mr William, rector of Kerretown, 17.
Balcarres, Colin, Earl of, 102, 104.
Baldi, Octavio, ambassador from Florence, cxxxii.
Balfour, Gilbert, lxx.
  Sir James, Lyon King of Arms, clxx, clxxii, ccxxix, ccxxx.
  Sir James, MS collection by, cxxxi.
Baliol, Edward, son of John, ccxxxviii.
Baliol, John, King of Scots, ccxxxviii.
Balliades, lands of, ccliv.
Ballywalter, Hamilton, minister of, ccxvi.
Balmaclellan, church of, xxxiv, xliii, cix, cxxxii, cxliv, 14, 25, 26; united to Chapel Royal, 42-48, 91, 92.
Bannock, the heights of, v.
Bannockburn, vi.
Bane, James, wright, ccxix.
Barbour, John, a luter, liii.
Bass Rock, 107.
Bastian, de, Queen Mary's French servant, lxxi.
Beaton, Sir David, of Balfour, xxxix.
  James, rector of Kirkinner, 35, 58.
  James, Archbishop of St Andrews, xxxix; dean of Chapel Royal, xliii; Archbishop of Glasgow, xliv; Bishop of Caithness, lxxiv, 98.
Bedford, Earl of, envoy to Scotland, lxvii, lxviii, lxix, lxx, lxxi, lxxii.
Bellenden, Adam, Bishop of Dunblane, cxl; his connection with the Chapel Royal, cxli-clviii; Bishop of Aberdeen, clxxxvii; deprived, cci; made rector of Portlock, and dies, cci.
  James, eldest son of the Bishop, cxlviii.
Belton, prebends of, xxxiv, cxxxiv, 14, 15, 26, 45.
Benedict VI., Pope, xxxvii.
Bennett, Mr William, parson of Ancrum, cciv.
Berkley, Walter de, x, xi.
Berwick, North, minister of (Turner), ccx.
Berwick, Pacification of, cii.
Betone, David, 17.
Binning, Thomas, Lord, 99, 100.
Birnie, Mr William, dean of Chapel Royal, cxii-cxvi.
Birnie of that Ilk, cxiv.
Birks, King Charles I. at, ccii.
Black, Mr David, minister, cxxiii.
Blackness, ministers confined at, cxv.
Blair, Robert, mason, cxcii, cxciii, cxciv.
  John, mason, cxii, cxciv.
Bonar, Alexander, town officer of Edinburgh, ccxlvi, 113.
Boniface VIII., Pope, 32, 59, 72.
Bosco, Ralph de, xi.
Bothkennar, cxxx.
Bothwell, Adam, commendator of Holyrood, ccxl.
  Adam, Bishop of Orkney, lxxxii.
  Mr John, abbot of Holyrood, lxxxii.

Bothwell, parish of, cxi.
  Earl of, lxviii, lxix, lxxiii, xcvi.
  Francis, Earl of, cxli, clxxii, clxxiii.
  Patrick, Earl of, 38.
Boyd, Lord, lxx.
Boyd, Lord, forfeiture of, xiii.
Boyde, John, mason, Glasgow, cxxi.
Braid, David, 52.
Brakis, rents of, ci.
Brand, Mr John, minister of Canongate, cxciv, ccxxxix.
Breadalbane, Earl of, 102.
Breda, in Holland, ccxii, ccxiii.
Breichen, Bishop of, cxxiii, clxxxii, cxci.
Brienne, Count de, French Ambassador, lxviii, lxix.
Broun, Sir John, vicar of Creiff, lvi, lvii, cxlvii, 90, 92.
  David, canon, xii.
  John, luter, xviii.
Bruce, Robert, King of Scots, ccxxx.
  Lieutenant, 112.
  Sir William, of Kinross, ccxiii, ccxv.
  ccxx, ccxlii.
Bruges, city of, xv, xviii, xix.
Brunswick, Duke of, lxxx.
Buccleuch, Earl of, cxxxi.
  Sir Walter Scott of, lxxxii.
  Sir Walter, Lord Scott of, cxxxiv-cxxxvii.
Buchan, Nicholas, chaplain, 93.
Buchan, John Stewart, Earl of, xii.
  James Stewart, Earl of, xix, xxi.
Buchanan, Sir Andrew, prebendary of Chapel Royal, ciii.
  George, the historian, xvii, xxii, lxxv, ccxxix.
  George, minister of Kilpatrick, cciii.
  Thomas, mason in Dundee, cxx.
Burntisland, xcvii.
Busso, Francisco de, musician, lxx.
Bute (Buitt), church of, xxxiv, xliii, cix, cxxxii, cxliv, 14, 15, 25, 26; united to Chapel Royal, 42-48.
  Donald of, dean of Dunblane, 97.

Caithness, bishopric of, lxxiv.
Calder, Captain, lxxvii.
Callander, John, smith, ccxix.
Cambusbarron, lands of, x.
Cambuskenneth, abbey of, vi, xv.
  Abbot of, xxxvi, xxxviii, xli, xlii, xliii, cxliv, 29.
Campbell, Alister, cxciv.
  Archibald, Abbot of Holyrood, ccxxxviii.
  James, musician in chapel royal, 93.
  Sir Colin, of Aberuchill, 111.
Canongate, church of, xcvi, ccxiv, ccxxxix.
  marriage register of, ccxxxix, ccxli.
  parishioners of, ccxxxii, ccxxxiv, ccxli.
  the cross of, 105, 112.
Canterbury, Archbishop of, cxxiv.

Canterbury, cathedral of, xlix; burial of Bishop Wedderburn therein, cci.
Carnoto, Thomas de, xi.
Carmichael, Sir James, of that ilk, ccvi.
Roland, musician in the Chapel Royal, 98.
Richard, singer in the Chapel Royal, lv.
William, 113.
Carstairs, Dr William, ccli,
Carswell, John, Bishop of the Isles, lvii, lviii.
Cartar, David, canon, 40.
Casaubon, Isaac, cxc.
Cassillis, Earl of, lxix.
Castellaw, Alexander, ccxi.
Sir James, preceptor of music, ci, cxxxi-cxxxiii, cxxxv, cxxxvii, cxxxix, cl.
John, ccxi, ccxvi.
lands of, xxxiii, ci, cix-ccxi, 11.
Castelnau, M. de Malvisie, lxv.
Catholic College at Holyrood, ccxlii.
Cavers, Andrew, Abbot of Lindores, xxxv.
Chalmer, Mr William, luter of Chapel Royal, ci, cii.
Chantry of the Chapel Royal, 27, 54-57, 65, 66.
Chapel Royal, Register of, xc, cxliii-cxlviii, 1-94.
Revenues of, xciii, xcix, ccli.
at Holyrood, lvi, lix, ccxlvii; modern deans of, and their incomes, ccli-ccliv; worship in, 99, 100.
at Stirling, v-ix, etc.; founded, xiv, xv; united with the see of Galloway, xlii; organs in, xlix; ornaments in, lx, lxi; baptism of James VI. in, lxv-lxxii; deanery of, lxxiv; baptism of Prince Henry in, lxxix-lxxxv; renovated, lxxix, lxxxi; repairs to be made on, lxxxv, lxxxix, cxvii; revisited by James VI., cxxvi, cxxxi, cxxxiii-cxxxix, cxliii-cxlviii, ccxl, ccxvi, ccxlvii, 1-94; erection of, as a collegiate church, with chantry, 18; treasurership of, 55; inventory of jewels and books belonging to, 72-78; Deanery of, 82, 83.
transferred from Stirling to Holyrood, lxii, lxxix, xciv, xcv; styled "Chapel Royal of Scotland," cxiii, cxxi; decorated for worship, cxxii, cxxiii; revenues of, cl-clxii; innovations in worship therein, clviii; musicians and music of, clxi-clxix; Charles I. worship in, clxix, clxxiv; "Articles" for worship therein, clxxvi, clxxviii; liturgical service in, clxxxix; repairs in, cxcii-cxciv, ccliii, ccliv; organs to be removed from, ccx; alterations in the structure of, ccxiii, ccxiv; converted into a conventual church,

ccxxiv; cost of ornaments for, ccxxxvi, ccxxxvii; question of Queen Mary's marriage in, ccxxxix, ccxl; as a Romish college, ccxlvii.
Charlemagne, Emperor, ccxxx.
Charles I., King of Great Britain, cl-clxviii; visits Scotland, clxix; his coronation, clxx-clxxii; opens Parliament, clxxii; touches people for "King's Evil," clxxiii; returns to London, clxxiv; his efforts to introduce the liturgy into the Church of Scotland, clxxxix-ccv; arrives at Holyrood, ccv; executed at Whitehall, ccx.
II., King of Great Britain, ccxi, ccxii, ccxxi, ccxli.
Charters, John, bailie of Edinburgh, 107.
Chatelherault, Duke of, lxvii, lxxvii.
Chepman, Walter, printer, l.
Chisholme, Alexander, musician, cxxv.
Chivalry, Order of, proposed by James VII., ccxxv, ccxxix, ccxlviii.
Cistercian order of monks, xxxvii.
Cither, musical instrument, xvii.
Claneboy, Viscount, ccxvi.
Clapperton, Sir George, subdean of Chapel Royal, lv, lviii.
Clarion, trumpet, xviii.
Clarsha, musical instrument, xxviii, xxix.
Cluniac order of monks, xxxvii.
Cochran, Robert, architect, xiv, xx, xxii.
Coins of Scotland, ccxxviii, ccxxix.
Coldingham, lxvii.
Herbert, prior of, viii, ix.
priory of, xxiii, cxxxiv.
Colistoun, rents of, ci.
Colkitto, ccxvi.
Cologne, town of, ccxxix.
Colt, Sir Robert, advocate, 111.
Colvile, Robert, of Hyltoun, 17.
Commission, Court of High, cci.
Compton, in Hants, cxc.
Conde, Servais de, the queen's valet, lix, lx.
Constantine, Emperor, ccxxvii.
Conynghaim, Cuthbert, 39.
James, canon, 40.
Cornets, for music in Chapel Royal, clxvii.
"Coronation, Form of," preserved in Chapel Royal, clxxvii.
Covenant, the National, renewed, cc; confirmed by the king, cciv.
Cowgate, the, Edinburgh, 105.
Cowper, William, Bishop of Galloway, cxvi, cxviii, cxxiii-cxxx, cxxxvi-cxxxix, cxlii, cxliii.
Andrew, brother of the Bishop of Galloway, cxxxi, cxxxii, cxxxix, cl.
James, nephew of the Bishop, cxxxii.
Thomas, nephew of the Bishop, cxxxii.
Cowye, John, mason, Pittenweyme, cxx.
William, mason, Pittenweyme, cxx.
Coylton, church of, ccix.
Craford, a singer li.

Craggroth, lands of, 95, 96.
Craig, Mr John, minister, xcvi, xcvii.
  Mr Thomas, advocate, cxli, ccxvii.
Craigmillar Castle, lxxii.
Crail, burgh of, cxix.
Crainthall, John, prebendar of Kells, cxxxix.
Cramond, Hamilton, minister of, ccxviii.
Cranschaws, church of, xxxiv, cxxxiv, 14, 15, 25, 26.
Craufurd, Mr Archibald, the queen's almoner, lix.
  Earl of, lxx, ccix.
  Robert, of Craufurdston, 107.
Craufurdland Castle, lix.
Crieff, church of, xxxiv, xxxvi, xxxviii, xliii, lvii, cix, cxxxiii, cxliv-cxlvii, 14, 15; union of, to Chapel Royal, 42-48, 60-66, 71, 89-94.
Crichton, James, singer in Chapel Royal, ccxi.
Crichtoun, Peter, 17.
Croc, Monsieur le, deputy from Savoy, lxviii, lxix.
Cromwell, Oliver, the Protector, ccxi, ccxv.
Croude, musical instrument, xvii.
Culross, workmen of, cxxi.
Cult-donald (Cuilte-dovenald), x.
Cultoun, rents of, cxxxii.
Cummyng, Mr James, of the Lyon Office, ccl.
Cuningbame, Captain James, 113.
Cunningham, Mr David, Bishop of Aberdeen, lxxxiii.
Cunnynghame, Archibald, of Ladyland, cxxxiii.
  Robert, father of Archibald, cxxxiii.
Cunynghame, a singer, xxx.
Cupar, Abbey of, xcviii.
Cymbaclanis Bells, musical instruments, xviii.

Dacia, 75.
Dacres, Lord, xcvi.
Dalam, Mr, organ maker, cxxv.
Dalkeith, cii.
Dalmellington, prebends of, xxxiv, ciii, cix, ccix, 14.
  parson of, cxxxii.
Dalrymple, Mr Hugh, advocate, 109, 111.
  James, lxxviii.
  church of, cix, cxxxii, ccix.
Dalyell, Sir John Graham, xc.
Darnley, Lord, lxiii, lxiv, lxii; his marriage to Queen Mary, ccxxxix; his skull exhumed, ccl.
David I., King of Scots, vii, viii, xi, ccxxxvii.
  II., King of Scots, xvi.
Davidson, Thomas, chaplain of the garrison of Stirling, lxxxix.
Days, Robert, pergeonar, cxciv.
Denmark, cxxxii.
Dennestoun, Mr William, notary, 89.
Donaldson, John, mason in Dundee, cxx.

Douglas, Gavin, the poet, li.
Douglas, Lady Margaret, Countess of Bothwell, cxli.
  Robert, Bishop of Brechin, ccxvii.
Dow, Moreis, musician, lxii.
  John, musician, lxii.
Down, Robert, Bishop of, ccxvi.
Drumlochy, Chalmers of, ci.
Drummond, James, Earl of Perth, ccxxiccxxv.
  John, Earl of Melfort, ccxx-ccxxv.
  John, architect, lxxxviii.
  John, receiver of royal rents, ccxxxv.
  Sir John, of Hawthornden, lxxxii, lxxxviii.
  Lord, xxiv.
  Sir Robert of Carnock, lxxviii, lxxxv, lxxxviii, xciv, ccxl.
  Sebastian, lii.
  William, canon of Chapel Royal, lxxviii.
  William, clerk to the artillery, 103.
  William, the poet, lxxxii, lxxxviii.
Duchell (Duthell), church of, xxxiv, xxxvi, xxxviii, cxxxiv, cxliv, 14, 15, 64, 65, 71.
Dulcet, musical instrument, xviii.
Dulcimer, musical instrument, xviii.
Dulsacord, musical instrument, xviii.
Dumbarton, castle of, 111.
Dumfries, William de, xi.
  the "cruikit" vicar of, lii.
Dunbar, Alexander, almoner of Chapel Royal, ccxxii-ccxxix.
  Gavin, dean of Moray, 38.
Dunbar, Captain, 107.
  castle of, xxiv.
  George, Earl of, cvii.
  rectory of, xxxiv, 15.
  collegiate church of, 3, 5, 8, 11, 14, 15, 20-25, 28, etc.
  prebends of, xliii, cxxxiv, cxliv, 3-5, 20, 42-48.
  school of, cxxix.
  Patrick, prebendar, cxxxii, cxxxiii, cxxxix, cl.
  William, the poet, ccxxviii.
Dunblane, Bishop of, lxix, clxxii, clxxiii.
  bishopric of, united to the deanery of the Chapel Royal, cxl, cxlii, ccli.
  diocese of, ccxii, ccxiv.
Duncan, Earl of Fife, viii, ix.
Duncanson, John, subdean of Chapel Royal, lvi, lxxv, xciii-xcvii, cxxxix.
  William, in Poland, cxxxiii.
Dundee, xi, cxix, cxc, ccxvii.
Dundrennan, barony of, cxli, cxcv, ccvi.
  abbey of, clv, clxxiii.
  church of, cxlii, ccvii.
Dunfermline, monastery of, vii, x.
  Galfrid, Abbot of, vii, viii.
  Abbot of, xlii, xliii.
  Earl of, cx.
Dunipace, parish of, vii.
Dunkeld, diocese of, xxxvi.
  church of, 14, 15, etc.

INDEX.

Dunkeld, Bishop of, xxxviii, lxix, clxxii.
Gregory, Bishop of, viii, ix.
Lord, xcvii.
Dunlop, John Mair, vicar of, liv.
Dunning, parish of, xcvii.
Dunse Law (Hill), ccii.
prebends of, xxxiv, cxxxiv, 14, 26, 45.
Duplin, George, Viscount, clxi, clxii.
Dura, Plain of, clviii.
Durrisdeer, xxix.
Dury, Andrew, Abbot of Melrose, lvii; treasurer of Chapel Royal, 97, 98.
George, archdean of St Andrews, 98.
John, of that ilk, 98.
Dysart, burgh of, cxix, cxx.

Eccles, parish church of, vii, ix.
Eckford, William, town officer of Edinburgh, ccxlvi, 113.
Edinburgh, castle of, vii, xxi, xxix, lxv, cxx, cxcvi; repairs on, ccxix, 107.
cross of, 112.
university of, cxxvi, ccx, ccli; chairs in connection with Chapel Royal, cclii-ccliv.
diocese of, erected, clxxv, ccxxxiii.
Bishop of, clxxxii.
magistrates of, ccxxxi-ccxlvi, 103-106.
Train Bands of, ccxliv.
Edmestoun, John, minister at Dunning, xcvii.
Edmondstone, Sir Archibald, of Duntreith, 17.
Edward IV., King of England, xiv, xv, xix.
Eglinton, Earl of, lxviii, lxx.
Elgin, grant to the burgh of, ccix.
lands in shire of, 12.
Elizabeth, Queen of England, lxvi, lxix, lxxii.
Ellem, church of, xxxiv, xliii, cxxxiv, cxliv, 14, 15, 25, 26; united to Chapel Royal, 42-48.
Elliot, Dr James, minister at Glasgow, cciii.
Ellon, parish of, ccxxxii.
Elphinstone, Robert, Lord, lxxxviii.
Ely, prebendary of, cxc.
England, musicians from, liii.
Erskine, Arthur, lxii.
Sir Robert, Sheriff of Stirling, xi.
Erroll, Countess of, lxxxii.
Erskine, Sir Charles, Lyon King of Arms, ccxxix.
Ertht, William of, Knight, 97.
Ettrick Forest, Kirk of the Lowes in, cxxxiv, cxxxv, 14, 15, 25, 26.
lands in parish of, ccliv.
Exchequer, commissioners of, cliii, clx, clxiii.

Falconer, Mr James, of Phesdo, 111.
Falkirk, vi.
Falkland, palace of, xxxv, 17.
Faslane (Fesulan), church of, xliii, 81.
Feldie, John, musician, lxii, lxiii.
Ferdinand II., King of Aragon, ccxxviii.

Ferguson, a trumpeter, cxxxii.
Ferny, Andrew, canon, 40.
Flanders, musical instruments from, liii.
Fleming, Marjorie, wife of Sir Robert Drummond, lxxxviii.
Flemings, musicians, lii.
Flodden, battle of, xcvi.
Florence, Duke of, cxxxii.
Forbes, Dr William, clxxiii, clxxiv; appointed first Bishop of Edinburgh, clxxv; his death, clxxxi, clxxxiii.
Fordun, John of, historian, ccxxvii.
Forest, church of the, xxxiv, xliii, 14, 15, 25, 26, 45.
Forrester, Sir Andrew, ccxxxi.
Mr Thomas, minister at Melrose, cciv.
Forth, Firth of, ccii.
river of, v, vi, lxxxvi.
Fowlis, Mr James, merchant in London, ccxxxv-ccxxxvii.
Fountainhall, Lord, ccxxi, ccxxxii, ccxli.
Fowlarton, Thomas, lxxiv.
Fowler, Susanna, wife of Sir John Drummond, lxxxii.
Mr William, Master of Works, lxxxii.
Fowlis, a harper, xxviii.
Fowlis-Easter, church of, xcvii.
France, xix, lxvi, xcvi.
musicians from, lii.
Fransche, James, 52.
Fraser, Henry, Rosse herald, ccxlv, ccxlvi, 113.
French Protestant Church in Edinburgh, ccxxxiii.
Fydell, musical instrument, xviii.
Fyndlater, a musician, lxx.
Fynn, William, cxcii.

Galbraith, Sir George, Master of Works at Dumbarton, li.
Sir Thomas, priest, li.
William, a luter, liii.
Galloway, Mr Patrick, minister of the king's house, lxxxii, xcvii, cxxiv.
bishopric of, xlii, cxi, cxvi; disunited from the deanery of Chapel Royal, cxl, 14.
David, Bishop of, 90, 91.
George, Bishop of, 33, 35, 37, 39.
Gaunt, John of, entertained in the Abbey Church of Holyrood, ccxxxviii.
George III., King, ccxlix.
IV., King, ccxlviii.
Gib, John, groom of the chamber, cii-cxii. cxiii, cxviii, cxxviii, cxxxii.
Sir George Duncan, baronet, cxxviii.
Sir John, of Knock, cxxviii.
Robert, cxxviii.
Gibson, Nicol, mason, Linlithgow, cxxi.
John, mason, Linlithgow, cxxi.
Gilleam, an organist, liii.
Gilmour, John, writer, cxxxix.
Gittern (Gythorn), musical instrument, xviii.
Glasgow, collegiate church of, lvii, 14, 15.
General Assembly at, cci, cciv, ccviii.

Glasgow, magistrates of, cxx.
  university of, endowed by Cromwell, ccxi; endowment of a Chair from funds of Chapel Royal, ccliii, ccliv.
  diocese of, xxxvi, ccxi.
  Archbishop of, xxxviii, cxii, clxx.
Glencairn, Earl of, ccxl.
Glencorse, parish of, ci, ccx.
Glenholm, church of, xxxiv, cix, cxxxii, 14, 15, 25, 26.
Glenluce, abbacy of, cxvi.
Glenshee, lands of, xxxiii, 11.
Goldsmyth, Sir John, canon, lvi.
  John, xxx, li, 90.
Gordon, Alexander, Bishop of Whithorn, lix; dean of Chapel Royal, etc., lxxiv, lxxv.
Gordon, Roger, son of William of Cracklaw, lviii.
Gospatric, Earl of Dunbar, viii, ix.
Gourlay, John, chaplain, 52.
Gowrie, Earl of, xcvii.
Graham, Archbishop, xxii.
  Captain, 103, 106, 112.
  James, bailie of Edinburgh, 113.
Grahame, Lieut.-Colonel, ccxlv, ccxlvi.
Gray, Andrew, musician, cii.
  Andrew, Lord, 38.
  Sir George, chanter of Chapel Royal, cliii, clxii.
  Mr James, master of the Chapel Royal, cxxxv.
  Nicholas, a minstrel, xxix.
  Mr Thomas, treasurer of the Chapel Royal, cxxxi, cxxxiii, cxxxv, cxxxvii, cxxxix.
  Lord, xxiv.
Graysteil, a song, xxx.
Green, Roger, wheelwright, St Andrews, cxx.
Greg, David, painter, St Andrews, cxx.
Greyfriars' Church, Edinburgh, cc.
Guidrig, Mathew, painter, cxxii.
Gulde, Alexander, custumar of Stirling, xii.
Guthrie, James, Dingwall pursevant, ccxlv, ccxlvi, 113.
  schoolmaster of Hoddesdon, cxxix, cxxx.

Haddington, Thomas, Earl of, 99.
Haddingtonshire, gentry of, lxvii.
Halkarstone, Mr Thomas, provost of Creichtoun, 17.
Hall, Mr John, minister, cxxiv.
Hamboys, a musician, xlii.
Hamilton, Duke of, keeper of Holyrood Palace, ccxix, ccxx.
  James, fourth Duke of, ccxlix.
  James, sixth Duke of, ccxlix.
  Gavin, Bishop of Galloway, cxl.
  James, Duke of, clxxv.
  Mr James, minister, ccxvi.
  John, subdean of Chapel Royal, ccxviii.
  Mr Robert, minister at Lesmahagow, cciii.

Hamilton, Thomas, Earl of Haddington, 99, 100.
  William, archdean of Chapel Royal, lvii.
  Archbishop of St Andrews, lxix.
  Sir Thomas, of Byres, clerk of register, cx.
Hannay, Mr James, minister of the Abbey Church, clxx; dean of Edinburgh, cxcviii.
Hardie, James, cxxxix.
Harpers, King James IV.'s, xxviii, xxix.
Hatton, Sir Christopher, lxxi.
Hay, George, slater, cciii.
  Mr John, parson of Renfrew, cciii.
  Mr Richard Augustine (Father), liv, xciii, ccxxiv, ccxxxiii, ccxlii.
  Dr Theodore, archdean of Glasgow, cciii.
  William, musician, lxii.
Hawyk, Andrew of, secretary to Duke of Albany, 97.
Helmburn, land of, ccliv.
Henderson, Mr Alexander, minister, ccv; Royal gift to him, ccvi; chaplain to the royal household, ccviii.
Henrietta Maria, Queen of Charles I., clxxxix.
Henry VI., King of England, xiv, xv.
  VII., King of England, xxiv.
Henry, Prince, son of James VI., lxxix; his baptism, lxxix-lxxxv, xcvii.
  Bishop of Galloway, 90.
  son of Swan, viii, ix.
  Prince, son of David I., vii, viii, xi.
  the minstrel, xxx.
Hepburn, Mr John, provost of Lincluden, 17.
  Patrick, of Smeaton, clix, clxi.
Hepburns, the family of, xxiv.
Heriot, Helen, wife of Mr Thomas Craig, cxli.
Herbert, the chamberlain, viii, ix.
Heron, James, musician, lxiii.
Heroun, clerk of the chapel, xviii.
Herries, Lord, lxxxii, ccxl.
Hert, John, a porter, xxix.
High School of Edinburgh, ccxxxiii.
Hird, Thomas, mason in Dysart, cxx.
Hoddesdon, cxxix.
Hoge, Thomas, cccl.
Holland, Sir Richard, xvii.
Holyrood, Abbot of, xxxv, xxxvi, cxliii, cxliv, 1, 21, 25.
  Abbey Church of, coronation of Charles I. in, clxx-clxxiv, ccxiv, ccxv; as a Romish convent, ccxxv; chapel for Knights of the Thistle, ccxxxi-ccxxxvi; historical sketch of the church, ccxxxvii, ccxliii; as Chapel Royal, ccxlvii; despoiled by mob, ccxlix; repaired, ccxlix; wreck of, 102-114.
  Alevin, Abbot of, viii, ix.
  a canon of, organist, liii.

INDEX. 121

Holyrood, Osbert, prior of, viii, ix.
Holyroodhouse, lxviii, xcviii, cxix, cxcviii, ccii ; designs for building, ccxlii.
Chapel Royal at, lix, lxii, cxiv.
palace of, xciv, xcv, cxiv, cxx, cxxi ; visited by Charles I., clxix, ccv ; partly burned, ccxi ; restoration of, ccxiii-ccxv ; repairs on, ccxix, 99, 108.
John, Lord, lxxxii.
Home, Mr David, of Crossrig, 111.
Baron James, xxiii, xxiv.
Patrick, xxiii, xxiv.
Homyll, James, robemaker, xix, xx, xxi.
Hope, Mr Archibald, of Rankeillour, 111.
Horne, James, smith, 113.
Howlat, the, poem of, xvii, li.
Hudsoun, "Mekill" Thomas, lxxiv, xcviii-c.
Robert, lxxiv.
James, lxxiv.
William, lxxiv.
Hume, Alexander, Lord, 17, 38.
Mr David, of Godscroft, cxxx.
John, chief luter, lxiii, lxxii.
Sir Patrick, advocate, 109, 111.
Hunnyman, James, mason in Dundee, cxx.
George, mason in Dundee, cxx.
Huntly, Earl of, lxviii.
John, Master of, lxxiv.

Icolmkill, abbey of, lviii.
Inch, John, stabler in Edinburgh, 113.
Inchcolm, Abbot of, liv, 78.
Inchmahome, priory of, cxlv.
Innocent III., Pope, xxiii.
Italy, minstrels from, lii.

Jacob, a musician, xxviii.
Jame, a piper, xxix.
James I., King of Scots, xii, xiii, xvi, xvii, ccxxxviii.
II., King, ccxxviii; born at Holyrood, ccxxxviii.
III., King of Scots, xii-xiv, xviii-xxv, lii, ccxxxviii, ccxxxviii, ccxlvi.
the queen of, ccxxxviii, ccxxxviii.
IV., King of Scots, xxvl, xxviii-liii, lvii, lxxxviii, cxiii, cxvii, cxxxi, cxxxiv ; his state robes, clxxi, ccxxviii, ccxxxviii, 1-28, etc., 79, 80.
V., King of Scots, liii, lxxiv, cxxxiv, ccxv ; collar worn by, ccxxviii, ccxxx, ccxxxvii ; his coffin opened, ccl, 97.
VI., King of Scots, born in Edinburgh, lxv ; his baptism, lxviii, lxix ; his household, lxxii, lxxiv, xciii, xcviii, cxv, cxix ; preparations for his visit to Scotland (1617), cxix-cxxvi; his efforts to decorate

the Chapel Royal, cxxiii-cxxvi, cxxxii, clxxxviii, clxxxix ; coins of, ccxxix, ccxli, 99.
VII., King, clxxv, ccxviii-ccxxxviii, ccxli, ccxliii, ccxlvi, ccl, 102.
Jamieson, Dr John, xxii.
Jane, natural daughter of James IV., lxxiv.
Jedburgh (Jedworth, etc.), Osbert, prior of, viii, ix.
John, a Court musician, lxxiii.
subprior of Whithorn, 39.
XII., Pope, 58.
Johnstone, Robert, historian, lxxxi.
Judas Cross, the, xxvii.
Bells, xlix, 77.
Julian II., Pope, xli-xliii, cxxxi, cxliv, cxlvii, 39.
III., Pope, xliii, cxxxi.
Juxon, Dr, Bishop of London, cxcvi.

Keir, Laurence, cxlviii.
Keith, James, cxxxiii.
Sir James, prebendary of Chapel Royal, cl.
Kellie, Edward, musician, clxi-clxix, clxxxv, clxxxvi.
Kells, church of, xxxiv, cii, cix, 14, 15, 25, 26, 91, 92
parson of, cxxxii.
Kenneth, son of Alpin, vi.
Kildean, vi.
Kilwinning, abbey lands of, lvi.
Kincardyn, church and chapel of, xxxiv, xxxvi, xxxviii, cxliv, 14, 15, 60-66, 71.
Kinkairn in Mar, kirk of, xxxiv.
Kingarth, parish of, lviii, cix.
Kinloch, Francis, of Gilmerton, ccxvii.
Kippen, prebendary of, ci.
Kirkaldy, Margaret, wife of Sir Robert Drummond, lxxxviii.
Thomas, a priest, cxlvi, 52, 53.
Sir William, of Grange, lxxvii, lxxxviii.
Kirkandrews, church of, xxxiv, xxxix-xli, 14, 15, 25, 26, 35, 38, 55, 57.
Kirkcowan, rector of, lviii.
teinds of, xcviii, cix, cxxxi.
Kirkcudbright, lands in, belonging to Chapel Royal, ccliv.
Kirkheugh, church of, St Andrews, xxxi ; separated from the Chapel Royal, xxxix.
provostry of, xlii.
Kirkhope, lands in parish of, ccliv.
Kirkinner, church of, xxxix-xli, lviii, lix, cix, cxxxi, cxlvi ; union of to Chapel Royal, 33-41, 49-52, 57.
James Beaton, rector of, xxxix-xli, 35, 49, 51, 52, 57-60.
teinds of, lvi, xcviii.
Kirk o' Field, lxvii, lxxiii.
Kirktoun, ci.

INDEX.

Kirktoun (Kirketun), lands of, x, ci.
Knox, John, the Reformer, lv, xcv.
Kynneir, Alexander, canon, 40.
Kyntore (Kintyr), lands of, xxxiii, xxxv, cxxxiii, 12, 68.
Kyrkaldy, Thomas, notary, xli.

Laing, Dr David, lv, lvi.
Lamb, Andrew, Bishop of Brechin, xcvii, xcviii, cxl.
Lambert, Sir John, prebendary, lvi, cxlvii.
Lamerol, David, lx.*
Lanark, vicarage of, cxi, cxv.
Larbert, parish of, vii.
Lateran Council, 59.
Laud, Archbishop, cxxiv, cxxvi, clxxii, clxxiv-clxxix; his correspondence for the introduction of a Liturgy into the Church of Scotland, clxxx-cxcvii; committed to the Tower of London and charged with treason, ccv ; ccxxi, ccxlvi, 99, 100.
Lauder, Sir John, of Fountainhall, 111.
  town of, xix.
  bridge of, xx.
Lauderdale, Earl of, ccxiii, ccxxix, ccxlvi.
Laurie, J., cl.
Law, Mr James, treasurer of the Chapel Royal, cxlviii-cl, 100, 101.
  James, Archbishop of Glasgow, cxlix.
Lee, Dr John, principal, xxii ; dean of Chapel Royal, cclii, ccliii.
  Dr Robert, dean of Chapel Royal, cclii.
Leighton, Dr Robert, Bishop, ccxii, ccxiv, ccxvii.
Leith, "the King's Work" at, cxxxii.
  Port of, cxciii, cxciv, ccxxxvii.
  South, xcviii.
  Hamilton, minister of, ccxviii.
Lennox, the, v, li.
  Duke of, clxxi.
  Mathew, Earl of, 38.
  The Regent, lxxv, lxxvii.
Leonard, skinner, xv.
Lermonthe, James, 51.
Leslie, General, ccii.
  Sir Patrick, commendator of Lindores, lxxxii.
Levingston, Lord, lxx, 103.
Levingstoun, Alexander, 52.
Liberton's Wynd, Edinburgh, 104.
Liltpipe, musical instrument, xviii.
Lincluden, provostry of, cxlv.
Lindsay, Bernard, cxxxii.
  Thomas, Searcher-General of Leith, cxxxii.
  Mr John, minister at Carstairs, cciii.
  Mr David, lxxviii ; Bishop of Brechin, clxx ; made Bishop of Edinburgh, clxxxii, clxxxviii, cxcviii.
  Sir David, of Balcarres, clvii.
  Mr Patrick, minister at Maxtoun, cciv.
  of Pitscottie, xxv.

Lindisfarne, priory of, xxiii.
Lindores, Andrew, Abbot of, xxxv, 17.
  Abbot of, xliii.
  a musician, xxviii.
Linlithgow, xxvi, xxvii, xxix, lii, cxx, cxxi, ccxxx.
Litlejohn, Thomas, tailor in Edinburgh, 113.
Livingston, James, clerk, 114.
  James, of the royal bedchamber ccviii.
Livingstone, Alexander, xli.
Lochaber, 107.
  lands of, xxxiii, xxxv, cxxxiii, 12, 68.
Lochill, lands of, cxxxii.
Loch Leven, ccxi.
Loch Lomond, lxxxvi.
Lochmaben, lii.
Lockhart, Sir William, 103, 109, 110, 111.
Lokart, Andrew, cxciv.
  Symon, ccxli.
London, cxxx, ccv, ccxxxvii, 76.
  Artists brought from, to Holyrood, cxxi.
Lothian, archdean of, xxxv, cxliv, 1, 21, 25.
  Robert, Earl of, Justice-General, 111.
Lourie, William, 113.
Louvain, city of, xxii.
Lowes, St Mary Kirk of, cvii, cix, cxxxi, cxxxiv-cxxxviii, cxliv, cliii, clxii, ccxvi.
Lowry, Adam, mason in Dundee, cxx.
Lundy, laird of, xxvii.
Lute, musical instrument, xviii.
Lyle, Lord, xxiv.
Lyndsay, Sir David, the poet, liv.

Mackenzie, Sir George, ccxxx.
Mackqueen, Mr John, subdean of Chapel Royal, ccl.
Macleod, Dr Norman, dean of Chapel Royal, cclii, ccliii.
Makgarwe, William, vicar of Peninghame, 39, 40.
Magdalene, Queen, her coffin rifled, ccl.
Magdeburg, Duke of, lxxx.
Mair (Major), Mr John, liv, 97, 98.
Makbuty, a harper, xxix.
Makclaouthan, Rolland, canon, 40.
Makcrekane, John, presbyter, 39, 41.
Makdowel, Fergus, official of Whithorn, xl, 39, 40.
Makkynnel, Henry, canon of Whithorn, 39.
Makneile, John, presbyter, 39.
Malvisie, M. Castelnau de, lxv.
Manfredonia, diocese of, xliii.
Manuel, nunnery of, ci.
Mar, Earl of, xix, xx, lxix, lxxv, lxxvi.
  Countess of, lxxiii.
Margaret, Queen, vii.
  . of Denmark, Queen of James III., ccxxxviii.
  the Princess, Queen of James IV., ccxxviii, ccxxxviii, 79.

INDEX. 123

Margaret, wife of Robert, Duke of Albany, 95.
Markill, lands and monastery of, cxli, clv, clix-clxi, clxxiii, cxcv, ccvii, ccxvii.
Mary, Queen of Scots, lxi-lxiii, lxv-lxix, lxxii, lxxiii, xcvi, ccxv, ccxxvi, ccxxxviii; place of her marriage with Darnley discussed, ccxxxix, ccxli.
Masoun, Thomas, mason in Pittenweyme, cxx.
Mauchline, 98.
Maximilian II., Emperor, xcvi.
Maxwell of Kirkconnell, ccxxxv.
  John, 51.
  John, Bishop of Ross, cxci.
  the Master of, lxx.
May, Andrew, prior of, 17.
M'Bretne, Martyn, a musician, xxix.
M'Gill, Captain, 106.
Meg, Mons, cannon, xxx.
Melfort, John, Earl of, ccxx-ccxxv, ccxxxi-ccxxxvii, ccxlvi, 105.
Melrose, abbey of, xvi, 98.
Melvill, Sir James, lxvi, lxxi, lxxiii, ccxl.
Melville, Katherine, wife of Sir John Arnot, xxxi.
  Earl of, secretary of state, ccxlix.
Melygam, Andrew, canon, 40.
Mennenius, author, ccxxix.
Menzies, Mr, an Edinburgh merchant, 102.
Mersington, Lord, 103.
Mildenhall, Suffolk, cxc.
Militia, the, ccxliv, ccxlv.
Millar, Mr Edward, musician, clxxxvii.
Miller, Alexander, mason, St Andrews, cxx.
Mingary Castle, ccxvi.
Minstrels, students, liii.
Monepenny, Robert, cxciii.
Monk, General, ccxiii.
Monteith, Earl of, clxi.
Montgomery, Alexander, poet, lxxxviii.
  Sir James, 103.
Montrose, Marquis of, ccxvi; executed, ccx.
  church of, xcvi.
Monycord, musical instrument, xvii.
Moodie, Dr Robert, minister of Clackmannan, lxxxix.
Moodie, Thomas, "mortification" by him, ccxxxii.
Moravia, State of, cci.
Moray, Earl of, lxviii, lxix, ccxxxiv-ccxxxvi, ccxlvi.
  diocese of, xxxvi, 14, 15.
  Bishop of, xxxviii, clxxi, clxxii.
Moret, Monsieur, ambassador of Savoy, lxiii.
Morton, Earl of, clxxix.
Morville, Richard de, constable, x, xi.
  Hugh de, constable, viii, ix.
Motto of Scottish coinage, ccxxix.
Mouat, James, singer in Chapel Royal, ccxi.

Mow, Henry, cxxxiii.
Murraw, Duncan, 39.
Murray, John, Earl of Annandale, his son's baptism, cxxvi, cxxvii, cxxix.
  John, of Lochmaben, cxli.
  W., parson of Creiff, cxxxix.
Muriel, wife of Robert, Duke of Albany, 95.
Music, instruments of, in Chapel Royal, clxvii, clxviii.
Musicians of Chapel Royal, c-cix, cxxix.
Mylne, Robert, the king's mason, ccxv.
Mylsone, James, a harper, xxviii.

Nairn, Mr Robert, advocate, cxliii, cxlviii.
Napier, Sir Alexander, cxlix.
Nebuchadnezzar, King of Babylon, clviii.
Neilston, William Semple, minister of, ccix.
Netherbow, the, Edinburgh, 105, 113.
Newburn, battle of, cciv.
Newcastle, capture of, cciv.
Newtoun, George, presbyter, 52.
Nicholson, Mr James, minister at Meigle, xcviii.
  Sir James, cxciv.
Nisbet, Alexander, heraldic writer, ccxxx, ccxliii.
Norie, Thomas, mason in Dundee, cxix.
  David, mason in Dundee, cxx.
  John, mason in Dundee, cxx.

Ochil Hills, v.
Olifard, David, justiciar of Lothian, viii, ix.
Ogilvie, Sir James, advocate, 111.
Oliphant, Mr William of Newtoun, cx.
Olmutz, in Moravia, cci.
Orbistoun, proprietor of, cxi.
Organ, musical, xviii.
Organist for Chapel Royal, clxvii.
Orr, Laurence, 111, 112.
Oxford, university of, cxc.

Padua, see of, xliii.
Pady, Thomas, mason, St Andrews, cxx.
Painter, Alexander, chaplain, 93.
Paisley, Abbot of, xxxvi, cxliv, 29.
Palatine, the Prince, clxxviii.
Paris hats for singers, lxiii.
  Scots College at, lxi.
Pate, the harper, xxviii, xxix.
Paterson, Alexander, sacristan of Chapel Royal, liv, lviii, 98.
  James, sacristan of Chapel Royal, lviii, lix.
  James, ccxi.
  Captain, in Leith Links, 113.
  John, 111.
  John, Archbishop of Glasgow, ccxxxii.
Patonson, Mr John, xvi.
Patrick, prior of Whithorn, 39.
Pattoun, William, bailie of Edinburgh, 113.
Paul IV., Pope, xcvi.

Paul II., Pope, 67.
Peblis, George, workman, cxciv.
"Peblis to the Play," the poem of, xvi.
Perth, old church of, xcvii.
  lands in county of, belonging to Chapel Royal, ccliv.
James, Earl of, ccxxi, ccxxv, ccxxxi, ccxxxvi, ccxlvi, 102, 105.
Pettybrachly, church of, xxxiv, xxxvi, xxxviii, cxxxiv, cxliv, cxlvi, 14, 15, 60-66, 71.
Pettygrew, Sir James, xlviii, 76.
Phrew, Hew, mason, St Andrews, cxx.
  James, mason, St Andrews, cxx.
Picts, the, vi.
Piedmont, lxiii.
Pinkartoun, prebends of, cxxxiv.
Pipers to James the Fourth, xxix.
Pitcairn, Henry, of Pitlour, 113.
Pitscottie, Lyndsay of, xiv.
Pittenweem, burgh of, cxix, cxx.
Pole, Cardinal, xcvi.
Pont, Mr Robert, provost of Trinity College, lvi.
Pope's, the, effigy, burned at Edinburgh, ccxxxvii.
Portative, musical instrument, xviii.
Portlock, in Somerset, rectory of, cci.
Pratt, William, 113.
Preistis Acres (Raploch), near Stirling Castle, cxxxiii.
Preshome, papers at, lxi.
Preston, Mr John, of Pennycuik, cviii.
Prestonkirk, parish of, cxli.
Primrose, Sir James, Clerk of the Privy Council, lvi, xc, cxliii, cxlv, cxlvii, cxlviii, 93.
Prince, Magnus, provost of Edinburgh, 104.
Psaltery, musical instrument, xvii.
Pyncartone, prebends of, xxxiv, 14, 26, 45.

Rae, James, merchant burgess of Edinburgh, cxxv.
Ralph, sheriff of Stirling, x, xi.
Ramsay of Balmain, ccix.
  Alexander, 93.
  Andrew, subdean of Chapel Royal, ccix, ccx.
  James, musician, lxiii.
  James, Bishop of Dunblane, ccxvii.
  John, xlv., xx.
  Sir John, 17.
  Symeon, student of music, cii.
Randolph, ambassador of England, lxii.
Raploch, lands of, cix, cxxxiii.
Rankine, James, mason, Glasgow, cxxi.
  John, mason, Glasgow, cxxi.
Ray, John, musician, lxiii.
Recorder, musical instrument, xvii.
Reid, Adam, 17.
Rhynd (Rende), Sir John of, xv, xxvi, xxvii.
Ribupe (Rebeck), musical instrument, xviii.

Riccarton, laird of, 103.
Richard II., King of England, ccxxxviii.
  the clerk, x, xi.
Richardson, John, custumar of Stirling, xii.
Richie, James, mason, Glasgow, cxxi.
Ripon, negotiations at, ccv.
Rist, musical instrument, xviii.
Rizzio, David, vocalist, etc., lxiii, lxiv, lxv, lxxii; his death, ccxxxix.
  Joseph, brother of David, lxv.
Robert II., King of Scots, ccxxvii.
  III., King of Scots, ccxxxviii.
  Earl of Fife, chamberlain, xi.
Robertson, David, gunner, 112.
  David, vintner, 113.
  Thomas, mason, St Andrews, cxx.
  David, mason, St Andrews, cxx.
  Dr William, historian, lxxxix.
Rogers, Sir William, doctor of music, xiii, xix, xx, xxii, xxviii.
  son of Odo, x.
Rome, court of, xxx, xxxi.
Ros, Robert, cl.
Roseneath (Rostnot ?) xxxii, xxxiv.
  Priory of, xciii, 3, 13, 20.
  chapel at, xliii.
Ross, John, prebendar of Strathbraan, cxxxix.
  Lord, lxviii.
  Bishop of, lxix clxxi, clxxii, clxxxv, clxxxvii, cxcvi.
  James, Duke of, Archbishop of St Andrews, 38.
Rostnot (Restenot, Roseneath) xxxii, xxxiv, cxxxiv, cxlv.
Rote, musical instrument, xviii.
Rothes, Earl of, lxx, lxxxii.
Rothesay, Duke of, xxiv, xxv.
Row, Mr John, historian, clxxxi.
Roulat, M., secretary to Queen Mary, lxiv.

Sakbuts, for music in Chapel Royal, clxvii.
Sauchie, battle of, xxv.
Sauchieball, laird of, younger, 113.
Saumur, university of, Andrew Ramsay professor in, ccix.
Savoy, Duke of, represented at baptism of James VI., lxviii.
Schalme, musical instrument, xviii.
Schevez, Robert, xxii.
  William, Archbishop of St Andrews, xxii, xxiv.
Sclaiter, David, mason in Glasgow, cxxi.
Scone, abbot of, xli, cxliii, cxlv, 1, 21, 25, 28.
  abbey of, ccxxx.
Scot, Andrew, surgeon, cxxxix.
  Mr James, servitor to the Bishop of Galloway, cxxxix.
Scott, Walter of Goldilands, cliii, clxii.
  Sir Walter, of Buccleuch, lxxxii, cvii.
  of Branxholme, ci.

Scott, William, chantor of Chapel Royal, cxxxi, cxxxv, cxxxvii, cxxxix, clii, clxii.
Scots College at Paris, lxi.
Scrymgeour, John, of Dudhope, cxix, cxx.
Selkirk, Earl of, lviii.
Sempill, Lord, lxviii.
Semple, Mr William, regent in Glasgow College, ccix.
Service Book, the, cxcviii, cci.
Seton, Alexander, Earl of Dunfermline, chancellor, cxxvii.
Seton, Sir George, ccxvii.
George Lord, lxx, ccxxx.
Shaw, laird of Sauchie, xxiv.
Mr Robert, clerk, 17.
Shaws, lands of, Selkirkshire, ccliv.
Sheriffmuir, vi.
Simson, Mr Patrick, minister at Stirling, cxxiv.
Sinclair, Andrew, prebendary, cxxxii, ccix, ccxvi.
Mr John, minister of Restalrig, ccxl.
Siponto, Archbishop of, xliii.
Sitharist, musical instrument, xvii.
Sitholis, musical instrument, xvii.
Skene, Mr Thomas, 111.
Skirling, Baron, (Livingstone), ccviii.
Smith, Mr James, overseer of works, ccxix.
James, ensign, 111.
Smyth, John, painter in Dundee, cxx.
Solomon, King of Israel, clxi.
Somerville, William de, of Carnwath, viii, ix.
Southwick (Suddick) parish church of, lviii, cix, cxxxii, 14, 15, 25, 26, 91, 92.
Spalding, John, historian, clxxii, clxxiv.
Spang, Mr William, clxxxviii.
Spence, laird of Wormiston, lxxvii.
Spot, prebends of, xxxiv, cxxxiv, 14, 26, 45.
Spottiswoode, Mr John, superintendent of Lothian, lxv.
Archbishop, clxxiv, clxxv, clxxxviii, clxxxix, cxcviii.
Ninian, archdean of Chapel Royal, 89, 93.
St Andrew, patron of Scotland, ccxxv-ccxxviii.
Order of, ccxxix, ccxxx.
St Andrews, Robert, Bishop of, vii, viii.
burgh of, cxix, cxx.
cathedral of, ccxxx.
university of, cxv, ccxviii.
Archbishop of, cxxiii, clxx-clxxii.
St Mary's College of, cxc, ccliii, ccliv.
St Anne's Yard, Edinburgh, ccxli.
St Anthony's Yards, near Holyrood, 104.
St Genevieve, Paris, canon of, ccxxiv.
St Giles, church of, Edinburgh, xli, xcvi, cxcvii, 51.
image of, 98.

St Leonard's, hospital of, cxv.
St Mary of the Rock, church of, xxxi, xxxiii; separated from Chapel Royal, xxxix, xlii, 2, 3, 4, etc.
of the Lewes, kirk of, cvii, cix, cxxxi, cxxxiv.
St Michael, chapel of, in Stirling Castle (or Chapel Royal), xi, xli, 2, 11, 18, etc.
Steill, Captain Patrick, 107.
Sterheid, Sir William, canon, lvi, 90.
Stevynson, Andrew, canon, 40.
Stewart, Alexander, Earl of Mar, 97.
Alexander, Earl of Moray, ccxxxiv.
James, advocate, 111.
John, Earl of Buchan, xii, 97.
John, Lord Lorne, 97.
Murdoch, Duke of Albany, 97.
Robert, eldest son of Murdoch, Duke of Albany, 97.
House of, vi, clxxv.
John, mason, Glasgow, cxxi.
Stirling (Strivelyn, etc.), v. vii, cxix, cxxvi, 2.
Parliament held at, lxxvii.
Privy Council retire to, cc.
haven, cxciv.
castle of, v, vi, xxiv, xxv, xxxv, lxvi, lxviii, lxxv, lxxx, lxxxv, lxxxvi, ccxlvii, 11, 18, 29, 37.
chaplaincy of, lxxxix, xc.
collegiate church of, xxxix-xliv; process for its erection, 1-18; confirmation thereof, 18-29; conservatory of, 29-33.
Palace of, lxvii, lxxxviii, 11, 18, 29.
William, Earl of, clxxx.
park of, x, lxxxvi,
rock, lxx.
Peter of, x.
George, apothecary, 102.
W., Abbot of, viii, ix.
Stone, Nicholas, carver, of London, cxxii.
Story, Sir John, xv.
Strathbraan, lands of, xxxiii, cix, cx, cxxxiii, 11.
Strathearn, 92, 93.
Swain, Will, xvi.
Sympsone, William, 17.

Talburn (or Tabor), musical instrument, xviii.
Tarbat, the Viscount of, 103.
Tassoni, the author, xvii.
Taylor, John, the "Water Poet," 99.
Teinds belonging to Chapel Royal, ccliv.
Teith, river, v, lxxxvi.
Tewkesbury, Thomas of, xiii.
Thistle, Order of, ccxxv, ccxxix-ccxxxi, ccxlviii, ccxlix.
Knights of, ccxxv, ccxxvi, ccxxx, ccxxxi, ccxlii, ccxlviii.
Officers of, ccxlix.
Star of the order, described, ccxlviii.
"Thistle and Rose," poem of, ccxxviii.

Thoirs, Sir David, advocate, 111.
Thomson, George, editor, lxi.
Tod, John, Chaplain, 93.
Towris, Clement, glass wright, cciii.
Train Bands, the, of Edinburgh, ccxliv, ccxlv.
Trail, Mr David, sacristan of Chapel Royal, xliv, cxlvi, 72.
Traprane, lands of, cxli, clix-clxi, clxxiii, cxcv, ccvii.
Traquair, lands of, xix.
Earl of, clxxix, clxxxvi, cciv.
Trinity College, Edinburgh, the Provost of, lv.
Troupe, Walter, cl.
Trumpe, musical instrument, xviii.
Tullideff, Stephen, prebendary of Chapel Royal, cxxxiii, cl.
Tulloch, George, sawyer, cciii.
Tungland, abbacy of, cxvi, 93.
Turing, Sanders of, xvi.
James of, xxvii.
Turner, Archibald, subdean of Chapel Royal, ccx.
Sir James, ccx.
Turnhouse-hill, ci.
Tympane, musical instrument, xviii.
Tyrie, the Jesuit, xcv.

University commissioners, their report as to revenues of Chapel Royal, ccii-ccliv.

Valoniis, Roger de, x, xi.
Vaus, George, prior of Whithorn, xlii.
Verrio, the painter, ccxviii.
Vienna, xcvi.

Walcar, Nycholas, canon, 40.
Wallace, George, "Spangeonar," cciii.
Wallace, Hugh, of Ingliston, ccxix.
Wallace, Captain John, his conduct at Holyrood-house, ccxliii-ccxlvi, 102-114.
Wallace, Sir William, xxx.
Wallat, Adam, musician, cxxv.
Walter, son of Alan the steward, viii, ix.
Walton, Sir Henry, cxxxii.
Wardlaw, John, a luter, xxviii.
Wardlaw, Robert, 51.

Wantones, a singer, lii.
Watergate, the, of Edinburgh, 111, 113.
Watson, James, 52.
Watson, Humphrey, cl.
John, cl.
Watson, Rev. Robert, chaplain of Stirling Castle, lxxxix.
Watt, Gilbert, cxl.
Waus, Alexander, canon, 40.
Wause, Patrick, of Berynberyth, 39.
Wedderburn, Dr James, Bishop of Dunblane, account of, cxc-cxcvii; deprived, his death and burial, cci.
Dr John, brother of the bishop, cci.
Peter, of Gosford, 113, 114.
Weir, John, mason, cciii.
Robert, cl.
Weland, Mr James, cl.
Wells, diocese of, cxc.
Wemyss, Henry, Bishop of Galloway, lvi, lvii, cxlvii, 90, 98.
Whitchurch, Wells, prebendary of, cxc.
Whithorn, George, Bishop of, xxxix, xli.
prior of, xxxix, xl, xli, lxix.
priory of, cxvi.
Widderspune, a fowler, xxix.
Wightman, John, town officer of Edinburgh, ccxlvi, 113.
Wigton, Earl of, cxxxii.
lands in, belonging to Chapel Royal, ccliv.
William, canon of Whithorn, 39.
William III., King of Great Britain, ccxvii, ccli.
William, a singer, xxx.
Bishop of Aberdeen, 38.
William the Lyon, King of Scots, ix, x.
Wilson, Andrew, mason of Dundee, cxix.
Andrew, mason, St Andrews, cxx.
John, mason, St Andrews, cxx.
Thomas, mason, St Andrews, cxx.
Windsor, 101.
St George's Chapel at, ccxviii.
Wishart, Sir John of Pitarrow, lxiv.
George, of Drymme, lxiv.
Wynram, Robert, albany herald, cl, clii, clxii.
Wynrams of Liberton, cl.

Young, Robert, printer, cxcvii.
Yester's, Lady, church, ccxxxiii, ccxxxiv.

www.ingramcontent.com/pod-product-compliance
Lightning Source LLC
Chambersburg PA
CBHW030356230426
43664CB00007BB/616